Inclusion *of* Exceptional Learners *in* Canadian Schools

a PRACTICAL HANDBOOK *for* TEACHERS

Nancy L. Hutchinson
Queen's University

Prentice Hall

TORONTO

For my daughter Jennifer who inspires me;
for all the children who enrich our lives

National Library of Canada Cataloguing in Publication Data

Inclusion of exceptional learners in Canadian schools: a practical handbook for teachers

Includes bibliographical references and index.
ISBN 0-13-939854-6

1. Inclusive education—Canada. 2. Special education—Canada. I. Title

LC3984.H88 2001   371.9'046   C2001-900471-0

ISBN 0-13-939854-6

Vice President, Editorial Director: Michael Young
Editor-in-Chief: David Stover
Acquisitions Editor: Andrew Wellner
Executive Marketing Manager: Christine Cozens
Signing Representative: Samantha Scully
Supervising Developmental Editor: Laura Paterson Forbes
Production Editor: Susan Adlam
Copy Editor: Susan Broadhurst
Production Coordinator: Peggy Brown
Art Direction: Mary Opper
Cover and Interior Design: Lisa Lapointe
Cover image: Andi Martin/Photonica
Page Layout: Janet Zanette

1 2 3 4 5   06 05 04 03 02

Printed and bound in Canada

Prentice
Hall

Brief Contents

Detailed Contents

List of Focus Boxes

Preface

Writing this book has taught me much. Some things I learned by doing background research in areas with which I was less familiar. Other things I learned through discussions with colleagues, graduate students, parents, teacher candidates, and individuals with exceptionalities. In particular, I have learned by challenging my assumptions about teaching exceptional children and adolescents. I believe that when we accept the challenges of teaching exceptional students in inclusive settings, we must be prepared to challenge assumptions about what exceptional students can and cannot do and to find new ways to help them reach their potential. Therefore, I hope this book helps you to challenge your assumptions and to reflect critically on what it means to include exceptional students.

I am frequently reminded of the way the rest of the world views Canadian approaches to inclusion and inclusive education. Educators in other countries look to Canada's commitment to inclusion as a model and an inspiration. The organizing body for the Commonwealth Games has committed to inclusive games in the future, modelled on the games held in Victoria in 1994. Our constitution has served as a model for countries developing constitutions since the early 1980s. Even Britain's charter of rights, approved by its upper and lower chambers in 2000, was compared to our Charter of Rights and Freedoms (1982) and was found to contain fewer guarantees of individual rights. In 1994–95, I spent time during my sabbatical leave working with colleagues at American universities, where I was inundated with questions from researchers, graduate students, and teachers about inclusive education in Canada. I was proud to describe the classrooms of Canadian teachers where I saw professionals "going the extra kilometre."

I continue to see teachers striving to make exceptional students part of the social and academic fabric of the classroom. I recently met with a group of parents of children, adolescents, and young adults with autism. They reminded me forcefully that to be effective, inclusion during the school years must mean inclusion in the community as well as in the school. Through all of this, I am aware of the incredible challenges facing parents, educators, employers, and exceptional individuals in making inclusion a reality. My hope in writing this book is that it may serve as a research-based, practically focused resource on inclusive education for teacher educators and pre-service and in-service teachers.

This textbook contains many references to Canadians—exceptional individuals, schools, educators, and educational researchers—including their locations in the country. I believe that it is critical that we know our history, stories, legislation, and heroes. We live next to a massive and influential power on the international stage. However, citizens, educators, and lawmakers in many countries respect us as a role model. I have observed that both Canadians and Americans are among those least likely to be aware of how Canada leads by example in our field. I have tried to point to the contributions of individuals such as Terry Fox and Rick Hansen, heroes and leaders of advocacy for the disabled, and of organizations such as the Canadian National Institute for the Blind, winner of national and international awards for advocacy and service. I believe that Aboriginal students, students from diverse cultures, and students at risk can benefit from inclusive environments and adapted teaching. I have tried to draw attention to significant, recent developments in Aboriginal education that coexist with the crisis of disappearing Aboriginal languages. Whenever possible, I have used Canadian examples and, at times, I may be guilty of citing Canadian research without including references to major research programs in other countries. I hope that the extensive listings of Canadian books, Web sites, and programs will help teacher candidates, teacher educators, and parents to locate our resources and our experts, of which there are many.

Perspective

For many years, I have organized my pre-service and in-service teaching about exceptional learners around topics such as planning, classroom organization and climate, and adapting teaching and assessment—a *non-categorical* approach. I am reminded each year, as I work in the university and in schools in our community, how much is expected of beginning teachers. If they are to meet these expectations, I think they must begin, from the first lesson they plan, by thinking about the range of individuals in the class. The question they need to ask is not how do I individualize for these students, an impossible task, but *how do I adapt my teaching to include these exceptional individuals?* That is the perspective you will find in this book. I have tried to focus on the kinds of information, skills, and strategies that recent teacher candidates have found both thought provoking and practical. I have taught in both elementary and secondary schools, I often teach classes with teacher candidates from both panels, and I have tried to acknowledge the different challenges in these different settings. There are examples relevant to elementary teachers and examples for junior and senior high school teachers, as well.

Organization

This textbook is divided into two main sections. Section one provides fundamental background knowledge in the field of exceptional education in Canada. Chapter 1 describes the current situation in Canada and provides a brief history of how we came to be where we are. It also includes a step-by-step strategy for adapting instruction, called ADAPT, that will help teachers to meet the needs of exceptional students. Chapter 2 describes the role of the classroom teacher in the education of exceptional learners and the kinds of partnerships that teachers forge with parents, paraprofessionls, and other professionals. Chapter 3 focuses on characteristics and strategies to meet the learning needs of exceptional students with six high-incidence exceptionalities (from giftedness to learning disabilities). Students with low-incidence exceptionalities and a range of health conditions are the focus of Chapter 4; the characteristics of these students and strategies to meet their learning needs are discussed. Chapter 5 turns attention to equity and diversity. There are strategies for adapting teaching for Aboriginal students, culturally diverse students, those who have English as a second language, and students at risk for a variety of reasons, including poverty and abuse.

Section two of this book presents the heart of any course on inclusive practices: instructional approaches that emphasize teaching students effectively regardless of exceptionality or other forms of diversity. Chapter 6 focuses on the climate, organization, and management of inclusive classrooms. Chapter 7 provides approaches to adapting teaching and Chapter 8 provides approaches to adapting assessment. There are many examples representing a range of grades, exceptionalities, and teaching subjects. In Chapter 9, you will find information on enhancing social relations of exceptional students. Chapter 10 deals with strategies for independent learning and independent living. The conclusion turns the focus on successful teachers and how they thrive on challenges and cope with stress in their professional lives.

Features

This textbook has the following features designed to help readers learn effectively:

- Vignettes serve as introductory cases to help readers relate the chapter content to teachers and students.
- Learning objectives at the beginning of each chapter point to key content within that chapter.
- Key terms throughout the chapters appear in boldface type, and easy-to-understand definitions often appear in the text and always appear in the glossary at the back of the book.
- Chapter summaries highlight important information in the chapters.
- Marginal notations are designed to stimulate critical reflection and to introduce additional resources, including Weblinks that have been researched and tested for quality and relevance. (Although all Weblinks were current as of the date of publication, the Internet is ever changing and some links may no longer be operative.)
- Focus sections help readers focus on inspiring examples of Canadian families, communities, schools, programs, and educators that may serve as models.
- Canadian references throughout help students locate practical supports, resources, research, curricula, people, and Web sites within the exceptional education community in Canada.

Supplements

An Instructor's Manual is available to instructors. For each chapter, it includes an overview outline, teaching ideas, activities, discussion questions, transparency masters, and handout masters. A computerized test item file is also available.

Acknowledgments

Many people have contributed to the completion of this project, so many that I will name only a few out of necessity. First, thank you to Hugh Munby for his love, unwavering support, and sense of humour. And then to outstanding graduate students Jenny Taylor and Nicole Lévesque for their persistence in locating elusive references and their positive perspectives no matter how much work was left to be done. Cheryl Schmid has been a great collaborator in the writing of the Instructor's Manual. In the early stages, library research was conducted diligently by Shelley Gauthier-McMahon, Cinde Lock, Lara Smith, Karin Steiner-Bell, and Beth Noble. All our library searches were made easier by the excellent work of our reference librarian, Brenda Reed. Many thanks to the professionals at Pearson Education Canada—to Cliff Newman who started me on this odyssey, and to Laura Paterson Forbes, Andrew Wellner, Su Mei Ku, and Susan Adlam who guided me at every stage of the journey. I am also grateful to Susan Broadhurst for her expert copy editing. Special thanks go to reviewers in the field who provided valuable feedback: Jane Barken, Anne Carr, Linda Chmiliar, D'Anne Epp, and Sandra Latchford. Finally, thank you to the thousands of parents, pre-service and in-service teachers, and exceptional students. You have been my teachers. I hope I have learned well and that this book does justice to your fine practice and your high ideals for including exceptional students in Canadian society and in Canadian classrooms.

Nancy L. Hutchinson
Queen's University
Kingston, Canada
December 2000

Introduction

So You Want to Be a Teacher

> One teacher's perspective: "I wish I had been made more knowledgeable about and sensitive to the realities of teaching real kids in a real school."
>
> Sarason (1993, p. xii).

This teacher voices a concern that is shared by many educators and administrators in Canadian schools. It can take this form: "I didn't realize there would be so many exceptional students in my classes." Or, "I wanted to teach English literature, not special education." This Introduction begins the process of talking directly with teachers, using the second person, "you"—so *you* want to be a teacher. One of the purposes of this book is to help you become more knowledgeable about the realities of teaching all the students who show up at school these days. In Canada, at the beginning of the twenty-first century, being a classroom teacher means there are certain to be exceptional children or adolescents in your classes, and you may feel like a special education teacher some days—even if you were hired to teach classes in advanced physics. This is because, as a country, we have made a commitment to the inclusion and participation of persons with disabilities in Canadian society. This commitment is expressed formally through federal and provincial legislation and supported by many court decisions of the past few years. Although you and your teaching colleagues were not consulted directly about inclusion, all Canadian citizens have been repeatedly consulted and informed indirectly—through elections, public debates, polls, and research.

The polls and research studies suggest that Canadians support inclusion, but individuals who must fulfil these expectations, whether they are employers or teachers, report that they need guidance and support. They repeatedly express that while they want to treat everyone fairly, they simply don't know enough about disabilities and about the changes that must be made in schools, workplaces, and the rest of society.

Three Canadian researchers—Gary Bunch (York University), Judy Lupart (University of Calgary), and Margie Brown (Acadia University)—interviewed and surveyed hundreds of teachers from three Canadian provinces about their attitudes toward inclusion. The following quotations drawn from interviews (Bunch, Lupart, & Brown, 1997) reflect the teachers' *support for inclusion* within six major themes: students' rights and equity, diversity within society, enhanced learning, mutual benefit for all students, benefits for included students, and benefits for regular students.

- "First of all, it comes back to one's rights" (teacher, p. 18).
- "I think we live in a heterogeneous society and the classroom should reflect our society as a whole" (teacher, p. 19).
- "I guess it comes from a basic philosophy about how children learn best and just the sense that all children can and should learn, that they should be together [in regular classrooms] as much as possible, that there are social benefits, large social benefits, to children from all different backgrounds to being together in one setting" (administrator, p. 22).
- "Having [exceptional students] in the regular classroom allows students to be made aware of their positive attributes and they become more familiar with them. I think it benefits most of society in that way. And it also benefits those who are disabled in some way" (teacher, p. 22).
- "They're part of a normal setting to grow socially and be part of the everyday affair of being at school" (teacher, p. 23).
- "It allows all of us to become more aware of people, more accepting of people with differences, that it makes us open to change, and to new ideas" (teacher, p. 26). (Quotations used by permission of the authors.)

The main *concerns about inclusion* that regular classroom teachers expressed to Bunch, Lupart, and Brown (1997) formed four groups or themes: professional adequacy, student progress, workload, and fear of insufficient support. The four quotations below reflect these four themes:

- "Some teachers are worried that they don't have the expertise to handle the problems that might come up with varying abilities in students" (teacher, p. 29).
- "Probably worrying about their other students' progress at the same time as they might be concerned that they might get a student who might fall behind" (teacher, p. 31).
- "There's a lot of meeting time [outside classroom hours]. You need to talk about certain students. You know there's an effect, but it doesn't bother me. Like, I think it's something that, as a professional, I do" (teacher, p. 34).
- The resource teacher's place is "in the classroom" and "there to help the classroom teacher with teaching the whole class." The one thing that could most meet teachers' concerns about inclusion was "they want to feel the administrator is supporting them." Other forms of support mentioned frequently were resources (material and human) and release time for planning and meeting. (Quotations used by permission of the authors.)

Bunch, Lupart, and Brown (1997) found that both pre-service and experienced teachers want more opportunities at all stages of their careers to learn about exceptional students, inclusion, and how to "make modification/adaptation to meet individual characteristics" (p. 124). This book is intended to meet this need for pre-service and in-service teachers. This Introduction begins the discussion of the issues surrounding inclusion and how they affect you, as a teacher, and your classroom. The discussion deepens in Chapter 1 and is elaborated on in every chapter of this book.

The Role of Classroom Teachers

As you can imagine, schools and classroom teachers have a pivotal role in the creation of an inclusive society. First, unlike other institutions, schools are legally responsible for preparing children and adolescents with disabilities to participate meaningfully as educated adults in a democratic society. This means that as teachers we are expected to teach exceptional children and adolescents the same kinds of knowledge and skills that we teach all other students, but in ways that are meaningful to them. We have in recent years adopted policies in every jurisdiction in Canada that reflect our commitment to carrying out this teaching in regular classrooms alongside peers without exceptionalities whenever this is possible (this topic is explored fully in Chapter 1). Second, schools have a legislated responsibility to prepare all children and adolescents to participate in an inclusive society and to accept individuals with disabilities as peers, co-workers, employees, employers, etc. This responsibility follows from one of the primary purposes of public education—to prepare citizens to live in the democratic society that we have shaped with its values, laws, and high expectations for participation. This means that Canadian educators, educational researchers, and policy-makers have to direct their efforts to understanding and reconciling these potentially conflicting responsibilities. As the discussion below suggests, it is impossible to conduct conversations in Canada about inclusive education without acknowledging and matching the extensive efforts of other institutions to include persons with disabilities.

While teachers are central to the Canadian project of inclusion, it is important for you as an individual teacher to remember that you are neither the cause of nor the solution to all of the problems that arise in your classroom. You can come to feel overwhelmed by guilt about your inability to be all things to all people. Crucial to your survival is judicious and frequent use of the resources provided to support classroom teachers and their exceptional students, the focus of much of this book. You also need to think about your advancement as inseparable from the advancement of the collective of educators in your school, your board, and your province. Seeing yourself as part of a collective and learning to collaborate are essential to your effectiveness and to your well-being as an inclusive educator.

The Place of Inclusion in Canadian Society

In Canada, inclusive education is an issue within the context of Canadian society, not just within the context of Canadian schools. In 1982 the Canadian constitution was repatriated from Britain. At that time, we adopted the Canadian Charter of Rights and Freedoms, which has influenced every aspect of our society. The Charter guarantees rights for minorities and specifically names persons with disabilities. The Charter not only guarantees rights, but also specifies responsibilities of the Canadian government, of provincial governments, and of institutions to ensure that these rights are attained and maintained. This means that in Canada inclusion is closely related to equity: inclusion of exceptional persons follows from our commitment to equitable treatment guaranteed in the Charter of Rights and Freedoms. For example, supplementary legislation to the Charter (Bill 62, Employment Equity Act, 1986) requires all employers with more than 100 employees to submit plans for employment equity to the federal government, and specifically names women, people with disabilities, visible minorities, and First Nations. At the same time, preschools, universities, community colleges, parks, libraries, shopping facilities, scout troops, and schools are consulting individuals with disabilities, their families, and the groups that speak for them.

Inclusive Schools

Thus inclusive schools are a natural part of inclusive society, and equitable treatment of students regardless of (dis)ability is closely related to equitable treatment of students regardless of gender, race, and so on. In Canada, if we choose to teach, we are choosing to teach in inclusive settings.

Dilemmas in Inclusive Schools

Dilemmas are a constant and pressing feature of teachers' lives (Berlak & Berlak, 1981; Brookfield, 1995). Rarely do we get through a day, let alone a week, of inclusive teaching without confronting some kind of a dilemma. Many of these may look, at first analysis, like they are only decisions about teaching methods. However, upon critical examination, they frequently turn out to have implicit ethical dimensions. Do I allow a student's insensitive comment to an exceptional classmate go unremarked? How much time do I spend preparing modified outcomes and assignments for two students, one who has a physical disability and another who is gifted, when I know I have not spent enough time thinking about the learning outcomes of the core activity? How far can I push my commitment to every student participating in hands-on learning when some can only complete the activities with so much assistance that finishing makes them feel more helpless than empowered? How much modification of assessment is fair, and why is it easier for us and for our students to accept these changes for blind students than for students with learning disabilities? The reality is that we live on the horns of complex ethical dilemmas every day of our teaching lives (Brookfield, 1995), and that these dilemmas are only intensified by our commitment in Canada to an inclusive society and inclusive classrooms.

Action Research: Teachers' Voices on Inclusive Education

Sometimes, there is little classroom research to guide teachers, and this Introduction closes with a challenge to teachers to become action researchers and to share their findings. Knowing how students are experiencing learning is fundamental to doing good work as teachers. Without this knowledge, we may unwittingly exercise our pedagogic skill in ways that confuse or intimidate learners. This insight has been accepted and acted on by a number of educators interested in what they describe as "action research" or "classroom research."

Action research is a way to study your own teaching practice. The intent is to change and improve your practice. Whether you focus on one student or your whole class, the question is: "How can I help my students improve the quality of their learning?"

The four steps to follow are:

1. Identify a concern in your practice.

2. Decide what you will do about this concern.

3. Select the evidence (one or more indicators) that will allow you to make a judgment about what is happening before, during, and after your action research.

4. Think about how you can validate any claims you might make about the success of your action research. Select evidence to show that you have done what you claim to have done.

You can see how action research could be an important vehicle for answering your own questions about what adaptations to your teaching work best for individual exceptional students. Typically, action research is carried out over several weeks or months. Some improvements in teaching practice take longer to accomplish than others and some require more time for you to demonstrate improvement. Teachers usually start with a concern that they can act on, something that is important to them and to their students. Talking about your action research with one or more colleagues (often called "critical friends") is a good idea.

What you do about this concern could be a small change, anything that will be likely to improve the quality of learning for students or even for one student. Starting small and achieving success is more likely to mean you will continue to use action research to improve your practice. When you try to find out if your actions have made a difference, look for indicators of improvement you can see in what the students do, or in what they learn, or in how they treat one another during discussions in the classroom. If you were focusing on the amount an exceptional student participated in class discussions, you could make a check mark each time she raised her hand and put a cross over it each time she spoke. You could ask her to put a check on a card taped to her desk each time she spoke in her small group.

In the fourth step, always prepare a written report, even if it is very brief. It should summarize the four steps you have taken. Discuss the report with other teachers and ask for suggestions. Perhaps you and your colleagues will find that you want to support one another in action research as each of you sets out to study your own teaching practice to improve it.

For examples of beginning attempts at action research, you might read some pieces by teacher candidates at Queen's University published in Featherstone, Munby, and Russell (1997) and in Upitis (2000). A highly readable introduction appears in *You and Your Action Research Project* by Jean McNiff and two colleagues (McNiff, Lomax, & Whitehead, 1996). These authors remind you that this approach focuses on "I," the researcher, changing "my practice" in ways that make a difference to "my students." Many examples help to show the wide range of aspects of professional practice that teachers could choose to improve in action research. Teachers' federations often produce hands-on materials aimed at teacher improvement. For example, Ontario Public School Teachers' Federation (1996) published *Act, Reflect, Revise, Revitalize: Action Research, Moving Beyond Problem Solving to Renewal*, which you and your colleagues could use to begin action research projects together. They also developed a kit entitled *Action Research*, which contains a video and a book (Delong & Wideman, 1998). Look to the journals and magazines published by provincial teachers' associations and by subject councils (e.g., teachers of mathematics) for examples of teachers' action research. One teacher reported on his experience in improving his practice with his peers to a focus group of the Ontario College of Teachers: "Instead of having some people come in and tell you what to do, it came out that people sitting as a group came to define their own goals." He continued, "I believe that's what changed the way I work" (Grant, 2000, p. 255).

Becoming a Teacher

Throughout this book, you will hear the voices of exceptional children, their parents, and teachers who are working together to enhance the learning experiences of exceptional students in regular classrooms. I hope that their words will strengthen and inspire you to use all your available resources, including action research, to meet the challenges of inclusive teaching! Finally, I hope this book will help you to become knowledgeable about and sensitive to the realities of teaching real kids in a real school.

Inclusion *of* Exceptional Learners *in* Canadian Schools

a PRACTICAL HANDBOOK *for* TEACHERS

LEARNER OBJECTIVES

After you have read this chapter, you will be able to:

1. Describe the current state of inclusion in Canadian society.

2. Describe the current state of inclusive education for exceptional students in Canada.

3. Trace highlights in the development of inclusive education in Canada.

4. Analyze the controversy over inclusive education for exceptional students.

5. Describe briefly various exceptionalities that are identified across Canada.

6. Discuss what it means to adapt teaching and classrooms to meet the needs of exceptional learners, and describe the steps of a strategy for ADAPTing teaching to include exceptional learners.

Chapter 1

Educating Exceptional Students: The Canadian Experience

Gurgit is a bright and articulate girl in grade 3 who was identified as gifted in grade 1. On the first day of the social studies unit about Canada, Gurgit answered all of Ms. Wang's questions about the provinces. She asked questions the teacher had not thought of, especially about the new territory of Nunavut. In a bored voice, Gurgit asked how long they would have to cover this material. Gurgit read reference books independently, surfed the Internet on her family's computer, and wrote pages while most of her classmates penned a few sentences. Gurgit had already met the unit's outcomes and needed a challenge. The next day, Ms. Wang assigned a province or territory to each group of students. She placed Gurgit in the group working on the Northwest Territories and challenged her to research the human and physical geography of Nunavut. Gurgit found information about Nunavut on the Web, and contributed many ideas to her group about life in the Northwest Territories. While the rest of the class prepared booklets about their provinces, Gurgit developed activities for her classmates to complete at a centre on Nunavut, which remained available to the grade 3 class for the next two months.

Ben has a learning disability that was identified when he was in grade 9. His grade 9 teachers said he rarely handed in assignments or contributed to class discussions, but when he did speak he had good ideas. Ben was often late for classes and forgot his books. His report card comments included, "Could work harder" and "Ben is disorganized." An assessment showed that Ben's reading comprehension was below grade level. He skipped over words he didn't understand and could not answer interpretive questions. At Ben's request and with the approval of his teachers, Ben transferred from the academic to the applied stream at the beginning of grade 10. The resource teacher, who began to work with Ben and his teachers in grade 10, focused on organizational strategies. She showed him how to use a daybook to keep track of the days, classes, and assignments, and how to break an assignment into parts and set a date for the completion of each part. The resource teacher also taught Ben to use the RAP strategy—Read, Ask yourself questions, Paraphrase—for comprehending one paragraph at a time. She encouraged Ben's teachers to make adaptations in their classrooms. One teacher used a paired reading strategy, another taught RAP to the entire class, and the chemistry teacher adopted occasional open-book tests. Ben passed all his applied courses in grade 10 but says that the courses were too easy. Now he wants to return to the academic stream.

1. Why are both Gurgit and Ben considered to be exceptional students?

2. How likely are you to teach students like Gurgit and Ben?

3. What should teachers be expected to do to meet the learning needs of students like Gurgit and Ben?

4. What expectations might Gurgit have after engaging in the enriched experience about Nunavut, while her classmates completed more traditional projects?

5. How do you think Ben's teachers and parents should respond to his request to return to the academic stream?

Gurgit and Ben are two of the approximately 600 000 exceptional learners in Canadian schools. As a classroom teacher, you will probably find students like Gurgit and Ben in every class you teach because learning disabilities and giftedness are common exceptionalities. Occasionally you will teach students with less common exceptionalities such as deafness and autism. This book will prepare you to include exceptional students in the life and learning of your classroom. You will find that Gurgit and Ben are like other students in most ways: first, they are children or adolescents; second, they have exceptionalities.

This chapter introduces you to the context in which we educate exceptional students. The discussion focuses on the current state of inclusion of persons with disabilities and of inclusive education, policies across the country, historical and legal roots, and controversies. This chapter is also concerned with how we can best help exceptional students to reach their potential. It includes brief descriptions of exceptionalities and closes by introducing a strategy for adapting teaching to include exceptional learners: ADAPT.

Exceptional Education in Canada

Weblinks

SPECIAL NEEDS OPPORTUNITY
WINDOWS (SNOW)
http://snow.utoronto.ca

COUNCIL FOR EXCEPTIONAL
CHILDREN
http://www.cec.sped.org

SPECIAL EDUCATION RESOURCES
ON SCHOOL NET
**http://www.schoolnet.ca/sne/
e/resources.html**

In Canada, **exceptional students** refers to students who are gifted as well as students with disabilities. Across the country, a number of terms are used interchangeably. Ontario uses *exceptional children,* while British Columbia and Alberta use *students with special needs.* For example, Alberta defines **students with special needs** as: "Students…including those who are gifted and talented [who] require specialized learning opportunities in order to receive the best education" (Alberta Education, 1997, p. 1). Some provinces acknowledge that students who are **at risk** due to poverty and other social conditions are more likely to develop special needs. Saskatchewan Special Education Unit posts a newsletter on its Web site called *Challenges, Choices, and Changes.* It begins: "Saskatchewan classrooms contain students with a wide range of physical, intellectual and emotional needs, as well as children exposed to sexual and physical abuse, children exposed to drugs, and other by-products of an increasingly complex and changing society" (http://www.sasked.gov.sk.ca/k/pecs/se/newsletter.html). Topics in the newsletter include the Young Offenders Act as well as disabilities.

Exceptional students in Canada are entitled to an adapted education program, sometimes called a special education program. **Special education** means "programs and/or services designed to accommodate pupils whose educational needs cannot adequately be met through the use of regular curriculum and services only" (Prince Edward Island Department of Education, 1997a). In British Columbia, an **adapted program** "retains the learning outcomes of the prescribed curriculum, but adaptations are provided so the student can participate in the program. These adaptations can include alternate formats (e.g., Braille, books-on-tape), instructional strategies (e.g., use of interpreters, visual cues and aids) and assessment procedures (e.g., oral exams, additional time)" (British Columbia Special Education Branch, 1995b, http://www.bced.gov.bc.ca/specialed/ppandg/toc.htm).

By contrast, a **modified program** has learning outcomes substantially different from the prescribed curriculum and specifically selected to meet the student's needs. You will see examples in upcoming chapters of a grade 5 student learning to use the telephone as part of her language arts program and a secondary student learning life skills such as making a sandwich.

You will need to become familiar with your provincial and school district documents about exceptional students. To examine the policies on an issue such as education of exceptional children, we must look at all ten provinces and three territories. Since Confederation, each province has had the authority to pass laws about education. However, all laws in Canada must be consistent with the Constitution Act, which contains the **Charter of Rights and Freedoms** (Government of Canada, 1982, http://laws.justice.gc.ca/en/charter/index.html). The **equality rights** that apply to education are contained in section 15(1): "Every individual is equal before and under the law and has a right to the equal protection and equal benefit of the law without discrimination based on race, national or ethnic origin, colour, religion, sex, age, or mental or physical disability."

Canada: Inclusive Society, Inclusive Schools

Participating in all facets of society, including educational institutions, is a fundamental right of all Canadians. Many developments worldwide contributed to Canada's adoption of the Charter of Rights and Freedoms in 1982. For example, all members of the United Nations adopted the Universal Declaration of Human Rights in 1948. Education was one of the fundamental human rights listed in the Declaration; however, there was no mention of people with disabilities. In 1975, the United Nations declared that disabled persons had the same rights as other people (including community living, education, work, voting, etc.) in the Declaration of Rights of Disabled Persons. The Canadian Human Rights Act of 1977 stated that no one should be discriminated against for reasons of physical or mental ability. Subsequently, 1981 was proclaimed the International Year of Disabled Persons, causing heightened awareness of disabilities and enhancing the self-advocacy of people with disabilities. That year, the Canadian parliament was debating the terms of the Charter of Rights and Freedoms. When people with disabilities were not named in an early draft of the Charter, they protested on Parliament Hill and got their story into the newspaper headlines and *Maclean's* magazine. The result was that when the Charter was passed, Canada became the first country to guarantee rights to people with disabilities in its constitution.

The United Nations continues to champion the rights of persons with disabilities, and in 1993 adopted the Standard Rules on the Equalization of Opportunities for Persons with Disabilities, targeting eight areas for **equal participation**, including education. "Persons with disabilities are members of society and have the right to remain within their local communities. They should receive the support they need within the ordinary structures of health, education, employment and social services" (United Nations Economic and Social Commission for Asia and the Pacific, http://unescap.org/decade/st-rules.htm).

Put Into Practice

Look at the Special Education Policies and Procedures Manual for your province or territory and for your local school district. Many schools also have their own protocols about exceptional students.

Weblinks

CANADIAN CHARTER OF RIGHTS AND FREEDOMS
http://laws.justice.gc.ca/en/charter/index.html

Further Reading

For teaching about human rights: W. Cassidy & R. Yates (1998). *Let's Talk About Law in Elementary School.* Calgary: Detselig Enterprises Ltd.

Public Legal Education Association of Saskatchewan (1997). *Teaching Human Rights.* Saskatoon: Public Legal Education Association of Saskatchewan.

Activists with developmental disabilities at the People First Conference. In 1981, people who are blind and people with physical disabilities and developmental disabilities held conferences and rallied on Parliament Hill demanding equality.

Canada's policy on persons with disabilities emphasizes **inclusion**. For example, the mandate of the Office of Disability Issues in the federal government is to "remove barriers and to improve the social and economic inclusion of Canadians with disabilities" (http://www.hrdc-drhc.gc.ca/bcph-odi/content/about.shtml). While progress is uneven, there are many indications of progress toward access and full participation for persons with disabilities. Parks Canada is making national parks accessible, and Canadian Heritage promotes and funds the inclusion of athletes with disabilities in mainstream sports. Universities are making their campuses and courses more accessible for students with disabilities (Careless, 1994), and exceptional children and adolescents are increasingly attending their neighbourhood schools. However, this is a time-consuming and expensive process. One only has to pick up a newspaper or magazine (e.g., *Abilities: Canada's Lifestyle Magazine for People with Disabilities*, http://www.abilities.ca) to see articles and letters to the editor about sites and events that are not yet accessible. Our aspirations to be inclusive still outstrip our accomplishments. However, schools play a key role in the process we have embarked on toward inclusion of persons with disabilities in all aspects of Canadian society.

Put Into Practice

Increase your awareness of the perspectives of people with disabilities. Visit an agency that advocates for people with disabilities (e.g., Association for Community Living). Read a publication written by and for people with disabilities (e.g., *Abilities* magazine).

Where We Are Now: The Current State of Inclusive Education for Exceptional Students

In 1998, a review of the policies and procedures across the country (Friend, Bursuck, & Hutchinson, 1998) showed two dominant themes in the education of exceptional learners: change and inclusion. Smith and Foster (1993) reviewed the platform of rights of exceptional children across Canada—non-discrimination and access—on which other more complex rights are constructed. Non-discrimination and access get exceptional learners inside the schoolhouse door. The changes we are experiencing currently are intended "to move from the goal of access for as many students as possible to success for as many as possible" (Gouvernement du Québec, Ministère de l'Éducation, 1999). Success for exceptional students depends on complex rights (Smith & Foster, 1994) that include identification of their educational needs and adapted teaching and services to meet those needs. This is usually accomplished through an **Individual Education Plan (IEP)**, a written plan developed for an exceptional student that describes the adaptations, modifications, and services to be provided. The next section contains descriptions of policies and procedures for exceptional learners in each province and territory, from west to east.

The Current State in Each Province and Territory

BRITISH COLUMBIA

British Columbia has thorough documents describing policies (1995b), IEPs (1996), and resource guides (e.g., *Gifted Education: A Resource Guide for Teachers*, 1995a). These were released after extensive consultation in 1995 and are available at the provincial Web site (http://www.bced.gov.bc.ca./specialed/docs.htm). B.C. defines **inclusive education** as "the value system which holds that all students are entitled to equitable access to learning, achievement and the pursuit of excellence in all aspects of their education. The practice of inclusion transcends the idea of physical location, and incorporates basic values that promote participation, friendship and interaction." The province provides a range of placements when necessary. Needs are identified during an assessment and the IEP provides a working document, "a plan to adapt materials, instructional strategies or assessment procedures, or to modify, supplement, or replace parts of the regular curriculum." *Individual Education Planning for Students with Special Needs* (British Columbia Special Education Branch, 1996) provides clear steps to develop, implement, and review an IEP.

While unemployment and underemployment remain higher for persons with disabilities, workplaces are being made accessible. Education is important to the careers of persons with disabilities, as it is to the careers of all Canadians.

YUKON

Yukon's *Special Programs Services: A Handbook of Procedures and Guidelines* (1995) is based on B.C.'s 1995 manual. The procedures and definitions are similar, but adapted for northern circumstances and a diverse population. The inclusive philosophy states, "School programs must recognize and be adapted to meet the wide range of needs and abilities of students." The **school-based team**, including the classroom teacher and within-school support staff, is involved in the assessment of exceptional students. After consulting with the parents and the student, the school-based team develops the IEP, "a concise and usable document which summarizes the plan for the student's educational program."

ALBERTA

Alberta engaged in wide consultation in the early 1990s and in December 2000 completed another special education review, this time focusing on streamlining administration and enhancing accountability (Alberta Learning, 2000, http://www.learning. gov. ab.ca/k_12/special/SpecialEdReview/). According to the *Guide to Education for Students with Special Needs* (Alberta Education, 1997), "students are placed in programs where their needs can best be met" (p. 12). While there is considerable emphasis in the review on inclusive classrooms and in the guide on providing classroom teachers with the resources and support they need, exceptional students have access to specialized classes and services as required. Assessment for identification of special needs is described in a guide for parents, *Partners During Changing Times* (Alberta Education, 1996), and in a general guide, *Individualized Program Plans* (IPP) (Alberta Education, 1995). The equivalent of the IEP, "The IPP is a written commitment of intent by an educational team" to ensure provision of services.

NORTHWEST TERRITORIES

The Education Act (Bill 25 Summary) (Northwest Territories Department of Education, Culture and Employment, 1995) clearly states the following policy: "Inclusive schooling—students whenever possible have access to the education program in a regular classroom setting in the community where they reside." *Educating All Our Children: Departmental Directive on Inclusive Schooling* (Northwest Territories Department of Education, Culture and Employment, 1996, http://www.learnnet.nt.ca) describes a team-based approach to educating and identifying the strengths and needs of *all* students. Program modifications occur at the classroom level and "where the education program, even with modification, is not suitable for the student, an Individualized Education Plan may be necessary to effectively meet the needs of the student." There are no definitions of exceptionalities, and no identifications of exceptionalities are made by the school, only identification of strengths and needs.

NUNAVUT

Nunavut became a territory on April 1, 1999; what had previously been the eastern two-thirds of the Northwest Territories is now a separate jurisdiction. Currently, Nunavut uses the Education Act (1995) and Inclusive Schooling (1996) policy of the Northwest Territories. Given that most inhabitants of Nunavut are Inuit, it is likely that this territory will develop unique educational policies just as it has developed a unique system of government that reflects its Inuit culture (see Government of Nunavut, http://www.gov.nu.ca).

SASKATCHEWAN

In 2000, Saskatchewan released both the final report of the Special Education Review Committee, *Directions for Diversity*, and the minister of education's response, *Strengthening Supports* (both are at http://www.sasked.gov.sk.ca/k/pecs/se/whatsnew.html). Consultation is underway. Both documents reiterate the commitment to inclusion that appears in the draft *Special Education Policy Manual* (Saskatchewan Department of Education, 1996): "Students with exceptional needs should experience education in settings that allow them to achieve their individual goals in inclusive settings. Other arrangements are to be used only when a legitimate case can be made for using such alternatives." Strengths and needs should be identified, "Students with designated disabilities should have a Personal Program Plan (PPP)," and disabilities are defined in the School Act for the purposes of funding.

MANITOBA

A major review of special education (Proactive Information Services, 1999) recommended that Manitoba continue the move toward inclusive education and clearer procedures, such as those in the handbook for developing and implementing IEPs (Manitoba Education and Training, 1998). The policy handbook *Special Education in Manitoba* (Manitoba Education and Training, 1989) is still in force, while the Special Education Review Initiative (SERI) (www2.edu.gov.mb.ca/metks4/instruct/specedu/review/default.htm) consults widely. On the Web site are SERI's recommendations for a "philosophy of inclusion" and plan for revising the policy handbook. A series of documents entitled *Towards Inclusion* prescribes curriculum modifications; for example, *Towards Inclusion: A Handbook for Modified Course Designation, Senior 1–4* (Manitoba Education and Training, 1995) focuses on students with "significant cognitive disabilities."

ONTARIO

In the past five years, Ontario has undergone massive change in all aspects of education (Gidney, 1999). The current policy states that an **Identification, Placement, and Review Committee (IPRC)** should use the definitions provided by the Ministry of Education to identify a student's exceptionality. While avoiding the word *inclusion,* it states that the IPRC should recommend placement in a "regular class, with appropriate special education services" whenever that meets the student's needs and the parents' preferences (Ontario Ministry of Education, Regulation 181/98; http://www.edu.gov.on.ca/eng/general/elemsec/speced/hilites.html). All recently developed curriculum guidelines include recommendations for adapting curriculum and assessment to meet individual needs. The *Individual Education Plan (IEP) Resource Guide* (Ontario Ministry of Education, 1998, http://www.edu.gov.on.ca/eng/general/elemsec/speced/individu.htm) describes five steps for educators to follow. Standards for IEPs are prescribed in *Individual Education Plans: Standards for Development, Program Planning, and Implementation* (Ontario Ministry of Education, 2000; http://www.edu.gov.on.ca/eng/general/elemsec/speced/iep/iep.html).

> **Cross-Reference**
> Chapter 2 describes IEPs, your role in the IEP process, and collaboration with parents.

QUEBEC

In 1999, Quebec released its draft policy on special education, *Adapting Our Schools to the Needs of All Students*, which recommends integration into regular classrooms and placement in neighbourhood schools whenever possible. There is a reference guide for developing IEPs (Gouvernement du Québec, Ministère de l'Éducation, 1993) that refers to section 10 of the Charter of Human Rights and Freedoms adopted by Quebec in place of Canada's Charter of Rights and Freedoms. Quebec's documents refer to students with handicaps ("a physical impairment may be a mild to severe motor impairment or an organic impairment"), students with social maladjustments, and students with learning disabilities.

NEW BRUNSWICK

In 1986, New Brunswick introduced legislation that stressed integration of exceptional students and in 1988, released *Working Guidelines on Integration* (N.B.

Table 1.1

SUMMARY OF PROVINCIAL AND TERRITORIAL APPROACHES
TO EDUCATION OF EXCEPTIONAL LEARNERS

Province/Territory	IEP or Equivalent	Description of Policy	Review of Special Education
British Columbia	Individual Education Plan	Inclusive education	1990s
Yukon	Individual Education Plan	Inclusive philosophy	1990s
Alberta	Individualized Program Plan	Most appropriate placement	1990s, 2000
Northwest Territories	Individual Education Plan	Inclusive schooling	1990s
Nunavut	Individual Education Plan (of NT)	Inclusive schooling (of NT)	Created in 1999
Saskatchewan	Personal Program Plan	Inclusive settings	Ongoing
Manitoba	Individual Education Plan	Philosophy of inclusion	Ongoing
Ontario	Individual Education Plan and Identification, Placement, and Review Committee	Regular class first	1990s
Quebec	Individual Education Plan	Integration, neighbourhood schools	Ongoing
New Brunswick	Individual Education Plan	Inclusive education	1990s
Nova Scotia	Individual Program Plan	Regular instructional settings	1990s
Prince Edward Island	Individual Education Plan	Most enabling environment	Ongoing
Newfoundland and Labrador	Individual Support Services Plan	Regular classroom and continuum of services	1990s

Department of Education). In 1991, the province issued a position statement on inclusive education emphasizing its commitment to: "a process of inclusive, quality education in which every effort is made to educate all students through instruction commensurate with their individual needs, in regular classes within neighbourhood schools." Extensive assessment of student needs is to precede the determination that a student requires a "special program," and a "special education plan" is to be developed for all exceptional children. This may vary from a short-term plan to a comprehensive IEP (New Brunswick Department of Education, *Guidelines for a Special Education Plan*, n.d.). In 1997, New Brunswick released *Gifted and Talented Students: A Resource Guide for Teachers* (http://www.gov.nb.ca/education/orgs/e/stuserv.htm).

NOVA SCOTIA

Nova Scotia's changes to the Education Act were completed in 1995–96. School boards are to "develop and implement educational programs for students with special needs within regular instructional settings with their peers in age." The *Special Education Policy Manual* (Nova Scotia Department of Education, 1997 (amended); http://doc-depot.ednet.ns.ca/) describes the goal of inclusion as facilitating the membership, participation, and learning of all students in school programs and activities. IPPs are based on an assessment of strengths and needs and are implemented for students for whom provincial curriculum outcomes are not applicable or attainable. A recent report suggests that while Nova Scotia teachers believe that IPPs have a positive impact on students, they also believe that teachers need more professional development on IPPs (French, 1999; http://www.nstu.ns.ca/aviso/Winter99/research.html).

PRINCE EDWARD ISLAND

Prince Edward Island has also seen change. In 1990, Prince Edward Island's Special Education Policy Statement emphasized that children with special needs "will be educated in the environment that is the most enabling and that allows opportunities for them to interact with their non-special needs peers." Subsequently, a non-categorical model of service delivery was developed called "a whole school approach" (P.E.I. Ministry of Education, 1995). This model involved school-based student services teams and IEPs, but did not focus on identification of specific exceptionalities. A Minister's Directive issued in 1997 made IEPs mandatory. A recent review of special education (Mackey & Associates, n.d.; http://www2.gov.pe.ca/educ/publications/reports/se/toc.asp) made 43 recommendations. These included "incorporating the best tenets of a continuum of services based on inclusionary practices," reinstating categories of exceptionality, and developing a practitioner's guide to IEPs.

NEWFOUNDLAND AND LABRADOR

Newfoundland and Labrador has also reviewed exceptional education (Canning, 1996; Newfoundland Classroom Issues Committee, 1995) and instituted change, including a new Schools Act in 1997. To integrate services and minimize duplication, Newfoundland initiated Individual Support Services Plans (ISSPs) involving the Departments of Education, Health, Human Resources and Employment, and Justice (*Coordination of Services to Children and Youth in Newfoundland & Labrador*, 1997; http://www.edu.gov.nf.ca/issp/table.htm). In 1998, the government released *Pathways to Programming and Graduation*, a handbook that describes five routes through the school curriculum with varying degrees of adaptation of the curriculum (Government of Newfoundland and Labrador, 1998), as shown in Table 1.2. The handbook also contains definitions of exceptionalities, lists of "supports which may be required" by exceptional students, and concrete programming suggestions. The final report of the Ministerial Panel on Educational Delivery in the Classroom included recommendations for streamlining *Pathways* and ISSPs (Government of Newfoundland, 2000, http://www.gov.nf.ca/edu/EDUPUB.HTM).

Table 1.2

SUMMARY OF THE FIVE PATHWAYS TO PROGRAMMING AND GRADUATION IN NEWFOUNDLAND

Pathways	Intended For	Decisions Made By	Program Defined By
1. Provincially approved programs	All students; groups of students who have particular interests, needs, or abilities	Students, classroom teachers, students' advisors, guidance personnel, parents/guardians	Provincially approved program outcomes
2. Provincially approved programs with additional supports (accommodations and adaptations)	An individual student who requires appropriate supports in order to meet provincially approved program outcomes or to be sufficiently challenged by the prescribed curriculum	Classroom teachers and special education teachers (and sometimes including other school & district personnel) in consultation with students and parents; Individual Support Services Planning Team	Provincially approved program outcomes/ Individual Support Services Plan
3. Modifications to prescribed programs	An individual student for whom some of the prescribed program outcomes are too challenging or not challenging enough	Individual Support Services Planning Team	Individual Support Services Plan
4. Alternate programs/ courses	Individual student for whom most/all of the provincially prescribed or modified outcomes are inappropriate	Individual Support Services Planning Team	Individual Support Services Plan
5. Alternate curriculum	Individual student who requires a curriculum alternate in all areas of development; i.e., students with moderate/global and severe cognitive delays	Individual Support Services Planning Team	Individual Support Services Plan

Source: Reprinted with permission of Newfoundland and Labrador Department of Education, from *Pathways to Programming and Graduation*, 1998, p. 5.

Summary of the State in Each Province and Territory

A recent document released in Newfoundland summarizes the current policies on inclusion across Canada: "most students can have their needs met in 'regular' diverse classroom environments and…whenever possible, supports and services should be provided in these settings. Students may, however, access special learning environments and/or community-based environments, when it will facilitate their programs, for specific and compelling reasons" (1996, p. 31). Change in exceptional education is everywhere. Most provinces and territories have adopted one of the following terms: "regular classroom first," "neighbourhood school," "inclusion," or "inclusive education." Although the predominant approach in Canada is inclusion, no jurisdiction uses the expression "full inclusion." All provide alternatives to the regular classroom when that choice clearly does not meet the student's needs. Documents, except for those of Northwest Territories and Prince Edward Island, include definitions to be used for identification of exceptional students; however, P.E.I.'s review suggests that categories of exceptionality will return. Finally, IEPs are ubiquitous, although they go by a variety of names and abbreviations. All jurisdictions have them, and Ontario retains IPRCs as well. Chapter 2 focuses on the development of IEPs and your role as a classroom teacher in this important process.

How We Got Here: Recent Highlights in the Development of Inclusive Education in Canada

In 1950, there was no obligation for schools to educate students with disabilities. In the 1950s, parents began schools for children with developmental disabilities (then called mental retardation) (Pletsch, 1997). The Canadian Association for Children with Learning Disabilities was formed in the 1960s (Wong & Hutchinson, in press). Between 1950 and 1970, many school districts developed segregated programs for exceptional students.

By 1970, researchers and parents in North America were beginning to question a special education system that paralleled regular education. In the United States, Dunn (1968) published an influential paper asking whether the ends (what was learned) justified the means (separate education for students by category of disability). In 1970, the first of a series of reports—the CELDIC report, *One Million Children* (Roberts & Lazure, 1970)—was released in Canada. Radical for 1970, it recommended integration, the right to free public education, and teaching based on an exceptional child's learning needs rather than on the category of exceptionality. In 1971, the SEECC report, *Standards for Education of Exceptional Children in Canada*, recommended that universities include courses about exceptional children in teacher education (Hardy, McLeod, Minto, Perkins, & Quance, 1971). Within a few years, such courses were being taught to classroom teachers in many provinces. The National Institute on Mental Retardation in Toronto promoted Wolfensberger's concept of **normalization**—that all persons, regardless of disability, should live and learn in environments as close to normal as possible (Wolfensberger, Nirge, Olshansky, Perske, & Roos, 1972).

As in the U.S., cases began to appear in the Canadian courts. Before the end of the decade, in 1978, an Alberta Supreme Court decision ordered Lamont County school board to widen doors, build a ramp, and educate Shelley Carrière, a student with cerebral palsy, in her community school. In 1980, the Ontario Education Act was amended to recognize the rights of students with disabilities to receive an appropriate education at public expense, and to permit parents to appeal the identification of their child as exceptional and the placement of their child.

The Charter was passed in 1982 and section 15 came into force in 1985. Since then, several court cases have been heard, mainly disputing a school district's decision to place a student with a severe disability in a segregated special education classroom. In 1991, in a case in Quebec (*Re: David M. and Commission scolaire*

Table 1.3

EVOLUTION TOWARD INCLUSION

1800s, Establishing a Country, Establishing Institutions

Developments in Canadian Society	*Developments in Education*
1815–50 The Great Migration brings thousands of new settlers to Upper and Lower Canada	1830–60 Orphanages open in Halifax, Montreal, Kingston, and Toronto
1850s Railway building joins the colonies together	1831–86 Schools for blind and deaf children open in Quebec, Ontario, Nova Scotia, and Manitoba
1867 Confederation; education becomes a provincial responsibility	1893 Children's Aid Societies start in Ontario

1900–50, Change and Growth

Developments in Canadian Society	*Developments in Education*
1914–18 First World War, followed by the economic boom of the 1920s and the Great Depression of the 1930s	By the 1920s Special education classes are offered in urban elementary schools
1939–45 Second World War increases Canada's international reputation	By 1923 Summer courses for teachers of special classes are available
1945 Fifty-one nations first meet to establish the United Nations, which has among its goals the promotion of equality among peoples	1940s Residential institutions are "home" to many people with disabilities (e.g., Weyburn, SK; Smith Falls, ON)

1950–70, The Impact of the Baby Boom Generation

Developments in Canadian Society	*Developments in Education*
1950s Baby boomers and immigrant families cause population increases, cultural diversity, and the construction of suburbs	Formation of the Canadian Association for the Mentally Retarded and the Canadian Association for Children with Learning Disabilities
Cold War and Sputnik lead to huge developments in technology	Parent associations establish schools for the education of retarded children
Television brings global events into Canadian homes; youth movement for civil rights and social justice worldwide	Growth of segregated programs for gifted students and students with disabilities
1964 Pearson government funds the Company of Young Canadians to give young activists the opportunity to work toward social change in local programs	Growth of post-secondary education: universities and community colleges

Saint-Jean-sur-Richelieu), a nine-year-old boy was found to be the victim of direct and indirect discrimination under the Quebec Charter. The school district was ordered to integrate him into a regular classroom with the necessary adaptations and support (Smith, 1991).

Table 1.3

EVOLUTION TOWARD INCLUSION (CONTINUED)

1970s and 1980s, Advocacy and Rights

Developments in Canadian Society	*Developments in Education*
1975 United Nations Declaration of the Rights of Disabled Persons	1970 *One Million Children* (Roberts & Lazure) advocates the integration of exceptional children and instruction based on individual learning needs
1977 Canadian Human Rights Act	1971 *Standards for Education of Exceptional Children in Canada* (Hardy, Minto, Perkins, & Quance) sparks teacher education on exceptional children at Canadian universities
April 12, 1980 Terry Fox begins his "Marathon of Hope" to promote public awareness of the abilities of persons with disabilities and to raise funds for cancer research	1978 Alberta's Supreme Court rules that the Lamont County school board must accommodate the physical and educational needs of Shelley Carrière, a student with cerebral palsy
1981 United Nations Year of the Disabled	1980 Bill 82 in Ontario guarantees the right of all exceptional students to an appropriate education with a new funding model
1981 Demonstrations by Canadians with disabilities on Parliament Hill to demand rights for people with disabilities in the Charter	Early 1980s Provinces develop IEPs; Ontario phases in the IPRC
March 21, 1985 Rick Hansen sets out on his "Man in Motion" tour of 34 countries to raise money for spinal-cord research	Mid-1980s Integration is adopted as the prevailing approach to educating exceptional students
1988 People with mental disabilities receive the right to vote	Late 1980s Educational reviews begin across Canada, including reviews of special education

1990s, Inclusion, Reform, and Challenges

Developments in Canadian Society	*Developments in Education*
Cutbacks in government funding to schools, social services, and universities	Parents demand inclusion in regular classroom settings
August 1994 First inclusive Commonwealth Games, hosted by Victoria, British Columbia	October 10, 1996 Supreme Court of Canada rules that Emily Eaton receive appropriate education to meet her individual needs in a segregated setting, reversing an earlier decision of a lower court
1997 Release of the Report of the Royal Commission on Aboriginal Peoples	Reviews and changes in exceptional education policies across Canada make inclusion the dominant policy

In the 1995 case *Eaton v. Brant County Board of Education,* the Ontario Court of Appeals stated that: "unless the parents of a child who has been identified as exceptional by reason of a physical or mental disability consent to the placement of that child in a segregated environment, the school board must provide a placement that is the least exclusionary from the mainstream and still reasonably capable of meeting the child's special needs" (*Eaton v. Brant Board of Education*, 1995, pp. 33–34).

Then, in 1996, the Supreme Court of Canada overturned the Ontario Court of Appeal's ruling on this case. While many saw this decision as a major setback for the equity of people with disabilities, Lepofsky (1996, p. 393), in a lengthy analysis, disagrees: "better seen as a mixed result for disability equality. It contains important principles which will serve disability equity well. However, these principles are followed by some judicial comments which are confused, contradictory and counterproductive." Lepofsky argues that the Supreme Court's approach rested on the foundation that the decision to remove a child from an integrated setting

Terry Fox

Terry Fox is a Canadian hero. When Canadians were asked to name their heroes in 1999, one of the most frequently chosen individuals was a young man who won Canadians' admiration and raised our awareness about people with disabilities. Terry Fox of Coquitlam, B.C., was only 19 years old when he lost his right leg to cancer in 1977. While he was recovering, he dreamed of inspiring others with cancer and raising money to fight the disease.

In April 1980, Fox set out from St. John's, Newfoundland, to run across Canada on a "Marathon of Hope." All summer he ran 40 kilometres a day, ignoring the pain, heading for the Pacific Ocean. Newspaper reporters described his run as "lift, hop, lift, hop, lift, hop" because he rocked back and forth between his left leg and his prosthetic right leg. Television cameras reported his daily progress and all of Canada began to watch. Thousands lined the streets as he passed through towns and cities. Money for cancer research poured in. Then, in September, after running 5300 kilometres and raising $2 million, Terry Fox stopped running on the north shore of Lake Superior. The cancer had returned; Fox died less than a year later.

Canadians were inspired by Terry Fox and his "Marathon of Hope." In the months following the end of his run, they donated $25 million for cancer research. Every fall, Canadians all over the world hold marathons in his name to raise funds and, annu-

ally, thousands visit the memorial marking the site where he halted his run. Since 1980, athletes with disabilities have become much more prominent in our communities and in the news, but Terry Fox was one of the first and has become a Canadian hero.

(always the preferred setting) must be governed solely by an individualized, case-specific consideration of what is in the best interests of that child. Such a decision cannot be made simply because of the existence of a disability.

We have arrived at our commitment to inclusive education through a complex set of circumstances that includes United Nations proclamations, repatriating our constitution during the International Year of the Disabled, protests, innovative legislation and human rights codes, and our idealistic notions of a multicultural, diverse, and equitable society. Canadian heroes and ordinary people with disabilities alike have advocated for themselves and raised our awareness that people with disabilities are "People First." When we choose to teach in the early twenty-first century, we are choosing to teach in inclusive schools in a society committed to inclusion. Although our reach exceeds our grasp, Canadian classrooms include exceptional learners and we must embrace this challenge.

While we followed one path to inclusive education, other countries pursued their own routes toward the same goal. Fullwood (1990) provides an Australian perspective on growing recognition of "social justice and equality," while Jenkinson (1997) of England reminds us that inclusion in the community is the important goal. Kauffman and Hallahan (1995) of the United States wrote a blistering critique of inclusive education. In the U.S., legislation was often enacted in response to litigation and parental advocacy, resulting in a patchwork of laws governing who must be integrated and to what extent. The essential legislation is reauthorized every five years, and each reauthorization has introduced changes (Smith, Polloway, Patton, & Dowdy, 1995). There is no doubt that Canadian advocacy groups and provincial legislators have been influenced by highlights on the American path to inclusion, especially by Public Law 94-142, passed in 1975 and implemented in 1978, with its emphasis on due process.

Further Reading

For an account of the development of educational services to students with developmental disabilities, read V.C. Pletsch (1997). *Not Wanted in the Classroom.* London, ON: Althouse Press.

"I Don't Agree!" The Controversies Over Inclusive Education

Inclusive education is a controversial topic in Canada and in other countries. *Inclusion* is a relatively new term. It has replaced **mainstreaming** and **integration**, which were used in the 1970s and 1980s and both of which referred to moving exceptional students from segregated settings into classrooms in the mainstream. **Inclusion**, however, suggests that people with exceptionalities ought to be part of the mainstream of society and all its institutions from birth onward. Inclusion suggests that they be ensured full social, educational, and economic participation in society and on their own terms as much as possible.

This is one of the main ways in which inclusion differs from its predecessors. Students with disabilities who had been placed in segregated settings were to be readied for re-entry. They were mainstreamed when they could meet traditional academic expectations with minimal support, or when traditional academic expectations were not relevant. Thus exceptional students were mainstreamed for physical education, health, music, art, assembly, and other parts of the day that were viewed as non-academic. They were often taught academic skills in a separate setting, but research suggested that exceptional students taught in segregated classes did not make more academic progress than exceptional students taught in mainstream settings (e.g., Dunn, 1968). With few exceptions, parents wanted their exceptional children to participate in society, and segregated classes did not provide good models of social participation. If segregated classes did not produce better academic learning, then how could they be justified?

Recent interviews with teachers suggest that some who express concerns about inclusion want to have in the classroom only those students who can keep up with all aspects of the curriculum. Angela Valeo and Gary Bunch (1998) of York University interviewed six experienced elementary teachers, each from a different school in the same district. One teacher said that for successful integration, a child had to participate "without too much interruption in the classroom both behaviourally and academically" (p. 13). Modifying curriculum was not a role these teachers saw themselves taking on: "It would be easier if he had someone [other than the classroom teacher] working with him" (p. 13).

In contrast, in an interview study with six teachers, Paula Stanovich of University of Toronto reported on focus groups (1999). Participants were four classroom teachers, one special education teacher, and one resource teacher, from a grade 7–8 school that was undergoing a transition from a self-contained special education model to inclusion. The teachers spoke of the benefits of inclusion and of "realities," rather than costs. Benefits included opportunities for students with disabilities to learn appropriate social behaviour and for students without disabilities to develop respect for their exceptional classmates. "There's a mutual respect now, and they're talking to each other outside of class" (p. 56). The teachers also recognized the motivating effects of inclusion on exceptional students who want to be accepted. They reported that the way they taught had a direct influence on the success of inclusion. For example, they made curriculum adaptations that included using materials of various reading levels; changing the length, time, or complexity of assignments; breaking assignments into smaller parts; and using cooperative groups. They also spoke of supports that would help inclusion, including more time, appropriate teaching materials, assistants in the classroom, and administrative support. However, these two sets of data underline some of the controversies about inclusion.

Perhaps these widely differing perspectives on inclusion can be explained in part by the recent work of Anne Jordan and Paula Stanovich of University of Toronto. They found that teachers effective in inclusive classrooms tend to have principals who believe that all children can and should learn in regular classrooms and that teachers should adapt teaching rather than expect exceptional children to adapt. In such schools, the prevailing norm of the school community supports inclusion. The second important predictor of effective teaching behaviour was teachers' responses to the same belief questionnaire completed by principals. These teachers believe that exceptional children should learn in regular classrooms and that teachers should collaborate and do their part to make inclusion work (Stanovich & Jordan, 1998). Teachers with these beliefs were observed to talk more with exceptional students, especially about academic matters, and at higher cognitive levels (Jordan, Lindsay, & Stanovich, 1997). They also reported that three exemplary inclusion teachers focused on helping exceptional learners become independent members of the classroom community and made many adaptations. These adaptations often applied in varying degrees to all students (Jordan & Stanovich, 1998). These studies suggest that when we work in schools that value inclusion, we do a better job of including exceptional students and that our beliefs about these students are closely related to our teaching actions. Thus, as teachers, we must examine our beliefs and assumptions about exceptional children, because they may explain conflicting views on inclusive education.

Community and Inclusive Education

There are a number of ways in which community is important to inclusive education. **Community** refers to a group of people who have shared interests and who mutually pursue the common good. Usually community members share an acceptance of group standards and a sense of identification with the group (Dewey, 1916; McCaleb, 1994). As discussed earlier, inclusion refers to acceptance and participation of all, a way of being together rather than a place, and inclusive classrooms ought to be communities. As well, inclusion is directed to the participation of all students in the community beyond the school. Thus it is important that the learning of all students, including exceptional students, takes place in the community that surrounds the school as well as in the classroom. These ideas arise frequently in subsequent chapters and are developed most fully in Chapters 6, 9, and 10.

Cross-Reference
Chapters 3 and 4 provide detailed information about the exceptionalities discussed in this chapter.

Who Are Exceptional Learners?

Earlier, we defined exceptional learners as both students who are gifted and students with disabilities. There are many definitions of disability. The World Health Organization (1997) set out three definitions that focus on interactions with the environment. **Impairment** refers to a loss or abnormality of body structure or of a physiological or psychological function (e.g., loss of vision); **disability** refers to the nature and extent of limitations to function (e.g., performing the activities required to read); and **handicap** refers to the nature and extent of restrictions on participation (e.g., being employed). While some provinces refer to students with special needs, I have chosen to use exceptional students and exceptionalities, more neutral terms.

This section contains brief descriptions of exceptionalities. These generic descriptions will not apply to all students with these exceptionalities, and they are quickly replaced by your description focusing on the most relevant characteristics of an individual learner. Exceptional learners are not their exceptionalities; rather, they are children and adolescents with exceptionalities. That is why we use person-first language (see Table 1.4).

Descriptions of Exceptional Students
STUDENTS WHO ARE GIFTED OR DEVELOPMENTALLY ADVANCED

Students who are **gifted** show exceptionally high abilities in one or several areas, including specific academic subjects, overall intellect, leadership, creativity, or the

Put Into Practice

Read about Sputnik, released by the Soviet Union in 1958, and think about why this might have caused North American educators to focus more on gifted students, especially in mathematics and science.

Table 1.4	

USING PERSON-FIRST LANGUAGE: STUDENTS WITH DISABILITIES

Terminology Guide Concerning Persons with Disabilities

Do not use or say	*Do use or say*
The blind; visually impaired	Person who is blind; person with a visual impairment
Confined to a wheelchair; wheelchair-bound	Person who uses a wheelchair; wheelchair user
Crippled	Person with a disability; person who has a spinal cord injury; etc.
The deaf	Person who is deaf (when referring to the entire deaf population and their culture, one can use "the deaf")
The hearing impaired	Person who is hard of hearing
Epileptic	Person who has epilepsy
Fit	Seizure
The handicapped	Person with a disability (unless referring to an environmental or attitudinal barrier)
Insane; mentally diseased	Person with a mental health disability; person who has schizophrenia; person who has depression
Mentally retarded	Person with a developmental disability
Normal	Person who is not disabled
Physically challenged	Person with a physical disability

Source: Adapted from Office for Disability Issues, *A Way with Words: Guidelines and Appropriate Terminology for the Portrayal of Persons with Disabilities* (Human Resources Development Canada, 1997). Copyright © 1997 by Human Resources Development Canada. Used with permission.

arts. Gurgit, described in the opening of this chapter, is gifted; she is eager to learn, sometimes reaches the outcomes for a unit before it has begun, and learns quickly, especially in language arts and social studies.

STUDENTS WITH LEARNING DISABILITIES (LD)

Weblinks

THE LEARNING DISABILITIES ASSOCIATION OF CANADA
http://www.ldac-taac.ca

Students with **learning disabilities** have dysfunctions in processing information. They may have disabilities in reading (dyslexia), writing, or arithmetic calculations. LD is often defined as a discrepancy between ability and achievement despite average or above-average intelligence. Learning disabilities are not a result of another disabling condition or of socioeconomic disadvantage. Ben, described at the beginning of this chapter, has a learning disability with difficulties in reading comprehension and organization.

STUDENTS WITH ATTENTION DEFICIT/HYPERACTIVITY DISORDER (AD/HD)

Students with **attention deficit/hyperactivity disorder** show a persistent pattern of inattention and impulsiveness that may be accompanied by hyperactivity and that hinders their social, academic, and vocational expectations. AD/HD is usually identified by physicians, and students with this exceptionality may take medications such as Ritalin to help them focus their attention and to make them more responsive to interventions.

> **Cross-Reference**
> Chapter 3 has information about medications prescribed to students with AD/HD, including Ritalin. Read about the potential benefits and side effects so you can ask questions about this common practice.

STUDENTS WITH SPEECH AND LANGUAGE EXCEPTIONALITIES

Students with **speech and language exceptionalities** may have a speech impairment (e.g., lisp or stutter) or may have an impairment in expressive or receptive language. Students with other disabilities (e.g., autism) may receive services to enhance communication.

STUDENTS WITH BEHAVIOURAL AND EMOTIONAL EXCEPTIONALITIES

Students who show dysfunctional interactions with their environment, including the classroom, home, and community, are described as having **behavioural or emotional exceptionalities**. Some provinces provide examples of characteristic behaviours (e.g., aggressive, extremely withdrawn, depressed, self-destructive, unable to build or maintain relationships with peers and teachers).

> **Cross-Reference**
> Chapter 9 focuses on promoting social relationships and handling challenging behaviours. It will help you respond to students with behavioural exceptionalities.

STUDENTS WITH DEVELOPMENTAL DISABILITIES

Students with **developmental disabilities** develop cognitive abilities and adaptive behaviours at a much slower rate than do their peers, which results in significant limitations in these areas. Despite these limitations, they can often participate in their community and neighbourhood school, and can lead productive adult lives if supported in employment. There are mild and severe levels of developmental disabilities.

> **Further Reading**
> For two first-person accounts of life with developmental disabilities: J. Kingsley & M. Levitz (1994). *Count Us In: Growing Up with Down Syndrome*. New York: Harcourt Brace & Co.

STUDENTS WITH AUTISM OR ASPERGER SYNDROME

Students with **autism** show limited development in communication and social interaction and a severe delay in intellectual, emotional, and behavioural development. Students with **Asperger syndrome** have a severe and sustained impairment in social interaction and develop restricted, repetitive patterns of behaviour, interests, and activities, with no significant delays in language acquisition or cognitive development.

STUDENTS WHO ARE HARD OF HEARING AND STUDENTS WHO ARE DEAF

Students who are **hard of hearing** or **deaf** have partial or complete hearing loss that interferes with the acquisition and maintenance of the auditory skills necessary to develop speech and oral language. They depend on visual sources of information to supplement or replace hearing.

>
> **Put Into Practice**
> Many people who are deaf view themselves as belonging to the Deaf Culture, and see themselves as different but not disabled. Find resources about the Deaf Culture. Learn about American Sign Language (ASL), the language of the Deaf Culture.

STUDENTS WITH VISUAL IMPAIRMENTS AND STUDENTS WHO ARE BLIND

Students with **visual impairment** or who are **blind** have partial or complete loss of sight and depend on auditory and tactile sources of information to supplement or replace sight.

STUDENTS WITH PHYSICAL DISABILITIES

Cross-Reference
Chapter 4 includes physical disabilities and chronic health conditions, along with Web sites about medical aspects and implications for mobility and classroom learning.

Weblinks
TOURETTE SYNDROME FOUNDATION OF CANADA
http://www.tourette.ca

Students with **physical disabilities** have a range of conditions restricting physical movement or motor abilities as a result of nervous system impairment, musculoskeletal conditions, or chronic medical disorders. I have included descriptions for a number of these because each is slightly different in cause, characteristics, and implications for the classroom.

Students with Cerebral Palsy. **Cerebral palsy** is a group of disorders impairing body movement and muscle coordination as a result of an interference in messages between the brain and the body (nervous system impairment).

Students with Spina Bifida. **Spina bifida** is a condition developed prenatally that disturbs proper development of the vertebrae or spinal cord and results in varying degrees of damage to the spinal cord and nervous system (nervous system impairment).

Students with Epilepsy. **Epilepsy** is a neurological disorder that occasionally produces brief disturbances in normal electrical functions in the brain that lead to sudden, brief seizures. Seizures vary in nature and intensity from person to person (nervous system impairment).

Students with Tourette Syndrome. Students with **Tourette syndrome** have a neurological disorder involving motor tics and uncontrollable vocal sounds or inappropriate words. These are often accompanied by obsessions and hyperactivity (nervous system impairment).

Students with Traumatic Brain Injury (TBI). Students with **traumatic brain injury** have damage to brain tissue as a result of a blow to the head or an accident. Brain injury can cause physical difficulties (e.g., paralysis) and cognitive problems (e.g., memory loss). The nature of school challenges varies widely depending on extent and location of the brain injury (nervous system impairment).

Students with Fetal Alcohol Syndrome (FAS). Students with **fetal alcohol syndrome** have physical and physiological abnormalities due to prenatal exposure to alcohol. There are delays in development, central nervous dysfunction, and a characteristic pattern of facial features. They experience learning and behavioural challenges in school (nervous system impairment).

Students with Muscular Dystrophy. **Muscular dystrophy** is a group of muscle disorders characterized by progressive weakness and wasting away of the voluntary muscles that control body movement (musculoskeletal condition).

Students with Juvenile Arthritis. **Juvenile arthritis** is a chronic arthritic condition with continuous inflammation of one or more joints. Students report stiffness and pain and the eyes can become involved (musculoskeletal condition).

Students with Diabetes. Students with **diabetes** have a condition of the pancreas that results in failure to produce a sufficient amount of the hormone insulin required for proper sugar absorption in the body. They may have restrictions on their physical activity at school (health condition).

Students with Life-Threatening Allergies. Students with **allergies** have an abnormal reaction to a normal substance (e.g., peanuts). They usually carry an EPIPEN® to provide an injection and need to be taken to the hospital immediately if they go into anaphylaxis (health condition).

Students with Asthma. Students with **asthma** experience obstructed airways that hinder the flow of air into and out of the lungs. An attack is characterized by persistent wheezing, chest tightness, and excess phlegm; can be life threatening; and requires that the student be rushed to hospital (health condition).

Students with Cystic Fibrosis. **Cystic fibrosis** causes increasingly severe respiratory problems and often involves extreme difficulty in digesting nutrients from food. Students may have to do breathing exercises during school to clear their lungs and passages (health condition).

Chapters 3 and 4 contain detailed information about all of the exceptionalities introduced in this chapter. They focus on educational implications for you as a classroom teacher.

Using the ADAPT Strategy for Adapting Teaching to Include Exceptional Learners

Recently, a pre-service teacher at Queen's University wrote: "Incorporating different learning strategies into a lesson should not be a 'modification.' I believe that it will become *my* norm. It facilitates and maximizes successful learning for everyone, which is what my job as a teacher is all about." You need strategies for adapting that are effective for your students, efficient for you, and become a regular part of your planning, teaching, and assessment.

This chapter introduces you to a systematic strategy called ADAPT for adapting teaching to include exceptional learners. This strategy is similar to others that serve the same purpose, but it includes considering the perspectives of those influenced by the decision to ADAPT and the consequences for them of the adaptation. This approach is elaborated on throughout the text with many examples, especially in Chapters 3, 4, 7, and 8. This strategy recognizes that both the characteristics of the student (**strengths** *and* **needs**) and the demands of the classroom environment have to be considered when devising adaptations.

The **ADAPT** strategy for adapting teaching to include exceptional learners has the following five steps:

Step 1	Accounts of students' strengths and needs
Step 2	Demands of the classroom
Step 3	Adaptations
Step 4	Perspectives and consequences
Step 5	Teach and assess the match

These five steps constitute a procedure that you can use in both elementary and secondary classrooms with learners who have a variety of exceptionalities.

Step 1: Accounts of Students' Strengths and Needs

This first step requires that you know each exceptional student well. Start with the student's confidential file. This file usually contains the IEP, assessment reports, anecdotal comments from previous teachers, and relevant medical information. It is your responsibility to be familiar with this file from the first day the student is a member of your class. Your own observations will quickly complement the views of others. The IEP includes specific statements of strengths and needs, usually in three general areas: social, emotional, and behavioural; physical; and academic.

Cross-Reference
In Chapter 2, you will find strengths and needs as described in a student's IEP. The IEP will supplement your own observations of a student.

Social, emotional, and behavioural strengths may include carrying on a conversation with peers, turn taking in a group activity, controlling anger, or being highly motivated to improve. You can use a strength such as high motivation to help a student focus on meeting personal goals. Conversely, social, emotional, and behavioural needs could mean that a student requires significant instruction and support because she cries when frustrated by academic tasks or interrupts the flow of the classroom by taunting peers and shouting out.

Physical strengths and weaknesses include motor skills, neurological functioning, and vision. A student may have strong mobility skills in spite of low vision and may be able to move around the school independently; however, her low vision may mean she needs significant instruction or adaptation to read, using a communication aid such as Braille or large print.

Academic strengths and weaknesses include the basic skills of reading, writing, mathematics, etc. They also include strategies for test taking, studying, and problem solving. Students can demonstrate strengths in completing calculations (with or without a calculator), organizing themselves, and answering questions orally. Needs can include requiring significant instruction and support to develop beginning reading, comprehend a textbook, solve word problems in mathematics, or study independently for a test.

The IEP is a working document, but it is usually confidential, and therefore should not be left where students can access it. Many teachers find it helpful to prepare a brief description of the strengths and needs of each exceptional student and tape it into their agenda. Focus on strengths and needs that are most relevant for your classroom environment and for the way you teach.

Step 2: Demands of the Classroom

Next, consider the social, emotional, and behavioural demands of your classroom. Do students learn individually or are they working with peers most of the time? A student with attention difficulties may find it hard to focus on and remember the steps in complex assignments without peer support, but also may be distracted by learning groups that are never really quiet. How long is the lecture or information-sharing section at the beginning of the class, and is it reasonable to expect a student with behavioural challenges to listen for that amount of time? Do you model positive interactions with and respect for all students?

When you consider physical demands, think about the frequency with which you move the furniture in the classroom. Ask yourself whether changes could be dangerous to anyone—especially to a student who is blind or in a wheelchair or who uses a walker. Do you rely on an overhead projector, and might some students experience difficulty seeing the projected images from where they sit in the classroom? What are the demands of your physical education classes, and could they endanger a student with asthma?

The academic demands of the classroom are manifested in the instructional materials you use, including textbooks, audiovisual aids, and manipulative devices. Do all of the children in grade 1 have the same basal readers, or do some have readers, others chapter books, and others instruction to learn the sounds in words, followed by reading of highly predictable rhyming books? Direct instruction followed by guided and, then, independent practice may enable students with learning disabilities to learn to solve complex mathematics problems (Hutchinson, 1993).

The academic demands of the classroom are also shown in your assessment and evaluation methods. Written reports, oral reports, drawings, three-dimensional models, and reports produced on CD-ROM represent different forms of assessment. Do you look for means of assessment that enable exceptional learners to show what they know rather than to show their disabilities? Adapting assessment is the topic of Chapter 8.

Cross-Reference
Chapter 7 focuses on adapting teaching and Chapter 8 focuses on adapting assessment.

Step 3: Adaptations

In this step you compare a student's learning needs to the demands of the classroom and identify potential mismatches and adaptations that will eliminate these mismatches. As we saw above, it is almost impossible to develop an account of a student's strengths and needs and to assess the demands of the classroom without thinking about adaptations that would bridge this gulf by taking advantage of the student's strengths. There are a number of ways to make adaptations, as we saw in the examples above.

You can ADAPT the fundamental organization and instruction of the classroom. For example, in a secondary history class one group may read speeches made by Canadian politicians during the Second World War and articles that appeared in Canadian newspapers of the same era to study divergent views on conscription. Students who are less competent readers may study political cartoons and view videotapes of historians discussing the issue of conscription. Both groups could use combinations of visual, oral, and written means to communicate their findings (with the emphasis on written communication varying between 20 and 80 percent).

Bypassing a student's learning need is another way to ADAPT. For example, Chung has not mastered the multiplication tables. In grade 5, his teacher shows the class how to use a calculator efficiently. The teacher reminds Chung to use his calculator and to request a "booster session" if he has forgotten any procedures. Bypassing his weakness in calculations enables Chung to work on the same authentic problems as the rest of the class. A peer editor or computerized spell checker bypasses poor spelling and Braille bypasses lack of vision. Bypass strategies minimize the impact of a disability.

Teaching students basic learning skills is also a way to ADAPT. Chung was taught two basic skills to use a calculator well: how to identify the series of operations required to solve a math problem and how to estimate the answer so he can check that his result is reasonable. Secondary teachers teach basic skills about note taking and test taking. While study skills may be an urgent need for students with LD, there are likely to be others in the class who benefit.

Step 4: Perspectives and Consequences

Reflect critically on adaptations and consider them from many perspectives. What is your experience of the adaptation? How time consuming is it? Does it change the fundamental nature of the teaching for you? Are you likely to find it satisfying? Your point of view is important because if you are uncomfortable with an adaptation, it is unlikely that you will continue with it. You have limited time and energy, so you want to choose the simplest adaptation that is effective. To get the most return for your effort, choose adaptations whenever you can that are beneficial for many (if not all) students in your class, and choose adaptations that have demonstrated effectiveness. Focus on Technology describes a strategy that is critical for students with learning disabilities, but that may benefit others. Validated practices are described in textbooks and in professional journals (see Figure 1.2), as well as on Web sites. For guidelines on evaluating Web sites, see Figure 1.1.

Next, take the perspective of the exceptional student. Is the adaptation age appropriate? Can it be conducted without drawing undue attention to the student? Is the return for effort worthwhile for the student? If you don't consider the student's perspective, you may find yourself putting in great effort, while the student is investing little. Observe and listen to the student to understand his or her point of view, and ADAPT in a way that is respectful of the student.

There are other perspectives to consider. How does the rest of the class view the adaptation? Do they notice; are they concerned, involved, and respectful? Do they feel ignored, or are they bored while you speak slowly to accommodate another student? How do the parents of the exceptional student view your adaptations? Other parents? Broaden the circle of concern to ask how the community views adapting teaching for exceptional students.

Consider consequences, intended and unintended. What are the consequences for the exceptional student—are participation and learning evident? Are there drawbacks? Pat, who has physical disabilities, may need more time and help to finish seasonal crafts in December. However, too much assistance may make Pat dependent, and the additional time may cause him to fall behind in math. Perhaps completing one craft well is more realistic and rewarding. What are the consequences of the adaptation for others in the class? Do any dilemmas arise? If you provide an open-ended assessment, you may be disappointed when students capable of writing an essay choose to develop a graphic representation of what they learned.

Step 5: Teach and Assess the Match

Ask how well the adaptation made a match between student strengths and needs and classroom demands. This analysis will help you decide whether to alter the adaptation while it takes place and whether to use the adaptation again. Remember that "things take time"; it is important to persevere and give an adaptation time to

Weblinks

MEDIA-AWARENESS: EVALUATION TECHNIQUES
http://www.media-awareness.ca/eng/med/class/teamed2/alextate.htm

KATHY SCHROCK'S GUIDE FOR EDUCATORS—CRITICAL EVALUATION SURVEYS
http://school.discovery.com/schrockguide/eval.html

QUEEN'S UNIVERSITY STAUFFER LIBRARY PAGE FOR EVALUATING WORLD WIDE WEB INFORMATION
http://stauffer.queensu.ca/inforef/tutorials/qcat/evalint.htm

While some students, especially those with learning disabilities, may *need* to write and revise their essays on a word processor, many students can benefit from such an activity. Computer activities can be planned for pairs and small groups to work cooperatively, so that students learn strategies and social skills while enhancing the quality of their written work.

In a recent study, Bernice Wong of Simon Fraser University and her associates taught low-achieving students and students with learning disabilities a strategy to plan, write, and revise opinion essays working in pairs at a computer. The steps in the writing strategy are:

- The teacher models the use of the planning strategy for the opinion essay, first outlining the reasons for taking one opinion on a controversial topic, then outlining the reasons for taking the opposite point of view. (Sample topic: Should high-school students have a dress code?)

- Pairs of students collaboratively plan one student's opinion essay, using planning sheets in two columns. The first student chooses a controversial topic. The two students then discuss pros and cons on the topic. The first student plans by listing what she knows or thinks about the topic, in the left column; her partner lists what he knows or thinks (an opposing opinion) in the right column. This is done through interactive dialogue and collaboration.

- Then, the second student of the pair plans his opinion essay in the same way with his partner providing the opposing view.

- The teacher models turning the points on the planning sheet into an essay in draft form, at the computer.

- Then, each student drafts his or her own essay at the keyboard. Charts posted around the room help students to formulate lead-in phrases, such as "In my opinion...""On the other hand..." and "After considering both sides..."

- The teacher demonstrates how to take the role of critic or editor and highlight ambiguous sections of a partner's writing with a coloured marking pen.

- Students return to their pairs to revise collaboratively, each in turn serving as critic for the other, using a coloured marking pen to highlight sections that were not clear to them.

- Students return to the computer to edit using the COPS strategy to check for errors: <u>C</u>apitalization, <u>O</u>rganization, <u>P</u>unctuation, <u>S</u>pelling. Grammar and spell checkers are helpful in this phase. After editing and checking the draft with their partners, students print their final copy.

Source: B.Y.L. Wong, D. Butler, S.A. Ficzere, and Sonia Kuperis, "Teaching Low Achievers and Students with Learning Disabilities to Plan, Write, and Revise Opinion Essays," *Journal of Learning Disabilities, 29* (1996), 197–212.

---

be effective. If you have tried everything, you may not have stayed with anything long enough. You can assess the match by observing how engaged the student is, asking how she finds the changes, charting her marks, analyzing her errors, and talking with her parents. You will think of many other sources of information to help you decide whether to continue or to rethink an adaptation.

Evaluating Internet Resources

Internet sites are identified throughout this book. I have visited these sites and found them useful; however, Web sites can change. Site addresses also change; but most Web browsers will automatically forward you to the new link. Each site

Figure 1.1

CRITERIA FOR EVALUATING INTERNET RESOURCES

1. Utility

   Before you start searching, define the research context and research needs. Then compare each site to the context and needs you have defined.

   - What are the intended purposes of this resource? Is the current Web page informational (ends in .edu or .gov), personal (includes ~), or an advocacy page (ends in .org)?
   - Who is the intended audience?
   - How current is the information and when was the site last updated?
   - Does the current Web-based resource meet your needs without causing overload?

2. Content

   Before you use the content of the current Web-based resource, consider the criteria you expect a conventional information resource to meet.

   - Do you have confidence in the content and the sources of the content provided in this resource?
   - Are the sources listed for factual information and claims so they can be verified in another source?
   - Can you obtain dates for data that you may need to compare over time?
   - Is there advertising on the site that causes you to question the objectivity of the content?

3. Authority

   Before you accept the authority of the current Web-based resource, consider whether the author would be credible if not on the Web.

   - Are the points of view of the author and organization presented clearly with arguments that are well supported?
   - Is the author identified so you know who is responsible for the content? Are the author's qualifications for writing on this topic clearly identified and credible?
   - If the source is an organization, is there a link to a page describing the function and nature of the sponsoring organization?
   - Is there a way of verifying the legitimacy of this organization? Is there more than an e-mail address, either a postal address or a telephone number?

4. Access

   - After you reach the site, evaluate its access and technical elements.
   - Can you connect quickly to the site, does access require a graphical user interface, and can the site be viewed with all Web browsers?
   - Can you tell from the first page how the site is organized and what options are available? Can you move easily from page to page? Does the site engage you?
   - Do all links work and can you see meaningful information within 30 seconds?
   - Can you print or download with ease, does the copyright notice appear prominently, and does the site name the contact for obtaining permission to copy from the site into another document?

address was verified shortly before this book went to press; the last date of address verification appears in the reference list. Before beginning to use any new information resource—print, online, or Web-based—take a few minutes to examine and evaluate the resource. This is particularly necessary for Web-based resources because they have not undergone the same rigorous process of review by experts in the field as most books and articles. Figure 1.1 contains a brief set of criteria to help you evaluate Web-based resources.

Reading the Journals to Remain Current

One of the strategies recommended for evaluating Web-based resources is to return to conventional sources, especially articles in reputable journals, to verify the information. Research journals provide one of the main routes professionals use to remain current in their field. Until Web-based resources undergo rigorous peer review, they will not take the place of journals. Peer review is the process by which a paper submitted to the editor of a journal is sent to prominent researchers in that field of research who subject it to a thorough analysis. They consider the research on which it is based, the design and method of the current study, and the analysis and interpretation of the data. Usually reviewers recommend changes that the author must make before the paper is published. Most peer-reviewed journals publish about 25 percent of the papers submitted. Figure 1.2 contains a list of peer-reviewed journals that will help you stay current as a professional educator.

Further Reading

For more information on evaluating Web sites consult: S. Mitchell & D. Wershler-Henry (2000). *Internet Directory 2000: A Canadian Guide to the Best Websites and Tools.* Toronto: Prentice Hall Canada.

N. Everhart (1998). Web page evaluation. *Emergency Librarian*, 25(5), 22.

Figure 1.2

READING THE JOURNALS

Special Education Journals

Education and Training in Mental Retardation

Exceptional Children

Exceptionality Education Canada

Focus on Exceptional Children

Intervention in School and Clinic

Journal of Learning Disabilities

Journal of Special Education

Learning Disabilities Research and Practice

Learning Disability Quarterly

Remedial and Special Education

Teaching Exceptional Children

General Education Journals

Canadian Journal of Education

Education Canada

Educational Leadership

Journal of Reading

Phi Delta Kappan

Reading Research Quarterly

Reading Teacher

Review of Educational Research

Key Terms

exceptional students (p. 4)

students with special needs (p. 4)

at risk (p. 4)

special education (p. 4)

adapted program (p. 4)

modified program (p. 5)

Charter of Rights and Freedoms (p. 5)

equality rights (p. 5)

equal participation (p. 5)

inclusion (p. 6)

Individual Education Plan (IEP) (p. 6)

inclusive education (p. 7)

school-based team (p. 7)

Identification, Placement, and Review Committee (IPRC) (p. 9)

normalization (p. 13)

mainstreaming (p. 17)

integration (p. 17)

inclusion (p. 17)

community (p. 19)

impairment (p. 19)

disability (p. 19)

handicap (p. 19)

gifted (p. 19)

learning disabilities (p. 20)

attention deficit/hyper-activity disorder (p. 21)

speech and language exceptionalities (p. 21)

behavioural or emotional exceptionalities (p. 21)

developmental disabilities (p. 21)

autism (p. 21)

Asperger syndrome (p. 21)

hard of hearing (p. 21)

deaf (p. 21)

visual impairment (p. 22)

blind (p. 22)

physical disabilities (p. 22)

cerebral palsy (p. 22)

spina bifida (p. 22)

epilepsy (p. 22)

Tourette syndrome (p. 22)

traumatic brain injury (p. 22)

fetal alcohol syndrome (p. 22)

muscular dystrophy (p. 22)

juvenile arthritis (p. 22)

diabetes (p. 22)

allergies (p. 23)

asthma (p. 23)

cystic fibrosis (p. 23)

strengths (p. 23)

needs (p. 23)

ADAPT (p. 23)

Summary

Exceptional education refers to the adapted teaching and specialized services that thousands of exceptional students in Canada receive every day. Current practices have developed out of our history, legislation, research, and commitment to an equitable society. The dominant approach currently is inclusive education—with some educators supporting inclusion and others questioning whether it is best for all exceptional learners. Many exceptionalities are recognized across Canada, including students who are gifted, those with learning disabilities, and students who have emotional disabilities and sensory disabilities. As a teacher, you will be expected to adapt your teaching and assessment for exceptional learners. The ADAPT strategy will help you meet the needs of exceptional students as you teach, and it will guide you as you learn strategies for the inclusive classroom in the upcoming chapters. ∎

- adapt/accomodate vs. modify
- equal participation → remove barriers.

- IEP outlines rights/needs

- Differentiated instruction!

- Gradual release of responsibility model

- necessary for some, good for all.

- Consider perspectives of all involved.

- continuously reflect/assess to see if the adaptations are working.

Chapter 2

The Teacher's Role in an Inclusive Classroom

Joan Hughes telephoned Silver Birch School to make an appointment with Andy's grade 2 teacher, Ms. Sauvé. Joan told Ms. Sauvé that Andy's report card—with many ratings of "needs improvement" and "is progressing with close supervision"—seemed poor for a bright young boy who likes to read, gets his friends to take part in plays, and is intensely curious. One comment sounded familiar: "Cannot listen to instructions and complete his work independently. Is easily distracted, and has a difficult time organizing his work and his belongings." Joan's older son, who is now in grade 7, had brought home similar report cards and was subsequently identified as having attention deficit disorder. Joan suggested to Ms. Sauvé that Andy be referred to the in-school team. Having an IEP had helped her older son—classroom teachers had adapted teaching and a resource teacher had taught him strategies to focus his attention and complete tasks. Ms. Sauvé was reluctant to make a referral based on a parent's request. As a new teacher, she was not certain if parents could make such referrals, or if teachers had to act on them. Ms. Sauvé kept thinking about the three students who seemed to have more difficulty learning than Andy did. She wondered, "How can I take Andy's case to the in-school team, if I don't take their cases, too?" Ms. Sauvé does not want the principal to think she cannot resolve her own challenges. She is not sure how she would feel about sharing her students with a resource teacher. Ms. Sauvé doesn't know what to do.

Brenda Piet has a learning disability and an IEP. It is September and she is hoping to complete grade 11 this year. Her school has instituted Teacher Adviser Groups (TAGs) this fall, and Brenda has asked her teacher adviser, Frank Bogg, to help her make a transition plan. She is worried about what she should do after secondary school. She has always wanted to be an architect, but she has heard recently that the local community college offers a program in architectural technology. She is wondering whether that might be a better option for her. Mr. Bogg has just become a teacher adviser in this new program of TAGs. It is not clear how much he needs to know about all of these career options. He understands that in the future exceptional students will be entitled to a transition plan, but he does not yet know who is responsible for making this plan or for implementing it. There are so many changes taking place in schools, and teachers are expected to take on so many new roles. Mr. Bogg used to feel that he knew what was expected of him. Now he's not so sure.

1. What is a teacher's responsibility when a parent or a student asks for a referral to an in-school team, asks for an assessment, or asks for help developing a transition plan?

2. What steps should Ms. Sauvé and Mr. Bogg take to respond to these requests?

3. Who should each of these teachers consult to help them decide what to do?

4. As the classroom teacher, what role might Ms. Sauvé expect to play if the in-school team decided to develop an IEP for Andy?

5. What can classroom teachers like Mr. Bogg do to advise students effectively about academic and career planning?

As a classroom teacher, you will know your students well. In an elementary classroom, you may be with the same students all day. As a middle school or secondary teacher, you may meet a hundred or more students each day. You will still come to know these students—their interests, their relationships with peers, and their strengths as classroom learners. When you encounter students in difficulty, you may wonder whether they should be identified as exceptional students and should have an IEP to guide you and other teachers. What is your role in this process? Who do you turn to for advice? How do teachers, parents, and paraprofessionals work together for the students' good? This chapter introduces you to the many roles expected of classroom teachers in the implementation of inclusive education. By following a classroom teacher through the steps, this chapter describes the kind of process followed in most parts of Canada after a teacher recognizes that a student may have exceptional learning needs. The teacher's roles are emphasized in relation to the school-based team that, after working with a teacher and a student, may suggest a fuller assessment. Depending on the assessment findings and the teacher's and the team's success in meeting the student's needs, an IEP could be developed for the student. The teacher also has key responsibilities in informing and supporting the exceptional child's parents, as well as directing the duties of a paraprofessional who might be assigned to work with the child, the teacher, or the class.

The Role of the Classroom Teacher in Identifying Needs of Exceptional Learners

Weblinks

TEACHERS HELPING TEACHERS FORUM
http://snow.utoronto.ca/cgi/ wbbb/teach_forum/config.pl

Cross-Reference
Chapter 4 contains descriptions of low-incidence exceptionalities and strategies for teaching students with each exceptionality.

Classroom teachers and parents usually have the most detailed knowledge about the strengths and needs of students with documented or suspected exceptionalities. Many exceptionalities, especially those that occur rarely, low-incidence exceptionalities, are identified early in a child's life. These include developmental disabilities, blindness, deafness, most physical disabilities (e.g., cerebral palsy), and chronic health conditions (e.g., diabetes). Teachers are usually informed about these exceptionalities before the students enrol in their classrooms, read the relevant student files and the IEP, and are responsible for carrying out the recommended adaptations and modifications in the classroom. Observing these students, talking to previous teachers, and reading about relevant teaching strategies will also help. Classroom teachers are also involved in regular reviews of the IEPs of students with low-incidence exceptionalities.

On the other hand, high-incidence exceptionalities such as learning disabilities, attention deficit disorder, and giftedness are most often identified after students enrol in school. All teachers need to be aware of the characteristics associated with these exceptionalities and of the key teaching strategies. However, secondary teachers frequently find that even students with high-incidence exceptionalities have been identified and have IEPs before they reach grade 9. Usually, the greater challenge for secondary teachers is finding ways to adapt complex curricula and teaching approaches. Thus while any teacher may be involved in recognizing students' exceptionalities, elementary teachers, especially those teaching in the primary grades, have a key role in the initial identification of exceptional students.

Teachers and parents bring individual students to the attention of other professionals when they suspect that a student needs a school-based intervention beyond the regular program. You may encounter a student who is reading below grade level and cannot get meaning from a textbook or a student who is restless and cannot focus on classroom tasks. A student's social interactions may be so different from those of the rest of the class that you suspect an emotional or behaviour disability. In the case at the beginning of the chapter, Ms. Sauvé wrote that Andy "cannot listen to instructions and complete his work independently. Is easily distracted and has a difficult time organizing his work and his belongings." She recognized that Andy was not thriving in the classroom, but was not confident that Andy was experiencing enough difficulty to warrant any action on her part. With experience, she will recognize that the first steps she can take are straightforward and focus on collecting relevant information to help in decision making. These are described in Figure 2.1.

Cross-Reference
For characteristics, identification strategies, and teaching approaches relevant to students with high-incidence exceptionalities, see Chapter 3.

FIRST STEPS

1. Document the student's characteristics, behaviours, and needs that led to your concern (or to the parent's concern), and the student's strengths. Analyze the demands of your classroom. Observe the student in your classroom.

2. Reread the student's file, test results, psychological reports, attendance records, and comments by previous teachers. Consult the protocol for identifying exceptional students.

3. Talk with the resource teacher. Share your observational notes, documentation, and ideas about how to address the student's needs.

4. Ask the resource teacher for suggestions and resources, including community associations. Plan pre-referral interventions. Inform the principal or the student's counsellor. The resource teacher may observe the student in your classroom.

5. Contact the parents to share your concerns and ideas for pre-referral interventions. Listen to the parents. The resource teacher may take part in this meeting. The protocol may recommend that you contact the parents before meeting with the resource teacher.

6. Make pre-referral adaptations, keep brief records of these and the student's responses. Use ADAPT and stay with any adaptation long enough for it to be effective. Reflect on your teaching. Could you be contributing to the student's learning needs? (This step may take from three weeks to three months.)

7. Analyze your records and make recommendations. Focus on the clearest examples of needs and strengths and the most effective adaptations. Look for patterns. Is there a need for further assessment or additional services?

Making Classroom Adaptations and Keeping Records

Ms. Sauvé described her meeting with Joan Hughes to the teacher assigned as her mentor. Ms. Sauvé's school had a formal mentoring program, but your school may simply encourage you to find a "soulmate" on staff who is willing to talk and help. Her mentor gave Ms. Sauvé a copy of the school's protocol, which is much like the list in Figure 2.1. Ms. Sauvé began recording the circumstances under which Andy did and did not follow instructions and complete assigned work. She noted when he seemed most distracted. By collecting samples of his work, she understood his organizational needs better. She also recorded what Andy did well and the times when he did not experience attention difficulties. Three weeks later, Ms. Sauvé showed the resource teacher her notes, which confirmed that most of Andy's inattentive behaviours and inability to follow instructions occurred at three times: during mathematics lessons, late in the day, and when other children were off-task. She learned how to cue Andy during oral instructions, especially in mathematics, and how to help him monitor his own behaviour. The resource teacher gave her two books to read and observed Andy twice in Ms. Sauvé's classroom. Armed with her own observations and the suggestions of the resource teacher, Ms. Sauvé telephoned Joan Hughes to report what she would be doing to adapt the classroom for Andy. They agreed to meet in six weeks.

Further Reading

On teaching students with attention deficit/hyperactivity disorder: S.F. Reif (1993). *How to Reach and Teach ADD/ADHD Children.* New York: The Center for Applied Research in Education.

K.G. Nadeau, E.B. Dixon, & S.H. Biggs (1993). *School Strategies for ADD Teens.* Annandale, VA: Chesapeake Psychological Publications.

Using the ADAPT Strategy

Ms. Sauvé was making **pre-referral interventions** to meet Andy's needs. Consider how the ADAPT strategy discussed in Chapter 1 might help if you were in Ms. Sauvé's place. First, it suggests you begin by providing an <u>A</u>ccount of the student's strengths and needs. Andy has many strengths, both social and academic: he likes to read (academic), he has friends in the class (social), he likes to get his friends to take part in plays (social), and he shows an intense curiosity about the world (academic). Andy also needs help focusing so that he can listen to instructions (academic), and he needs to learn to concentrate on his assigned work and complete it more independently (academic). He is easily distracted and needs to learn to ignore other children when they are off-task (social). He also needs strategies for organizing his work and his belongings (academic). Developing this account of strengths and needs will involve some informal assessment of the student's current knowledge and learning approaches.

Informal assessment includes asking a child to think aloud while solving a problem.

ASSESSING THE DEMANDS OF YOUR CLASSROOM

Teacher _____ Classroom/Course _____
Student _____

1. For what percentage of class time do students typically listen to lectures or instructions?

2. How many pages of in-class reading do you assign to be done in a typical class?

3. How many pages of out-of-class reading do you assign to be done in a typical evening?

4. List typical classroom activities (e.g., lectures, demonstrations, labs, co-operative learning, independent work, discussion, pairs, videos, etc.).

5. How many hours of homework do you typically assign in a week?

6. Describe the typical assignment and the number of days from assignment given to assignment due.

7. Do you assign projects or long-term assignments? (If so, how much structure or guidance is given?)

8. Do you give a final test at the end of each unit?

9. How are grades assigned?

10. What are your expectations for student behaviour in class?

After answering these questions, star up to 3 items where you perceive a mismatch between the strengths of the named student and the demands of your classroom or course.

―――

Source: Nancy L. Hutchinson, *Teaching Exceptional Children and Adolescents: A Canadian Casebook*, p. 119. Copyright © 1999 by Prentice Hall Allyn and Bacon Canada. Reprinted by permission.

Second, the ADAPT strategy suggests that you next describe the Demands of your classroom. Ms. Sauvé read the questionnaire (shown in Figure 2.2) given to her by the resource teacher. Afterwards, she wrote the following list:

- Most math classes start with a 15-minute "lecture" that introduces a new concept or activity. Andy interrupts by talking or I interrupt to ask him to sit still.

- I expect students to work in groups, and sometimes the noise is distracting. I often have to ask Andy to move to the quiet table at the back of the room because he "clowns around" when in a group.

- I am growing to dread the last half-hour of the day. During this "catch-up time" I want the children to finish anything not completed, and ask about anything not understood. Andy wanders around the classroom and talks to his friends rather than catching up.

The third step in ADAPT is making Adaptations that help to eliminate the kinds of mismatches seen in Ms. Sauvé's list. After talking with the resource teacher, Ms. Sauvé reduced the introduction to new math concepts and activities from 15 to 10

What do you think?

Ms. Sauvé knows that Chen can help Andy by reviewing the teacher's instructions with him to ensure that he understands. What are the advantages and disadvantages of this strategy for each boy?

minutes. The resource teacher hinted that 15 minutes was perhaps too long for grade 2 students. Ms. Sauvé also told Andy to check with his friend Chen to be sure that he understood what to do after she had given instructions. She also arranged a cue with Andy. When she snapped her fingers, it was a reminder to him to "sit up straight and listen." During group work, Andy had to "work hard" or move himself to the quiet table before Ms. Sauvé asked him to move. Andy was told to consult with Ms. Sauvé at the beginning of catch-up time. She recommended that he sit with a friend who would refuse to chat with him while he was catching up.

Every day, Ms. Sauvé jotted informal observations about Andy on yellow Post-it Notes. At the end of the day, she copied all of these notes onto one page. Usually she had made about five short comments or observations. Below is her summary for one day:

- Had to snap my fingers three times in a 10-minute period while introducing the math activity "Halloween sets." Andy did not understand the activity until I explained it to him individually.

- Andy moved to the quiet table by himself during math. He stayed quiet for about five minutes. Then he argued with the next child who came to the quiet table. Andy completed only half the examples, although he could do the questions. Quiet table only works when Andy is there alone.

- Andy fidgeted through the Halloween story. He didn't remember any characters except for the witch. He had great ideas for a play after Chen told him what had happened in the story.

- Andy spent catch-up time discussing the play with two children. No catching up was done.

The fourth step in ADAPT is to consider Perspectives and consequences. The fifth step is to Teach and assess the match. If you were in Ms. Sauvé's place, what would your view be of the pre-referral adaptations already made for Andy and how successful they had been? Ms. Sauvé felt that she had made considerable effort to change her math teaching for all students. The changes were an improvement, but Andy needed even more effective strategies for staying focused. Andy told her he was trying to work hard, but that he didn't know how. She believed him. Ms. Sauvé was concerned that the consequences of pushing Andy to work harder would be frustration and self-criticism.

By the next parent–teacher meeting, Ms. Sauvé had come to agree with Joan Hughes and the resource teacher that further assessment and services might be a good idea. Although he had tried to follow Ms. Sauvé's cues and to monitor his own attention, Andy continued to distract himself and others. This occurred mainly during mathematics and following a disruption. Andy needed more consistent and intensive intervention to learn **self-monitoring** strategies (to monitor his own behaviour, especially focus) than Ms. Sauvé could provide within her grade 2 classroom of 31 children. Joan Hughes agreed. Ms. Sauvé told the resource teacher and the principal about her observations, documentation, parent meeting, and recommendations. Together, they decided it was time for more collaboration—time for a meeting of the school-based team.

Put Into Practice

Interview a resource teacher from the panel in which you teach (elementary or secondary) about the pre-referral interventions teachers in that panel might take if they were in Ms. Sauvé's position.

Collaboration: Working with the Resource Teacher and Other Professionals

We saw in Chapter 1 that any school's success in responding to the needs of exceptional students in inclusive classrooms depends on the beliefs and actions of its teachers and administrators (Stanovich & Jordan, 1998). Another critical factor is collaboration. **Collaboration** refers to teachers and other professionals learning from each other's experiences and working in teams where all members feel that their contributions are valued (Jordan, 1994). Collaboration is joint planning, decision making, and problem solving directed toward a common goal (Stanovich, 1996). As a classroom teacher, you are central to collaboration—you are the expert on the curriculum, organization, and management of your classroom. However, you do not have to be an expert on every aspect of the exceptional student's needs. Collaboration provides you with a built-in support network, and you can draw on the expertise and resources of many individuals. You will work closely with fellow educators, including resource teachers, special educators, guidance counsellors, district consultants, and your principal. Other professionals you may collaborate with include speech therapists, rehabilitation therapists, social workers, and psychologists. Paraprofessionals and parents also play important roles in collaboration.

Creating collaborative relationships requires effort on the part of everyone. First, you need team members who hold positive beliefs about inclusion and about working together. Anne Beveridge (1997) of Queen's University described the beliefs and practices of four elementary teachers who were recognized as outstanding in their inclusion of exceptional learners. These four teachers shared beliefs about inclusion that could be described as "build communities, not ghettos." All valued and demonstrated excellent collaboration and communication with colleagues, parents, and administrators. In a study of school-level restructuring, Michael Kamann and Nancy Perry (1994) of the University of British Columbia described changes that enabled classroom teachers and other members of the school to function as a collaborative team and to share responsibility for exceptional students.

Similar findings have emerged about the beliefs and collaborative practices of secondary teachers who are acknowledged as leaders in inclusive education. Karol Lyn Edwards (2000) of Queen's University interviewed secondary science teachers known for their effective inclusion of students with learning disabilities. She found that these teachers expressed positive beliefs about inclusion and adapted teaching to meet individual needs. Similar findings regarding beliefs about collaboration and inclusion emerged in a description of Nova Scotia secondary teachers when James Fasano and Margaret Brown (1992) of Acadia University studied teachers who were successful in accommodating adolescents with developmental disabilities. Cheryl Duquette (1996) of the University of Ottawa observed three secondary teachers (teaching science, mathematics, and English/history) viewed as successful at inclusion. These teachers shared positive beliefs about collaboration and inclu-

> **Cross-Reference**
> Chapter 7 focuses on adapting teaching and Chapter 9 describes best practices for enhancing social relations, including collaborative learning and peer tutoring.

sion, as well as common teaching behaviours. While their styles varied considerably, all three teachers:

- Planned thoroughly and implemented their plans flexibly.
- Used teaching methods that engaged students.
- Used preventive and caring classroom and behaviour management so that almost all classroom time was focused on learning.
- Were positive about including exceptional adolescents in their classes.
- Worked collaboratively with the administration and, especially, with the resource teachers in the school.

These studies highlight the importance of your role as a classroom teacher in the inclusion of exceptional learners. Your beliefs and your willingness to collaborate will contribute to your ability to teach exceptional students effectively as part of a team. In her study of successful inclusion in elementary schools, Duquette (1992) wrote: "Perhaps the most important element is the quality and quantity of support for the classroom teacher. The classroom teacher needs to be part of an in-school team that can provide him or her with information, strategies that work and moral support" (p. 151).

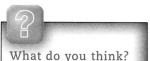

What do you think?

How would you answer the kinds of questions asked of teachers in the interview studies reported here? What are your beliefs about including exceptional students in regular classrooms?

The Classroom Teacher and the School-Based Team

As policies emphasizing neighbourhood schools and inclusive education have been adopted across Canada, more school districts are developing school-based teams or in-school teams to share the responsibility for exceptional students. These teams are usually composed of members of the school staff and the parents. Occasionally professionals from the school district or community may be added if they have particular expertise relevant for the child's education and not available in the school.

Suggesting a Meeting of the School-Based Team

When should you suggest that the in-school team meet to discuss a student in your class? You and the resource teacher have carried out all of the steps in the pre-referral stage (see Figure 2.1), and you feel that the adaptations you have tried in your classroom are not sufficient to meet the student's needs. That is usually a sign that the in-school team should consider the child's case. After Ms. Sauvé's initial meeting with Andy's mother, she collected information about Andy and the demands of her classroom and she tried to eliminate mismatches between the two by adapting her teaching. While Andy paid more attention and completed more of his assignments, Ms. Sauvé could see that he would benefit from intensive teaching of these strategies over a period of time. She was not certain how to teach these strategies and recognized that she did not have time for such concentrated work with one student.

Ms. Sauvé worked closely with the resource teacher. A **resource teacher** can have many titles, including learning assistance teacher, learning program teacher, tutor, and curriculum resource teacher. Resource teachers support teachers and exceptional students, usually by consulting to teachers and offering some direct services to exceptional students, either in the classroom or in the resource room.

If you and the resource teacher believe that the first level of intervention has not been effective, then you will approach the **school-based team**. The team has been described as "a school-based, solution-finding group, the purpose of which is to provide a forum for dialogue on specific needs of students, by parents, teachers, and other professionals" (Napier, 1995, p. 15). As the classroom teacher or referring teacher, you are a key member of the in-school team, along with the principal and the resource teacher. Usually the parents are invited to take part and sometimes the student is as well. Parental consent is sought for decisions that significantly alter the education of an exceptional student. If a school-based team is meeting about a student to whom a **paraprofessional** has been assigned, the paraprofessional is normally part of the in-school team. Paraprofessionals are employed to assist teachers in carrying out the program and care of exceptional students. Teachers of English as a second language and Aboriginal community representatives are often members of the team for students of diverse cultural groups. School-based teams make the best possible use of the resources within a school, and supplement with key professionals from the school district or the community whose knowledge is especially relevant for the individual student. Other professionals who may be asked to join the school-based team include a district special education consultant, psychologist, nurse, social worker, behaviour specialist, speech and language therapist, occupational or physical therapist, child-care worker, mobility teacher, and sign language interpreter. Usually in-school teams work better when they are small and focused.

Put Into Practice

Problem-solving teams that meet before an IEP is considered for a student have a variety of names. Talk with educators and principals to learn what these teams are called in your school district and how their role is described.

The Work of the School-Based Team

What does the school-based team do? According to British Columbia's *Manual of Policies, Procedures, and Guidelines*, "It provides support through extended consultation on possible classroom strategies, and may become a central focus for case management, referrals and resource decisions" (1995b, Section C, p. 4). Usually the team appoints a case coordinator and problem solves informally. As the **referring teacher**, you will be asked to present the student data from the pre-referral interventions already carried out. The team brainstorms and suggests additional assessment strategies and additional teaching strategies. The assessment strategies could include **informal assessment** conducted by you or the resource teacher and formal assessment conducted by the resource teacher, a psychologist, or another professional.

When the team recommends that you and the resource teacher continue with assessment and intervention, then the team continues to monitor and support your actions. In some jurisdictions, the team would prepare an IEP at this point. As the referring teacher, you supply the relevant classroom information. Regardless of the decision to pursue an IEP at this time, members will confer with you informally and another meeting of the team will likely take place to assess what has been accomplished. Steps in the school-based team process are shown in Figure 2.3.

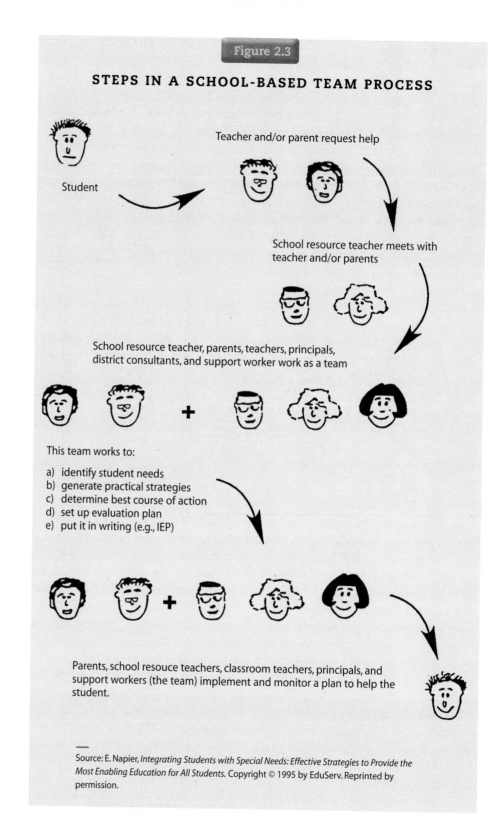

Figure 2.3

STEPS IN A SCHOOL-BASED TEAM PROCESS

Student

Teacher and/or parent request help

School resource teacher meets with teacher and/or parents

School resource teacher, parents, teachers, principals, district consultants, and support worker work as a team

+

This team works to:

a) identify student needs
b) generate practical strategies
c) determine best course of action
d) set up evaluation plan
e) put it in writing (e.g., IEP)

+

Parents, school resouce teachers, classroom teachers, principals, and support workers (the team) implement and monitor a plan to help the student.

Source: E. Napier, *Integrating Students with Special Needs: Effective Strategies to Provide the Most Enabling Education for All Students.* Copyright © 1995 by EduServ. Reprinted by permission.

This working group, the in-school team, is the "cornerstone of the process of identification, assessment and planning." If the decision of the team is to seek an extended assessment, to access other school district or community-based services, and to seek an IEP, then other **formal assessments** will be conducted. These could include an intelligence test; behaviour observation checklists; vision, hearing, or language assessments; medical tests; and others. In some school districts, there is a long waiting list for assessment services, and parents may choose to pay for assessments administered outside the school system. When results are available, the in-school team, including the parents, meets to consider the recommendations. Figure 2.4 contains tips to help parents prepare for IEP conferences. In most provinces, the IEP would be written at this stage; again, you will likely play a large role in this. In Ontario, there is a two-stage process in which an **Identification, Placement, and Review Committee (IPRC)** meets to consider whether the child is exceptional and recommends a placement. This is followed by an IEP, usually written by the teacher and the resource teacher in elementary schools and by the resource teacher with input from the classroom teachers in secondary schools

---

Figure 2.4

TIPS TO HELP PARENTS PREPARE FOR CONFERENCES ABOUT INDIVIDUAL PROGRAM PLANS

General Tips

_____ maintain ongoing contact with the school

_____ take an active role in decision making

_____ ask about other parents who may be in a similar situation; they can be a valuable resource

_____ ask about the services and resources available

Tips for Participating in the IPP Process

Before the Meeting

_____ find out the agenda in advance

_____ discuss your child's involvement in the process

_____ jot down your comments and questions in advance

_____ think about your goals and expectations for your child

At the Meeting

_____ make time limits known if you have other commitments

_____ provide samples of your child's work done at home if you think they can be useful

_____ ask questions if anything is unclear to you

_____ ask how you can help achieve some of the goals at home

Source: Alberta Education, Special Education Branch, *Partners During Changing Times: An Information Booklet for Parents of Children with Special Needs.* Copyright © 1996 by Alberta Education. Reprinted by permission.

(Pincivero, 2000), and participation by the parents or guardians. Ask about the procedures in your school, because there are slight variations from school to school even within a district.

THE SCHOOL-BASED TEAM AND THE IEP PROCESS

The IEP process addresses all areas of student need, including adaptations in the regular classroom, supports and services to be provided there, and other services the student may receive. With inclusive education as the predominant approach, services are increasingly offered within the neighbourhood school, and even within the classroom. However, some students still require and receive services outside the neighbourhood school. For example, Patricia MacCuspie (1993), a researcher in the Maritimes, has argued that students who are blind may benefit from short-term placements in residential schools to learn Braille and mobility. As another example, an IEP may recommend that a violent student attend a board-wide program for anger management and self-control until he can cope with the social demands of the classroom.

The educators on the school-based team share with the teacher the ongoing responsibility for the student's program when they hold brief, frequent, and informal meetings, even after the IEP has been established. Iain Davidson and Judy Wiener (1991) of the University of Toronto found that participating in in-school teams has other benefits for teachers. "Teachers claimed that they learned a great deal from their association with team members, whom they viewed as supportive and helpful co-workers" (p. 29). Participation in the in-school team was a professional development experience that teachers viewed as contributing to better teaching for exceptional students.

Teachers with experience in collaboration say it is worth the effort. In-school teams share the responsibility for exceptional students.

Occasionally, in-school team meetings can be frustrating and threatening for classroom teachers. What can you do to ensure that this does not happen to you? One month into her second year of teaching, Leanne was reassigned from a grade 6 class to a grade 3 class, due to increases in enrolment. One of her new students, Mickey, had autism and needed many adaptations and modifications to function in the classroom. By the end of the first week with her new class, Leanne felt that she was beginning to make progress with Mickey. A few days later, the resource teacher told Leanne that Mickey's parents had requested a meeting to discuss his program. They were wondering whether his needs might be better served in a special education class. Leanne asked the resource teacher, "What should I do to prepare? I've never been to an in-school team meeting." The resource teacher replied that people could hardly expect Leanne to present the case when she had only taught Mickey for two weeks. On the day of the meeting, the vice-principal decided to chair. At the beginning of the meeting, he asked Leanne to present Mickey's history from his arrival at the school up to the current adaptations she was making in her classroom. Leanne had read Mickey's file, but she had not brought her notes to the team meeting. After some initial panic, she described Mickey's history from memory, feeling frustrated and defensive. The parents were pleased with the adaptations Leanne described, and decided to leave Mickey in the inclusive grade 3 class. Everyone else judged the meeting a success, but Leanne felt that she had appeared unprepared and unprofessional. Leanne, Mickey, and the rest of the grade 3 class went on to have a very successful year. However, Leanne still describes this meeting as the worst experience in her professional life. What could she have done before the meeting so that she would have felt prepared for any eventuality? Figure 2.5 contains suggestions for preparing for and participating in an in-school team meeting.

The Teacher and the Individual Education Plan (IEP)

Individual Education Plan (IEP) refers to the formal document that is used to plan an exceptional student's program and serves as the blueprint for that student's education. In some provinces (e.g., Alberta), it is called an **Individualized Program Plan (IPP)** and in others (e.g., Saskatchewan) it is called a **Personal Program Plan (PPP)**. Generally, across Canada, whenever significant changes in learning expectations, curriculum, or teaching approaches are made to a student's educational program over the long term, an IEP must be prepared.

Components of an IEP

An IEP is a written plan. It is a working document which describes the strengths and needs of an individual exceptional pupil, the special education program and services established to meet that pupil's needs and how the program and services will be delivered. It also describes the student's progress

Ontario Ministry of Education, 1998, p. 5.

Figure 2.5

PREPARING FOR AND PARTICIPATING IN AN IN-SCHOOL TEAM MEETING

Communicate Regularly with Parents

Send out a monthly newsletter with space for parents' comments.

Host a class curriculum night to communicate your curriculum and expectations.

Make a positive contact with parents of exceptional students before you make a negative contact.

If you have not met the parents, make telephone contact before an in-school team meeting.

Respond to parents' notes and telephone calls promptly.

Look at Each Student as an Individual

Read all of the student files before the term starts.

Make notes on the files, reports, IEPs, and medical information of exceptional students.

Make written observations of all exceptional students early in the term.

Meet with the resource teacher, ask questions, secure resources, and learn strategies to adapt teaching; make written notes.

Collect work samples that demonstrate the student's strengths and needs in your class.

Prepare for the In-School Team Meeting

Ask for and read the information about responsibilities of the members at in-school team meetings.

Ask the chair of the meeting what will be expected of you.

Discuss the student's case thoroughly with your best source of information, probably the resource teacher; ask her opinion on what you plan to say.

Prepare to give briefly the student's history in the school as well as in your classroom.

Bring *all* of your written notes to the in-school team meeting.

Bring work samples to show the student's strengths and needs in your classroom.

During the In-School Team Meeting

Approach the meeting in a spirit of goodwill.

Think about how stressful these meetings can be for parents.

Listen actively to what others have to say; take notes; do not interrupt.

Answer questions briefly and honestly without becoming defensive.

Ask questions if you do not understand; do not agree to commitments you cannot keep.

Make your presentations brief, clear, and to the point; be positive and realistic in saying what you can do to meet the student's needs.

Ensure that the meeting is summarized and ends on a positive note; thank the parents and other team members for their participation.

Clarify when the next meeting is likely to occur and what is expected of you.

In a practical handbook, Napier, an educator in British Columbia, defines an IEP as "a description of an instructional program that has been modified to suit a particular student" (1995, p. 72). Different names may be given to the components, and different emphasis may be placed on those components. Wherever you teach in Canada, IEPs are likely to include the following seven **components**:

1. a description of the present level of functioning;
2. long-term goals;
3. short-term goals;
4. instructional strategies, materials, and services;
5. dates for review;
6. identification of the case coordinator and participants (including parents) and their responsibilities;
7. evaluation procedures.

Present level of functioning refers to recent test results, observations of the student, medical and school history, and degree of participation in current classes. "If there is sufficient information to plan for and implement programming, no further assessment is necessary" (Alberta Education, 1995, p. 6). **Long-term goals** may include learning goals within the curriculum, independence goals within the community, and career goals. Setting these goals involves considering parental and student values and priorities as well as what is age-appropriate and realistic. **Short-term goals** are usually steps on the way to the long-term goals, and may be goals for a term or half-term.

Instructional strategies, materials, and services refers to the adaptations to teaching and modifications to curriculum as well as other efforts made to provide an appropriate education for the student. **Related services** include such things as speech therapy, physical therapy, and alternate transportation. **Equipment** includes tape recorders, wheelchairs, computers, and other technological devices. **Evaluation** or assessment procedures refer to how the in-school team will demonstrate accountability by showing that the student is making reasonable progress. "If the student is progressing slowly toward the objectives, alternate instructional strategies should be employed before revisions to the goals and objectives are made" (British Columbia Special Education Branch, 1996). Look for assessment strategies that are simple and that occur naturally in the context of learning in the classroom. When students are receiving adapted teaching and adapted assessment, asterisks may be used beside letter and mark grades on their report cards to indicate the adaptations to those who read the students' transcripts. Anecdotal comments may be more appropriate than letter or mark grades when students experience major modifications to the grade-level curriculum.

Dates for review are usually set for the end of the school year in which the IEP is established or renewed. Identification of participants allows parents and educators to consult the members of the team in the future, when they wish to know more about effective strategies and other aspects of the child's program. In most provinces, parents have the right to appeal the IEP. The appeal process varies from province to province, but all appeals are time consuming and tend to destroy the

What do you think?

Take the parent's perspective and consider what it might feel like to be one parent among four or five educators. Look at the documents for your school or school district—what is the appeal process and can parents involve an advocate? What could you do to help parents feel comfortable and to play a constructive role in an in-school team?

good working relationships that enable schools and parents to collaborate on behalf of exceptional students. As a classroom teacher, your responsibility is to make a good-faith effort to accomplish the short-term goals on the IEP and to keep the in-school team informed of the student's accomplishments.

Planning to Meet Individual Needs

The IEP demands that you and your colleagues make an individual plan for an exceptional student. However, that does not mean that you must teach the student individually. Gail Lennon, an Ontario teacher, describes how teachers can meet society's expectations of inclusion and adapted curriculum for exceptional students: "A separate and distinctly different curriculum is not the answer. Parents and students want a program which includes the student as part of the class. Students want to be just like the rest of the class" (1995, p. 24). The ministry of education prescribes most curriculum content. Often the content does not need to be changed for exceptional students.

However, what may need to be changed is the amount of time the student takes to learn the skill. As well, the content may be modified so that certain skills are selected for the exceptional student and others are deleted from her program plan. In rare cases, the entire content may be replaced by more appropriate learning experiences. "The measuring stick in teacher decision making should be: *To what extent can the exceptional student learn the content which is being presented to the rest of the class?*" (Lennon, 1995, p. 24)

The way the content will be learned might include cooperative learning, teacher demonstration, student presentations, etc.; often the exceptional student will benefit from the same teaching approaches used for the other students. Sometimes learning time might be extended, or a tutor (peer, older student, community volunteer, paraprofessional, resource teacher) might assist the exceptional student. Learning or physical challenges might mean that in rare instances the entire process of learning is altered for an exceptional student. Again, the question to be asked is: *To what extent can the exceptional student learn in the same way as the rest of the class, and what adaptations do I need to make to the way I teach, based on the student's unique learning needs?*

Exceptional students sometimes need a different way to demonstrate the learning outcomes they have accomplished. Whenever the same outcome is appropriate, maintain that outcome. When necessary, choose alternate formats or products that enable students to show what they have learned rather than to show the impact of their disabilities. Widely used adaptations are more time for tests, speaking into a tape recorder, and using a scribe.

Example of an IEP

Brenda Piet, a secondary student, was introduced at the beginning of the chapter. Her teacher adviser was not certain about his role in developing a transition plan for Brenda, who had been identified as an exceptional student with learning disabilities. Increasingly, provinces (e.g., Ontario, British Columbia, Alberta) are requiring that a transition plan form part of the IEP for exceptional secondary stu-

Put Into Practice

Obtain a copy of the IEP form used in your school district. Compare it to the IEP for Brenda Piet shown in Figure 2.6.

dents. As Brenda's teacher adviser in the **Teacher Advisor Groups (TAGs)** program, Mr. Bogg may be a member of the in-school team or IEP team for Brenda. However, the **transition plan** to her post-secondary destination forms part of Brenda's IEP, so Mr. Bogg will not have to prepare it alone. Figure 2.6 shows an IEP for Brenda Piet that includes participation in **cooperative education** (that is, learning in the workplace for course credit) as a strategy to respond to her need for increased career maturity. Other actions that are intended to contribute to Brenda's greater independent use of compensatory strategies and study and time management skills are implemented and reviewed.

Cross-Reference
In Chapter 10, you can read about strategies for encouraging independent living, including both career education and cooperative education.

Figure 2.6

CLEAR LAKE DISTRICT SCHOOL BOARD
INDIVIDUAL EDUCATION PLAN
YEAR: 1999–2000

Student: Brenda Piet   DOB: April 23, 1983   IEP Date: Oct. 1, 1999
Parent/Guardian: Ben & Lois Piet
Identification: Learning Disabilities   Grade: 11

Areas of Strength

Strong math skills
Creative artist, especially
   line drawing
Motivated to succeed
Participates in sports

Statement of Need

To practise compensatory skills for
   written expression
To continue to develop organizational
   skills
To improve reading comprehension
To enhance career awareness

Current Achievement Level

Grade 11 in math

Grade 9 in reading comprehension; reading rate slow

Overview and Goals for the Year

Adapted program:

Brenda will develop greater independence in application of compensatory strategies for written expression and reading comprehension.

Brenda will choose and carry out a study and time management plan.

Brenda will participate in workplace learning.

Response to Statement	*Support Personnel*	*Specialized Equipment of Needs*
Curriculum adaptations	Classroom teachers	Laptop computer for
	Resource teacher	assignments
		Texts on tape and tape player
Study skills and	Resource teacher	Study skills group (weekly)
study plan	Classroom teachers	Agenda book entries for tests
Workplace experience	Co-op ed teacher	Laptop computer for
	Resource teacher	assignments
		Agenda book entries for
		assignments

Further Reading
About career education and workplace preparation for exceptional adolescents: N.L. Hutchinson, & J.G. Freeman (1994). *Pathways* (a five-volume instructional program). Scarborough, ON: ITP Nelson Canada.

M.E. Morningstar (1997). Critical issues in career development and employment preparation for adolescents with disabilities. *Remedial and Special Education, 18*, 307–20.

Figure 2.6

CONTINUED

Transition Plan

Workplace experience in grades 11 and 12. Investigate special needs resources at Clear Lake Community College and Plains University for architecture and architectural technologist programs.

Year-End Review Summary

Brenda used the laptop for all of her classes and assignments. She used taped texts whenever available. She needed assistance all year in setting up and following study plans. She was successful in and pleased with a co-op placement in an architectural firm.

Goals for 2000–2001: continue to develop test strategies and study plans for all tests as preparation for grade 12 examinations and for college or university course demands; continue curriculum adaptations; continue cooperative education.

Date of Review Meeting: June 10, 2000

IEP Team Members: Mona Simpson (resource teacher), Brian Smith (co-op education teacher), Frank Bogg (TAG teacher), Leila Chan (English teacher)

Case Coordinator: Mona Simpson (informs all other teachers about Brenda's IEP)

_____

Parent Who Was Consulted in Development of IEP (signature): Lois Piet

_____

Student Who Was Consulted in Development of IEP (signature): Brenda Piet

The Teacher and the Paraprofessional

Most members of the team working with an exceptional student will be qualified professionals—teachers, psychologists, social workers, physical therapists, or speech pathologists. However, there are important team members in inclusive schools who are not usually certified professionals. Your team may include a paraprofessional. These non-certified staff members are employed to assist teachers in carrying out the program and to support the personal care, behaviour management, and instruction of exceptional students.

The qualifications required of paraprofessionals vary from province to province. A recent issue of the newsletter *Keeping in Touch* (Spring/Summer 1999), published by the Canadian Council for Exceptional Children, described "Qualifications of Paraprofessionals" in Alberta, British Columbia, Manitoba, Ontario, and Saskatchewan. Overall, post-secondary educational qualifications were set by individual school districts rather than by the provinces. Typically, requirements included experience working with exceptional children or adolescents and a certificate from a one- or two-year community college program in a relevant area. The titles given to paraprofessionals also vary considerably—teacher assistants, teaching assistants, educational assistants, and educational aides.

The Role of the Paraprofessional

Sometimes paraprofessionals are assigned to work full-time or part-time with an exceptional student in your classroom, while other times they are assigned to support your work with the entire class while monitoring the progress of the exceptional students and offering them assistance at key times. You may be wondering who assigns these responsibilities to teacher assistants and how you can know what to expect. Often the IEP includes information about the role of the paraprofessional in the program of an exceptional student and may identify where that role is to take place. The paraprofessional could work in one or all of the following places: in the classroom (e.g., supporting completion of assigned work), at a separate workspace in the classroom (e.g., teaching a strategy for organizing an essay), or in a space outside of the classroom (e.g., administering medication). The principal is responsible for the paraprofessionals' roles in your school, but usually consults with you when one of your students is involved, and normally the paraprofessional works under your direction or the direction of the school-based team.

Put Into Practice

Look for provincial and district policies about paraprofessionals. Interview a paraprofessional about his or her working relationship with teachers and in-school teams.

The research suggests that in successful inclusive schools, paraprofessionals and teachers work as partners (Beveridge, 1997; Gauldnau, 1996; Kamann & Perry, 1994; Working Forum on Inclusive Schools, 1994). The paraprofessional in your classroom can provide continuity for staff, parents, and exceptional learners and can contribute a great deal to the planning and delivery of services. As the classroom teacher, you should ensure that the paraprofessional has a workstation in the classroom and that the two of you have a shared understanding of his or her role. Include the paraprofessional in the discussions of the school-based team and value his or her contributions (Hammeken, 1996; Yssel & Hadadian, 1998).

When you learn that you will be teaming with a paraprofessional, read the job description and expectations of paraprofessionals in your province and in your school district. Ask for your own copy of these documents, and reread the IEPs of any exceptional children in your upcoming class for guidelines about the role of the paraprofessional with regards to these children. Be sure to familiarize yourself with the roles that cannot be assumed by paraprofessionals due to the fact that they are not certified teachers.

This student with cerebral palsy is included in a secondary school in Vancouver with the support of an educational assistant. The student does not speak and uses a wheelchair and a computer. His intellectual abilities are unaffected by cerebral palsy.

Your Role in Working with a Paraprofessional

It is important to clarify your own role and that of the principal before beginning a partnership with a paraprofessional (see Figure 2.7). You may be expected to prepare materials that the paraprofessional will use with an individual or a group of students, to provide informal training to the paraprofessional about new programs and strategies, and to inform this partner about the expectations, routines, and transitions you set for the class. Many classroom teachers have not supervised another team member. Some find it difficult to assign tasks they feel they should do themselves. As you have seen, these dilemmas abound in inclusive classrooms. While there may be a few more dilemmas when you work closely with a paraprofessional, you can also share the responsibility and ideas with an enthusiastic partner who may have worked with the exceptional student for many years.

In writing about schools in New Brunswick, Cripps (1991) described how some paraprofessionals have worked with the same exceptional child for many years. At the beginning of the year or term, the paraprofessional may know the child or adolescent much better than the classroom or subject teacher does. This gives the paraprofessional a key role on the team. The most important thing for you to remember is that paraprofessionals always complete their job assignments under the supervision of a qualified teacher. They only act on teaching decisions or adapt materials and modify programs with your direction.

Figure 2.7

ROLE OF CLASSROOM TEACHERS IN WORKING WITH PARAPROFESSIONALS

- Classroom teachers who receive support from a teacher assistant have the following responsibilities:

- Informing teacher assistants of classroom procedures and rules, and methods of classroom management.

- In collaboration with teacher assistants, discussing and clarifying specific job functions based on the needs of the student(s).

- Documenting identified job functions that are to be in accordance with the teacher assistant's job specifications, and ensuring that the principal has a copy of the job functions.

- Providing input regarding the supervision and evaluation of teacher assistants.

- Informing school principals when students whom teacher assistants are supporting are absent so that the teacher assistants' schedules can be changed.

- Ensuring communication with teacher assistants through documentation (e.g., communication book, logbook, regular meetings for collaborative monitoring, and ongoing discussion).

- Modelling the confidentiality of the student–school relationship.

- Resolving conflicts with teacher assistants at the classroom level first, school level second, and regional school board level third.

Source: Adapted from Nova Scotia Department of Education and Culture (1998). *Teacher Assistant Guidelines*. Used by permission.

How do teachers and paraprofessionals view the role of the paraprofessional? In a study conducted in five school districts in British Columbia, Lamont and Hill (1991) found that the two groups generally held similar views about the roles and responsibilities of paraprofessionals in regular classrooms. The major difference was that paraprofessionals thought they should take more responsibility for instructional support, diagnostic support, and classroom organization than teachers thought was appropriate. To make the partnership work smoothly, establish clear communication and a good working relationship with each paraprofessional who will work in your classroom. Consider the point of view of this member of the team. Look for his or her unique strengths and then work together, because the two of you are the heart of the in-school team for students who require the support of a paraprofessional in order to learn in an inclusive classroom.

Further Reading

About working with parapro-fessionals: P.A. Hammeken (1996). *Inclusion: An Essential Guide for the Paraprofessional*. Minnetonks, MN: Peytral Publications.

The Teacher and the Parents

Canadian parents have developed an increasing awareness of their own and their children's legal and social rights recently, and are asserting themselves more with school personnel (Hoffman, 1999; MacLeod, 1997). Being aware of these rights and making an effort to understand and support parents who exercise them is likely to enhance your relations with parents. These families have to meet the challenges that accompany the disability as well as all the normal pressures of family life. Families of children with disabilities spend significant amounts of time interacting with educational professionals. By becoming sensitive to their needs, you will facilitate these interactions.

Understanding the Parents' Perspective

A recurring theme in this book is the importance of taking others' perspectives. This section focuses on the perspectives of the parents of exceptional students. Living with an exceptional child or adolescent creates challenges for a family, with both positive and negative effects. Lily Dyson of the University of Victoria has studied how a child's disability influences parents and siblings (1993, 1992a). These families experience higher levels of stress because of the responsibilities of caring for and advocating for exceptional children and because of parental worry about the child's future.

CARING FOR EXCEPTIONAL CHILDREN AND ADOLESCENTS

Parents are first faced with accepting their child's disability. Lorraine Wilgosh (1990) of the University of Alberta writes that most parents of children with disabilities go through active adjustment to increasing and changing demands. However, you may see recurring parental sorrow when new challenges arise at each major developmental stage. Parents of exceptional children reported dreading transitions (e.g., from preschool to kindergarten) (Schmid & Hutchinson, 1994). It may help parents, young exceptional children, and their siblings to read books about children with disabilities—in order to teach all members of the family about the nature of the exceptionality and what exceptional children can accomplish. For examples of such books, see Figure 2.8.

What do you think?

Parents in Prince Albert, Saskatchewan, recently sued school boards and the Ministry of Education over the education of students with learning disabilities. See J. Hoffman (1999). The learning channels: How to navigate the special-ed system. *Today's Parent*, 16(3), 56–62. What do you think of their actions?

Weblinks

PARENTBOOKS (A BOOKSTORE)
http://parentbooks.com/

Families of exceptional children in Calgary published a book entitled *Letters to Our Children.*

Letter to Andrew Ziebell, who was born three weeks prematurely with cerebral palsy that affects all four limbs. Andrew has some hearing and vision loss.

Dear Andrew:

You, my love, turned seven years old on March 3, 1993. In your short lifetime you have had a long, hard road to follow. And that road will not get any easier. Always know, Andrew, that I love you more than anything in the world and I will always be there right beside you, helping your every step, sharing in your dreams, your hopes, your tears and your fears.

You have a circle of friends who love you and love to share in your life. These friends are special in every way because they see you as Andrew, a person first and foremost, and your disability doesn't matter.

The sky was the limit when you entered preschool. Your teachers, Jill, Jo-Anne, and Val took you through two years of learning, socializing, and fun-filled experiences. Your summer program there was just as wonderful because I could see the look of excitement on your face each and every day when you came home from the Leisure Centre. You had a great year at your community school where you moved mountains and acquired lifelong friendships.

In the beginning of 1993, another chapter opened in your life. You entered the world of Scouting. In full uniform you and your brother proudly stand united with all Boy Scouts of Canada. We are all proud to feel your sense of belonging.

Your world is not always full of joy and not all people see your strength, but dwell on your disabilities. The most difficult challenge began in June 1992 when you were not allowed to continue in your community school placement. Not only did this cost you a year of education, but the emotional devastation this inflicted on your brother and sister, who could not understand why you were not allowed to go to school with them, has been very traumatic. We will continue to fight to obtain your right to a fair and equal education in your community school, no matter how long it takes.

What your future holds for you, my son, I cannot say; but what I hope it holds for you is full acceptance into society and a world that is kind and full of love; a circle of friends and independence.

Lovingly,
Your Mom, Dad, Jennifer-Lea, Christopher and last, but not least, your watchful puppy Kelsey

Parental challenges in caring for exceptional children and adolescents vary greatly. Some children require physical and personal care daily and need to be lifted frequently. Others have life-threatening allergies that require parents to be constantly vigilant. Some children look different from their peers, and families may have to provide emotional support to overcome the potentially destructive effects of rejection. An eight-year-old boy with facial disfigurement, Lee, reported being bullied at school. His mother described consoling Lee, teaching him to respond to his tormentors, and moving him to a new school when the situation became intolerable (Valpy, 1998, p. D2).

Because learning disabilities are an invisible handicap, parents sometimes delay identification and acceptance of their child's exceptionality (Dyson, 1992b). Parents may not receive the same support as they would if their children had more visible disabilities (Waggoner & Wilgosh, 1990, p. 98). Gifted children and adolescents also feel different and can be teased and ridiculed at school. Alisha, who tied for second place in a National Mathematics League test, described her school experiences: She was in the school choir, play, and soccer team, but had only one friend. When asked where she got her support, Alisha answered without hesita-

BOOKS FOR PARENTS TO READ WITH EXCEPTIONAL CHILDREN AND THEIR SIBLINGS

For Preschoolers and Children in Grades 1 to 3

Allergies:	Aaron Zevy, & Susan Tebbutt (1995). *No Nuts for Me!* Downsview, ON: Tumbleweed Press.
	L. Habkirk (1995). *A Preschooler's Guide to Peanut Allergy.* London, ON: Ticketar Co.
Asthma:	Eileen Dolan, (1996). *Winning Over Asthma.* Amherst, MA: Pedipress.
Attention deficit/ hyperactivity disorder:	Clifford Corman, & Esther Trevino (1995). *Eukee: The Jumpy, Jumpy Elephant.* New York: Specialty Press.
Autism:	Becky Edwards, & David Armitage (1999). *My Brother Sammy.* Brookfield, CT: Millbrook Press.
Cerebral palsy:	Sarah Yates (1994). *Nobody Knows.* Winnipeg: Gemma B. Pub.
Deaf:	Judith E. Greenberg, (1985). *What Is the Sign for Friend?* New York: F. Watts.
Developmental disabilities:	Lucille Clifton, & Thomas DiGrazia (1980). *My Friend Jacob.* New York: E.P. Dutton.
Learning disabilities:	Kathryn Boesel Dunn, & Allison Boesel Dunn (1993). *Trouble with School: A Family Story About Learning Disabilities.* Bethseda, MD: Woodbine House, Pub.
Physical disabilities:	William Roy Brownridge, (1995). *The Moccasin Goalie.* Victoria, BC: Orca Book Publishers.
Speech disabilities:	Muriel Stanek, (1979). *Growl When You Say R.* Chicago: A. Whitman & Co.

Figure 2.8

tion, "My mom" (Wong, 2000, p. R7). A parent who tells you there is no time or energy for a parent–teacher meeting may have good reason to feel tired and discouraged.

EFFECTS ON FAMILIES

Siblings of children and adolescents with disabilities tend to show more social competence and to display the same level of self-concept and behaviour problems as comparable siblings of children without disabilities (Dyson, 1992a). However, school-age siblings of children with disabilities have stresses and needs (Alper, Schloss, & Schloss, 1996). They need to be informed about their sibling's disability, because they are often expected to supply information at school and to act as a caretaker at home. Siblings may need help handling teasing and feelings of embarrassment. However, positive effects have also been observed: "Having a brother with a learning disability has taught his sister tolerance. The kids have gained values well beyond their years, that will stay with them forever" (Wilgosh, 1990, p. 307). One mother said of inclusion, "It's our philosophy of family life, not just an educational practice; this is how we choose to value our family" (Wilgosh & Chomicki, 1994).

PARENTS' TEACHING AND ADVOCATING FOR EXCEPTIONAL YOUTH

Parents assume the roles of teachers and advocates (Waggoner & Wilgosh, 1990). They often spend long hours helping their children with disabilities complete unfinished school work. A "communication book" for children or an agenda book for adolescents may remind the students about assignments and may enable parents to see what is expected. Sometimes parents report that their teaching role interferes with their parenting role. It seems more important for exceptional children and adolescents to have accepting and supportive parents than to have another academic teacher. Teaching is, after all, your role. Many parents also assume the role of **advocate**: "I really didn't know, when I became a mother, that I was supposed to be a warrior. Yet as I am talking, I am aware that I need to fight if I want things to change" (Wilgosh, 1990, p. 304). Advocating can be an emotional and satisfying experience for parents; many join community associations to share experiences and learn with other parents.

CONCERN FOR THE FUTURE

Depending on the nature and severity of their disabilities, some individuals may not be able to live independently (Waggoner & Wilgosh, 1990), and children and adolescents with disabilities often face an uncertain future in career and work (Annable, 1993). Focus on Community describes one successful plan that is working for many Canadian families. Strategies to prepare students for adulthood include workplace learning and cooperative education during secondary school (Tennant, Hutchinson, & Freeman, 1992), and early planning of the transition from school to work. The case of Brenda Piet illustrated that, increasingly, IEPs contain such transition plans.

Collaborating with Parents

It would be difficult to overstate the importance of parents in the lives of their offspring. Many teachers recognize that the real experts on a student are usually the parents. In turn, some parents recognize the pressure that teachers are under and can be a source of support and advocacy for additional resources (Jory, 1991). Research suggests that the more extensive the collaboration between schools and families, the more successful children with exceptionalities are likely to be (Gallegos & Medina, 1995). Not all parents choose to collaborate with teachers and schools, but parents are more likely to cooperate with educators if the school, program, and teacher make them feel welcome (Stanovich & Jordan, 1995).

What will parents of exceptional students expect of you? Many Canadian parents believe that excellence in teaching leads to school success for children with special needs. The qualities they look for in teachers include patience, approachability, comfort, flexibility, a positive attitude, and adequate training (Wilgosh, 1990). Waggoner and Wilgosh (1990) reported that parents feel that teacher–parent communication is important, the teacher must accept the child's disability, and

Weblinks

CANADIAN NATIONAL INSTITUTE FOR THE BLIND (FOR HELP WITH ADVOCACY)
http://www.cnib.ca/library/ general_information/ advocacy. htm

Further Reading

On parents' planning for the future of their children with disabilities: K. Pike & P. Steinemann (1997). *Connections: A Planning Guide for Parents of Sons and Daughters with a Mental Handicap.* Brampton, ON: Brampton Caledon Community Living (available from 34 Church St. West, Brampton, ON L6X 1H3).

The Planned Lifetime Advocacy Network (PLAN)

At some point, parents of children with disabilities recognize that they will not personally be able to provide emotional support and financial security in their children's later years. PLAN is based in Burnaby, B.C., and was started by parents of children with disabilities.

PLAN tries to help create a good life for every member, regardless of level of disability, age, or income, by working with parents, friends, and existing social services. At its Web site, www.plan.ca, the organization writes: "At PLAN we believe that the best guarantee of a safe and secure future for persons with disabilities is the number of caring, committed friends, family members, acquaintances and supporters actively involved in their life. As parents, we at PLAN share your concerns about the future of your child with a disability. We know how hard you are working to secure a good life for them. No one can ever take your place. However, one day someone will have to assume the responsibility of caring for your relative in the event of your illness or death. We work hand in hand with families to build a network of caring people, friends and advocates for your loved one."

Josh is 14 years old and has severe epilepsy and brain damage. His parents have established a plan that will take care of Josh financially, and Josh has a circle of friends at his neighbourhood school, where he is in grade 8. His family plans to establish a formal network for Josh in his last year of secondary school, a time when adolescents with disabilities and their families can feel abandoned.

Josh, sitting beside his father, has always been included in all family activities and attends a neighbourhood school. His father wants him to become a member of the community as an adult.

A network of support usually consists of 4 to 12 people who pledge to look out for and remain involved with Josh for the rest of his life. Families pay fees to join and remain members of PLAN. For lifetime members, PLAN promises that a network will ensure that the child, regardless of age, is cared for his or her entire life (Picard, 1998).

Source: Based on A. Picard (1998). When disabled kids grow up. *Globe and Mail*, August 7, pp. A1, A4.

teacher–parent cooperation is essential. Parents also want to feel supported (Kimber & Kysela, 1998). Wilgosh and Chomicki (1994) interviewed four mothers of exceptional children. For them, inclusion meant: "The child is a fully participating, valued, and contributing member of a regular classroom of age appropriate peers. The child should feel safe, accepted and encouraged, being given choices and making decisions in a learning environment rich with opportunities" (p. 30).

Parent–Teacher Conferences

Parent–teacher conferences are "one of the most effective and commonly used methods to facilitate productive partnerships between parents and professionals" (Turnbull & Turnbull, 1990). To ensure strong working relationships with the parents of exceptional students, you can try to communicate effectively with them at every opportunity. In spite of your busy schedule, try to make calls to these parents yourselves, rather than ask the school secretary to do it. Prepare well by being informed about the student and the resources available in the school and community. Figure 2.9 shows a worksheet developed by a parent advocacy group to help parents prepare to be full participants in a parent–teacher conference.

DURING PARENT-TEACHER CONFERENCES

The message you want to convey is that there is a team approach between home and school, between students and teachers, and among teachers (Wilgosh, 1992). Parents report that they find an "us versus them" atmosphere to be a serious impediment to communication (Alper, Schloss, & Schloss, 1995). Create a comfortable atmosphere. Parents prefer to receive information about their children informally, in conversational meetings with teachers, so avoid jargon and give examples to show what you mean (Schmid & Hutchinson, 1994). While you may want to focus on teaching methods, parents are usually most interested in the outcomes for their children, so be prepared to discuss frankly the goals for the next week, month, and term (MacLeod, 1997). Parents aren't always honest with themselves about their children's progress, and this can put both parties on the defensive. You may need to remind them gently about what the student is accomplishing now and what is reasonable to expect in the upcoming months. Rather than forecasting far into the future, focus on what is feasible in your classroom if everyone makes a concerted and collaborative effort.

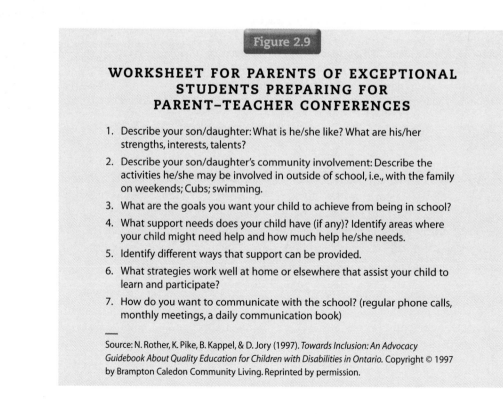

Figure 2.9

WORKSHEET FOR PARENTS OF EXCEPTIONAL STUDENTS PREPARING FOR PARENT–TEACHER CONFERENCES

1. Describe your son/daughter: What is he/she like? What are his/her strengths, interests, talents?
2. Describe your son/daughter's community involvement: Describe the activities he/she may be involved in outside of school, i.e., with the family on weekends; Cubs; swimming.
3. What are the goals you want your child to achieve from being in school?
4. What support needs does your child have (if any)? Identify areas where your child might need help and how much help he/she needs.
5. Identify different ways that support can be provided.
6. What strategies work well at home or elsewhere that assist your child to learn and participate?
7. How do you want to communicate with the school? (regular phone calls, monthly meetings, a daily communication book)

Source: N. Rother, K. Pike, B. Kappel, & D. Jory (1997). *Towards Inclusion: An Advocacy Guidebook About Quality Education for Children with Disabilities in Ontario.* Copyright © 1997 by Brampton Caledon Community Living. Reprinted by permission.

Exceptional adolescents are expected to learn to **self-advocacy** (Hutchinson & Taves, 1994). Then they can negotiate with their teachers for accommodations consistent with the IEP and with the recommendations of the resource teacher or case manager. Taking part in parent–teacher conferences may help adolescents to articulate their strengths and needs and advocate for themselves (Van Reusen & Bos, 1990). Adolescence is a period of development toward autonomy, responsibility, and personally relevant life goals. Participating in parent–teacher conferences may contribute to this development. Remember to prepare the students to take part and prepare their parents for the idea that the adolescent should join the conference.

AFTER PARENT–TEACHER CONFERENCES

After a conference, you have several additional responsibilities. First, write notes to remind yourself of the important points discussed. Second, if you and the parents have made any major decisions, you may want to write a brief note to the parents to confirm what was decided. Third, if you agreed to take any action (such as consulting the resource teacher or asking the principal to contact the parents), carry it out as soon as possible. Provide other educators who work with the child with a brief update on the outcomes. Some schools require that an update be entered in the "Parent–Teacher Conference Log" so the principal and other educators can access it.

It also can be helpful to take the parents' perspective when reflecting on the parent–teacher conference. While you may find it challenging to include their child in your classroom for one year, remember that the parents have this challenge for their entire lives. While you have an important job—to teach this child and include him or her in your classroom—these parents also have an important job. Theirs is to love and care for this child and to be the child's advocate. This is the basis from which you can expect them to communicate with you. Partnerships are built and cannot be achieved instantly; both you and the parents may have to challenge long-held beliefs and, in some cases, live through a few mistakes.

There may be families who do not form partnerships with you. Because of situations families face—including homelessness, unemployment, discrimination, poverty, and violence—parents may not choose to, or may not be able to, engage in collaboration. As educators, we have to respect their decisions and encourage them to attend the next parent–teacher conference.

> **Cross-Reference**
> Chapter 5 describes many situations that place families at risk—homelessness, unemployment, discrimination, poverty, violence—and might reduce their collaboration with schools.

Key Terms

pre-referral interventions (p. 36)

self-monitoring (p. 38)

collaboration (p. 39)

resource teacher (p. 40)

school-based team (p. 41)

paraprofessional (p. 41)

referring teacher (p. 41)

informal assessment (p. 41)

formal assessments (p. 43)

Identification, Placement, and Review Committee (IPRC) (p. 43)

Individualized Program Plan (IPP) (p. 45)

Personal Program Plan (PPP) (p. 45)

components of an IEP (p. 47)

present level of functioning (p. 47)

long-term goals (p. 47)

short-term goals (p. 47)

instructional strategies, materials, and services (p. 47)

related services (p. 47)

equipment (p. 47)

evaluation (p. 47)

dates for review (p. 47)

Teacher Advisor Groups (TAGs) (p. 49)

transition plan (p. 49)

cooperative education (p. 49)

advocate (p. 56)

parent–teacher conferences (p. 57)

self-advocacy (p. 59)

Summary

"Partners During Changing Times" is the title the Special Education Branch of Alberta Education gave to its resource guide for parents and teachers of exceptional students. This seems a particularly apt title in these times, when two prominent themes in exceptional education are change and inclusion. The role of the classroom teacher in the education of exceptional children is increasing. Teachers identify the needs of exceptional students, carry out pre-referral adaptations, and collaborate with school-based teams to facilitate inclusion. Teachers also play a central role in developing IEPs and carrying out these IEPs by using a variety of techniques to ADAPT their teaching and classroom organization and management. Strategies for meeting these challenges appear in upcoming chapters. Both parents and paraprofessionals are partners in the education of exceptional students and can work with you to share the responsibility in these changing times. ■

LEARNER OBJECTIVES

After you have read this chapter, you will be able to:

1. Define high-incidence exceptionalities, including giftedness, learning disabilities, attention deficit/hyperactivity disorder (AD/HD), communication exceptionalities, behavioural exceptionalities, and mild developmental disabilities.

2. Describe adaptations you can make in regular classrooms for students who are gifted or developmentally advanced.

3. Discuss adapted teaching to meet the needs of students with learning disabilities.

4. Describe classroom adaptations for students with attention deficit/hyperactivity disorder.

5. Describe adaptations needed by students with communication disorders.

6. For students with behavioural and emotional exceptionalities, discuss adapted teaching.

7. Discuss classroom adaptations appropriate for students with mild developmental disabilities.

Chapter 3

Exceptional Students: High-Incidence Exceptionalities

Urjo is 15 years old and in grade 10. His teachers describe him as non-compliant and underachieving. Their observations describe a boy who fails to complete assignments in class, refuses to do his homework, has difficulty following instructions, and rarely cooperates with teachers or classmates. Teachers describe him muttering under his breath, folding his arms across his chest, and shouting at peers. However, in art class, he excels. While he engages in loud, verbal, power struggles with most teachers, Urjo is quiet and engrossed when drawing or painting. The counsellor who interviewed him suggests that Urjo uses power struggles to avoid work he finds boring and pointless and to exert control over others. In an interview, Urjo's parents report that he initiates the same battles at home and that his younger brothers are starting to engage in the same behaviours. When teachers pressure Urjo to comply, he "badmouths" them and indulges in negative self-talk. Achievement tests show that Urjo is slightly below grade level in reading, written expression, and mathematics, and is easily distracted but does not have a learning disability. His difficulties have been described as a behavioural exceptionality, with a focus on defiant behaviours and disruptions to the classroom.

Scott is included in a grade 3 classroom and learns to read in a small group in the resource room. Scott was born with Down syndrome. His family has always involved him in all their activities and he has always been in regular education programs. After participating in early intervention (from the age of two months to four years) and attending the neighbourhood preschool, he moved with his classmates to kindergarten. At his teacher's suggestion, Scott stayed in kindergarten for a second year. Since then, he has moved to the next grade each year. Like many people with Down syndrome, Scott learns much by watching. For the past two years, he has watched and asked Billy, a friend and classmate with AD/HD, whenever he didn't know what to do. Scott's parents and teachers know that the gap between Scott's academic achievement and that of his classmates will gradually increase. However, Scott works hard, likes school, and especially likes learning to read. Scott recognizes and sounds out many words, is reading small books with predictable stories, and has recognized the names of all the students in his class for the past year. In math, Scott can add and subtract numbers less than 10 and hopes to learn to use his new calculator this year. He loves environmental science, discusses issues such as recycling, watches nature programs on television, and attends the "young naturalists" program in his community. Scott hopes to work in environmental protection when he grows up. Scott's IEP (part of which appears in Figure 3.7) lists his exceptionality as mild developmental disabilities, and refers to Scott's lower-than-average intellectual, social, and adaptive functioning.

1. Which of the characteristics of each student are most likely to affect learning and participation in the regular classroom? What learning needs are implied by these characteristics?

2. With such a range of characteristics and learning needs, what do exceptional students like Urjo and Scott who are learning in inclusive classrooms have in common?

3. How frequently is a teacher likely to be teaching a student with each of these exceptionalities?

4. What types of adaptations does each student need in order to be included in the social life and the group learning activities of the classroom?

5. What community resources can a teacher draw on to supplement in-school resources when teaching each of these students?

Introduction

In this chapter, you will learn about the characteristics and needs of students with a range of **high-incidence exceptionalities** and about classroom adaptations that help these students to learn. Our review of current policies in Chapter 1 showed that some territories and provinces are placing less emphasis on identifying and labelling specific exceptionalities and are paying more attention to meeting individual student needs. When you read the definitions and characteristics of exceptionalities, try to think of individual, exceptional students whom you have met or taught. Definitions enable communication, but they never capture the essence of the individual exceptional learner. Our language must be respectful and professional; for example, don't refer to exceptional children "with learning disabilities" as "the learning disableds." Keeping two things in mind may help you to use person-first language: (1) exceptional students are children and adolescents *first* and (2) they also have *some* characteristics associated with their exceptionality; think about how you would want teachers to speak if you were the parent of an exceptional student. We usually refer to the student first and describe the student as *having* an exceptionality second. The exception to this general rule, for the exceptionalities described in this chapter, is the expression "children who *are* gifted."

Cross-Reference
Chapter 4 focuses on descriptions of and adaptations for students with low-incidence exceptionalities, physical disabilities, and chronic health conditions.

This chapter focuses on teaching students with each of six high-incidence or frequently occurring exceptionalities. For each exceptionality, the section begins with the words of a child or adolescent, modelled on sources like *The Kids on the Block* book series (Aiello & Shulman, 1988a, b, c, d; 1989a, b) that contain the diaries or personal stories of exceptional individuals. The remainder of each entry follows a pattern: first, the exceptionality is described with information about its incidence or frequency. Then we focus on characteristics and on implications for learning and for classroom adaptations. There are examples of teachers' ADAPTing in elementary and secondary classrooms. The implications for social participation and for adult participation in employment and community life are explored briefly because these are important in a society committed to inclusion. Throughout the chapter, you will find reminders that exceptional students are most successful when their teachers and parents hold realistic but high expectations for them. The intent of this chapter is to provide a resource to which you can return when you encounter exceptional learners in other chapters of this book and in your classroom.

Students with high-incidence exceptionalities are gifted, or have learning disabilities, attention deficit/hyperactivity disorder, speech or language disabilities, behavioural or emotional exceptionalities, or mild developmental disabilities. It is usually thought that they make up approximately 75 percent of the exceptional student population in Canadian schools. (This may be a bit misleading, because some of these students will also have asthma, allergies, diabetes, and other chronic health conditions described in Chapter 4.) The definitional terms and characteristics for high-incidence exceptionalities are summarized in Table 3.1. These students are often difficult to distinguish from peers without exceptionalities, especially outside school settings. Students with high-incidence exceptionalities frequently show a combination of behaviour, social, and academic needs. Gifted students usually benefit from challenges and opportunities to work with develop-

Table 3.1

STUDENTS WITH HIGH-INCIDENCE EXCEPTIONALITIES

Exceptionality	Description
Gifted or developmentally advanced	Demonstrated or potential abilities show exceptionally high capability in specific disciplines, intellect, or creativity
Learning disabilities	Dysfunctions in processing information. Often defined as a discrepancy between ability and school achievement. Difference in ability/achievement not due to (a) visual, hearing, or motor disability; (b) emotional disturbance; (c) environmental, cultural, or economic disadvantage. General intellectual functioning within normal range.
Attention deficit/hyperactivity disorder	Persistent pattern of inattention and impulsiveness that may be accompanied by hyperactivity.
Communication exceptionalities	Refers to exceptionalities in speech or language. Speech is disordered when it deviates so far from the speech of other people that it calls attention to itself, interferes with communication, or causes the speaker or listeners distress. Language is disordered when student has impairment in expressive or receptive language.
Behavioural and emotional exceptionalities	Dysfunctional interactions between a student and his or her environment, including the classroom, home, and community. Can be seen in inability to build or maintain satisfactory interpersonal relationships with peers and teachers.
Mild developmental disabilities	Lower-than-average intellectual functioning and adaptive behaviour. Knows a great deal about living in the community without supervision; requires some instruction that could be provided under relatively non-intensive conditions.

mentally advanced peers. Other students with high-incidence exceptionalities usually benefit from systematic, structured, instructional interventions such as those described in this chapter and throughout this book.

Teaching Students Who Are Gifted or Developmentally Advanced

Teacher: How can I help you stay out of trouble?

Brian: I don't want to be bored. Challenge me. Let me work ahead on things that really interest me.

Brian is a gifted Aboriginal boy in grade 3. This exchange took place after his teacher had intervened in a scuffle between Brian and a classmate for the third time in a week.

Teacher: Why did you push Larry?

Brian: When I have nothing to do, he gets to me. He calls me "brainer" and tells me that I'm weird. When I'm busy, I don't notice as much. I need more stuff to do … please.

Weblinks

COUNCIL FOR EXCEPTIONAL
CHILDREN (TEACHING GIFTED
STUDENTS)
http://www.cec.sped.org/
ericec/digests/e513.html

GIFTED CANADA
http://www3.bc.sympatico.ca/
giftedcanada/

UNIVERSITY OF CALGARY CENTRE
FOR GIFTED EDUCATION
http://www.educ.ucalgary.ca/
altagift/

Description of Gifted Students

Students who are advanced in one or many areas of development are described as gifted or talented. They exceed teachers' and parents' expectations in specific areas of development or of the school curriculum. Over the years, definitions of gifted-ness have provoked controversy; for example, see a 1988 paper by Robert Hoge of Carleton University. In the past, gifted students were identified by high scores on intelligence tests, and often were assumed to be advanced in all areas. However, recent provincial definitions reflect the research of Dan Keating (1990, 1991) and Dona Matthews (1996; Matthews & Steinhauer, 1998) of the University of Toronto. They emphasize that gifted learners are **developmentally advanced** in specific **domains**.

"A student is considered gifted when she/he possesses demonstrated or poten-tial abilities that give evidence of exceptionally high capability with respect to intel-lect, creativity, or the skills associated with specific disciplines. Students who are gifted often demonstrate outstanding abilities in more than one area. They may demonstrate extraordinary intensity of focus in their particular areas of talent or interest. However, they may also have accompanying disabilities and should not be expected to have strengths in all areas of intellectual functioning" (British Columbia Special Education Branch, 1995b, p. E17).

Incidence of Giftedness

Incidence of giftedness is estimated at 2 to 5 percent of school-aged children (Winzer, 1999). Although some gifted students can be easily identified because they use their abilities and are willing to be recognized for them, some gifted stu-dents go unnoticed. Groups at risk for being unidentified include young boys, ado-lescent girls, students from diverse cultural groups, and students with disabilities (Lupart & Pyryt, 1996; Whitmore, 1988). Judy Lupart of the University of Calgary has studied the career aspirations of adolescent girls who are gifted in science (e.g., Lupart & Cannon, 2000) and the accomplishments of gifted women (Lupart, Barva, & Cannon, 2000). Women consider their personal accomplishments, as well as their career accomplishments, important.

Characteristics of Students Who Are Gifted

What should you look for to ensure that you recognize students who are gifted? No student will show all of the characteristics described here. Gurgit, who was described in the case study that opened Chapter 1, could meet most, if not all, of the learning outcomes for a social studies unit before it began. Gurgit's in-class questions indicated she was bored by the discussion. On challenging tasks, she read and wrote more and at a higher level of complexity than her classmates. Like many gifted students, Gurgit was articulate. Often gifted students' vocabulary is sophisticated for their age. They may show an unusual degree of curiosity, of ingenuity in seeking answers, and of persistence with tasks they enjoy. The same students may surprise you with their ordinary performance in subjects in which they do not excel.

COGNITIVE CHARACTERISTICS

In general, students gifted in academic skills and cognitive functioning differ from their classmates on three key dimensions: (1) the rate at which they learn new knowledge or skills, (2) the depth of their comprehension, and (3) the range of their interests (Parke, 1992). They often demonstrate enhanced **metacognition** or ability to decide when and where to use their knowledge and skills. Characteristics that suggest advanced cognitive development include:

- Has large vocabulary and high verbal fluency.
- Shows excellent retention of new knowledge.
- Learns quickly and easily.
- Demonstrates ability to generalize information.
- Makes abstractions readily.
- Uses good observational skills; identifies similarities, differences, and relationships.
- Has good organizational and planning skills.

Renzulli's Enrichment Triad Model (MacRae & Lupart, 1991; Reis & Renzulli, 1985; Renzulli & Reis, 1985) describes giftedness as an interaction among three primary clusters of characteristics: (1) above-average **cognitive abilities**, as described above, (2) high levels of task commitment, and (3) high levels of creativity. High **task commitment** refers not only to students' working hard but also to students' needing little external motivation, especially in areas that interest them. In general, they set their own goals, embrace new challenges, show perseverance, and enjoy sharing their projects with peers. However, high task commitment sometimes results in perfectionism that can be destructive or paralyzing. Gifted students may chastise themselves when they make a mistake or misbehave, and may think they should excel at everything. High levels of **creativity** are demonstrated by students' contributing many ideas, transforming and combining ideas, asking questions, and being insatiably curious about many topics.

BEHAVIOUR CHARACTERISTICS

The behaviour of gifted students varies. Frequently, gifted students are more advanced intellectually than emotionally (Colangelo, 1991; Delisle, 1992). They may show an enhanced concern for justice and a sharp sense of humour that can contribute positively or negatively to the classroom atmosphere (Friend, Bursuck, & Hutchinson, 1998).

Implications for Learning and Classroom Adaptations for Students Who Are Gifted

To teach students who are gifted effectively, you need to discover what challenges the individual students. In areas of the curriculum where a student is not challenged, look for the easiest way to remedy that. Research suggests that they need to be with their intellectual peers for at least part of the school day, so they are stimulated in areas in which they are advanced (Keating, 1991). However, they also benefit from learning with same-age peers during each school day. Strategies for adapting the curriculum to meet the needs of gifted students appear in Table 3.2. Figure 3.1 is an example of an **open-ended assignment**.

Implications for Social and Career Participation of Students Who Are Gifted

Surprisingly, gifted adolescents often find it difficult to focus their career aspirations and to make appropriate course selections. This may be because they have so many talents and interests. Allen is a talented musician and a top student in almost every curriculum subject. He has been invited to audition for the Canadian Youth

Gifted students are challenged by authentic problem solving in sites such as the Toronto Zoo. These students examine butterfly specimens in the butterfly meadows, a natural habitat area at the zoo.

Table 3.2

ENRICHMENT STRATEGIES FOR TEACHING GIFTED STUDENTS

Strategies	Descriptions and Examples
Sophistication	Introduce students to the theories and concepts that underlie the content being learned by the class. *Example:* When teaching about child development in a secondary course on psychology, provide gifted students with writings by Piaget and Montessori and encourage them to make systematic observations in a preschool.
Novelty	Students explore required curricular content from different and unique perspectives. *Example:* In history, gifted students write from the perspective of the oxen pulling the Red River cart across the Canadian West, or of the child who lived in Montreal while her father was a member of the North West Trading Company.
Authentic problem solving	Students apply their knowledge and skills to problems that are significant to their own lives. *Example:* When studying watersheds, gifted students test the water quality of a stream that runs through a park or that collects runoff from a parking lot in their community and prepare a report for town council.
Independent studies	Students pursue an area of personal interest or investigate a topic from the curriculum on their own. *Example:* Students select a character from *Hamlet* and prepare a resumé for that character based on their knowledge of the play.
Telescoping	Taking advantage of the overlap in curricula of adjacent grades, students do two curricula in a year. *Example:* Students complete grades 7 and 8 science in one year.
Compacting	After discerning what the student already knows of the unit, provide assignments so the student can master unfamiliar material. Then provide enrichment activities in the compacted area. *Example:* For a student who has already read and understood many of the events and issues of WWII as they appear in the curriculum, assign readings and written synopses of unfamiliar topics. When these are completed, encourage the student to choose a topic of interest about the role of the war in changing Canadian society, communicate with the War Museum, use the Internet, conference with you regularly, and prepare a multimedia presentation on the chosen topic.
Ability grouping	Students work with their intellectual peers on a regular, part-time basis, within the classroom or outside the classroom, providing social and emotional support, as well as intellectual stimulation. *Example:* An advanced reading or math work group, perhaps with peers from other classes, for enrichment in one or more subject areas.
Mentor programs	Students apply their knowledge and skills in a hands-on, real-life setting under the supervision of an adult in the community. They can pursue special interests, grow in self-confidence, and try out possible career paths. *Example:* A student who has considerable skill as an artist might be partnered with a painter who invites her to visit her studio and share the experience of being a working artist preparing for an upcoming show.
Open-ended assignments	Students are given options for completing an assignment and decide how far to take their learning. *Example:* In a kindergarten unit on whales, provide required assignments that must be completed by all students about the habitat and diet of the whales studied; provide optional assignments that require more writing, allow children to create games for whales based on knowledge of whales' particular skills and characteristics, etc. See Figure 3.1 for an example of an open-ended assignment on whales.
Tiered assignments	You prepare a range of distinct assignments, from fairly simple to complex, all focusing on key learning outcomes for the lesson or unit. Students may be assigned a particular activity or activities, you may select one activity to be completed by everyone and allow students to choose another, or students may choose the level of assignments they will complete. *Example:* In a secondary drama unit, the tiers for a culminating assignment might include preparing a scene, an act, or a short play while employing two, three, or more actors, and embodying one or more of the themes from a list generated by the class. Each tier can be described separately so students see that they have choices with regard to degrees of complexity.

Figure 3.1

AN OPEN-ENDED ASSIGNMENT FOR A KINDERGARTEN CLASS CONTAINING GIFTED STUDENTS

A Whale of a Party!
Kindergarten Independent Project
Due Date: January 29, 1999

Dear Parents,
The following is an outline of the Independent Project for term two. The format I have set out does not have to be followed strictly, so if you or your child has something to add or change, please feel free to do so. The items that are starred (*) are optional. The written sections may be typed on a computer, but I would encourage student printing wherever possible. Obviously, I would like the students to do as much of the work as possible and to be making the decisions regarding their projects. However, this should be an enjoyable experience, so if they have reached their limit, feel free to give extra help or to cut something out. Stress quality over quantity and the experience/process over the final product. Finally, if you have any questions, don't hesitate to ask me in person or via the homework books.

You are going to throw a party, and all of your friends are whales. Pick two different kinds of whales to invite (three, if you are feeling extra keen) and fill out the following party plan. Plan on having 10 whale guests.

The Guest List
(a) What kind of whales did you choose to invite and why? Make sure you invite whales that will get along (i.e., whales that will not eat each other!).
(b) Make a list of their names (e.g., Ollie Orca, Mandy Minke, etc.).
(c) *List the general address you would send an invitation to in January for each type of whale (e.g., Arctic Ocean).

The Invitation
Hand in a sample of the invitation you would send out to your guests.
Your invitation should include:
(a) A cover design.
(b) The name and type of whale (e.g., Ollie Orca) to whom the invitation is addressed.
(c) *Location of the party (consider the size of your guests, but you can pretend that the whales can be out of the water for your wingding).
(d) Date and time of the party.
(e) R.S.V.P. address or telephone number.

The Party
(a) Draw me a picture of how you would decorate the party location to make your guests feel at home.
(b) Draw and/or print a menu of the food you will serve your guests.
On another piece of paper, list the following:
(c) *The kind of music you will listen to at your party (this can be people music—Spice Girls rock!)
(d) *Will you ask your guests to do any tricks or play any games at your party (find out if your guests are especially good at something)?
(e) *Will you send your guests home with a party favour? What will it be?

The Party's Over
(a) Draw me a picture of what a photograph taken at your party might look like.
(b) *Write a thank-you letter that you think one of your guests might have sent you after the party.

Source: Developed by Jennifer A. Taylor of Kingston, Ontario, 1999, for a kindergarten class that included a number of students who were developmentally advanced in reading and writing. Used by permission.

Orchestra (CYO) this spring. If Allen attends CYO, he cannot take part in an archaeological "dig" for which only eight students have been accepted. Allen says that after every cello lesson, he knows that he wants to be a professional musician.

However, after spending a day at the "dig," he is just as passionate about becoming an archaeologist. Allen's guidance counsellor invited him to a seminar on careers and course choices. After the seminar, Allen told the counsellor he had not realized that there were prerequisite courses for entering a university program in archaeology. Allen also enrolled in a cooperative education placement with an archaeologist, for which he received a secondary credit. Recent research in Ontario (Chin, Munby, Hutchinson, & Steiner-Bell, in press) reports that many university and community college students have completed cooperative education placements to try out careers they think they want to pursue. For example, one college student described taking a co-op placement in a veterinary clinic to decide whether she wanted to be a veterinarian technologist. Like over 95 percent of the former co-op education students questioned, she recommended co-op education to others (Chin et al., in press).

Weblinks

YOUTH ORCHESTRA OF CANADA (FOR TALENTED YOUTH)
www.nyco.org

COLONY OF AVALON AT FERRYLAND, NEWFOUNDLAND (CANADIAN ARCHAEOLOGICAL SITE)
www.heritage.nf.ca/avalon/

Teaching Students with Learning Disabilities

Frank watched his teacher putting a schedule for the afternoon on the board. The list included reading, social studies, and journal writing. Did that mean oral reading? Frank had not practised the next story in the book. If the teacher asked him to read, he would die, the other kids would laugh, and… He tried to think of a way to get out of class before oral reading started. He felt his chest tightening, his stomach flipping, and his palms growing damp. Frank hated to stutter and stumble. He slouched down in his seat and worried. He kept asking himself, "How bad can it be?" But he knew the answer: "Bad!" When you can't read in grade 6, it's bad.

Description of Students with Learning Disabilities

Above are the words of a grade 6 student with learning disabilities. Students with learning disabilities have dysfunction in **information processing**. They may have disabilities in reading (**dyslexia**), writing (**dysgraphia**), or arithmetic (**dyscalculia**). In the provincial documents, the term *learning disabilities* (LD) is usually used to refer to exceptional students with a **discrepancy** between ability (usually measured by an intelligence test) and achievement in one or more of the following areas: reading, writing, language acquisition, mathematics, reasoning, and listening. This discrepancy is not primarily the result of a visual, hearing, or motor disability; emotional or behavioural disability; or environmental, cultural, or economic disadvantage. Usually the term LD is used to describe students who have at least average ability from whom we would expect better achievement. Much of the research on LD focuses on inefficient cognitive processing and the need for direct teaching.

CONTROVERSIES

Controversies surround definitions of LD. The Learning Disabilities Association of Ontario has recently proposed a new definition that emphasizes impairments in psychological processes related to learning that cause difficulties in skills such as oral language, reading, written language, and mathematics. While the definition is still in draft form, it is gaining support (http://www.ldao.on.ca/pei/defdraft.html).

Linda Siegel (e.g., 1999) of the University of British Columbia has argued against using discrepancy formulas as most provinces do. She argues that all students who show disabilities in learning (e.g., in phonological processing in beginning reading) should be identified as having LD. Some jurisdictions state that learning disabilities are apparent in both academic and social situations (e.g., Ontario Ministry of Education, 1999). Researchers debate whether **social skills difficulties** are a **primary disability** or a **secondary disability** that arises from living with a learning disability (see a paper by Richard Conte and Jac Andrews (1993) of the University of Calgary). Research findings about social skills are inconsistent. Teachers report that *most* students with LD experience social skills difficulties and peers report that *many* have low **social status**; however, only a *few* children with LD report low social **self-concept** (for reviews, see Bryan, 1999; Chan, 2000; Kavale & Forness, 1996).

READING DISABILITIES

Most students with LD experience difficulties learning to read. Recent research strongly supports insufficiently developed phonemic awareness as a characteristic of most children with reading disabilities in the primary grades. **Phonemic awareness** refers to the awareness that words can be segmented into component sounds, identifying sounds in various positions in words, and manipulating sounds in words. Studies by Keith Stanovich of University of Toronto (e.g., 1996; Gottardo, Chiappe, Siegel, & Stanovich, 1999) and John Kirby of Queen's University (e.g., Kirby & Parrila, 1999) contribute to this literature. One Canadian study reported that phonemic processing in grade 1 was the best predictor of grade 6 reading (Cunningham & Stanovich, 1997). Phonemic awareness interventions are effective in helping *most* children with learning disabilities to read (e.g., Martinussen, Kirby, & Das, 1998; Schneider, Ennemoser, Roth, & Kuspert, 1999).

Incidence of Learning Disabilities

Provinces report that about half of exceptional students have learning disabilities, making this the highest incidence exceptionality (Friend et al., 1998). Some people suggest that schools overidentify learning disabilities to support students who otherwise would not receive services (read Sheila Landucci and Dan Bachor (1992) of the University of Victoria). Definitional controversies and inconsistent identification procedures influence Canadian estimates, which suggest that 2 to 4 percent of the school-age population has LD. Boys outnumber girls, although the reasons for this are still unclear (Winzer, 1999). In some provinces, students with AD/HD, another 3 to 5 percent, are considered to have LD.

Characteristics of Students with LD

Teachers are the most likely people to suspect learning disabilities because the characteristics interfere with classroom learning. However, characteristics vary greatly from student to student.

Cross-Reference
Chapter 7 contains practical strategies to implement phonemic awareness interventions. Consult: M.J. Adams, B.R. Foorman, I. Lundberg, & T. Beeler (1998). *Phonemic Awareness in Young Children: A Classroom Curriculum.* Toronto: Irwin Publishers.

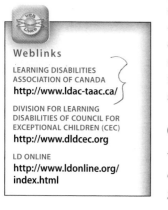

Weblinks

LEARNING DISABILITIES ASSOCIATION OF CANADA
http://www.ldac-taac.ca/

DIVISION FOR LEARNING DISABILITIES OF COUNCIL FOR EXCEPTIONAL CHILDREN (CEC)
http://www.dldcec.org

LD ONLINE
http://www.ldonline.org/index.html

COGNITIVE CHARACTERISTICS

Students with LD demonstrate lower-than-expected achievement in one area or in many areas. You will also see academic strengths on which you can build and for which you can give sincere praise. Frequently these students perform poorly on tasks requiring memory, focused attention, organization, metacognition, and information processing. These characteristics are elaborated on in Table 3.3. You may see inaccurate, seemingly careless, reproductions of teacher-created notes, with words omitted and organizational details overlooked. These students sometimes process information slowly, do not finish work in class, and appear to manage time poorly. Possibly they cannot start assignments because they don't know how to tackle them (Weber, 1993), so you may be able to develop a strategy to help them begin promptly.

Students with learning disabilities often receive tutoring in math as well as reading.

CHARACTERISTICS: LEARNING TO READ

The subjects in which students with LD have academic needs are usually reading, writing, spelling, and mathematics. Adapting teaching and assessment in each of these subjects is discussed further in Chapters 7 and 8. In reading, insufficiently developed phonological processing (already discussed in this chapter) is often followed by challenges in **reading comprehension** (Cunningham & Stanovich, 1997). Bernice Wong of Simon Fraser University has described these challenges for older students, which include missing the main idea, getting events out of sequence, and deducing content that is not there (e.g., Graham & Wong, 1993). The printed or written letters of students with LD can be distorted in size and shape, mirrored or reversed, and barely legible. Because all students tend to reverse letters until about the age of eight, reversals are only a problem when they persist past age eight. Some students also have difficulty learning to spell (James, 1996; Lennox & Siegel, 1996).

CHARACTERISTICS: LEARNING MATH

Researchers suggest that **number sense** may be the mathematical equivalent of phonemic processing in reading, that is, the bottleneck for students with LD learning mathematics (Gersten & Chard, 1999). According to Robbie Case (1998; Griffin & Case, 1997) of the University of Toronto, number sense refers to children's flexibility with numbers, the sense of what numbers mean, and an ability to look at the world and make mental comparisons about quantities. Older students find it challenging to represent mathematical relations in math and science word problems (Hutchinson, 1993; Montague, 1997). Perhaps this is a complex form of number sense. Challenges often arise in learning multiplication tables, and students may ignore columns in computations and carry or borrow incorrectly.

Table 3.3

WHAT ARE CHILDREN AND ADOLESCENTS WITH LEARNING DISABILITIES LIKE?

Hard question. They are all different. No list of characteristics would describe every student with learning disabilities. Frequently they puzzle us because they strike us as bright kids, but on closer inspection, they have real strengths and real weaknesses. Often they are overwhelmed by the volume of work they must do in the classroom, and always behind. They can feel frustrated by these things. They do have average or better ability, but achievement lags behind ability.

Let's think about how students with learning disabilities learn. Definitions suggest they have "a disorder in one or more of the basic psychological processes involved in understanding or using language." Language refers to symbols of communication—spoken, written, or even behavioural. Basic psychological processes refers to taking in information (listening, reading, observing), making sense of information (relating, remembering, evaluating), and showing (speaking, writing, calculating). They seem to be less active as learners, to do less meaning-making, to be less strategic.

Psychological Processes	What We Can Do
1. PERCEPTION: organizing, interpreting what we experience; most impact when perception is critical to learning—early years; may confuse letters when learning to read, more often and longer.	**WE CAN:** pieces of information that are perceptually confusing should not be presented together until at least one is learned well; important characteristics of information need to be highlighted.
2. ATTENTION: refers to focusing on information; coming to and maintaining attention; some identified as having attention deficit disorder (ADD) or attention deficit disorder with hyperactivity (AD/HD); "in her/his own world"; distracted, in constant motion.	**WE CAN:** break task into smaller segments; gradually build up; cues can bring attention to key words in explanations; meaning-check for instructions; help identify the important, independently.
3. MEMORY: arranging what they have perceived and attended to; many processes; e.g., problems in working memory (storing and retrieving information); too much so they only take in part of it (e.g., notetaking during a lecture); may not make connections.	**WE CAN:** help develop strategies for remembering (e.g., minute hand is longer than hour hand, minute is longer word); more practice; remind to find relationships; make it meaningful; teach strategies.
4. METACOGNITION: monitoring and evaluating own learning; identifying most effective way to learn; key to learning from experience, generalizing, and applying; may act impulsively, not monitor or plan.	**WE CAN:** teach self-monitoring; model thinking out loud; ask student to give reasons, give cues, give feedback, encourage, be clear, teach strategies.
5. ORGANIZATION: come without pencil; lose papers; have difficulty getting good ideas into an essay or assignment; lose track of goal, especially if it is long-term.	**WE CAN:** teach routines, put checklist on desk or notebook, break task into steps, put agenda on board, warn about major changes, ask questions to keep putting the onus on the student.

Source: Nancy L. Hutchinson (1999). *Teaching Exceptional Children and Adolescents: A Canadian Casebook*, p. 121. Copyright Prentice Hall Canada. Used by permission.

SOCIAL AND BEHAVIOURAL CHARACTERISTICS

Some students' social and behavioural needs are expressed in task avoidance, social withdrawal, frustration, and **depression**. Nancy Heath of McGill University found that while more children with LD may have depressive symptoms, the relationship between depression and LD is complex (1995, 1996; Heath & Ross, 2000). Judy Wiener of the University of Toronto found that students with LD generally have low

Subtypes of Learning Disabilities

During the past 20 years, researchers like Byron Rourke at University of Windsor and Linda Siegel of University of British Columbia have investigated the heterogeneity among children and adolescents with learning disabilities. While reading disability is dominant, it is not the only kind of disability. Both researchers have found students with reading disability who have concomitant disability in mathematics. The older the student, the more likely reading disability will be accompanied by learning problems in mathematics.

These learning problems in mathematics are shown in a wide range of errors. These include problems with spatial organization, aligning numbers in columns, and difficulties with visual details, like reading mathematical signs. Procedural errors in the steps in mathematical operations are common. They also tend to experience difficulties with the logic and reasoning that go into understanding mathematical problems and into generalizing from what is known to new problems.

Rourke and his associates have also shown that there is a group of students with learning disabilities whose problems in mathematics are primarily centred on poor memory. These students fail to remember the multiplication tables and the steps in computation. They are likely to avoid math problems that demand reading.

While the research on subtypes of students with learning disabilities is complex, it is clear that there are many students with learning disabilities in mathematics. However, there is much more research on learning problems in reading and more learning assistance for reading disabilities than for mathematics disabilities.

To read more about students with learning disabilities in mathematics, consult any of the following research sources:

- Montague, M., & Applegate, B. (1993). Mathematical problem-solving characteristics of middle-school students with learning disabilities. *The Journal of Special Education, 27*, 175–201.

- Rourke, B.P. (1989). *Nonverbal learning disabilities: The syndrome and the model.* New York: Guilford Press.

- Shafrir, U., & Siegel, L.S. (1994). Subtypes of learning disabilities in adolescents and adults. *Journal of Learning Disabilities, 27*, 123–134.

- Two chapters in Wong, B.Y.L. (1996). *The ABCs of learning disabilities,* address mathematics disabilities and subtypes of learning disabilities:

  - Chapter 3: An Overview on Subtyping Research in Learning Disabilities, pp. 49–65.

  - Chapter 8: Arithmetic and Mathematics and Students with Learning Disabilities, pp. 169–194.

Source: Nancy L. Hutchinson (1999). *Teaching Exceptional Children and Adolescents: A Canadian Casebook*, p. 137. Copyright Prentice Hall Canada. Used by permission.

social status in the eyes of their peers (Kuhne & Wiener, 1999; Weiner, Harris, & Duval, 1993). However, in a series of qualitative studies on social relations of children and adolescents with LD, graduate students at Queen's University reported more positive results. Some students with LD show well-developed social skills and peer relations (for two case studies, see Lévesque, 1997), while others show better social skills, peer acceptance, and peer relations in some contexts than in others (Chan, 2000, Stoch, 1999). As teachers, we may be able to create classroom contexts in which students with LD can participate socially as well as academically.

Implications for Learning and Classroom Adaptations: Students with LD

Most students with LD require adaptations in instruction and in the learning environment. They are usually taught in inclusive classrooms and may receive services in resource rooms.

ESTABLISHING AN INCLUSIVE CLASSROOM

Establishing a safe classroom characterized by understanding and acceptance is the first step. In a study of inclusive secondary science teachers, Karol Lyn Edwards (2000) of Queen's University found that exemplary teachers helped students with LD to participate by using interactive teaching, checked the understanding of individual students, and eliminated bullying.

ADAPTING TEACHING

You can build on an inclusive learning environment by adapting your instructional techniques to make them more accessible to students with LD (Newfoundland and Labrador Department of Education, 1998). These adaptations include:

- Providing overviews of lessons in chart form.
- Varying the **mode of presentation** (oral, visual, discussion, activity-based).
- **Cueing** students to listen to or make notes about important points.
- Relating material to students' lives and using experiential teaching approaches.
- Making directions short, and reinforcing oral directions with visual cues.
- Clarifying definitions and ensuring understanding by having students repeat definitions.
- Breaking a large topic or task into manageable parts with individual deadlines.
- Using collaborative and cooperative learning approaches.
- Offering assistance when it is needed, after students have asked their peers.
- Preparing **study guides** of key words and concepts so students have clear notes from which to study.

Students with LD may find **colour-coded** materials easier to organize, and may benefit from manipulative learning materials. They may be able to complete a partially filled-in task. A tape recorder can provide a textbook in an alternate format, enable an older student to tape a complex lecture, and give almost immediate feedback for oral reading practice. It can also serve as a scribe to record an assessment or a composition. Cross-age tutoring can help students with LD to learn by either teaching younger children or being befriended by older role models.

TEACHING STRATEGIES

It is important that you demonstrate how to learn for the benefit of students with LD and allow students with LD time to practise the skills they find difficult. General strategies such as organizational strategies and note-taking strategies can be taught to the whole class; then provide additional practice for those who need it. For example, introduce agenda books and model how to make entries, and put a daily agenda on the board. Teach outlining by providing a partial outline of your notes for students to complete, and teach highlighting by having pairs of students decide what to highlight. Model on an overhead before the students begin and debrief with reasons at the end of the lesson.

Further Reading

On learning disabilities: B.Y.L. Wong (1996). *The ABCs of Learning Disabilities.* Toronto: Academic Press.

G. Markel & J. Greenbaum (1996). *Performance Breakthroughs for Adolescents with Learning Disabilities or ADD: How to Help Students Succeed in the Regular Classroom.* Champaign, IL: Research Press.

Put Into Practice

Observe an experienced teacher with students with learning disabilities in his or her inclusive classroom. Focus on how the teacher makes everyone feel like a valued member and adapts teaching.

Students with LD are frequently taught **cognitive strategies** for reading comprehension (Graham & Wong, 1993) and math problem solving (Hutchinson, 1993). Alan Edmunds (1999) of St. Francis Xavier University developed an individualized approach to learning strategies to provide students with cues. Edmunds suggests that teachers "talk out" the cues with an individual student, key the steps into the computer, and print them out on a credit card–sized space. By laminating the card, punching a hole in one of its corners, and affixing a cable tie, the student can attach the cognitive credit card (CCC) to his pencil case. Figure 3.2 contains an example of a history CCC developed by a grade 11 student.

Implications for Social and Career Participation of Students with Learning Disabilities

There are successful adults with learning disabilities in almost every career, but many other adults with LD experience underemployment (Gerber et al., 1992). Brenda Tennant, an Ontario teacher, found that cooperative education employers recommended adolescents with LD receive explicit instruction in interpersonal skills, job preparation, career awareness, etc. (Tennant, Hutchinson, & Freeman, 1992). **Career development** programs have used cognitive strategy approaches to teach

---

Figure 3.2

HISTORY COGNITIVE CREDIT CARD (CCC)

This Cognitive Credit Card, designed by an 11th-grade student, was primarily used to alleviate his perennial problem of not being able to take good notes during class. He did not seem to understand the purpose of taking notes—he just did it because everyone else did it and he had done so since about grade 6. He did not know where to start, what was important, what was not important, or what to do with the notes once he was finished. It is evident from the card that he needed numerous cues to manage what he thought about during class time. His note-taking skills were not bad—he got the information down on paper—he just felt that he needed to be a more active learner/listener, an idea he got from one of his teachers. The primary benefits of his use of the card were that he "learned to take a lot fewer notes—just the important ones," and he did not feel lost when it came time to study for a test. After initial success with this CCC, he designed a similar one for taking notes from the readings he did while away from the classroom.

Taking Notes in History Class
What did I read/study about last night?
How was it related to what we did last class?
What do I predict the topic will be about today?
What is the introduction of today's topic?
Why is this topic important to what I already know?
How many major/minor points *will* the teacher make?
How many major/minor points *did* the teacher make?
What kind of questions could be asked on a test?
Do I have any concerns that need to be cleared up?
Do I need to talk to the teacher?

Source: A.L. Edmunds (1999). Cognitive credit cards: Acquiring learning strategies. *Teaching Exceptional Children, 31*(4), 68–73. Used by permission.

employment readiness and career awareness explicitly. Effective Canadian programs of career development for adolescents with LD include *The BreakAway Company* (Campbell, Serff, & Williams, 1994) and *Pathways* (Hutchinson & Freeman, 1994), which provide teachers with collaborative activities that accommodate heterogeneity. Such programs help reduce the underemployment of adults with LD.

Teaching Students with Attention Deficit/Hyperactivity Disorder

I have Attention Deficit Disorder, which is often called ADD for short. I forget to take my homework to school because my thoughts run ahead of me. That's why I bump into things, too. All that energy keeps me awake into the night. Dad says that I have eagle eyes; I notice everything. But eagles know when to stop looking around and zoom in on their prey. Me, I just keep noticing more things and miss my catch.

Once when Dad and Emily and I hiked at Birdsong Trail, a thunderstorm sent us rushing back toward the car. Dad tripped over a rock and twisted his knee. His face wrinkled with pain. He asked Emily to go for help, but she was not sure of the way.

"I can find it, Dad!" I interrupted. And I told him the whole route. "Ben, I knew those eagle eyes of yours would come in handy," Dad replied. "You'll find the way just fine. Emily can stay here to keep me company." As I turned to go, Dad called, "Hurry, Ben! I need you." Swift as an eagle, I zoomed off toward the ranger station and got help for Dad. I was the only one who could do it. And that's when I realized it's good to be me.

Gehret, 1991, p. 11.

Description of Students with Attention Deficit/Hyperactivity Disorder (AD/HD)

The above quotation might have been drawn from the autobiography of a grade 4 student with AD/HD. Children and adolescents with AD/HD display chronic and serious **inattentiveness**, **hyperactivity**, and/or **impulsivity**. They have difficulty staying focused on instructions, schoolwork, and chores; are easily distracted and forgetful; and are constantly on the go and into everything. These characteristics occur prior to age seven, but may not be observed that early because young children typically experience few demands for sustained attention. At school, these students are often described as having LD because there is no separate category of AD/HD in most provinces. For example, "for the purposes of this document the term 'learning disability' … may include students with Attention Deficit/Hyperactivity Disorder" (B.C. Special Education Branch, 1995b, section E, p. 11).

Incidence of Attention Deficit/Hyperactivity Disorder

In Canada, the prevalence of AD/HD is estimated at 3 to 5 percent of school-aged students (B.C. Special Education Branch, 1995b, p. 21), consistent with estimates

Weblinks

ATTENTION DEFICIT DISORDER ONTARIO FOUNDATION
http://www.addofoundation. org

CH.A.D.D.—CHILDREN AND ADULTS WITH ATTENTION DEFICIT DISORDERS (CANADIAN SITE)
http://www.vcn.bc.ca/ chaddvan/

CH.A.D.D.—CHILDREN AND ADULTS WITH ATTENTION DEFICIT DISORDERS
http://www.chadd.org

in the U.S. (Barkley, 1990). Boys are three times more likely to be affected than girls, and neurological causes are suspected (Hynd, Hern, Voeller, & Marshall, 1991). Usually, a diagnosis is the result of individualized testing for cognitive ability and achievement, a medical screening, and **behaviour ratings** completed by parents and teachers (McBurnett, Lahey, & Pfiffner, 1993).

Characteristics of Students with AD/HD

The characteristics and learning needs of students with AD/HD vary. *The Diagnostic and Statistical Manual of Mental Disorders* (DSM-IV) (American Psychiatric Association, 1994) defines three subtypes of AD/HD: Predominantly Inattentive, Predominantly Hyperactive-Impulsive, and Combined Type.

CHARACTERISTICS OF AD/HD, PREDOMINANTLY INATTENTIVE

Students with AD/HD, Predominantly Inattentive, display many more characteristics of inattention than hyperactivity-impulsivity. They may ignore details, make careless errors, or have trouble staying on-task while working or playing. They do not seem to listen when you speak to them directly; often they do not follow through on instructions, and do not complete homework and classroom tasks. Students who are predominantly inattentive may have difficulty organizing their activities, and lose or forget things. They dislike or try to avoid becoming involved in work that requires them to concentrate for long periods of time, and may be easily distracted by movement, objects, or noises in the classroom.

CHARACTERISTICS OF AD/HD, PREDOMINANTLY HYPERACTIVE-IMPULSIVE

Students with AD/HD, Predominantly Hyperactive-Impulsive, display many more characteristics of hyperactivity-impulsivity than inattention. They may fidget and squirm, leave their desks, and run and climb at inappropriate times. They usually find it challenging to play or work quietly, they move constantly, and they talk excessively. Impulsivity characteristics include blurting out answers before you have finished asking a question, not waiting for their turn, and interrupting other students.

CHARACTERISTICS OF AD/HD, COMBINED TYPE

Most students with AD/HD have the Combined Type. These students display many characteristics of both inattention and hyperactivity-impulsivity. The key behaviour patterns you may recognize in your students are (1) not listening when you speak to them directly, (2) difficulty making and keeping a schedule for assignments and activities, (3) fidgeting, (4) difficulty paying attention for sustained periods of time, (5) answering questions before they are called on, and (6) always "on the go."

CHARACTERISTICS OF SOCIAL INTERACTIONS

AD/HD influences all aspects of an individual's life, including social interactions. Figure 3.3 provides descriptors of peer relations and what a student with AD/HD would like others to know. The classroom is the most problematic environment for

Further Reading

On teaching students with AD/HD: K.G. Nadeau (1993). *School Strategies for ADD Teens: Guidelines for Schools, Parents, & Students: Grades 6–12.* Annandale, VA: Chesapeake Psychological Publications.

S.F. Reif (1993). *How to Reach and Teach ADD/ADHD Children.* West Nyack, NY: The Center for Applied Research in Education.

students with AD/HD due to their impulsivity, distractibility, and overactivity (Roberts, White, & McLaughlin, 1997). These characteristics can cause both students and teachers to react negatively. Treat students with AD/HD respectfully and patiently to enhance your relationship with them and serve as a model for the class.

Implications for Learning and Classroom Adaptations: Students with AD/HD

Because students with AD/HD often have difficulty getting started on, and then concentrating on, assignments, help them to begin. Try scheduling frequent, but short and specific, break times. "**Checkpoints**" for project completion and homework journals for nightly assignments can help many students. Providing students with clear, numbered, and written as well as verbal instructions will help them complete tasks.

ADAPTING CLASSROOM ORGANIZATION

There are strategies for classroom organization to enhance the learning of students with AD/HD that may benefit other students. For example, minimize distracting factors. A **carrel** is a protected space, with wooden walls or made of cardboard, that blocks out distractions. You may be able to borrow a carrel from your school library or make one from the carton for a large appliance. If you introduce a carrel, be sure to use it yourself, so it is seen as a high-status opportunity, not a punishment. Provide a predictable structured environment, so students know what

---

Figure 3.3

With My Friends
I get mad easily when I play with my friends.
I don't know why, but a lot of times other kids don't want to play with me.
Sometimes other kids complain about me to the teacher.
Most of my friends are younger than I am.
I'm not very good at making friends.
My mom or dad tells me I'm too bossy with other kids.
Some kids in my class pick on me and tease me.
I wish I had more friends.
It's easy to make friends at first, but pretty soon they're not my friends anymore.

What I Wish Other People Knew About Me
I really do care about my schoolwork.
I'm not getting in trouble on purpose.
I don't mean to be bossy.
I hate it when people tell me I'm not trying.
Lots of the time it's really confusing to be me.
I want my mom and dad to be proud of me.

Source: K.G. Nadeau & E.B. Dixon (1997). *Learning to Slow Down and Pay Attention: A Book for Kids About ADD,* Second edition. Washington: Magination Press. Used by permission.

you expect of them and what they can expect of you. Communicate explicitly about predictability and structure to ensure that students with AD/HD have understood. When you teach, ADAPT, maintain the students' interest, model by **thinking aloud**, and ensure adequate opportunities for practice.

RESPONDING TO INAPPROPRIATE BEHAVIOUR

In spite of your best efforts, on occasion you will have to respond to inappropriate behaviour by students with AD/HD. The best response is to give inappropriate behaviour as little attention as possible and instead provide positive reinforcement for appropriate behaviour as soon as it occurs (Roberts et al., 1997). However, a **verbal reprimand** may be necessary when behaviour is getting out of hand. To be effective, reprimands should be immediate, unemotional, brief, and backed up with a time out or loss of privileges. Sometimes you will need to follow up with the consequences developed at the beginning of the year.

In-school teams sometimes develop **time-out** procedures for children with AD/HD. A time out can be carried out in the classroom or away from the immediate setting that is reinforcing the behaviour, for example, in the hall. Time out is a type of removal punishment in which a student is removed from opportunities for reward. Consult Chapter 6 for more information on time out. Roberts et al. (1997) suggest that a one- to five-minute time out will have the same effect as a longer one. A rule of thumb is to assign one minute per two years of age.

STRATEGIES FOR SELF-MANAGEMENT

Cognitive-behaviour management (CBM) programs teach students how to use cognition to control behaviour. Usually you and the student agree on a problem that is getting in the way of learning (e.g., looking around instead of completing assignments). You develop steps for the student to follow, put these on a cue card, and model their use. The student practises using the steps aloud, and gradually covertly, to solve the problem. The student monitors his own performance of the steps. Some teachers use a signal to remind the student to begin using the CBM steps. Chapters 6 and 9 contain examples of CBM programs developed for students. These take considerable thought and time in the early stages, but are worth the effort when they are effective. The student must know the steps and be able to carry them out individually. At first, the student can be cued, but eventually must initiate the steps independently. Other ways to encourage self-management include giving students with AD/HD responsibilities they can handle so they feel they are contributing to the school environment, as well as working with the in-school team to help the student develop better social and academic skills and improve time management and organization.

MEDICATION

Medication is probably the most controversial issue surrounding AD/HD. Two classes of medication are commonly used to treat children with AD/HD: **psychostimulant medications** and **antidepressants**. The amount of the stimulant Ritalin consumed in Canada increased more than fivefold from 1990 to 1997 (Health

Put Into Practice

Develop a set of consequences for a class you have taught or may be teaching in the near future. Describe the characteristics of a student with AD/HD who is a member of this class, and consider how the consequences will apply in this case. Consult Chapter 6.

Canada, 1997, cited in Maté, 2000). A *Globe and Mail* article suggested that in Quebec, the increases were mainly due to schools that asked parents to have their children use Ritalin (Paradis, P. 1998, May 27. The *Globe and Mail*, cited in Maté, 2000). Nearly 2 percent of the American school-age population receives stimulant medications for AD/HD (Barkley, 1990), despite concerns about abuse and addiction. The most commonly prescribed are Ritalin, Dexedrine, and Cylert (Sweeney, Forness, Kavale, & Levitt, 1997). Researchers have reported a decrease in classroom performance in some children treated with psychostimulants. They have questioned whether the resultant decrease in behaviour problems or relative gains in attention are worth the loss of learning performance in some children (Forness et al., 1992; Forness & Kavale, 1988). The most common side effects of the stimulants are insomnia, decrease in appetite, gastrointestinal problems, irritability, increase in heart rate, and sometimes a worsening of the presenting symptoms. Uncommon side effects are depression, cognitive impairment, growth retardation, tic disorders (e.g., Tourette syndrome), and impaired liver function (Sweeney et al., 1997).

The current best practice in the management of AD/HD requires combining a psychosocial approach with medical intervention (Cantwell, 1996). The recommended psychosocial approach includes cognitive-behaviour management programs for the child, interventions that focus on the family as well as the classroom, and individual psychotherapy for the child, if depression occurs. Cantwell (1996) suggests that 70 percent of children with AD/HD respond to one of the stimulants on the first trial and if all three are tried, the likelihood of positive response increases to between 85 and 90 percent. The other class of medication prescribed frequently for AD/HD is antidepressants. Drugs in this class can cause an array of side effects, including cardiac complications, nervousness, insomnia, and seizures in rare cases.

A recent book, *Scattered Minds* by Gabor Maté (2000), a Vancouver physician who has AD/HD, recommends a balanced view. While there are strongly held views on both sides of this issue, parents make the decisions about medication and receive prescriptions from physicians. Consider Paradis's claim (cited in Maté, 2000) that teachers are causing the increase in use of stimulant drugs in Quebec. As teachers, we lack knowledge about psychopharmacologic medications and, given the serious **side effects** and **contraindications**, it seems irresponsible of us to recommend blithely to parents that they should place their children on medication. However, parents may seek our advice. Figure 3.4 contains questions for parents and teachers to ask physicians about medication.

Implications for Social and Career Participation of Students with AD/HD

The account by Ben at the beginning of this section illustrates that people with AD/HD have many strengths and plenty of energy. Like people with LD, they may find themselves underemployed as adults unless they have opportunities for hands-on learning and for acquiring career awareness through explicit teaching. In his book *ADD Success Stories*, Hartmann (1995) suggests that adults with AD/HD need to choose careers that are particularly suited to their characteristics.

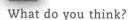

What do you think?

Read about both sides of the debate on medication and AD/HD:

<u>Pro</u>: L.B. Silver (1999). *Attention-Deficit/ Hyperactivity Disorder: A Clinical Guide to Diagnosis and Treatment for Health and Mental Health.* Washington, DC: American Psychiatric Press.

<u>Con</u>: D.B. Stein (1999). *Ritalin Is Not the Answer: A Drug-Free, Practical Program for Children Diagnosed with ADD or ADHD.* San Francisco: Jossey- Bass.

QUESTIONS FOR PARENTS AND TEACHERS TO ASK PHYSICIANS ABOUT MEDICATIONS PRESCRIBED FOR AD/HD

1. What are the effects and side effects, both short-term and long-term, of this particular medication?

2. What doses will be used, and by what schedule should they be given?

3. How often should you see the child for reevaluation while he or she is taking this medication?

4. When should the medication be stopped briefly to see if it is still required for the treatment of ADHD?

5. Are there foods, beverages, or other substances the child should not consume while taking this medication?

6. Will you be in contact with the school periodically to determine how the child is responding to the medication in that environment, or am I expected to do that?

7. If the child accidentally takes an overdose of the medication, what procedures should I follow?

8. Do you have a fact sheet about the medication that I can have to read?

Source: R.A. Barkley (1995). *Taking Charge of ADHD: The Complete, Authoritative Guide for Parents*, p. 250. Copyright © The Guilford Press, New York. Used by permission.

Teaching Students with Communication Exceptionalities

Writing in my journal every day helps me feel better and write better. I used to go to speech therapy every week. Now my therapist comes to school once a month. In between, I practice my sounds with helpers. Today my speech therapist told me that I am really getting better at making my sounds. She recorded me talking and I listened to myself on the tape recorder. I felt proud. I have to talk like that in my class so the other kids will stop saying that I talk like a baby. I am going to ask if I can be in the next play for social studies. So they can see that I talk like them now.

From the journal of Ruth, a grade 2 student with an articulation speech disorder

Description of Communication Exceptionalities

Generally, communication exceptionalities include disorders of speech (**articulation**, voice, and fluency) and disorders of language (expressive or receptive). The term *speech impairment* is widely used to refer to a disorder that involves the perceptual motor aspects of transmitting oral messages. The Ontario Ministry of Education (1999) describes language impairment as "an impairment in comprehension and/or use of verbal communication or the written or other symbol systems of communication, which may be associated with neurological, psychological, physical, or sensory factors" (p. 2). Usually language impairment is described as involving one or more of the form, content, and function of language in communication and is characterized by language delay. You usually see delayed development of expressive language, receptive language, or both.

Incidence of Communication Exceptionalities

Generally, school districts in Ontario report that 3 to 5 percent of the school population receives "speech help" (Weber, 1993). However, recent funding cutbacks have reduced services for communication exceptionalities across the country. Incidence data for speech and language disorders are uncertain because criteria and levels of service vary widely from district to district and even across schools within a district. Sometimes services are provided by the health care system, and some parents seek private therapy rather than face waiting lists. Boys with communication disorders outnumber girls by about two to one.

Characteristics of Students with Communication Exceptionalities

Most students with communication disorders experience difficulties with both speech and language, but some students have difficulty in only one of these areas. Many students with other exceptionalities (e.g., learning disabilities, cerebral palsy, developmental disabilities) have communication disorders as a secondary disability. However, the designation "communication disorders" is most often used when speech or language is the primary exceptionality. There is a wide variety of communication disorders. You may recognize students with communication disorders in your classroom from some of the characteristics listed in Table 3.4. If you suspect that a young child has a speech or language disorder, talk with the parents. Recommend a thorough evaluation by a speech-language pathologist to determine the child's communication strengths and weaknesses. This professional can provide a plan for meeting the child's needs, and can recommend services within the school district and other agencies.

Put Into Practice

Seek resources to help you understand the level of language development of children entering grade 1. Look for books. Consider videos such as *Children Learning Language: How Adults Can Help* (1997). Lake Zurich, IL: Learning Seed.

Implications for Learning and Classroom Adaptations: Students with Communication Exceptionalities

Historically, speech and language disorders have been the responsibility of speech and language therapists and students have been removed from the classroom for short periods of time for therapy. Teachers carried out follow-up exercises in the classroom. In the scenario presented at the opening of this section, Ruth practises with helpers or volunteers between visits to the specialist. Today, many teachers rely on volunteers from the community for individual activities such as articulation practice.

You can assist students with communication disorders. Create an accepting atmosphere and never allow classmates to mock or tease. Collaborate with the student, the parents, and the speech and language specialist to obtain suggestions and goals. Be proactive: give students opportunities to answer questions that require brief responses, and teach them to monitor their speech.

Table 3.4

SPEECH AND LANGUAGE DISORDERS AND THEIR CHARACTERISTICS

Communication Disorder	Example of Characteristics
Language delay	For young students, at least six months behind in reaching language milestones; a grade 2 student uses three words rather than full sentences.
Receptive language	Student in grade 6 consistently fails to understand an oral instruction, even when given individually.
Expressive language	Student in grade 10 begins each sentence four or five times and cannot be understood by peers; refuses to speak in front of class.
Aphasia	Student cannot understand speech or produce meaningful sentences.
Apraxia	Student cannot sequence muscle movements and thus does not produce meaningful speech.
Articulation	Student in grade 2 cannot produce the s sound. This results in teasing by classmates.
Dysfluency	Student in grade 12 stutters, but persists to express ideas.
Voice disorders	Student speaks slowly and softly in a husky voice (does not speak with normal pitch, loudness, duration, or quality); is shy about expressing ideas.
Orofacial defects	Student in grade 5 with cleft palate has difficulties with speech and feeding.
Dysarthria	Grade 9 student's speech is distorted due to paralysis of speaking muscles.

You can help students who have difficulty responding orally by taking some simple actions. Be a good role model for all students in the class when speaking to students with communication disorders. Speak clearly and a bit slower than normal, pause at appropriate times, and use straightforward language and simple grammatical structures. When responding to a student with a communication disorder, respond to the meaning of the student's speech rather than to how the student speaks. Resist the temptation to interrupt students or to finish their sentences when they stutter or pause. Make eye contact with the speaker, and wait for a few seconds before responding (Salend, 1998).

Early language development underpins much of academic learning. Thus many children with communication disorders also experience difficulty with academics. Problems with speech sounds can result in underdeveloped phonemic awareness, which is required for learning to read and spell. Receptive language delays can contribute to difficulties in reading comprehension and in understanding specialized terms in mathematics (e.g., carry, regroup, minus, times) and other subjects. Language disabilities can seriously impede content-area learning in upper grades, where lectures and independent reading provide complex conceptual information.

Implications for Social and Career Participation of Students with Communication Exceptionalities

Being unable to communicate effectively can contribute to social needs. Children with speech and language disorders can feel neglected or even rejected if their peers cease to include them in games and classroom activities. These pressures can be felt acutely during adolescence when peer acceptance is so highly valued. However, many adults are able to overcome speech disorders if these are their only exceptionalities. Not developing either comprehension or production of language may prevent adults from participating fully in the workplace unless adaptations are provided.

Teaching Students with Behavioural and Emotional Exceptionalities

I don't like the work we do here. It is easy and boring. I can figure out the questions and after that I don't feel like doing them, so I don't. Most of the teachers back off when a student yells at them. They don't make me do it then. Other guys leave me alone when they see I can make the teacher afraid. I don't know what good this boring stuff is. I like to draw. I'm awesome at drawing. I should just do drawing all day at school so I can be an artist. I want to draw comic books and stuff like that.

From Urjo's interview with a counsellor about his experiences at school. Urjo, who is 15 years old, was identified as having a behaviour exceptionality.

Description of Students with Behaviour Exceptionalities

Urjo was described at the opening of this chapter as refusing to do his homework, engaging in loud, verbal disagreements with teachers, and having a behaviour exceptionality or disorder. *Behaviour disorder* is a generic term. In a recent analysis of the definitions used across Canada, Don Dworet of Brock University and Arthur Rathgeber of Nipissing University (1998) demonstrate the range of meanings given to this generic term. This heterogeneous group of disorders refers to dysfunctional interactions between a student and his or her environments, including the classroom, home, and community. Behaviour disorders can vary in severity and in effect on interpersonal relations and personal adjustment.

MILD AND MODERATE TO SEVERE BEHAVIOURAL EXCEPTIONALITIES

Students with mild behavioural exceptionalities usually can be supported in the classroom with the assistance of a resource teacher, counsellor, or other in-school resources. Students with moderate and severe behaviour disorders may require more intensive interventions in addition to classroom adaptations. Students with moderate behaviour disorders demonstrate one or more of:

- **aggression** (physical, emotional, or sexual) and/or hyperactivity
- **negative psychological states** (such as anxiety, depression, stress-related disorders)
- behaviours related to **social problems** (such as delinquency, substance abuse, neglect)

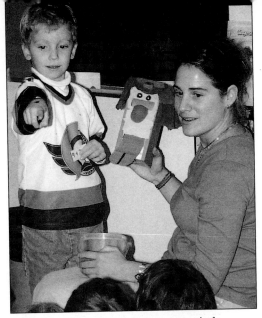

Help all students to participate constructively. This boy is demonstrating a puppet he has made.

These students have a disruptive effect on the classroom learning environment, social relations, or personal adjustment. They have demonstrated these behaviours over an extended period of time, in more than one setting, and with more than one person (teachers, peers, parents, siblings). In addition, they have not responded to interventions provided through classroom management strategies (B.C. Special Education Branch, 1995b). Students with more severe behaviour disorders than those described above are likely to require intensive intervention over a period of time from community as well as school personnel.

Incidence of Behaviour Exceptionalities

Educators treat behaviour exceptionalities as denoting behaviour that varies markedly and chronically from the accepted norm and that interferes with the student's own learning or the learning of others. That is, educators refer to educationally relevant characteristics. In contrast, psychologists and psychiatrists focus on more clinical characteristics. Variations in expectations and norms across communities also contribute to difficulties in estimating incidence of behaviour exceptionalities. Who makes the identification—educators or clinical personnel—varies and contributes to variation in incidence. The British Columbia Special Education Branch recognizes that about 2 percent of students may have a moderate behaviour disorder (1995b).

Characteristics of Students with Behaviour Exceptionalities

Because students who experience behaviour exceptionalities make up an extremely heterogeneous population, any list of characteristics must be highly varied in type and intensity. No student would exhibit all of the following characteristics. However, you are likely to observe some of these characteristics in students with mild or moderate behaviour disorders (Smith, Polloway, Patton, & Dowdy, 1998):

- aggressive acting-out behaviours
- social deficits, irresponsibility
- inadequate peer relationships
- hyperactivity
- distractibility
- lying and stealing
- academic deficits
- depression
- anxiety

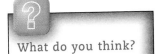

What do you think?

The characteristics in this list can be seen on occasion in many students; what distinguishes those with behavioural and emotional difficulties from other students?

If a student has a moderate behaviour disorder, you are likely to see that the student needs some or all of the following while in the classroom (Reithaug, 1998):

- **structure**, predictability, and consistency
- immediate, frequent, and specific **feedback** with consequences
- academic success
- responsibility and independence
- positive problem solving
- positive alternatives to current behaviours
- enhanced self-confidence
- positive school-to-home support systems
- evidence that he or she is making change for the better

In addition, most students with behaviour exceptionalities need challenging, respectful, and cognitively engaging activities. Sometimes we think we must lower our expectations or excuse the student from learning; however, as Urjo suggests, boredom often contributes to students' acting out their behaviour disorders in the classroom.

Implications for Learning and Classroom Adaptations: Students with Behaviour Exceptionalities

Students with behavioural exceptionalities, like Urjo, can be a disruptive force in the classroom and affect everyone present. When teacher candidates and experienced teachers tell me that they have reservations about inclusion, most of their negative personal experiences focus on children with behaviour exceptionalities who have been disruptive to the learning of the entire class.

HELPING STUDENTS TO IMPROVE THEIR BEHAVIOUR

You can help students improve their behaviour in many ways, ranging from preventive measures to direct responses. Figure 3.5 focuses on preventive measures and ways to ensure they are effective for students with behaviour exceptionalities. Focus on People describes a teacher who is effective in teaching students with behaviour exceptionalities.

STRUCTURING THE CURRICULUM AND THE CLASSROOM

Structure the curriculum and classroom environment to take advantage of "getting off to a good start." Apply your procedures, rules, and consequences consistently and discuss any changes (reasons and implementation) with the class. Develop a behaviour or learning **contract** with a student with a behaviour disorder that is specific to his or her greatest challenge, and ensure that it is realistic and immediate. Both of you should sign it. Contracts are described in Chapter 6. Use the resources of the school, the school district, and the community—to secure group intervention for the class—to teach **prosocial behaviours** and to develop cooperation. Some police services offer a VIP program; find a local equivalent and work

Figure 3.5

PREVENTIVE MEASURES AND ADAPTATIONS FOR STUDENTS WITH BEHAVIOURAL DISORDERS

Establish an orderly and predictable classroom:

- Inform students of what is expected of them and of the consequences of not meeting your expectations.
- Check to ensure that the student with a behaviour disorder understands both expectations and consequences.

Then establish a positive climate for participating and learning:

- Model behaviour that treats everyone fairly, makes everyone feel included, and challenges but does not threaten.
- Talk with the student with a behaviour disorder about what each of you can do to ensure that he or she feels part of the class.
- Focus on the positive, rather than the negative, by exhibiting your self-confidence and building the self-confidence of your students.
- Encourage the student with a history of behaviour problems to believe that the two of you can work together for a positive experience.
- Recognize positive student attributes; catch students "being good."
- Focus on recognizing the positive attributes of the student with a behaviour disorder at optimal times; be vigilant so you don't miss the times when he or she is cooperating, etc.

FOCUS ON PEOPLE

Milly Fraser, Grade 4, Alexander Forbes School, Grande Prairie, Alberta

A teacher who catches students being good and much more.

"Stop, Drop, and Phone" Award
Milly Fraser will drop everything in the middle of the school day and phone parents, even at work, to let them know their child did especially well on a test. Milly Fraser might even suggest that mom or dad make the child a favourite meal as a reward.

Best Supporting Role
When Nancy Goheen's son, Taylor, was in a church play, Milly Fraser took in a rehearsal—because she couldn't make the performance. On skate night, she showed her support by coming, even though she doesn't skate. And when she heard that a local missionary group was going to help children in Nicaragua, Milly Fraser organized a class bake sale to raise money for school supplies for them. The kids saw their charitable efforts in action when the missionaries returned with a video of the Nicaraguan schoolchildren.

A Rewarding Experience
Taylor Goheen, a bright but troubled boy, was in danger of becoming the class outcast, but Milly Fraser brought him into the fold by employing savvy behavioural modification techniques that engaged the whole class. She put Taylor on a program where he was marked on his conduct. When he behaved well, he got to choose an enjoyable activity for everyone in the class—not just himself. Fraser also rewarded him, personally, with stickers and other little gifts. "She has given so much to my son," says Nancy Goheen, "that it has totally changed the person he is."

From Dorothy Nixon (2000). Inspiring teachers. *Today's Parent*, September. Today's Parent Online, September 4, 2000 (http://www.todaysparent.com).

Further Reading

On behaviour exceptionalities: B.C. Special Education Branch (1996). *Teaching Students with Learning and Behavioural Differences: A Resource Guide for Teachers* (http://www.bced.gov.bc.ca/specialed/docs.htm).

D. Reithaug (1998). *Orchestrating Positive and Practical Behaviour Plans.* Vancouver: Stirling Head Enterprises.

S. Rockwell (1995). *Back Off, Cool Down, Try Again: Teaching Students How to Control Aggressive Behaviour.* Reston, VA: Council for Exceptional Children.

Put Into Practice

Interview an adult who immigrated to Canada. Ask about behaviours of children recently immigrated from his or her country that could be misunderstood at school. Compare notes with classmates.

collaboratively. (The VIP program focuses on Values, Influences, and Peers. It is a joint program of the Ontario Ministry of Education and the Ministry of the Solicitor-General. Topics include peer pressure, responsible citizenship, and interpersonal skills.) Be persistent in securing individual therapy, counselling, instruction in self-management strategies (whatever is needed for the student with a behaviour exceptionality), consistent with the group intervention. Teach so that all of your students feel that they are learning; engage your students fully. You can use the ADAPT strategy to ensure that a student with a behaviour exceptionality finds classes meaningful, and work with a resource teacher, paraprofessional, or volunteer to ensure that individual tutoring reinforces your adaptations. Although time consuming and challenging, these actions can get the student with behaviour exceptionalities "onside" from the first day of term.

CLASSROOM PROGRAMS IN PROSOCIAL BEHAVIOUR

You may feel that your efforts, as a teacher with these students, are insignificant compared to the work of psychologists and psychiatrists. However, you are understating your importance. A recent report from the National Institute for Mental Health (Teens: The Company They Keep, http://www.nimh.nih.gov/publicat/teens.cfm) in the United States highlights the roles of teachers and schools. It suggests that many attempts to "reform" severely delinquent youths have had little positive effect. Typically these programs place delinquent youth together in settings such as group homes. "The association with delinquent peers precedes the initiation and progression to serious violent offenses in 90% of cases." Research suggests that we prevent anti-social behavior through interventions aimed at peers and other key people in the students' social environment. "The challenge of contemporary prevention … is to alter these adolescent norms [where] … an aggressive reputation is positively related to adolescent peer popularity. The primary strategy currently employed to achieve this goal is through the use of classroom and school-based programs in social problem solving, conflict management, violence prevention, and more broad-based curriculum for promoting emotional and social development in the total school population."

OTHER CONTRIBUTING FACTORS AND APPROACHES

School violence has many causes, including community factors (e.g., portrayal of violence in the media), school administrative and policy issues (e.g., lack of proactive approaches aimed at peer pressure to take drugs), and school building–level factors (e.g., lack of enforced schoolwide policies). All of these are important, as are the individual student factors and classroom strategies that we have discussed in this section.

Implications for Social and Career Participation of Students with Behaviour and Emotional Exceptionalities

Students with behaviour and emotional exceptionalities tend to lack advocates (Dworet & Rathgeber, 1998). There is no high-profile national organization like the Learning Disabilities Association of Canada that offers workshops to teachers and community support to parents. Perhaps the stigma associated with emotional problems contributes to the lack of advocacy, or perhaps this is due to the higher preponderance of emotional disorders in children from communities characterized by poverty. In most communities, you and your school can enlist the support of the local mental health association and other community organizations, depending on the nature of the behavioural exceptionality. These organizations provide employment support to adolescents and adults with emotional and mental health disorders.

Weblinks

CANADIAN MENTAL HEALTH ASSOCIATION
http://www.cmha.ca/

NATIONAL INSTITUTE FOR MENTAL HEALTH (CHILD AND ADOLESCENT MENTAL HEALTH)
http://www.nimh.nih.gov

Teaching Students with Mild Developmental Disabilities

To Ms. Starr: I want to work in recycling. Because I want to help the environment and I won't need to read too much. I'm not too good at reading or writing, but I am learning this year. I like this class. You and Mr. T. [Mr. Tymchuk, the resource teacher] make me want to learn. You let me try my way. Thank you. That's why I want to be in recycling. The end.

Dictated to the resource teacher, following a lesson about careers, by Scott, who is in grade 3 and has mild developmental disabilities.

Perspectives on a Problematic Concept: Description of Developmental Disabilities

The term *developmental disabilities* refers to disabilities that affect all aspects of development and is widely used in Canada to replace *mental retardation*, a term unacceptable to most people but still in use, particularly by the American Association on Mental Retardation (AAMR). We are referring here to "a state of functioning that begins in childhood and is characterized by limitation in both **intelligence** and **adaptive skills**" (http://www.aamr.org). Recently, some of the international community has begun to use the term *intellectual disabilities*.

In Chapters 1 and 2, we considered a range of perspectives on exceptionality. All of these perspectives are represented in the field of developmental disabilities. A human rights perspective emphasizes what persons with disabilities are entitled to (e.g., the Canadian Association of Independent Living Centres, http://www.cailc.ca). An educational perspective emphasizes the learning needs of individuals with exceptionalities and of professionals who work with them (e.g., the Ontario Association on Developmental Disabilities, and the J.P. Das Developmental Disabilities Centre, http://www.quasar.ualberta.ca/ddc/INDEX.html). A medical or psychological perspective emphasizes limitations experienced by these individuals (e.g., the Developmental Disabilities Program at University of Western Ontario, http://www.psychiatry.med.uwo.ca/).

The AAMR definition lists 10 adaptive skill areas, two of which must show limitation: communication, home living, community use, health and safety, leisure, self-care, social skills, self-direction, functional academics, and work. This definition rests on four assumptions:

What do you think?

Visit the Web sites representing the various perspectives on mild developmental disabilities. How can teachers become effective advocates for students with developmental disabilities?

- To be valid, assessment must consider cultural diversity.
- Limitations in adaptive skills are indexed to the individual's need for supports.
- Limitations in adaptive skills coexist with strengths.
- With sustained, appropriate supports, life functioning will generally improve.

This definition, adopted in 1993, focuses on the individual's functioning within the community, rather than emphasizing scores on IQ and adaptive behaviour tests.

The AAMR (1993) recommended the language of levels of support, ranging from *intermittent* (on an "as needed" basis), through *limited* (consistent but time limited) and *extensive* (daily in at least some environments and long term), to *pervasive* (constant, high intensity, potentially life-sustaining). This system classifies needs rather than deficits, and focuses on the 10 specific adaptive skills areas in the new definition. None of the ministries of education in Canada has yet adopted this system of levels of support for describing developmental disabilities, but a number have adopted the two categories of mild and severe, as described below.

TWO LEVELS OF DEVELOPMENTAL DISABILITIES: MILD AND SEVERE

In the past, four categories—mild, moderate, severe, and profound—were used, primarily associated with IQ score ranges. Recently, practitioners have begun to use two levels of functioning—mild and severe—to describe individuals with developmental disabilities, primarily associated with level of adaptive functioning. Mild developmental disabilities are discussed in this chapter as a high-incidence exceptionality, while severe developmental disabilities are discussed in Chapter 4.

MILD DEVELOPMENTAL DISABILITIES

Weblinks

CANADIAN DOWN SYNDROME
SOCIETY
http://www.cdss.ca

"Persons with mild [developmental disabilities] are those who know a great deal about living in the community without supervision and who require some instruction that could be provided under relatively non-intensive conditions" (Dever, 1990, p. 150). Besides the ongoing debates about terminology, recent research has dispelled the earlier belief that individuals with **Down syndrome** necessarily function at a moderate level of developmental disability. Research shows that many individuals with Down syndrome have mild developmental disabilities (Rynders & Horrobin, 1990) similar to those of Scott, whose case is highlighted at the opening of this chapter. Figures 3.6 and 3.7 provide information about Down syndrome and an excerpt from Scott's IEP, respectively.

Incidence of Mild Developmental Disabilities

It is estimated that about 2 percent of the general population has mild developmental disabilities. In a school of 400 students, this would be about eight students, but there is variation from one community to another, with a higher rate associated with psychosocial disadvantage (B.C. Special Education Branch, 1995b, 1998).

Figure 3.6

INFORMATION ABOUT DOWN SYNDROME

Down syndrome is a genetic defect causing limitations in physical and cognitive development. It is the result of a chromosomal error, not any fault of either parent. One in every 700–800 live births will be affected by Down syndrome. Though the likelihood of having a child with Down syndrome increases to some degree with the age of the mother, three-quarters of all children with the syndrome are born to mothers under 35.

Recent studies show that, though all children with Down syndrome have some degree of intellectual disability, other factors, such as environment, misinformation and low expectations, have a considerable impact on their learning potential. Generally, progress will be slow, and certain complex skills may be difficult. Each individual has unique strengths and weaknesses.

Physically, children with Down syndrome have low muscle tone and a generalized looseness of the ligaments. The Canadian Down Syndrome Society recommends that children be assessed by x-ray at age three to four (before kindergarten) and again at age 10–12 to look for instability at the two top neck vertebrae. This instability must be carefully considered during any planning for physical activity to avoid serious injury. There is also a strong susceptibility to hearing and vision difficulties. At least one-third of the children will have heart defects.

Classroom Strategies

Teaching

- Discuss scheduling and activities before they happen: use wall charts, calendars, photos of a single activity or a single day. These activities reinforce structure and sequencing.

- Allow time to finish a task.

- Help the student to structure play as well as work or the activity may become confusing.

- Break up tasks into small steps; use short blocks of time.

- Avoid the abstract in favour of the concrete and the visual.

- Phrase questions simply, and allow response time. Use short sentences.

- Encourage speech by having the student express wants, rather than forming simple "yes" or "no" responses.

- Gain attention by using simple commands, e.g., use eye contact. Be precise.

- Help the child focus on the task—remove items that might distract.

- Expect appropriate behaviour. All students are accountable for their behaviour.

- Cooperate with the parents in integrating learning activities, e.g., shopping, banking, renting a video, travel. Be mutually aware of what the student knows and is learning.

- Be aware of the available specialized computer software especially designed to facilitate reading and communication.

Social

- Help the student develop independence; this will both increase self-esteem and improve social relationships.

- Help the student and others understand Down syndrome. Initiate open discussion, considering individual differences and wide variations of abilities. Your own behaviour and acceptance will serve as a model.

- Encourage interaction and involvement with other students through play and classroom activities.

Source: British Columbia Ministry of Education (1996). *Awareness of Chronic Health Conditions: What the Teacher Needs to Know.* Victoria: Queen's Printer for British Columbia. Used with permission.

Figure 3.7

SECOND PAGE OF INDIVIDUAL EDUCATION PLAN (GOALS FOR THE YEAR/ADAPTATIONS)

Student: Scott Boudin　　　　Teacher: Pat Kostas
Exceptionality: Mild developmental disabilities (Down syndrome)

LONG-TERM GOALS FOR THE YEAR	ADAPTATIONS
1. Reading: Scott will continue to develop phonemic awareness and reading comprehension.	1. Materials at his level; individualized instruction (resource teacher).
2. Writing: Scott will improve his written expression using full sentences in his journal and curriculum areas.	2. Using drawings or pictures from magazines as necessary (support of educational assistant).
3. Listening: Scott will improve listening to and following instructions.	3. Using comprehension check (repeating instructions to educational assistant or classroom buddy).
4. Speaking: Scott will speak clearly in social and learning situations, asking questions when he does not understand.	4. Asking educational assistant or classroom buddy about what to say.
5. Math: Scott will improve counting, use of money, addition and subtraction of numbers to 10.	5. Using coins, other concrete materials for addition and subtraction.
6. Social and environmental studies: Scott will participate in collaborative learning group.	6. Asking educational assistant or classroom buddy when unsure what to do.
7. Motor development: Scott will engage in games, increase independence in eating lunch, increase hand–eye coordination.	7. Assistance with eating lunch, using computer (educational assistant).
8. Art and music: Scott will gain experience with various art media.	8. Tasks at level.
9. Self-management: Scott will follow lunch routines, join an extracurricular activity.	9. Adult volunteer to support in eating and cleaning up lunch.
10. Social: Scott will develop close relationships with several peers and participate in group activities.	10. Watching and following positive actions of peers (encouraged by educational assistant).

Source: Adapted from Nancy L. Hutchinson (1999). *Teaching Exceptional Children and Adolescents: A Canadian Casebook*, p. 30. Copyright Prentice Hall Canada. Used by permission.

Characteristics of Students with Mild Developmental Disabilities

DELAYED DEVELOPMENT: COGNITIVE AND PHYSICAL

Usually, students with mild developmental disabilities learn to meet the everyday demands of living and develop into self-sufficient adults. However, "In school, they may have difficulty attaining the academic skills associated with their grade level, ... often have difficulty understanding concepts of the same complexity and acquiring skills and knowledge at the same rates as other students" (British Columbia Special Education Branch, 1998, p. 7).

Students with mild developmental disabilities pass through the same developmental stages as other students, but at a much slower rate. Delays can be seen in physical, cognitive, language, and social development. In physical development, fine motor coordination may be delayed, affecting cutting, colouring, printing, etc. Cognitive delays affect short-term memory, attention, and ability to generalize and to recognize similarities and differences. Frequently these students are less interested in letters, words, reading, and numbers than their classmates in the early school years. They are likely to find reading comprehension, arithmetic reasoning, and problem solving most difficult, but may attain lower levels of achievement in all curriculum areas. Exceptions may be curriculum areas where they can use experiential learning, such as Scott's expertise about recycling and nature acquired by camping and watching television programs. Figure 3.7 includes an excerpt from Scott's IEP.

DELAYED DEVELOPMENT: COMMUNICATION AND SOCIAL ADJUSTMENT

In speech and language development, you may see delay—less-developed expressive and receptive vocabulary. Students may not understand long sentences or complex ideas presented for the first time. Characteristics include articulation disorders, concrete language, and difficulty with advanced grammar rules. Students with developmental disabilities usually experience challenges in social adjustment, part of adaptive behaviour. They may lack initiative and sometimes display "**learned helplessness**." Thus they are less socially prepared to pay attention, initiate conversation, and cooperate, and they may appear immature or shy. During the adolescent years, this can be especially difficult.

TEACHER REFERRALS

Some students will be identified before they start school, for example, those with Down syndrome who have physically distinguishing characteristics. Other students with mild developmental disabilities may be identified after starting school. Teachers frequently make pre-referral adaptations, consult with resource teachers, and refer these students for assessment (as described in Chapter 2). This exceptionality has been referred to as the "**six-hour handicap**," because students who lag behind their peers at school may meet the everyday demands of living. Occasionally school districts describe these students as "slow learners." They often are advised to register in the **applied or basic stream** in secondary schools. When there is no clear evidence of an **organic cause** for delay, the suspected causes include disadvantage—poverty, inadequate nutrition, family instability, and lack of stimulation and opportunity to learn.

Implications for Learning and Classroom Adaptations

ADAPTATIONS TO SUPPORT COGNITIVE DEVELOPMENT

To promote cognitive development, encourage students with developmental disabilities to interact with the environment and with other students. Arrange the environment to provide sensory and intellectual stimulation. Structure and consistency will help them function in a world that can seem chaotic (Weber, 1993). Set cognitive goals and use action-oriented activities to facilitate their attainment (Smith, Polloway, Patton, & Dowdy, 1998). Other organizational strategies, such as colour-coding notebooks, reducing choices, and highlighting key text, make learning easier because students can focus on the important parts of a lesson (Department of Education, Government of Newfoundland, 1998; Weber, 1993). Extending deadlines and arranging for peers to create social opportunities can improve the learning environment for students with mild developmental disabilities. Learn what alternative resources are available, such as parallel textbooks at **lower reading levels**, audiotaped texts, manipulatives that appeal to the senses, and games to practise important concepts. Students with developmental disabilities will benefit from reteaching, practice, and application of skills and concepts.

ADAPTATIONS TO SUPPORT LANGUAGE DEVELOPMENT

To promote language development, simplify the language you use in instructions and relate new ideas to the student's experiences. Provide opportunities for students to use speech and language, without fear of correction or criticism, for a variety of communication purposes. These kinds of activities may also promote social development. Ensure that classmates treat the student with mild developmental disabilities with respect, and create many contexts in which students learn by collaborating and using strengths other than traditional academic knowledge. To adapt assessment procedures for students with mild developmental disabilities, look for ways to simplify, shorten, and make clearer what you are looking for in an answer. Alternatives may also include oral exams, portfolios, or interviews.

Further Reading

About collaborative and cooperative learning: E.G. Cohen (1994). *Designing Groupwork: Strategies for the Heterogeneous Classroom,* Second edition. New York: Teachers College, Columbia University.

P.J. Vermette (1998). *Making Cooperative Learning Work: Student Teams in K-12 Classrooms.* Upper Saddle River, NJ: Merrill.

Implications for Social and Career Participation of Students with Developmental Disabilities

During the secondary years, the focus usually shifts to functional, vocational, or applied learning, and students may learn in the community and in specialized classes as well as in regular classes. Adolescents and young adults with mild developmental disabilities benefit from learning through experience in programs like cooperative education and on-the-job training. Some seek programs in community colleges. People with mild developmental disabilities are primarily disadvantaged in formal school settings and thrive in the community, where they can use their life experience and are not required to use literacy skills or grapple with abstract concepts. In my community, young adults with Down syndrome deliver mail in a large institution, organize audiovisual equipment in a university department, do cleaning in a small business, and work in food preparation. They have found niches as volunteers or employees in the service sector or in predictable jobs that don't require high levels of problem solving or literacy. However, data suggest that less than half of those with developmental disabilities are involved in work or training 30 months after leaving secondary school (Edgar, 1988).

It is thought that the vast majority of adults with mild developmental disabilities can obtain and maintain gainful employment (Smith et al., 1998). However, to do this they must develop personal and social behaviours appropriate to the workplace through transition experiences that prepare them for the expectations of employers. This means that to be successful, inclusion must mean inclusion in the community, not just within the four walls of schools.

Adults with development disabilities in H'Art studio in Kingston, Ontario, feel empowered by producing and selling folk art.

Key Terms

high-incidence exceptionalities (p. 64)

developmentally advanced (p. 66)

domains (p. 66)

metacognition (p. 67)

cognitive abilities (p. 67)

task commitment (p. 67)

creativity (p. 67)

open-ended assignment (p. 68)

information processing (p. 71)

dyslexia (p. 71)

dysgraphia (p. 71)

dyscalculia (p. 71)

discrepancy (p. 71)

social skills difficulties (p. 72)

primary disability (p. 72)

secondary disability (p. 72)

social status (p. 72)

self-concept (p. 72)

phonemic awareness (p. 72)

reading comprehension (p. 73)

number sense (p. 73)

depression (p. 74)

mode of presentation (p. 76)

cueing (p. 76)

study guides (p. 76)

colour-coded (p. 76)

cognitive strategies (p. 77)

career development (p. 77)

inattentiveness (p. 78)

hyperactivity (p. 78)

impulsivity (p. 78)

Summary

Students with high-incidence exceptionalities include students who are gifted or who have learning disabilities, attention deficit/hyperactivity disorder, communication exceptionalities, behaviour exceptionalities, or mild developmental disabilities. They comprise about 75 percent of exceptional students. This means that you will be teaching these students frequently. In fact, many educators say that it is unusual, these days, to teach a class that does not contain at least one student with a learning disability or attention deficit/hyperactivity disorder. These students may be inefficient at making sense of what you are teaching and may require encouragement and learning strategies that help them stay on-task and complete assignments.

Gifted students will thrive with assignments that offer choice, challenge them, and enable them to go beyond regular curriculum expectations. Students with speech and language exceptionalities may require opportunities to practise in the classroom what they learn with a specialist, and volunteers may assume this responsibility. Expect to seek the assistance of other team members for students who have behaviour exceptionalities. They can be very challenging and often require individual counselling that you simply cannot provide in a classroom setting. Asking for help when you really need it is a sign of strength, not weakness. Students with mild developmental disabilities will probably not keep pace with the regular curriculum, and you can expect to see the gap widen over time. However, they benefit greatly from observing their peers in a regular class and are likely to participate in regular classrooms during the elementary years and to be enrolled in streams or programs that emphasize inclusion in the community, more than in regular classrooms, during the secondary years.

It is often difficult to distinguish students with high-incidence exceptionalities from their peers, because their exceptionalities are not always obvious, with the exception of students with Down syndrome, who have characteristic facial features. Using the ADAPT strategy, in combination with students' IEPs, will help you to change elements of the classroom so that, with no more effort than is necessary, you can meet individual needs. Most of these students will benefit from a structured, predictable, engaging class with a positive tone, in which everyone is treated with respect by you and taught that that is how they are expected to treat one another. ■

Key Terms *continued*

behaviour ratings (p. 79)

checkpoints (p. 80)

carrel (p. 80)

thinking aloud (p. 81)

verbal reprimand (p. 81)

time out (p. 81)

cognitive-behaviour management (CBM) (p. 81)

psychostimulant medications (p. 81)

antidepressants (p. 81)

side effects (p. 82)

contraindications (p. 82)

articulation (p. 83)

aggression (p. 87)

negative psychological states (p. 87)

social problems (p. 87)

structure (p. 88)

feedback (p. 88)

contract (p. 88)

prosocial behaviours (p. 88)

intelligence (p. 91)

adaptive skills (p. 91)

Down syndrome (p. 92)

learned helplessness (p. 95)

six-hour handicap (p. 95)

applied or basic stream (p. 95)

organic cause (p. 96)

lower reading level materials (p. 96)

Chapter 4

Exceptional Students: Low-Incidence Exceptionalities, Physical Exceptionalities, and Chronic Health Conditions

Pam is in senior kindergarten at Grove Elementary School. She likes playing with water, making towers of blocks, being near the teacher, and exploring the materials the teacher is demonstrating. The classroom is often busy and noisy. For example, today a visitor is teaching the children to drum on the tomato juice–can drums they made last week. While the others sit in a circle, Pam is running from one side of the room to the other, waving her arms. She has a short attention span for activities with a social component and becomes agitated when the classroom is too busy or too noisy. Pam wants to sit on the chair beside the visitor and touch his drum. When she can't have her way, she has a tantrum. She repeats, "I like the big chair. I like the big chair," and "Thump the drum. Thump the drum," which she has heard the visitor say to the class. Pam communicates through echolalia, gestures, and limited functional speech, including, "No," "Help me," and "Get that one." Pam's IEP states that she has autism and developmental disabilities.

Brittany has cystic fibrosis and coughs constantly. Although she is in grade 7, she is as small as most girls in grade 4. She has just returned to school after being hospitalized for two months. Each year, Brittany had told teachers and students in other classes about how her body produces abnormally thick and sticky secretions that cause problems in her respiratory and digestive systems. This mucus builds up in her lungs and also makes it difficult for her to digest her food. Brittany has always left class willingly to take her medication and receive therapy to clear her airways. Most teachers have found that Brittany needs encouragement to follow her regime of medication and treatment. This year she also needs emotional support to deal with the recent insertion of a feeding tube that will ensure that she continues to grow and has enough energy. Brittany's health condition has an impact on her school life, mainly on her social and emotional well-being.

1. Which of the characteristics of each student are most likely to affect learning? What learning needs are implied by these characteristics?

2. With such a range of learning needs, what do exceptional students like Pam and Brittany have in common?

3. How frequently is a teacher likely to be teaching a student with each of these exceptionalities?

4. What types of adaptations does each of these students need in order to be included in the social life and the learning activities of the classroom?

5. What community resources can a teacher draw on to supplement in-school resources to teach each of these students?

Introduction

In this chapter, you will learn about the characteristics, needs, and strengths of students with a number of **low-incidence exceptionalities**, **physical disabilities**, and **chronic health conditions**. The emphasis is on classroom adaptations you can make. Students with many of the exceptionalities described in this chapter are identified soon after birth because their needs are high and their disabilities or conditions are severe. Many, identified by doctors or psychologists, start school with a detailed IEP.

While reading this chapter, think about children and adolescents you have known with these exceptionalities or other conditions with similar implications for learning. Labels give us a shared language, but it is important that, as teachers, our language is respectful and professional. Labels never capture the essence of the individual's experience of an exceptionality or health condition.

Cross-Reference
For descriptions of and adaptations for students with high-incidence exceptionalities, see Chapter 3.

As you read about students in this chapter, consider the parents' perspective. The parents of children with low-incidence exceptionalities tend to be very involved in the lives of their offspring (Bluebond-Langner, 1996). They may assume the role of **case coordinator**, and are often better informed than classroom teachers about particular exceptionalities and conditions. You may teach a child with muscular dystrophy twice in your career. The parents teach their child with muscular dystrophy every day. I have used person-first language, for example, students with cerebral palsy. This means we refer to the student first and describe the student as *having* an exceptionality second.

Each section on an exceptionality begins with the words of a child or adolescent. Frequently these are based on questions asked by a student (in sources like Miriam Kauffman's 1995 book, *Easy for You to Say*) or on sources such as *The Kids on the Block* book series (Aiello & Shulman, 1988, 1989). Each entry follows a pattern: the exceptionality is described with information about its incidence or frequency, followed by characteristics, classroom implications, and often implications for career participation. For low-incidence exceptionalities, teachers must seek information on a need-to-know basis. It is almost impossible for you to remember the details of 15 or more low-incidence conditions. However, the principles of inclusion and adapting always apply. Information is provided about responding to life-threatening and extremely disruptive conditions—for example, teachers who are knowledgeable about allergic reactions and asthma can save lives.

Teaching Students with Severe Developmental Disabilities

My dream: My name is Reid. I am 17 and I have developmental delay. Caused by a genetic condition—called Coffin-Lowry syndrome. Some people say I am retarded. I don't like to hear that. I am in a life-skills class at Campbell Collegiate. My favourite part is my work placement. Every morning, I clean the cages and walk the animals for a pet store. I also sweep the floors, and do odd jobs. Sometimes I sell kittens. My boss is my neighbour, Ms. Boychuk. I have known her all my life. That makes it easier.

Table 4.1

STUDENTS WITH LOW-INCIDENCE EXCEPTIONALITIES, PHYSICAL DISABILITIES, AND CHRONIC MEDICAL CONDITIONS

Exceptionality	Description
Low-Incidence Exceptionalities	
Severe developmental disabilities	Severe limitation in both intellectual functioning and adaptive behaviour; focus is on the individual's need for support to function in the community
Autism	Impairments in verbal and nonverbal communication and reciprocal social interaction; restricted, repetitive patterns of behaviour; and intellectual disability
Asperger syndrome	Severe and sustained impairment in social interaction, and development of restricted, repetitive patterns of behaviour and interests
Hard of hearing and deaf	Hearing loss that has significantly affected development of speech and/or language and caused students to need adaptations to learn
Visual impairments	Blind or partially sighted students who need adaptations to learn through channels other than visual
Physical Disabilities and Chronic Medical Conditions *Nervous System Impairment*	
Cerebral palsy	Disorders affecting body movement and muscle coordination resulting from damage to brain during pregnancy or first three years
Spina bifida	Neural tube defect that occurs during first four weeks of pregnancy causing vertebrae or spinal cord to fail to develop properly
Epilepsy	Neurological disorder involving sudden bursts of electrical energy in the brain
Tourette syndrome	Neurological disorder characterized by tics
Brain injury	Damage to brain tissue that prevents it from functioning properly
Fetal alcohol syndrome	Neurological disorder caused by significant prenatal exposure to alcohol
Musculoskeletal Conditions	
Muscular dystrophy	Genetically based muscle disorders that result in progressive muscle weakness
Juvenile arthritis	Continuous inflammation of joints in young people under 16
Chronic Health Impairments	
Diabetes	Condition in which the body does not make enough insulin and has problems absorbing and storing sugars
Allergies	Sensitivity or abnormal immune response to normal substance, which can cause anaphylactic shock
Asthma	Chronic lung condition, characterized by difficulty breathing, in which airways are obstructed by inflammation, muscle spasms, and excess mucus
Cystic fibrosis	Incurable disorder caused by inherited genetic defect, affecting mainly the lungs and the digestive system

My goal is to live in my own place with my friend Dan. I want to move out like my brother did. My mom says she hopes that I can do that, but she will miss me. We need people to help us. I use my wheelchair more. But I think we can do it. You will see. That is my dream.

Generated by Reid Ford and his mother in conversation

Description of Severe Developmental Disabilities

The term *severe developmental disabilities* focuses on an individual's functioning within the community and refers to severe limitations in both intelligence and adaptive skills. The adaptive skills in which one would expect to see individuals challenged by the expectations of their environment include communication, home living, community use, health and safety, leisure, self-care, social skills, self-direction, functional academics, and work. The use of the term *developmental disabilities* makes four assumptions. These are that valid assessment considers cultural diversity, and limitations in adaptive skills are indexed to an individual's need for support. As well, individuals have strengths as well as limitations, and support will enable life functioning to improve (see the Web site of the American Association on Mental Retardation, http://www.aamr.org).

Using Reid as an example may clarify the meaning of these four assumptions. Because Reid's first language is English and he was born in the community in which his assessments have taken place, the issue of cultural diversity does not arise for him. It would be much more pertinent if his parents had arrived in Canada from Somalia when he was three years old. Under these conditions, an assessment conducted in English when he began school might have been primarily a reflection of his cultural background and lack of opportunity to learn English. Reid is clear about his need for supports—and knows that he and his friend Dan need paid assistants to help them with bathing, taking medications, etc. Reid and Dan can read environmental print (e.g., the symbol for Coke) and functional signs like Exit, but not labels on pill bottles. Reid has many strengths—he communicates well orally, is a hard worker, knows himself, and uses this self-knowledge to make good decisions. With excellent support at home, at school, and in the neighbourhood, his life functioning has surpassed early predictions, but he is aware that he will increasingly need his wheelchair for mobility. He wants to be as independent as possible, but accepts that he will always need support to manage in his environment.

Incidence of Severe Developmental Disabilities

In the general population, severe developmental disabilities occur at a rate of about 1 per 1000 people (B.C. Special Education Branch, 1995b). Developmental disabilities are often the result of conditions described in the section of this chapter on physical disabilities and health conditions. For example, among the leading causes of developmental disabilities are fetal alcohol syndrome, cerebral palsy, and spina bifida, as well as Down syndrome, fragile X, and other **chromosomal abnormalities**.

Tiffany Dawe was born with severe physical and developmental disabilities. However, because of an inspiring community effort, Tiffany moved into her own apartment in Rougemont Co-op, a 105-unit, non-profit housing cooperative in Pickering, Ontario. She lives a full and rewarding life: attending school, shopping (with the aid of paid support workers, family, and friends), visiting friends, and participating in the Rougemont choir.

Ten families of youth with severe disabilities worked for five years to provide safe, affordable, inclusive housing where their children could live as independently as possible. They wanted a co-op and an "intentional community," a combination of residents committed to sharing their lives. The families knew that their offspring were accustomed to living in a neighbourhood, attending school and church, and being part of the community. They did not want to live in group homes. The 10 families applied for and obtained joint federal–provincial funding, which the governments will recoup through Canada Mortgage and Housing Corporation, to build a co-op. The building has 105 units, of which 25 are designed for disabled residents—9 for people in wheelchairs and 16 that accommodate people with either hearing or vision impairment—and spread throughout the building to ensure full integration of those residents.

People who live in the "intentional" community must agree to be helpful, supportive, accepting, and friendly to all the residents of the co-op, including the 10 who have severe disabilities. Then a second community was created, called the Deohaeko Support Network, taken from the Iroquois word for "spirit-supporters of life." Each family has created a volunteer support network specifically to meet the needs of the individuals with severe developmental disabilities.

The intentional community is proving to be a great success. For example, Brenda Gray's family believed she would require 24-hour care. However, since moving to the co-op, Brenda has grown socially and increased her independence. Her close friendship with a senior citizen neighbour, Hilda Hawkes, has helped Brenda to be able to stay alone for several hours at a time. Another resident, Rose Connors, explained why she moved to Rougemont, "I really liked the idea of living in this community with people working together to provide security for each other. We all need help at some point in one way or another."

In 1997, the Rougemont Co-op won a Caring Community Award, given by the Ontario Trillium Foundation (http://www.trilliumfoundation.org/english/cca/our_award_recipients/97_awards/finalist_23.html).

Friendship from Hilda Hawkes, left, is credited with helping her neighbour, Brenda Gray, need less attendant care. Both are residents of Rougemont Co-op, an "intentional" community.

CONTRADICTORY AND CONTROVERSIAL TRENDS WITH IMPLICATIONS FOR INCIDENCE

Two recent developments could influence the incidence of severe developmental disabilities. Medical advances save the lives of babies who would have died in the past and are now born with severe developmental disabilities (Alper, Schloss, & Schloss, 1994). However, **genetic screening** and **amniocentesis** enable parents to prevent the birth of babies with severe developmental disabilities, although this raises ethical questions about the value we place on members of our society with developmental disabilities (Miller-Chenier, 1996; Smith, 1998).

What do you think?

Does it devalue people in our community with severe developmental disabilities when parents terminate pregnancies that would result in the birth of infants with severe developmental disabilities?

Characteristics of Students with Severe Developmental Disabilities

Severe developmental disabilities now include students previously considered to have moderate, severe, or profound disabilities. They span a wide range of abilities, from those who can acquire academic skills to those who will require assistance with **self-care** for their entire lives.

You will usually find in the psychological reports and IEPs that students' strengths and weaknesses have been assessed across four dimensions:

- intellectual or cognitive and adaptive behaviour skills;
- psychological, emotional, and social considerations;
- physical and health considerations; and
- environmental considerations.

Cognitive characteristics include difficulties focusing attention and getting information into memory; however, long-term memory may be excellent. Language is likely to be delayed, and in the most severe cases verbal language may not develop. Adaptive behaviours refer to coping with the demands of daily living. Psychological characteristics often include frustration and impulsivity. Students with developmental disabilities find social interactions challenging; they may miss social cues, and often they do not know how to make friends, even though they may be loyal and caring. They may withdraw or develop repetitive behaviours that seem bizarre to their peers.

Physical and health considerations may depend on concomitant conditions such as cerebral palsy. Less physical dexterity and coordination than others of the same age are to be expected, and in the most severe cases there may be limited locomotion. Environmental considerations refer to such things as requiring a wheelchair that holds the head in a specific position or a **voice synthesizer** to produce speech.

Focus on the strengths and weaknesses in the functional and educational assessments of students with developmental disabilities and on teaching strategies that can make a difference. "Teachers should not see these disabilities as predicting a limit to their potential" (B.C. Special Education Branch, 1998, p. 2).

Adapting Curriculum and Teaching for Students with Severe Developmental Disabilities

Many of the adaptations discussed in Chapter 3 for students with high-incidence exceptionalities are suitable for some students with severe developmental disabilities. The curriculum outcomes will be appropriate, but materials or presentation need to be changed. For example, you can adapt the environment by positioning the student where there are the fewest distractions, and the desk may be adapted to suit a wheelchair or a laptop computer. An agenda and list of assignments may be taped to the student's desk. You can highlight key points in the text, break information into steps, and complete the first example with the student. Use concrete examples. You could videotape a lesson so the student can review it at home (B.C. Special Education Branch, 1998). Allow extra time to complete tasks and tests. The student may draw or write individual words rather than sentences and paragraphs to communicate her understanding. Jim Fasano and Margaret Brown (1992) of Acadia University reported on a project called SCAMP (Secondary Curriculum Adapted Materials Project), in which pre-service teachers developed adapted materials for students with developmental disabilities to use in curriculum units in secondary classrooms. Adapted materials included game boards with cards containing questions at varying levels of complexity.

MODIFYING CURRICULUM

You may also need to modify the learning outcomes for students with severe developmental disabilities. Your guide for modifying outcomes is the goals section of the student's IEP. Consult with other members of the in-school team. Two principles usually guide the development of modified curriculum for these students (Ford, Davern, & Schnorr, 1990). The first is the principle of a **functional curriculum**, in which the goals for a student are based on life skills. At his co-op placement in the pet store, Reid learned to be punctual and how to speak to customers, co-workers, and pets. The second principle is that education should be **community-based** and relate what is learned in school to what occurs in the community. While other students in Reid's high-school economics class are learning about the role of the Bank of Canada, Reid benefits from learning to cash a cheque, to pay bills at the instant teller, and to withdraw cash from his account at the neighbourhood bank. Robert Sandieson of University of Western Ontario (1994) reports that activities such as using money take considerable practice for youth with severe developmental disabilities.

There will be great variation from one IEP to the next. Each IEP will include a detailed description of strengths and needs, but the goals of the modified program usually include

- functional academic skills
- physical development and personal care
- communication skills and social interaction skills
- community living skills
- career development, work experience, and transition planning

Figure 4.1 contains examples of curriculum modifications.

How can you explain to other students why a student like Reid has different learning activities than they do? Younger children sometimes ask about this out of curiosity, whereas older students are likely to raise issues of fairness. If you have set a climate of inclusion in which differences are seen as normal, expected, and valued, you may have fewer questions and the ones you do encounter will probably be easier to answer.

Explain the **principles of fairness** so that your students, no matter how young they are, understand that fairness does not mean sameness. You might use examples of different but fair treatment for exceptionalities not represented in your class. Ask whether it is fair to expect a student with no legs to climb stairs, or whether it is fair to expect a blind student to read a paper-and-pencil test. Most students can see that not everyone needs the elevator or Braille, and in fact would be disadvan-

CURRICULUM MODIFICATIONS FOR STUDENTS WITH SEVERE DEVELOPMENTAL DISABILITIES

- Give more concrete assignments on a related topic.

- Change learning tasks with a similar topic by simplifying or condensing, combining or grouping, or by using special coding.

- Give easier questions on the same concept.

- Assign the same materials on another concept. For example, addition instead of multiplication.

- Use high interest/low vocabulary resources.

- Provide community preparation such as:
  - trips to community locations such as stores.
  - opportunities to apply functional skills in different settings.
  - job related experiences such as running a small business.
  - individualize community tasks for each student based on different needs.

When making modifications the teacher should change only that which is necessary to meet the needs of the student, with a view to fostering inclusion.

Source: B.C. Special Education Branch (1998). *Students with Intellectual Disabilities: A Resource Guide for Teachers.* Used by permission.

taged by Braille. To ensure equity, use routines for exceptional students that are similar to the routines you use for the rest of the class. Students with severe developmental disabilities should be assigned homework, tests, and projects at the same time as the rest of the class, and theirs should be as challenging for them as the assignments given to the rest of the class.

Teaching Students with Autism and Asperger Syndrome

I love buses. I know all the routes. And I can tell you anything about buses in Fredericton—the history, the kinds of buses, how they are serviced. But I wish there were no other people on the buses. The people bug me. When I ride the bus, I always get into trouble because of the people. They make noise and come near me. And I get mad at them. My favourite thing is to ride the bus with my dad while all the people are at work and school. We talk to the driver. Buses are my hobby.

From the free-writing book of Jason, who is 12 and has Asperger syndrome

This section focuses on autism and Asperger syndrome. These two exceptionalities may prove to be quite similar; Asperger syndrome may be what we have previously called "high-functioning autism." Some people speak of a **spectrum of autistic**

disorders and others of **pervasive developmental disabilities (PDD),** which include autism and Asperger syndrome. For an explanation of these terms, see *APA Diagnostic and Statistical Manual of Mental Disorders* (4th ed., 1994). Autism is discussed first, followed by Asperger syndrome.

Weblinks

GENEVA CENTRE FOR AUTISM, TORONTO
http://www.autism.net

SASKATCHEWAN EDUCATION, TEACHING STUDENTS WITH AUTISM: A GUIDE FOR EDUCATORS
http://www.sasked.gov.sk.ca/k/pecs/se/docs/autism/hero.html

Autism: Description and Incidence

One of the cases at the beginning of this chapter describes Pam, a kindergarten student who has autism with developmental disabilities. Pam communicates mainly by echoing the words of others, socializes little with her classmates, and sometimes runs from one side of the room to the other waving her arms. Autism affects the functioning of the brain and is believed to be genetic in origin, although diagnosis is based on a child's behaviours and must be evident before the child is three years old. It has been commonly estimated that there are 4 to 5 persons with autism in every 10 000 births. However, recent estimates are as high as 10 in every 10 000 (Bristol et al., 1996; Bryson, Clark, & Smith, 1988). The incidence is higher among males, with the ratio estimated to be three males for every female (Bryson, 1996, 1997).

Autism: Characteristics

Autism is characterized by (American Psychiatric Association, 1994):

- impairments in verbal and nonverbal communication
- impairments in reciprocal social interaction
- impairments in imaginative creativity
- restricted, repetitive, and stereotypic patterns of behaviour, interests, and activities

Most people with autism have some level of intellectual disability ranging from mild to severe.

Language often shows **perseveration** on one topic or echoing what is said (**echolalia**). It is estimated that about 50 percent of those with autism never develop functional speech. It is *not* that students with autism do not want to interact reciprocally with others; rather, they are unable to read and understand social situations. Their lack of imaginative creativity can be seen in their inability to understand or even acknowledge the perspective of others; this has been described as lacking a "**theory of mind**" (Baron-Cohen, 1995). It seems that they are unaware that people have intentions, emotions, etc. Unusual and distinctive behaviours you might observe in students with autism include (http://www.sasked.gov.ca/k/pecs/se/docs/autism/def.html):

- a restricted range of interests with a preoccupation with one specific interest or object
- an inflexible adherence to nonfunctional routine
- stereotypic and repetitive motor mannerisms, such as hand flapping, finger licking, rocking, spinning, walking on tiptoes, spinning objects
- a preoccupation with parts of objects

- a fascination with movement, such as the spinning of a fan or wheels on toys
- an insistence on sameness and resistance to change
- unusual responses to sensory stimuli

Autism: Implications for Learning and Classroom Adaptations

The IEPs of students with autism usually include goals in the areas used to identify the exceptionality—communication, social interaction, stereotypic behaviours, and, sometimes, imaginative creativity—as well as in functional skills.

ENHANCING COMMUNICATION

To enhance communication, it may be necessary to teach the student to listen by facing the speaker, remaining still, and focusing on what is being said. Speak in sentences to the student with autism; if you are not understood, use more concrete words and repeat as necessary. Use visual aids at an appropriate level; objects are the most concrete, followed by photographs, and then line drawings. A Polaroid camera enables you to "catch the student doing good" and record the action. You can make a personalized schedule showing the student completing each activity of the day, or a sequence of photographs of the student carrying out the steps in a complex activity. To encourage oral language expression, accept limited verbal attempts and nonverbal behaviour as communication. Use specific praise.

ENHANCING SOCIAL COGNITION AND BEHAVIOUR

To improve social interaction, social skills, and social cognition, students with autism require explicit teaching and practice. Carol Gray (1993) has developed **social stories** that describe a situation from the perspective of the student, direct the student to do the appropriate behaviour, and are in the first person. Each page in a booklet of up to five pages contains one sentence (or two). There is a directive behaviour on one of the five pages. For an example of a social story, see Figure 4.2. Interventions have been developed using videotape to explicitly teach children with autism that others have intentions and emotions. Karin Steiner-Bell of Queen's University (1998) used narratives of children's happy, sad, and surprising experiences. You may be successful in having a student with autism learn classroom routines by observing others. You can also model for other children how to interact with their classmate with autism.

GENERAL ADAPTATIONS AND MODIFICATIONS

For all teaching, use visual approaches, **reinforcers** that you know work for this student, and task analysis to keep tasks at a level that minimizes frustration. Try to keep the theme of the learning consistent with the lesson for others in the class. For example, if others are writing about highlights of the day in a journal, then try teaching the child with autism to take a photograph from a magazine or a Polaroid photograph that communicates "something fun" that she has done today. She can

Figure 4.2

A SOCIAL STORY FOR PAM

A social story describes a social situation and includes social cues and appropriate responses. It is written for a specific situation for an individual student. The story can be used to:

- facilitate the inclusion of the student in regular classes

- introduce changes and new routines

- explain reasons for the behaviour of others

- teach situation-specific social skills

- assist in teaching new academic skills

Stories can be read, listened to on audiotape, or watched on videotape. The language must be understood by the child. The story should be from the child's perspective, using "I," and should direct the child to perform the appropriate behaviour. Social stories use descriptive sentences (which provide information on the setting and people), directive statements (i.e., positive statements about the desired response for a specific situation), and perspective statements (which describe the possible reactions of others).

Use two to five descriptive statements and one directive statement. Put only one or two sentences on a page. Symbols, drawings, or pictures can be included to support the meaning for the student.

Pam tends to run and wave her arms while the other children sit on their chairs in a circle. Her teacher has made a social story for Pam. The first page includes a photograph of the children smiling, sitting in a circle while the teacher reads a story. The second page shows Pam smiling, sitting on her chair while the teacher holds a book. Page three shows a smiling child sitting on each side of Pam, one speaking to her and the other offering her a toy. Each day, before the children sit in their circle, the teacher reads the story twice to Pam and then reads each sentence and waits for Pam to repeat it. Pam has a videotape of the story at home that she watches with her mother.

Page 1:   Other kids like to hear the teacher.

Page 2:   **I will sit on my chair when the teacher talks.**

Page 3:   Everyone likes me when I sit on my chair.

Based on C. Gray (1993). *The Social Story Book*. Jenison, MI: Jenison Public Schools.

name the picture or dictate a sentence. Use concrete examples and hands-on activities, and allow as much time as the child requires.

It helps to provide a structured, predictable classroom environment. Make a customized visual daily schedule, and give advance warning of any changes from the usual schedule and of transitions from one activity to another. Minimize auditory stimuli such as noisy fans, reduce distracting visual stimuli around the student's desk, and try to remove textures the student finds aversive to maintain a calm learning environment.

Further Reading

To learn more about teaching students with autism: P. Howlin (1998). *Children with Autism and Asperger Syndrome: A Guide for Practitioners and Carers.* Chichester, NY: John Wiley.

Asperger Syndrome: Description and Incidence

Asperger syndrome is a lifelong developmental condition, characterized by a severe and sustained impairment in social interaction and the development of restricted, repetitive patterns of behaviour, interests, and activities. In contrast to autism, a child with Asperger syndrome will experience no significant delays in the acquisition of language, adaptive behaviour (other than social interaction), cognitive development, and development of age-appropriate self-help skills, or in curiosity about the environment. Incidence for Asperger syndrome is unclear, and some cases are believed to be included in the numbers used to calculate the incidence of autism.

Asperger Syndrome: Characteristics and Teaching Strategies

Students with Asperger syndrome are characterterized by a qualitative impairment in social interaction. They are often enthusiastic about relating to others and speak fluently, but are challenged by the complexity of the language, and approach others in unusual ways. You will observe these students misinterpret social cues, lack empathy, appear socially awkward, and be unaware of the rules of conversation. They need explicit instruction in social skills. With average or better intelligence, they tend to excel at learning facts but need intensive teaching in reading comprehension, problem solving, organizational skills, and inference making. Frequently, students with Asperger syndrome are **hypersensitive** to sensory stimuli and may engage in unusual behaviour to obtain a particular sensory stimulation. They may be inattentive, easily distracted, and anxious. Some strategies for teaching students with autism will apply, but consider the student's unique learning characteristics and build on their considerable strengths. Draw on the expertise of the in-school resource team, too.

Implication for Social and Career Participation of Students with Autism and Students with Asperger Syndrome

Transition planning from secondary school to adult life should continue throughout the high-school years. Areas to consider include employment options, post-secondary training or education options, residential options, transportation and medical needs, as well as income support opportunities. Advocacy, recreation, and relationships with family and friends are also important. The **McGill Action Planning System (MAPS)** may prove helpful for promoting these (Alper, Ryndak, & Lea, 1992; Forest & Lusthaus, 1987). The MAPS process involves gathering key people in the student's life who cooperatively answer such questions as: What is the student's history? What is your dream for the child? What are the student's gifts? What would an ideal day at school be like? Plans for structured friendship or peer programs are usually suggested as part of the MAPS meeting. Work experiences, participation in co-curricular activities, and help with developing hygiene, appropriate dress, and self-management are all necessary during the secondary years for students with autism and for many with Asperger syndrome.

Teaching Students Who Are Hard of Hearing or Deaf

> I am deaf and have always gone to school with kids who can hear. I lip read and learned some Sign last summer at camp. Ever since then I have wanted to go to a school where all the kids are deaf.
>
> *Kauffman, 1995, p. 114*

Description and Incidence of Students Who Are Hard of Hearing or Deaf

Students who have a hearing loss that has significantly affected the development of speech and/or language and who require adapted teaching to participate effectively and benefit from instruction are described as being deaf or hard of hearing (Manitoba Special Education Review, Proactive Information Services, 1998). This includes children who have a hearing impairment at birth and those who develop hearing loss later (Alberta Education, 1995).

Estimates vary, but about 1 infant in every 1000 is born profoundly deaf or is deaf before the age of three (Ruppert & Buhrer, 1992). In the general population, about 1 in 10 people has some form of hearing impairment and 1 in 40 has an impairment serious enough to affect communication (Ontario Ministry of Health, 1978).

Characteristics of Students Who Are Hard of Hearing or Deaf

The main characteristics of students with hearing impairments are that they cannot hear well enough to use hearing as a primary channel for learning without significant assistance and that their language development is likely to be influenced.

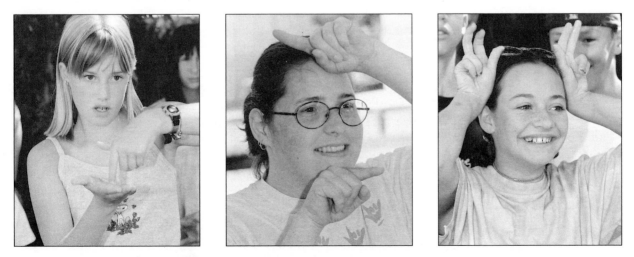

Young classmates of students who are deaf or hard of hearing are taught sign language by an instructor from the Canadian Hearing Society.

A complex array of factors influence learning development. Two students with similar hearing loss may have completely different experiences before they arrive at school, and may communicate in quite different ways. Language development and communication can be affected by:

- the student's age at the onset of the exceptionality, especially whether they had already developed spoken language
- the severity of the hearing loss
- intelligence
- **hearing status** of the family (a student who is deaf tends to experience higher academic success if the parents are deaf as well)
- means of communication chosen by the family

FOCUS ON FAMILIES

One of the most difficult decisions faced by many families of newly diagnosed children who are hard of hearing or deaf is how to communicate with their child. If the parents are deaf and are members of the deaf community, who use American Sign Language (ASL), they will likely choose to initiate their child into their culture and to communicate with their child through ASL. However, if the parents are part of the hearing culture and do not know ASL, they may be apprehensive about being unable to communicate with their child if ASL becomes the child's first language. Ninety percent of parents whose children are deaf or hard of hearing have hearing themselves. These families receive advice and predictions from a variety of professionals. The amount of information is overwhelming, and opposing views are advanced forcefully and convincingly.

There are books to help parents decide on the best approach for their child:

- S. Schwartz (ed.) (1996). *Choices in Deafness: A Parent's Guide,* Second edition. Bethesda, MD: Woodbine House.

- M. Marschark (1997). *Raising and Educating a Deaf Child: A Comprehensive Guide to the Choices, Controversies, and Decisions Faced by Parents and Educators.* New York: Oxford University Press.

- D. Luterman, with E. Kurtyzer-White and R.C. Seewald (1999). *The Young Deaf Child.* Baltimore, MD: York Press, Inc.

There are helpful Web sites. For example, http://www.entnet.org/agbell8.html provides information for parents about their options that prompts them to consider the merits and drawbacks of the five approaches that appear in Table 4.2.

In Canada, parents can consult the Canadian Association of the Deaf (http://www.cad.ca), which focuses on "protecting and promoting the rights, needs and concerns of deaf Canadians," in particular those who are profoundly deaf and whose preferred mode of communication is sign language. On the other hand, parents might consult Voice for Hearing Impaired Children (http://www.voicefordeafkids.com), whose mission is "To ensure that all hearing impaired children have the right to develop their ability to listen and speak and have access to services which will enable them to listen and speak." Even greater controversy is sparked by the cochlear implant, an electronic device that bypasses a non-functional inner ear and delivers sound directly to auditory nerves linked to the brain. Data suggest that children with implants can expect to detect conversation and environmental sounds (*Sound Matters*, 1996). Richard Seewald (1999) of the University of Western Ontario suggests that matching an implant to the needs of children is challenging (Luterman, Kurtyzer-White, & Seewald, 1999). The deaf community raises issues of invasion of one's person when cochlear implants are chosen. They argue that this decision by parents forces young children to "choose" the hearing society over the Deaf Culture, and that those who are deaf can never use spoken language with the facility they can have with ASL. When you teach students who are deaf or hard of hearing in inclusive classrooms, you can expect parents to be coping with all of these dilemmas and more.

Web sites:

http://www.entnet.org/agbell8.html

http://www.cad.ca

http://www.voicefordeafkids.com

Some young children experience hearing loss when fluid builds up in the middle ear. Characteristics you might see include children failing to respond to their name, asking for directions to be repeated, turning the head to hear, and speaking too loudly or too softly. You might also see a change in behaviour or academic performance or hear the child complain of recurring earaches. Physicians can insert ventilating tubes that drain fluid, reversing the temporary loss of hearing. Teachers of young children who spot these characteristics play an important role in preventing hearing loss and subsequent language delays.

While students who are hard of hearing or deaf tend to fall behind in reading and other language skills, they often meet or exceed expectations in subjects like

Table 4.2

EDUCATIONAL OPTIONS FOR CHILDREN WHO ARE HARD OF HEARING OR DEAF

Options	How Language Is Taught	School Placement	Additional Information
Auditory-Verbal	Emphasizes use of residual hearing to learn spoken English; amplification	Usually regular class from the beginning	Parents communicate through spoken language; early amplification
Auditory-Oral	Emphasizes use of residual hearing to learn spoken English *and* visual information (speech-reading); amplification *and* speech-reading	Usually regular class after success is certain	Emphasis on the two approaches varies from program to program; parents communicate through spoken language; early amplification
Cued Speech	Uses eight handshapes in four locations near the face to give phonemic cues that assist speech-reading; can be used with all other approaches that include listening; amplification *and* speech-reading *and* phonemic cues	Depends on approach with which it is combined	Claims to enhance learning to read; has enabled second language learning
Total Communication	Child's environment contains access to full range of communication methods; amplification *and* speech-reading *and* sign language	Congregated school or class for deaf students; regular class with interpreter	Uses three means of communication simultaneously
American Sign Language (ASL)	Language system that is completely visual rather than auditory; for educational purposes; English also taught	Congregated school or class for deaf students; regular class with interpreter	Emphasis on English varies from program to program; proponents consider ASL natural language for the deaf; sense of belonging to Deaf Culture encouraged; young adults sometimes choose this option so they can participate in Deaf Culture

Based on Communications Options Reference Chart, http://www.beginningssvcs.com.

science and math. As with other exceptionalities, difficulty with a subject does not necessarily imply lack of ability. When fatigued and frustrated by their difficulties in communicating, these students can be disruptive and inattentive.

Implications for Learning and Classroom Adaptations for Students with Hearing Loss

The implications for classroom learning and participation are related to the choices parents make for their children in the preschool years. These issues are explored in Focus on Families. Table 4.2 describes the options that parents have for communication and education for their children. Be sensitive to parents' concerns about whether they have made the best choice for their child. In inclusive classrooms, you may be teaching children whose parents have chosen auditory-verbal, auditory-oral, cued speech, or total communication. It is less likely that you will teach children who use only **American Sign Language (ASL)**. Many students who learn in inclusive classrooms use amplification to help them hear. At first, you may experience difficulty understanding their speech, but teachers usually grow accustomed to their manner of speaking in a few days. Ask a student who is reluctant to speak in front of the class to speak with you individually so you can learn the speech patterns.

ENHANCING SPEECH-READING

There are many actions you can take to adapt your teaching. For students who are **speech-reading**, arrange the classroom so the student can see your face at all times. Allow the student to move during a lesson, and ensure that you don't turn your back (use an overhead projector instead of the blackboard) or put your hands in front of your face. Speak normally and avoid making distracting gestures. Some words, such as bat, pat, and mat, look the same when you pronounce them. Try to put words like this into context, especially during spelling dictation. If other students ask questions, repeat them so the student who is deaf or hard of hearing knows what was asked. Summaries at the end of lessons give all students a second chance to take in information. During group discussions, sit the class in a circle.

You can convey important messages visually as well as orally—for example, many students will benefit from having an agenda and assignments listed on the board. Use visual aids, written summaries, and **manipulatives**. The student with hearing loss will benefit from your **preteaching** new vocabulary. Pay attention to and try to diffuse the student's frustration. You can plan the day's work so periods of intense concentration are interspersed with less-demanding activities.

SYSTEMS OF AMPLIFICATION

Two common systems of **amplification** are **hearing aids** and **frequency modulation (FM) systems**. Carpeted classrooms are best for both systems; alternatively, place tennis balls over the feet of the desks. Hearing aids make speech louder, not clearer, and also amplify background noise. They typically have a range of two metres. A classroom FM system transmits sound through the air from a teacher-worn microphone to a student-worn receiver that enables the student to hear the teacher clearly from any location in the classroom. Expect new devices based on technological advances. Some students who use ASL have an interpreter who signs the words of the teacher and classmates. You should address the student, not the interpreter, and treat the interpreter as an instrument that facilitates communication for the student, not as a teaching assistant. You may find this difficult at first.

Implications for Social and Career Participation of Students with Hearing Loss

Social participation is challenging for students with hearing loss or deafness because their exceptionality affects communication. Their system of communication is also influential. As the opening of this section suggests, some adolescents and adults who are deaf or hard of hearing choose to learn ASL and to join the **deaf community**, in spite of their parents' earlier choice of oral language. This group of exceptional adults has a higher rate of underemployment and unemployment than the general population. However, there are strong lobby groups to assist adults, and career education and cooperative education can help these adolescents learn about themselves and about careers.

Teaching Children with Vision Disabilities and Blindness

"See you tomorrow, Ms. Fine!" The grade 3 students shouted goodbye to Marie Fine. Marie watched Amber painstakingly packing her books on tape and thick pages of Braille into her backpack. Marie stood nearby in case Amber needed help. However, Amber did the same thing every day; she put everything into her knapsack herself and then asked, "Did I get everything I need to finish my work?" Marie thought about how hard Amber would work at home to complete the day's school tasks. "Good night, Amber. Don't work too hard." As Amber lifted the heavy bag, she answered, "'Night, I'll try not to. But I still have a lot of questions to do in math." Her voice sounded as heavy as her book bag. Amber knew that when you can't see, everything takes longer.

Adapted from Hutchinson, 1999, p. 9.

Description and Incidence of Students with Visual Impairment

Students with total or partial visual impairment who require adapted teaching, even with correction, are described as having visual disabilities. For educational purposes, a student with visual impairment is one whose visual acuity is not sufficient "to participate with ease in everyday activities" and "can result in a substantial educational disadvantage, unless adaptations are made" in the environment, learning materials, teaching, and assessment (B.C. Special Education Branch, 1995, p. E-45). The IEP will include the student's need for orientation and mobility skills; efficient use of vision, **Braille**, and/or alternate formats such as **taped**

books; access to technology; and daily living skills. These are usually the responsibility of a **vision teacher** or paraprofessional. The IEP will also refer to classroom adaptations that are your responsibility. Approximately 1 in 1000 students in Canada is visually impaired. Of these, 80 percent are print users and 20 percent are potential Braille users (Ontario Ministry of Education, 1987).

Characteristics of Students with Visual Impairments

For two reasons, it is important that you know the characteristics that accompany visual impairment. First, children and adolescents can experience deteriorating vision at any age. Teachers often identify students who need to be assessed. Complaints of blurred print or headaches may signal a need for correction, but can also signal conditions such as brain tumours. Pay attention to the appearance of the eyes (e.g., reddened, encrusted, frequent sties or tears). Listen to student complaints (e.g., headaches, burning eyes after use, nausea, blurred print). Also observe behavioural signs (e.g., squints or closes one eye, tilts head extremely, rubs eyes, turns head while reading across a page) (Weber, 1993). Record your observations and encourage the parents to seek a vision assessment.

Second, knowing the characteristics of students with visual exceptionalities will help you understand their actions, postures, and developmental histories. Because they cannot learn social skills through observation, they may need specific instruction in areas such as body language and eye contact. Because vision plays a key role in young children's exploration of their environment, students with vision disabilities and blindness have often had a limited range of experiences and restricted movement in their environment. This may result in global delays in development (cognitive, motor, social, and emotional) due to lack of experience rather than lack of ability.

Implications for Learning and Classroom Adaptations for Visual Impairments

Students with visual disabilities and blindness are likely to need adaptations in four areas: presentation of information, classroom environment and organization, learning resources, and assessment (Department of Education, Government of Newfoundland, 1998). Figure 4.3 includes tips for teaching students with visual impairments.

ADAPTING PRESENTATION OF INFORMATION

In adapting the presentation of information, you will work closely with a vision teacher, paraprofessional, or resource teacher. The specific adaptations depend on how the student acquires information—substituting other senses for vision, using partial vision, or both. For students who do not acquire information visually, give directions and notes verbally as well as visually, and provide the opportunity to explore three-dimensional models of visual concepts. For students with partial vision, enlarge print (usually to 130 percent on a photocopier or 18-point font size on your computer) and enhance contrast of written materials. Experiment to see whether coloured acetate (e.g., yellow or pale blue) enhances the contrast or if par-

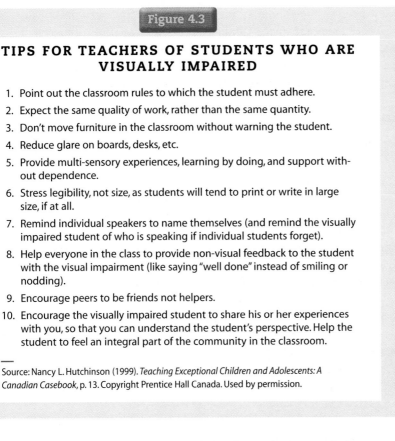

Figure 4.3

TIPS FOR TEACHERS OF STUDENTS WHO ARE VISUALLY IMPAIRED

1. Point out the classroom rules to which the student must adhere.
2. Expect the same quality of work, rather than the same quantity.
3. Don't move furniture in the classroom without warning the student.
4. Reduce glare on boards, desks, etc.
5. Provide multi-sensory experiences, learning by doing, and support without dependence.
6. Stress legibility, not size, as students will tend to print or write in large size, if at all.
7. Remind individual speakers to name themselves (and remind the visually impaired student of who is speaking if individual students forget).
8. Help everyone in the class to provide non-visual feedback to the student with the visual impairment (like saying "well done" instead of smiling or nodding).
9. Encourage peers to be friends not helpers.
10. Encourage the visually impaired student to share his or her experiences with you, so that you can understand the student's perspective. Help the student to feel an integral part of the community in the classroom.

Source: Nancy L. Hutchinson (1999). *Teaching Exceptional Children and Adolescents: A Canadian Casebook*, p. 13. Copyright Prentice Hall Canada. Used by permission.

ticular contrasts of paper and print are easiest for the student to read. A peer may serve as a note taker. You can make large-print copies of chalkboard notes and overheads (Ontario Ministry of Education, 1987).

ADAPTING ORGANIZATION

Organize your classroom and use a seating arrangement so that students with partial vision have the best view possible of chalkboard work and demonstrations. Enclosed (rather than open-concept) classrooms with reduced clutter are better for these students. Ensure that everyone keeps possessions off the floor. To ensure safety, move the furniture as little as possible and always warn the student who cannot easily see any changes. The organization of learning activities can also foster the inclusion of students with visual impairments. Form groups that enable them to practise social and communication skills with empathic peers. Work closely with the vision or resource teacher who may be instructing them in eye contact, body language, facial expression, and alternatives to behaviour patterns such as rocking and eye poking.

ADAPTING RESOURCES AND ASSESSMENT

There are many learning resources for students with visual impairments, including large-print books and Braille books, typewriters, and computer keyboards. Computer technology includes Braillers combined with word processors, programs

Further Reading

On students who are deaf-blind: J.M. McInnes (ed.) (1999). *A Guide to Planning and Support for Individuals Who Are Deafblind.* Toronto: University of Toronto Press.

On students who are blind: P.A. MacCuspie (1996). *Promoting Acceptance of Children with Disabilities: From Tolerance to Inclusion.* Halifax: Atlantic Provinces Special Education Authority.

that convert print to audio output, and **speech-activated** word processors. An IEP usually ensures provincial funding for technology, three-dimensional maps and tape measures, and other learning materials. You may need to plan six months ahead to ensure receipt of Braille textbooks, books on tape, and large-print learning materials by the time they are needed by the student.

The work and learning of students with vision disabilities and blindness can be evaluated effectively by extending time frames for test taking and homework assignments and by testing students orally. Braille or large-print formats may be necessary, or assessments can be completed on a computer or under supervision in a resource room.

Implications for Social and Career Participation of Students with Visual Impairment

Adults with visual impairments experience higher-than-average rates of unemployment and underemployment. These students need to explore a wide variety of career options while developing a realistic understanding of their potential through a transition plan, adapted career education, job shadowing, and cooperative education (Hutchinson et al., 1999). *Take Charge* (Rabby & Croft, 1989), a career development program, is available in Braille.

Majed Al Kayed, age 14, checking out Rick Hansen Secondary School before it opened in 1999. The school was built with input from Rick Hansen to give students in wheelchairs full access. Visit the school's Web site at http://www.peel.edu.on.ca/rickhansen/.

Teaching Students with Physical Disabilities and Chronic Medical Conditions

Many physical disabilities and chronic medical disorders influence the social participation and learning of children and adolescents at school. These issues are explored in a new book, *Cognitive Aspects of Chronic Illness in Children* (Brown, 1999). These conditions result from genetic, environmental, and unknown causes and may be transient, lifelong, or life threatening. Many students experience unpredictable changes due to deteriorating health, recurring surgery, **remission**, and increasing doses and side effects of medication. Each physical condition can present differently from case to case, and how families and individuals cope interacts with the physical condition. When you are teaching a student with a physical disability or chronic medical disorder, it will be critical for you to familiarize yourself with characteristics, emergency responses, and teaching strategies—on a need-to-know basis.

Physical and chronic health disorders are difficult to categorize. The description depends on whether the focus is on the area of dysfunction, the cause, or the impact. For example, muscular dystrophy can be described as a musculoskeletal impairment, a health disorder, or a motor disability. A student is considered to have a physical disability or chronic medical disorder, based on the need for adapted teaching or special education services, due to one or more of the following: (1) nervous system impairment, (2) musculoskeletal condition, (3) chronic health impairment (B.C. Special Education Branch, 1998).

Nervous System Impairment

Nervous system impairment or **neurological dysfunction** results from damage or dysfunction of the brain or spinal cord that may have occurred before, during, or after birth. The exceptionalities discussed are cerebral palsy, spina bifida, epilepsy, Tourette syndrome, brain injury, and fetal alcohol syndrome.

CEREBRAL PALSY

> On Wednesday, nobody understood what I wanted. Most days I can point at it or just wheel over in my walker. I've got lots of words inside my head but people don't seem to hear them like I do. Some days, even my mum doesn't know what I mean. Wednesday was a bad day. Nobody understood. My big yellow school bus was on my top shelf and I wanted to play with it. Dad handed me the blocks instead. Bbbusss… That's a hard word to say.
>
> Yates, 1994, pp. 3–5.

This young girl has cerebral palsy. Although she speaks little and cannot walk, she has thoughts to express and can become frustrated. Cerebral palsy (CP) describes a group of disorders affecting body movement and muscle coordination resulting from damage to the brain during pregnancy or before age three. This damage interferes with messages in both directions between brain and body. Approximately 1 in every 550 people in Canada has CP.

The effects vary widely. At its mildest, CP causes awkward movement or hand control. At its most severe, CP may result in almost no muscle control, profoundly affecting movement and speech. Depending on which areas of the brain have been damaged, one or more of the following may occur:

- muscle tightness or spasm
- involuntary movement
- difficulty with gross motor skills such as walking or running
- difficulty with fine motor skills such as writing and speaking
- abnormal perception and sensation

The brain damage that caused CP may also lead to other conditions such as seizures, learning disabilities, or developmental delay. The degree of physical disability experienced by a person with cerebral palsy is not an indication of level of intelligence.

> **Put Into Practice**
>
> Interview an adult with cerebral palsy. View the 11-minute video *Never Say Never*, available from Cerebral Palsy Association in Alberta, fax: 403-543-1168. Consult Provincial Associations for Cerebral Palsy, http://www.cerebral palsycanada.com.

Treat students with cerebral palsy as normally as possible and don't underestimate their ability to learn and participate. They may need more time to complete a task or to respond verbally, and they may need to repeat themselves when misunderstood. Learn to help to position and transfer students who use wheelchairs and how to push wheelchairs by asking the student, a parent, and a physiotherapist. Felt-tipped pens and soft-lead pencils enable the student to exert less pressure when writing. A rubber grip around the shaft may help with pencil grip. You can help the student set and reach realistic goals in your classroom.

SPINA BIFIDA

> I am going to try out for the swim team this year, even though I may not be chosen. I have been swimming since I was very young because my parents thought I might get hurt in rough team sports. I have always swum by myself, but I really want to be part of a team.
>
> *Excerpt from the diary of a 15-year-old male with spina bifida who wears leg braces and uses crutches.*

Spina bifida is a neural tube defect that occurs within the first four weeks of pregnancy. The vertebrae or spinal cord fails to develop properly, causing damage to the spinal cord and nervous system. Spina bifida often results in paralysis of the lower limbs as well as loss of bladder control, and is often accompanied by **hydrocephalus**, the accumulation of cerebrospinal fluid surrounding the brain. This fluid can cause brain injury if not treated immediately; usually a **shunt** is installed to drain the fluid for reabsorption. About 1 in every 750 babies born in Canada has spina bifida and 80 percent of these have hydrocephalus (http://www.chebucto.ns.ca/Health/SBANS/index.html).

You may be asked to watch for signs of headaches, coordination difficulties, vomiting, and seizures—indications of shunt blockage. If the student lacks bladder or bowel control, this can be a barrier to peer acceptance. You can model acceptance and be sensitive to the student's need to leave the classroom unexpectedly. Encourage independence and ensure privacy. Usually a paraprofessional assists young students with these functions.

Sitting in a wheelchair makes one vulnerable to sores and skin breakdown. Students need to be positioned properly and moved periodically and may be advised to use prone standers, braces, or crutches for part of the day. Treat changes in position as normal occurrences and assist students without drawing undue attention to them. Be prepared to accommodate extended absences from school that result from skin breakdown, bladder infections, etc. Encourage students with spina bifida to use computers, cassette tapes, and calculators, and give them two copies of books: one for school and one for home. By working closely with the family, you can help minimize the impact of spina bifida on school participation.

Weblinks

SPINA BIFIDA ASSOCIATION OF AMERICA
http://www.sbaa.org

EPILEPSY

> Last week I had a seizure at school. I have only one or two a year, and this is the first one I've had at this school since I started a year ago. Fortunately, my best friend was in the class and stopped some guy from sticking his pencil in my mouth so I would-

n't 'swallow my tongue.' She also told the other kids it was no big deal and not to worry. My friend says the teacher fluttered around like she didn't know what to do. Now the teacher is being kind of gooey sweet and sympathetic to me. I think my classmates would forget the whole thing if she would act normal.

Kaufman, 1995, p. 99.

Epilepsy is a neurological disorder involving sudden bursts of electrical energy in the brain. It is characterized by sudden, brief **seizures** that can last from 10 seconds to 5 minutes. If a seizure lasts longer than 10 minutes, medical attention may be needed (Epilepsy Association, Metro Toronto). About 1 percent of the population has epilepsy, and in many cases the causes are unknown. Contributing causes include chemical imbalance and head injury.

The two main categories of seizures are partial and generalized. **Partial seizures** involve one area of the brain, while **generalized seizures** involve the whole brain. In a partial seizure there may be strange sensations, possibly accompanied by inappropriate movements such as plucking at clothes or books, smacking the lips, or aimless wandering. Complete consciousness is not lost and confusion usually follows the partial seizure.

Generalized seizures are of two types—simple absence and tonic-clonic. The **simple absence seizure (petit mal)** occurs in children; they stare or daydream for 5 to 15 seconds. There may be small muscle movements in the face, the eyes may roll upward or to one side, and the child may be confused about the seconds "missed." If these seizures are not treated, serious learning problems can result. Teachers most often notice these seizures and urge parents to seek a neurological assessment (Epilepsy Association, Metro Toronto).

The **tonic-clonic (grand mal) seizure** can be frightening when it occurs in the classroom. Sometimes the student gives a sharp cry before falling to the floor, the muscles stiffen, then begin to jerk rhythmically. There may be loss of bladder control, some breathing difficulty, and saliva may gather at the mouth. In most cases, the seizure will not hurt the student and there is no emergency; some school policies require that the student be taken to the hospital. Medical attention is required if the seizure "lasts more than ten minutes or is repeated without full recovery" (Epilepsy Association, Metro Toronto, p. 4).

Figure 4.4 lists the specific actions to take during a generalized seizure. Familiarize yourself with the student's condition; school performance can be affected, but each case is unique. Students may be excused from activities such as climbing high ropes or operating power tools. Side effects from medications include drowsiness and blurred vision, and repeated seizure activity can contribute to inattentiveness and distractibility. Students with epilepsy need you to be calm, respectful, understanding, and knowledgeable.

What do you think?

Many people with epilepsy feel they are discriminated against. View the Web site of Epilepsy Canada and then discuss with your classmates this charge of unfair treatment: http://www.epilepsy.ca/eng/basic.html.

TOURETTE SYNDROME

Dear Kellie, Kamilla and Magrau—Hi! My name is Russell. I am nine years old and I have TS. I have tics. They really bother me because they keep me awake at night. I get what I call 'buggie' when something is frustrating and it makes it hard to work. At school it is sometimes hard to work, I get really hot and my teacher says I can leave the classroom if I want to and get a drink. I don't like it when other kids ask me why I make funny noises. These are some of the tics I have: twirling my hair, arm movements, shrugging my shoulders, sticking my pinky finger in the air and some others. This web site is really cool.—From Russell

Excerpt from a letter written to Kellie at Kids Korner on the Tourette Syndrome Foundation of Canada Web site, http://www.tourette.ca.

Tourette syndrome (TS) is a complex neurological disorder modulated by psychological and social factors. It is characterized by **tics**: involuntary, rapid, sudden

Figure 4.4

STRATEGIES FOR HANDLING A GENERALIZED SEIZURE IN THE CLASSROOM

Before a Seizure

- Meet with the parents and student at the beginning of the year. Learn the characteristics of the student's seizures.
- Familiarize yourself with the school's policies.
- Discuss with the family how to inform the class that a seizure may occur.
- Keep the area surrounding the student's desk free of objects that could cause harm to the student during a seizure.

During a Seizure

- Stay calm, and keep the students calm. Remind them that the seizure is painless. Ask another teacher to remove excited students from the classroom.
- Ease the student to the floor and loosen clothing.
- Try to remove any hard, sharp, or hot objects that might injure the student.
- Place a blanket, coat, or cushion under the student's head to soften the impact of the seizure.
- Place the student on his or her side to allow saliva to flow from the mouth.
- Write down the time the seizure began. If a seizure lasts longer than 10 minutes, medical attention may be needed.
- Refrain from restraining the student or placing objects in the student's mouth.
- Refrain from giving the student food or drink.

After a Seizure

- Allow the student to rest or sleep and then offer the opportunity to resume classroom activities.
- Be attuned to the student's emotional state, as most but not all students can rejoin classroom activities.
- The student should not leave the school alone if weakness or convulsive behaviour persist.
- Refrain from "fussing over" the student with epilepsy. Foster an attitude of understanding and acceptance. The student with epilepsy needs support from you and peers.

muscular movements; uncontrollable vocal sounds; and inappropriate words. Symptoms appear between the ages of 2 and 18 and change over time. Often one type of tic replaces another and the syndrome is mistaken for a psychological disorder. Stress aggravates TS symptoms; thus more structure and predictability result in fewer disruptions. Typically, tics decrease with concentration on an absorbing task, so engaging teaching will help students with TS. These children may also have learning disabilities, obsessive-compulsive behaviours, and attentional difficulties. The need to accept themselves and to have others accept them is critical to youth with TS.

Controversial issues include incidence. According to the American Psychiatric Association (1994), this is a relatively rare disorder affecting about 1 individual per 2200. "Recent genetic studies suggest that the figure may be one in two hundred when those with chronic and transient tics are included in the count" (Tourette Syndrome Foundation of Canada, http://www.tourette.ca/whatists.html). Symptoms also appear to be more severe in students with concomitant identifications such as attention deficit disorder.

When teaching a student with Tourette syndrome in a classroom:

- Be patient and engage all students fully.
- Respond to tics with tolerance, not anger; the student with TS cannot control them.
- Encourage the student to leave the room for a short time when tics become distracting.
- Provide a quiet place for the student to work or take tests, preferably in the classroom.
- Minimize stress by adapting teaching and assignments, using structure, and eliminating chaos.
- Seek assistance for yourself and the student with TS from counsellors, psychologists, and parents.

BRAIN INJURY

> How I hated going to school! It was almost a year after my brain injury. I was still relearning to read and write and even to remember. I felt myself getting more and more down. Most of my teachers were helpful, and I had a tutor who helped me write my assignments and read my textbooks. But it was really the counsellor who got me through those 'dark periods' until I finished school.
>
> *Mark, reflecting on returning to school after his brain injury. Based on Acorn and Offer (1998).*

Brain injury happens when the brain's tissue is damaged or is not able to function properly. It is sometimes called **head injury** or **traumatic brain injury**. Many brain injuries are traumatic, the result of a blow to the head from a fall, a sports injury, an assault, or a cycling or motor vehicle accident. Cycling and motor vehicle accidents are responsible for most brain injuries to youth. About 56 000 new cases of traumatic brain injury occur each year in Canada and 9000 have significant long-term rehabilitation needs (Higenbottam, 1998).

Further Reading

S. Acorn & P. Offer (eds.) (1998). *Living with Brain Injury: A Guide for Families and Caregivers.* Toronto: University of Toronto Press.

M. Bergland & D. Hoffbauer. New opportunities for students with traumatic brain injuries: Transition to postsecondary education. *Teaching Exceptional Children, 28*(2), 54–57.

Students with brain injury experience difficulties remembering, understanding, organizing, and planning that interfere with their ability to function in school. They often have physical effects such as paralysis and vision and hearing loss and experience socioemotional challenges. Anti-social behaviour, impulsiveness, confusion, and inappropriate or immature language and behaviour can result. Not surprisingly, these students have decreased interactions with peers and reduced self-esteem. Because they know themselves as they were prior to the brain injury, they may hold onto their pre-trauma academic and career aspirations, although these have become unrealistic. Realistic goals are essential, but can be discouraging. Figure 4.5 contains strategies for physical, language, cognitive, and social adaptations in the classroom.

FETAL ALCOHOL SYNDROME (FAS)

> John [my son] doesn't have an easy time in school. He doesn't have any close friends except for his doggy. You see, John has fetal alcohol syndrome (FAS), a disorder caused by prenatal exposure to alcohol. His birth mother's drinking during pregnancy caused John's mild retardation, small stature, unusual facial features, and damage to his central nervous system. He has a hard time learning the rules of life. John needs reminders about how to behave normally around people. I give him verbal cues for everything from how to get ready for school in the morning, to taking care of his dog, to how to behave in public, to how to interact with company, and so on and so on, day after day. His brain just doesn't function like yours and mine.
>
> *http://www.specialchild.com/archives/dz-011.html*

Fetal Alcohol Syndrome (FAS) is a neurological disorder caused by significant **prenatal exposure to alcohol**. In addition to maternal use of alcohol, the following criteria are present:

- slowed growth and weight, and height below normal;
- brain damage, ranging from mild to severe; and
- characteristic facial features (short eye openings, an elongated flattened mid-face, a long indistinct space between the nose and upper lip, and a thin upper lip).

Further Reading

British Columbia Ministry of Education, Skills and Training (1996). *Teaching Students with Fetal Alcohol Syndrome/ Effects: A Resource Guide for Teachers.* Victoria: Queen's Printer for British Columbia.

D.M. Burgess & A.P. Streissguth (1992). Fetal alcohol syndrome and fetal alcohol effects: Principles for educators. *Phi Delta Kappan,* 74(1), 24–30.

FAS is difficult to diagnose. Reasons include the similarity of its characteristics to those of other exceptionalities and the resistance of some mothers to the idea that they are responsible for their children's disabilities. The term **fetal alcohol effects (FAE)** is used to describe individuals with a documented history of prenatal alcohol exposure and the presence of some, but not all, of the other diagnostic criteria for FAS. Those with FAE may be just as severely affected cognitively as those with FAS (Streissguth, 1997). Prevalence estimates for FAS and FAE are about 1 for every 3000 births, with large geographical differences. A recent study suggests that teachers in northern Canada are more aware of the presence and needs of students with FAS than teachers in southern Canada (Beddard, 1996).

Students with FAS can be chatty and charming, and this may initially mask their learning and behaviour difficulties. They usually show impaired rates of learning, poor memory, and difficulty generalizing. They often act impulsively, exhibit short attention span, and are distractible. Parents describe examples of

Figure 4.5

STRATEGIES FOR TEACHING STUDENTS WITH BRAIN INJURY IN A CLASSROOM SETTING

Strategies for Physical Adaptations

- Schedule rest breaks; have a shortened day.
- Schedule more difficult classes early in the day.
- Provide adapted equipment or assistance, including computers and scribes, without drawing undue attention.

Strategies for Language Adaptations

- Use shorter, simpler sentences, with pictures and gestures to aid comprehension.
- Teach the student to ask for clarification or repetition at a slower rate.
- To aid student communication, use pictures, an alphabet chart, etc.

Strategies for Cognitive Adaptations

- Remove distractions and limit the amount of information on a page.
- Provide focusing cues and visual cues or a set of steps to follow.
- Adjust the length of assignments to the student's attention span; limit the number of steps.
- Use rehearsal to strengthen memory; have the student practise aloud.
- Use a tape recorder instead of having the student write notes or information about assignments.
- Teach the student to compensate for word-finding problems by describing the size, function, etc., of items that cannot be recalled.
- Praise the student once they begin a task; remind them they are capable of completing the activity.
- Give prior warning for transitions; make transitions clear and structured.
- Role-play appropriate responses and stop inappropriate responses as soon as they begin.

Strategies for Social Adaptations

- Make asking for assistance a student goal; remind the student to seek assistance.
- Check work after a small amount is begun, to reassure the student that he or she can complete the task.
- Emphasize personal progress; discourage comparisons to classmates.
- Arrange for counselling to deal with frustration and aggression.
- Model patience and understanding to the class in your relations with the student.

fearlessness, lack of social judgment, and lack of internalization of modelled behaviour. Difficulty understanding cause and effect appears to be an integral part of learning and behaviour difficulties for individuals with FAS (Kleinfeld & Westcott, 1994). Consistency in behaviour management across home and school usually helps children and adolescents with FAS. Figure 4.6 includes strategies for behaviour management and discipline that can be used in both environments.

Excerpt from http://www.nofas.org. Used by permission.

Figure 4.6

STRATEGIES FOR CLASSROOM MANAGEMENT AND DISCIPLINE OF STUDENTS WITH FAS

- Set limits and follow them consistently.
- Change rewards often to keep interest in rewards high.
- Have pre-established consequences for misbehavior.
- Review and repeat consequences of behaviors. Ask them to tell you consequences.
- Do not debate or argue over rules already established. "Just do it."
- Notice and comment when the child's doing well or behaving appropriately.
- Avoid threats.
- Redirect behavior.
- Intervene before behavior escalates.
- Avoid situations where child will be overstimulated.
- Have child repeat back their understanding of directions.
- Protect them from being exploited. They are naïve.

Musculoskeletal Conditions

Two **musculoskeletal conditions** that can affect all aspects of a student's life are muscular dystrophy and juvenile arthritis. They have different characteristics, treatments, and educational implications.

MUSCULAR DYSTROPHY

In March 1999, Jérémie Girard, a young artist in Quebec, painted a work called "Secret" on a pizza box for his art class. His art teacher recognized the merit of the work, as did a neighbour who suggested that Jérémie have it framed. When the neighbour took the painting to a gallery to be framed for Jérémie, the owner of the gallery offered to promote this new artist. She admired the way he had captured themes of life and death in his painting. Jérémie has muscular dystrophy and was 10 years old when he painted "Secret." His story appeared on the Web site of the Muscular Dystrophy Association of Canada (http://www.mdac.ca).

Muscular dystrophy (MD) refers to a group of genetically based muscle disorders that result in progressive muscle weakness. Muscle tissue is replaced by fatty tissue and connective tissue, which causes the muscles to weaken and eventually waste away. About 28 000 people in Canada have MD. Duchenne muscular dystrophy is the most common form of MD and affects approximately 1 in 3300 male births

(Heller, Alberto, Forney, & Schwartzman, 1996). In **Duchenne muscular dystrophy (DMD)**, marked physical degeneration occurs during the school years, so teachers need to provide adaptations and a supportive school environment.

Symptoms of DMD are first noted between two and five years of age, and include difficulty in rising from the floor and climbing stairs. The calf muscles become prominent. A wheelchair is usually necessary by early adolescence, and breathing is increasingly affected. Most adolescents with DMD are prone to respiratory infections. Lifespan is shortened, with death typically occurring during the twenties. Other forms of MD include Becker MD and Myotonic MD (Steinart's disease), neither of which is as severe as DMD during the school years.

A physical therapist will be a member of the in-school team and exercise will form part of the treatment, but care must be taken to avoid overactivity and fatigue. Because the disease is progressive, the needs of the student are continually changing—including physical adaptations, adjustment to a wheelchair, exercising to avoid obesity, and coping with the prospect of a reduced lifespan. Emotional support is critical. You may have to cope with the attitudes of people who feel that youth with terminal diseases should not demand your effort because they won't live long enough to benefit from adapted schooling. However, these students are entitled to an education, as are all other youth in Canada. As well, recent advances in gene therapy research may soon change the lives of children and adolescents with MD.

Weblinks

MUSCULAR DYSTROPHY
ASSOCIATION OF CANADA
http://www.mdac.ca

ARTHRITIS CANADA
http://www.arthritis.ca

JUVENILE ARTHRITIS

> No one knows for sure what causes juvenile arthritis. Mine was diagnosed when I was eight. I was upset because I played sports, played the piano, and was good at art. My treatment team has helped me to take charge of my life. I play the piano even though I can't practise when my hands are swollen. I continued the sports with the least chance of body contact. Now I am 18. Some days I can't get out of bed, but those days are rare. When my fingers are too swollen to write, my friends at school take turns making carbon copies of their notes for me. With the help of my family, friends, and teachers I do well in school and will go to university next year. You can take charge of your arthritis, too.
>
> *From Helen's speech to children recently diagnosed with juvenile arthritis, at a conference for families.*

Juvenile arthritis (JA)—continuous **inflammation** of one or more joints lasting at least six weeks for which no other cause can be found—is a chronic arthritic condition present before the age of 16. Approximately 1 in 100 children under age 16 has JA. This condition can be difficult to detect. Doctors look for signs of joint swelling or loss of mobility that suggest inflamed joints. Students may complain of stiffness or pain, walk with a limp, or have difficulty using an arm or leg. The **immune system** seems to be overactive, inflaming joints as if fighting an infection when none is present. Most children have an up-and-down course for many years; physiotherapy and occupational therapy are essential parts of the treatment program.

Students with JA will tend to feel stiffness and pain after sitting in one position. They may need to stand in the middle of a class period or move around. Because of low stamina, they may require a shorter day or rest breaks during the day. Medication will probably have to be taken during the school day, and often must be taken with food to prevent adverse effects on the gastrointestinal tract. Fever is a symptom of JA and does not indicate an infectious disease. Because eyes can become involved in arthritis, you will need to be alert for any indications of a visual problem and notify the parents.

You may need to make adaptations. The physical education program should take into account decreased stamina and limit strenuous games that put pressure on joints or limbs. Pain can interfere with concentration, so break tasks into shorter segments and check comprehension of the instructions. Students may have a **limited range of motion** in affected limbs and swollen fingers that prevent them from grasping pencils and pens. Because symptoms vary from day to day, you must be accepting of a wide range of variation in the students' functioning and independence. Encourage as much independence as possible while reassuring the students that support is available.

Chronic Health Impairment

Students with **chronic health impairment** or **chronic medical disorder** have been assessed by a qualified medical practitioner who certifies that the student requires:

- medical procedures, excluding administration of medication only, to ensure the health and safety of the student while in school; or
- ongoing special education interventions due to the student's limited school attendance for health reasons or because the condition adversely affects the student's educational performance at school (Saskatchewan Education, 1996).

Conditions discussed in this section include diabetes, allergies, asthma, and cystic fibrosis. There are many other chronic health impairments, including congenital and acquired heart disease, gastrointestinal system diseases such as Crohn's disease and ulcerative colitis, as well as hemophilia, cancer, and AIDS. In each case, you can obtain relevant information from the family, community agencies, Web sites, and print sources of information, including pamphlets, resource books, and books to be read to children and by adolescents about these conditions.

DIABETES

I stayed after school to talk to my homeroom teacher. I told her that I have diabetes. She already knew from my file. I said I don't want the other kids to know I am diabetic until I get to know them better. I told her that I keep juice in my backpack and that if I ask to leave class, it will be because I need sugar or insulin and she should let me go right away. Tomorrow I have to talk with my physical education teacher because I always need to eat after exercising. Today was good—a practice run for tomorrow.

Phil, describing his first day of high school to his parents.

For those with diabetes, the body does not make enough insulin and has problems absorbing and storing sugars. Most children with diabetes receive two **insulin**

injections daily. Adolescents give themselves insulin injections and check their blood sugar regularly. Diabetes is controlled somewhat through planned eating, insulin supplementation, and regular physical activity.

Most students with diabetes do not need undue attention from you. However, there are two types of diabetic emergencies that you could face: low blood sugar and high blood sugar. The symptoms appear similar, but low blood sugar is the more dangerous, so if you are unsure which is occurring, give sugar. The symptoms of **low blood sugar (hypoglycemia)** occur suddenly: cold, clammy, or sweaty skin; trembling; confusion; difficulty speaking; and eventually fainting or unconsciousness. The student may report hunger, headache, dizziness, blurry vision, and abdominal pain. If the student is conscious, give a regular soft drink or juice that contains sugar or 2 teaspoons of sugar. The amounts may be specified in the student's file. This should be followed by a snack that includes complex carbohydrates and protein (e.g., a nutrient bar). The student may carry such a snack in his or her backpack. The causes include too much insulin, delayed or missed meals, and more exercise than usual without extra food. Contact the parents or a physician, or take the student to hospital. Follow the school's protocol.

High blood sugar (hyperglycemia) symptoms show gradually, even over days. Causes include overeating, too little insulin, and stress. You may see thirst, flushed dry skin, nausea, drowsiness, and eventually unconsciousness. Contact the parents or a physician. It may be necessary to take the student to the hospital.

Your school will probably have **diabetes emergency kits** containing juice, raisins, or dextrose. Know the location of these kits and take one on field trips. Explain to younger children the importance of eating their own snacks, without focusing undue attention on the child with diabetes. Speak with the parents about appropriate activity levels, etc. Supervise the student at all times after a reaction and inform the parents. Most students know about their condition, and require support, respect, and information about changes in the routine, especially the timing of snacks and meals.

Diabetes can affect students in the classroom. They need a specific eating schedule. When students are experiencing a high or a low, or the day after they have had high or low blood sugar during the night, they may be weak, tired, irritable, and unable to concentrate. Some students have characteristic high or low periods that cause them to arrive late in the morning. Encourage students with diabetes to speak with you confidentially, develop a sign to be used in class when the student needs to leave quickly, and talk regularly with parents of younger children so they are comfortable telling you about their child's changing condition. Beware of the three misconceptions about diabetes (Rosenthal-Malek & Greenspan, 1999):

- that the student will inform you of highs or lows; sometimes they don't know
- that only food affects the level of blood sugar; activity level also influences it
- that bathroom privileges can wait; a few minutes can put a student into a coma

Your understanding will make a difference to the well-being and learning of students with diabetes.

Put Into Practice

Make a contingency plan for when a student has high blood sugar and has to be rushed to hospital. Consult A. Rosenthal-Malek & J. Greenspan (1999). A student with diabetes is in my class. *Teaching Exceptional Children, 31*(3), 38–43, and Canadian Diabetes Association, http://www. diabetes.ca/.

Dear Parents of Children in Room 4:

I am asking for your help, as the mother of a seven-year-old boy with a life-threatening allergy to peanuts. I want my son Silas to attend school and play with his friends, but I also want to protect him from exposure to minute amounts of some of the most common childhood foods—peanuts and peanut butter. That is why I am asking you to read the accompanying letter by the principal of Grove School and asking you not to send food to school with your child that contains any trace of peanuts. I am asking you to give up some of your child's freedom and some of your time. But think what could be lost if you don't agree. Silas has been rushed to hospital with anaphylactic shock three times; each time his reaction has been more severe. Because of the understanding and cooperation of teachers, classmates, and families at Grove, Silas has never had a severe reaction at school. You can contact me at 555-1212. Thank you for considering my request.

Sincerely,

Alison Cohen

Letter from a parent to the families of the children in her son's class

Isabel Grant, a lawyer at the University of British Columbia, has argued persuasively that a child with allergies has the law on his or her side. "Provincial human-rights legislation prohibits discrimination on the basis of disability for services customarily available to the public. It is clear that a life-threatening medical condition that greatly restricts the activities of daily living is a disability" (1997, p. A24). She argues that other students' rights are not interfered with because the "rights of others" does not include a right to eat peanut butter and because all Canadian children have a right to a safe education in the public school system.

An allergy is an abnormal immune response to a substance that is tolerated by non-allergic people. It results in individual signs and symptoms that vary in range and severity and that can occur up to 72 hours after exposure to the allergen. **Anaphylaxis** or **anaphylactic shock** is a sudden, severe allergic reaction that causes breathing difficulties. Death can occur within minutes unless an injection is administered. About 20 percent of the school population have a major allergy, and a smaller percentage has anaphylaxis (British Columbia Special Education Branch, 1996).

Allergens, which cause allergic reactions, can enter the body:

- breathed through the nose or mouth—including dust; pollen; molds; odours from chemicals, markers, perfumes, etc.
- ingested through the mouth—including food such as peanuts, shellfish, and milk; drugs such as aspirin (ASA), penicillin, and other antibiotics
- by contact with the skin—including powders; lotions; metals such as jean snaps; latex; peanut butter
- through stings of insects—including venom of bees and wasps

Other factors that may aggravate the allergy include weather changes; extremes of heat, cold, and humidity; infections; and second-hand smoke.

Weblinks

ALLERGY/ASTHMA INFORMATION ASSOCIATION
http://cgi.cadvision.com/
~allergy/aaia.html

For the allergic student, reactions often accompany changes in routine, and anaphylactic shock is more likely to take place at school than at home. Before the start of the school year, read the school policy on allergies and meet with the family. Because characteristics of allergic reactions vary, it is important to learn each student's signs and symptoms. The main symptoms are itchy, watery eyes and itchy, runny nose. Other signs include itching, eczema, hives, dark circles under the eyes, headache, shortness of breath, wheezing, cough, diarrhea, and stomach cramps. Some teachers watch for what has been called "the **allergic salute**"—pushing up on a runny nose.

If you read the school policy first and bring it to the meeting, you can tell the parents how it compares with their expectations (e.g., some policies name the adults who can administer an injection). Inform the principal and invite others who teach the student to the meeting. The Canadian School Boards Association (1996) has prepared a handbook to help school boards clarify the responsibilities of principals, parents, teachers, and students. An emergency allergy alert form appears in Figure 4.7. Many schools are posting these.

You should know the steps in the emergency plan that has been developed for each student with severe allergies and the location of the injector for each student (in the student's fanny pack, in a cupboard, etc.). The general steps in an emergency plan are:

- administer **epinephrine** immediately (**EPIPEN**® or **ANA-KIT**®)—follow directions on the injector; this can save a life, but is only first aid

- call 911 or an ambulance, or transport student to the nearest emergency facility—warn that there is anaphylaxis; more serious reactions may follow, so a hospital is essential

- ensure that you have additional epinephrine available, in case it is needed—may be necessary every 15 minutes if breathing difficulties persist, until patient reaches hospital

- call parents or next of kin—administer the injection immediately; don't delay by calling parents first

Children and adolescents with severe allergies can feel anxious and isolated because they feel "different than everyone else." They usually wear a **MedicAlert**® identification bracelet and carry an injector in a fanny pack. Sometimes adolescents leave their "uncool" fanny pack in their locker or engage in risky behaviours, such as eating cafeteria food, with their peers (Lightfoot, 1997). You can enhance self-acceptance by respecting feelings, accepting differences, and supporting personal decisions. Try to include the student in all activities, even if this means providing an **allergen-free alternative**.

ASTHMA

> Ms. Aboul: I need to talk with you. Grade 9 is hard. I'm so far behind. I've missed a lot of classes this year because of my asthma and doctors' appointments. I hate carrying my puffer around at school and trying to avoid stressful situations that make my wheezing worse. Most of all I'm afraid of having a really big attack and not making it to the hospital. I need to talk with you. My homeroom teacher is Mr. Wong.
>
> Meghan Lowie, 9D

A note left for a guidance counsellor by a student with asthma

Further Reading

J. Engel (1997). *The Complete Allergy Book.* Toronto: University of Toronto Press.

B. Zimmerman, M. Gold, S. Lavi, S. Feanny, & E. Brownridge (1997). *The Canadian Allergy and Asthma Handbook.* Mississauga, ON: Random House.

Put Into Practice

Learn what to do in an emergency. Consult *Anaphylaxis Reference Kit,* which you can order from AAIA National Anaphylaxis Committee, 20 South Road, Doaktown, NB E9C 1G1 (506) 365-4501, and Health Canada and Canadian School Boards Association (1996). *Anaphylaxis: A Handbook for School Boards.* Ottawa: Health Canada, Minister of Supply and Services.

Figure 4.7

EMERGENCY ALLERGY ALERT FORM

Name:_____

ALLERGY—DESCRIPTION
This child has a DANGEROUS, life threatening Allergy to the following foods:

_____
_____
_____

And all foods containing them in any form in any amount, including the following kinds of items:

_____
_____
_____

FOR USE IN:
Classroom
Lunchroom
Staff Room
Office
Fanny Pack

PLACE CHILD'S
PHOTO HERE

AVOIDANCE
The key to preventing an emergency is ABSOLUTE AVOIDANCE of these foods at all times. WITHOUT EPIPEN®/ANA-KIT®, THIS CHILD MUST NOT BE ALLOWED TO EAT ANYTHING.

EATING RULES (List eating rules for your child, if any, in this space)

_____
_____
_____

POSSIBLE SYMPTOMS
- flushed face, hives, swelling or itchy lips, tongue, eyes
- tightness in throat, mouth, chest
- difficulty breathing or swallowing, wheezing, coughing, choking
- vomiting, nausea, diarrhea, stomach pains
- dizziness, unsteadiness, sudden fatigue, rapid heartbeat
- loss of consciousness

ACTION—EMERGENCY PLAN
- Use EPIPEN®/ANA-KIT® immediately!
- HAVE SOMEONE CALL AN AMBULANCE and advise the dispatcher that a child is having an anaphylactic reaction.
- If ambulance has not arrived in 10–15 minutes and breathing difficulties are present (e.g., wheeze, cough, throat clearing) give a second EPIPEN® if available.
- Even if symptoms subside entirely, this child must be taken to hospital immediately.
- EPIPENS®/ANA-KITS® are kept _____

_____   _____
Doctor/Date   Parent/Date

From Allergy/Asthma Information Association's *Parent Package for School-Age Children with Anaphylaxis*, p. 39 of handbook. Used by permission.

Asthma is a chronic lung condition that can develop at any age but is most common in childhood. The most important characteristic is difficulty breathing. The airways are obstructed by inflammation, muscle spasm, and excess mucus. It is estimated that 7 to 10 percent of children and adolescents under age 16 have asthma, and that asthma accounts for 25 percent of school absenteeism (http://www.lung.ca/asthma/asthma1.html). Twice as many boys as girls are affected in childhood, but more girls than boys develop asthma during adolescence.

The airways respond in an exaggerated way to common irritants (e.g., smoke, smog, scents in markers), allergens (e.g., pollen, foods such as nuts and shellfish), and other triggers (e.g., viral head colds, exercise, cold air). To treat asthma effectively, the individual must know what may trigger an attack and avoid contact with these triggers. Two categories of medication are used for treating

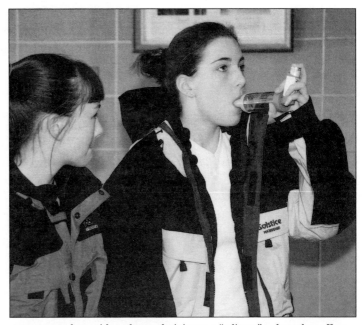

A young student with asthma administers a "reliever," a drug that offers short-term relief, during the onset of an asthma episode by using what is commonly called a puffer or an inhaler.

asthma. **Preventers** are anti-inflammatory drugs taken regularly to prevent and treat inflammation. **Relievers** are used as rescue medications to relax the muscles of the airways and provide quick relief of breathing problems. They are usually inhaled with a **puffer** or **nebulizer**.

Symptoms of asthma include persistent coughing, **wheezing**, chest tightness, and shortness of breath. Those with asthma are affected to varying degrees, from mild (only during vigorous exercise) to severe (with daily symptoms that cause lifestyle restrictions). In Canada, about 20 children die annually from asthma. An asthma episode can lead to life-threatening anaphylactic shock. If you can identify the warning signs, you can help prevent an episode. Watch for coughing, consistent rubbing of the nose or throat, increasing breathing rate, fatigue, irritability, restlessness, obvious discomfort, and increasing exercise intolerance. As breathing becomes more difficult, signs of an asthma episode become more evident:

- wheezing
- rapid shallow breathing
- complaints of chest tightness
- lips and nails greyish or bluish in colour
- neck muscles contract and bulge; nasal flaring and mouth breathing

When you see these signs, start asthma first aid treatment (see Figure 4.8). Time is critical, so you must know what to do before an episode occurs. Your familiarity with the information in the file of a student with asthma could save the student's life. Read the school policy on asthma and advise the principal of your upcoming meeting; then meet with the student and parents before school begins. Learn the

Weblinks

A TEACHER'S GUIDE TO ASTHMA
**http://cgi.cadvision.com/
~allergy/teacherast.html**

THE LUNG ASSOCIATION
http://www.lung.ca

Figure 4.8

ASTHMA FIRST AID TREATMENT

In case of breathing difficulty:

- Have the child *stop all activity*.

- Help the child assume an upright position; sitting with legs crossed and elbows on knees may ease breathing somewhat.

- Stay with the child; talk reassuringly and calmly.

- Have the child take the *appropriate medication*; it is more detrimental to withhold medication than to give the child medication when it is not needed. This is usually taken by means of an inhaler or nebulizer.

- Notify the proper person, in accordance with school policy. This usually means contacting the parents; if the child's condition does not improve or becomes worse 15 minutes after giving the medication, call an ambulance.

Based on information provided by The Lung Association at http://www.lung.ca/asthma/. Used by permission.

student's triggers, warning signs and symptoms, and how the asthma medications (relievers) are administered. Have the parents detail the steps they follow in first aid treatment, and together compare these to the school policy. If the two are not the same, consult your principal. Some schools have a form that parents of students with asthma must complete to describe medications, symptoms, prevention, and first aid.

Always believe students with asthma. Do not make them wait for medication; asthma can be life threatening! If you think these students are using their symptoms to get attention, discuss your concerns with the parents and encourage the students to talk with a counsellor. Students with asthma can be at risk for decreased school performance due to (Celano & Geller, 1993; Neuharth-Pritchett & Getch, 1999):

- stress

- acute exacerbation of symptoms

- adverse effects of medication

- incorrect perceptions that the student is too vulnerable to participate in school activities

Encourage physical activities and remind students to monitor their symptoms. Their level of activity can change daily with their condition. Inform students and parents about potential triggers likely to be introduced into the classroom. Medications may cause behaviour changes in children and adolescents, including poor attention span, lethargy, and irritability (Lowenthal, 1993). Taking medication and having asthmatic episodes at school can make students self-conscious. You can help by arranging for the student to leave unobtrusively when necessary, a quiet supervised location in which the student can relax and take medication, and someone to remain with your class while you monitor the student with asthma.

CYSTIC FIBROSIS

> Today my mom told me I had no choice, and here I am in the hospital with pneumonia again. I'm sorry I can't be in our class play on Friday. I was really looking forward to that. Mom says I probably got overtired from all the rehearsals, and that might be why I am sick again. But I'm still glad I tried out for the play. I don't want CF to get in the way of having a life. I miss my friends from school. I hope they visit tomorrow.
>
> *From the diary of Brittany, a grade 6 student with CF*

Cystic fibrosis (CF) is incurable, caused by an inherited genetic defect, and causes chronic lung problems and digestive disorders. It affects about 1 person in 10 000. Their lungs become covered with sticky mucus that is difficult to remove and promotes infection by bacteria. Most people with CF require frequent hospitalizations and continuous use of antibiotics. They take **enzyme supplements** so they can digest adequate nutrients from their food. Life expectancy has increased from 8 to 32 years. Still, most persons with cystic fibrosis eventually die of lung disease (Korneluk, MacDonald, Cappelli, McGrath, & Heick, 1996).

The student with CF copes with a chronic cough and may need to have therapy during school to remove mucus from her airways. She will probably have an excessive appetite, combined with weight loss, and may need to eat during school hours. Bowel disturbances are common and embarrassing. Repeated bouts of pneumonia mean frequent absences, and communication with the family eases shifting learning to the hospital room. During adolescence you may witness a rebellion against treatments. Adolescents often need counselling to accept that their life expectancy is only about 32.

Weblinks

CANADIAN CYSTIC FIBROSIS FOUNDATION
http://www.cysticfibrosis.ca

AMERICAN CYSTIC FIBROSIS FOUNDATION
http://www.cff.org

INTERNATIONAL CYSTIC FIBROSIS ASSOCIATION
http://www.icfma.org

Key Terms

low-incidence exceptionalities (p. 102)

physical disabilities (p. 102)

chronic health conditions (p. 102)

case coordinator (p. 102)

chromosomal abnormalities (p. 104)

genetic screening (p. 105)

amniocentesis (p. 105)

self-care (p. 106)

voice synthesizer (p. 106)

functional curriculum (p. 107)

community-based (p. 107)

principles of fairness (p. 107)

spectrum of autistic disorders (p. 108)

pervasive developmental disabilities (PDD) (p. 109)

perseveration (p. 109)

echolalia (p. 109)

theory of mind (p. 109)

social stories (p. 110)

reinforcers (p. 110)

hypersensitive (p. 112)

McGill Action Planning System (MAPS) (p. 112)

hearing status (p. 114)

American Sign Language (ASL) (p. 116)

speech-reading (p. 116)

manipulatives (p. 116)

preteaching (p. 116)

amplification (p. 116)

hearing aids (p. 116)

frequency modulation (FM) systems (p. 116)

deaf community (p. 117)

Braille (p. 117)

taped books (p. 117)

vision teacher (p. 118)

speech-activated (p. 120)

remission (p. 120)

nervous system impairment (p. 121)

neurological dysfunction (p. 121)

hydrocephalus (p. 122)

shunt (p. 122)

seizures (p. 123)

Summary

Students with low-incidence exceptionalities comprise only about 15 to 25 percent of all exceptional students. However, the numbers of students with chronic health conditions like asthma and allergies are growing quickly in Canada (Zimmerman et al., 1991). Taken together, the students discussed in this chapter have diverse strengths, challenges, and needs. Many of them can succeed in your classroom. Remember that you will only teach two or three students in your career who have, for example, cystic fibrosis, and are never likely to be teaching more than one or two students at a time who have low-incidence exceptionalities. Many of the teaching strategies you have already learned will be effective in teaching these students, and you should draw on the experience and expertise of parents and in-school team members. While adaptations will usually be adequate, on occasion you may need to modify the curriculum, especially for students with severe developmental disabilities and autism.

In this chapter, we focused on making adaptations and modifying curriculum for students with a number of low-incidence exceptionalities, including severe developmental disabilities, autism, and

Asperger syndrome. We considered adaptations for students who are deaf, who are hard of hearing, or who have visual impairments. The range of needs and strengths in students with these low-incidence exceptionalities is huge. Students with physical exceptionalities also benefit from adaptations. We focused on students with nervous system impairment—cerebral palsy, spina bifida, epilepsy, Tourette syndrome, brain injury, and fetal alcohol syndrome—as well as two musculoskeletal conditions (muscular dystrophy and juvenile arthritis). The final area of concentration was chronic health conditions such as diabetes, allergies, asthma, and cystic fibrosis. It is customary to think of the physical and stamina limitations of students with physical and health conditions, as well as the possibility that they will need medication at school. However, meeting the social and emotional needs of many of these students is also important. Inclusion means more than the physical presence of students with low-incidence exceptionalities in regular classrooms for all or part of the day. Inclusion means making them feel part of the social and academic life of the class and the broader community. ■

Key Terms (continued)

partial seizures (p. 123)

generalized seizures (p. 123)

simple absence seizure (petit mal) (p. 123)

tonic-clonic (grand mal) seizure (p. 123)

tics (p. 124)

head injury (p. 125)

traumatic brain injury (p. 125)

prenatal exposure to alcohol (p. 126)

fetal alcohol effects (FAE) (p. 126)

musculoskeletal conditions (p. 128)

Duchenne muscular dystrophy (DMD) (p. 129)

inflammation (p. 129)

immune system (p. 129)

limited range of motion (p. 130)

chronic health impairment (p. 130)

chronic medical disorder (p. 130)

insulin injections (p. 131)

low blood sugar (hypoglycemia) (p. 131)

high blood sugar (hyperglycemia) (p. 131)

diabetes emergency kits (p. 131)

anaphylaxis (p. 132)

anaphylactic shock (p. 132)

allergic salute (p. 133)

epinephrine (p. 133)

EPIPEN® (p. 133)

ANA-KIT® (p. 133)

MedicAlert® (p. 133)

allergen-free alternative (p. 133)

preventers (p. 135)

relievers (p. 135)

puffer (p. 135)

nebulizer (p. 135)

wheezing (p. 135)

enzyme supplements (p. 137)

Chapter 5

Teaching for Diversity: Including Aboriginal Students, Students from Diverse Cultural Backgrounds, and Students Who Are at Risk

Ragu is in Dan Borenstein's grade 5 class. This is Dan's fifth year teaching, but his first year teaching in the inner city. Ragu arrived in Canada recently from Sri Lanka by way of a refugee camp. Most days Ragu wanders the classroom or sits with his head on his arms. He enjoys his ESL tutorial, where he is beginning to dictate stories to his tutor and read them back. All of Ragu's stories are about violence and killing, except one about games Ragu used to play with his best friend. Ragu told Dan that soldiers attacked them and his friend died. Ragu still has nightmares about it. Until he had to leave school two years ago, Ragu was a quick learner with high grades. Dan tries to communicate his high expectations to Ragu without making him feel pressured. Dan wonders how long he will have to wait for schoolwork to re-emerge as a priority for Ragu.

Anita Harper is proud of her Aboriginal heritage. She is a ceremonial dancer and her mother is a leader in her Nation. Anita always spoke openly about her heritage in elementary school, and expected to do the same when she entered South River Secondary School two months ago. Then two grade 12 boys began taunting Anita after school while she waits for the bus. They call her "squaw" and humiliate her. Anita asks her homeroom teacher, Betty Bird, who is also Aboriginal, for advice. Anita says, "I should be able to work this out myself. But I can't. Teachers don't usually do anything. But you are different; you are like me." Betty Bird knows that only with support will Anita report the racist incidents to the administration. She wishes there were an Aboriginal counsellor at South River for the 120 Aboriginal students in this school of 700. There are so few Aboriginal educators that Betty knows they are fortunate to have three at South River. She will talk with the other two Aboriginal teachers about how they can support Anita and increase their efforts to make South River Secondary more inclusive for Aboriginal students.

1. How can teachers respond to the situations of Ragu and Anita described in these case studies? What aspects of each situation are most likely to affect learning?

2. With such a range of characteristics and learning needs, what do students like Ragu and Anita have in common?

3. How frequently is a teacher likely to be teaching an Aboriginal student or a refugee student?

4. What does each of these students need in order to be included in the social life of the classroom and of the school?

5. What community resources can a teacher access to ensure that each student learns?

Introduction

This chapter illustrates the conceptual and pragmatic ties between exceptionality and other manifestations of diversity in Canadian society. Equity is the common driving force. You will learn about teaching students from Aboriginal cultures and from other diverse cultural backgrounds. There are issues unique to the education of Aboriginal students, including the threat of extinction of Aboriginal languages and cultures. You will be challenged to identify your perspectives and question your stereotypes about diversity. This chapter also focuses on students who are at risk for school failure for a variety of reasons. Poverty, homelessness, abuse, and other conditions are explored for their impact on learning and participation.

Making adaptations for these students is similar to the process explored earlier in this book. However, fluctuations in students' circumstances and lack of documentation (e.g., no IEP) may mean that you receive less direction. School teams may not include these students in their mandates, although in some provinces funding is directed to the needs of diverse and at-risk students. While the specific causes of the need for sensitive and adapted teaching vary greatly in the examples throughout this chapter, the process of ADAPTing is consistent, and equity and respect for diversity are central.

Diversity and Equity in Canadian Society

Communities and schools in Canada are increasing in **diversity**. Sources of this diversity include immigration to Canada and our willingness to receive refugees. For example, from 1991 to 1996, the number of immigrant children grew by 26 percent (Canadian Council on Social Development, 1998, http://www.ccsd.ca/facts.html). Aboriginal families continue to move into urban areas (Royal Commission on Aboriginal Peoples, 1996). Other sources include the growth of poverty, homelessness, and other social conditions that place Canadian youth at risk for failing to learn in school and for leaving school early (Valpy, 1993).

In Chapter 1, we referred to the Charter of Rights and Freedoms; the equality rights that apply to education refer to the rights of all students: "Every individual is equal before and under the law and has a right to the equal protection of and equal benefit of the law without discrimination and, in particular, without discrimination based on race, national or ethnic origin, colour, religion, sex, age, or mental or physical disability" (section 15(1)). This section of the Charter applies to the courts and other institutions as well as to schools.

The Unique Role of Education, Schools, and Educators

Schools have a unique role in the creation of an inclusive society for two reasons. First, unlike other institutions, schools are legally responsible for preparing all children and adolescents (including those who have disabilities or are members of minorities) to take meaningful roles as adults in our society. Second, schools have a legislated responsibility to prepare all children and adolescents to participate in an inclusive democracy. This implies that you must prepare our youth to accept all individuals (including those who have disabilities or are members of minorities) as fellow citizens.

TEACHING CHALLENGES

There are many reasons for including a broad discussion of teaching for **equity** in this text. Creating an inclusive classroom means creating a learning community in which *all* students feel accepted and safe. The students described in this chapter often benefit from adaptations similar to those that meet the needs of exceptional students. This serves as a powerful reminder that the strategies you learn throughout this book apply to many of your students, not only to students with IEPs.

Student needs are complex. A gifted student like Gurgit, described in Chapter 1, can also be a member of a cultural minority. A student with a behaviour disability like Urjo, described in Chapter 3, might have English as his second language (ESL). Children who live in poverty can be at risk because of drug abuse in their family, and so on. To teach students with multiple needs you will make use of any supports your community can provide—parents, cross-age tutors, volunteers, social workers, public health nurses, police officers, immigration counsellors, translators—in addition to school psychologists, consultants, and resource and ESL teachers. We are challenged to create classrooms that respect diversity and foster learning for *all* students.

Aboriginal Education

This section begins with a description of the history of **Aboriginal cultures** in Canada and of recent attempts to negotiate education that will help to preserve Aboriginal languages. The focus moves to strategies for teaching Aboriginal students and for teaching all Canadian students about Aboriginal cultures.

History of Aboriginal Cultures in Canada

It is impossible to say how many people lived in North America in 1492, but estimates range from 1 to 18 million (Wright, 1991). Archaeological evidence suggests that when Christopher Columbus visited, the Americas were inhabited, in large part, to their carrying capacities for the ways of life being followed (Dickason, 1992). There were 12 language families and about 50 languages. Several regional economies coexisted. These were hunting-and-gathering cultures in the north and east, partly agricultural economies in the St. Lawrence River valley, buffalo-centred cultures on the plains, and salmon- and whale-based economies in the Pacific west coast. All of these cultures emphasized the group as well as the self (Dickason, 1992). All had delicate relationships with their natural environments, until the Europeans brought epidemics with them. Then the population was decimated by smallpox, and the traditional ways were altered forever. In light of history, the first sentence of the *Report of the Royal Commission on Aboriginal Peoples* (1996) sounds conciliatory: "Canada is a test case for a grand notion—the notion that dis-

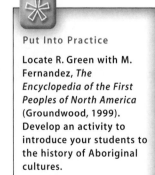

Put Into Practice

Locate R. Green with M. Fernandez, *The Encyclopedia of the First Peoples of North America* (Groundwood, 1999). Develop an activity to introduce your students to the history of Aboriginal cultures.

Weblinks

DEPARTMENT OF INDIAN AND
NORTHERN AFFAIRS CANADA
http://www.ainc-inac.gc.ca/

HIGHLIGHTS OF THE REPORT OF
THE ROYAL COMMISSION ON
ABORIGINAL PEOPLES
**http://www.ainc-inac.gc.ca/
ch/rcap/rpt/index_e.html**

similar peoples can share lands, resources, power and dreams while respecting and sustaining their differences. The story of Canada is the story of many such peoples, trying and failing and trying again to live together in peace and harmony."

In 1991, four Aboriginal and three non-Aboriginal commissioners were appointed to investigate Aboriginal issues and advise the federal government. Canadians had just watched an armed conflict between Aboriginal and non-Aboriginal forces at Kanesatake (Oka). High rates of Aboriginal poverty, disease, and suicide were in the news (Dickason, 1992). The central conclusion of the Report (1996, http://www.ainc-inac.gc.ca/ch/rcap/rpt/) was that the policy of assimilation pursued by Canadian governments for 150 years must change. "To bring about this fundamental change, Canadians need to understand that Aboriginal peoples are nations ... political and cultural groups with values and lifeways distinct from those of other Canadians." Figure 5.1 answers questions about Aboriginal peoples.

Differences Between Issues in Aboriginal Education and Multicultural Education

Aboriginal issues are distinct from multicultural issues. For example, "Native peoples did not immigrate to a different cultural context thinking that they might have to change their ways in order to fit into the society of a foreign country" (Witt, 1998, p. 269). Rather, the country "became foreign" to them with the arrival of other peoples and they had to deal with "forced assimilation." Eber Hampton, of Saskatchewan Indian Federated College, writes about "the world-shattering difference [in perspective] between the conquered and the conqueror" (1995, p. 41). Binding treaties were ignored, spiritual activities were outlawed, and children were forced to attend residential schools. Figure 5.2 provides a brief timeline showing examples of the treatment of Aboriginal peoples.

The Importance of Education and Community in Preserving Disappearing Cultures

"The future of our people in Canada and the survival of our cultures, languages, and all that we value are directly linked to the education of our children" (George Erasmus, 1988, cited in the Report, 1996). The Report (1996) describes the goals of Aboriginal peoples for schools: First, to help children and adolescents learn the skills they need to participate fully in the economy.

Larry Pierre of the Okanagan on the occasion of the First Nations Constitutional Conference, 1980, demanding Aboriginal participation in constitutional talks.

Figure 5.1

ABORIGINAL PEOPLES IN CANADA

Who are the Aboriginal peoples in Canada?
They are descendants of the original inhabitants of North America. The Canadian Constitution Act (1982) recognizes three separate Aboriginal peoples with unique heritages: Indians, Métis, and Inuit. Aboriginal peoples make up 4.4 percent of the Canadian population (799 010 in 1996 census).

What is a First Nation?
This is a term that came into use in the 1970s to replace the word *Indian*, which many people found offensive. No legal definition of First Nation exists. There are 609 First Nations in Canada.

Who are Indians?
Although many Aboriginal people find the term Indian outdated and offensive, the Constitution Act (1982) uses this term to describe all Aboriginal people in Canada who are not Métis or Inuit. In the 1996 census, 554 000 people identified themselves as North American Indian.

Who are Métis people?
They are people of mixed First Nation and European ancestry who identify themselves as Métis people, as distinct from First Nation people, Inuit, or non-Aboriginal people. About 210 000 people identified themselves as Métis in the 1996 census.

Who are Inuit people?
They are Aboriginal people in northern Canada who live above the treeline in Nunavut, the Northwest Territories, northern Quebec, and Labrador. About 41 000 people identified themselves as Inuit in the 1996 census.

Who are Status, Non-Status, and Treaty Indians?
A Status Indian is a person who is registered under the Indian Act, while a Non-Status Indian is not registered as an Indian under the Indian Act. This may be because his or her ancestors were never registered or because he or she lost Indian status under former provisions of the Indian Act. A Treaty Indian is a Status Indian who belongs to a First Nation that signed a treaty with the Crown.

How many Aboriginal people live on reserves?
About 60 percent of the Aboriginal people in Canada are Status Indians and more than half of all Status Indians live on 2370 reserves. Thus about 30 percent of Aboriginal people live on reserves.

How many Aboriginal people live in urban areas?
About 45 percent (320 000) of self-identified Aboriginal people live in cities according to the *Report of the Royal Commission on Aboriginal Peoples* (1996).

—

Based on information from the Web site of Indian and Northern Affairs Canada (http://www.ainc-inac.gc.ca) and *Highlights from the Report of the Royal Commission on Aboriginal Peoples: People to People, Nation to Nation* (1996) (http://www.ainc-inac.gc.ca/ch/rcap/rpt/).

Weblinks

THE FIRST PERSPECTIVE, NEWS OF INDIGENOUS PEOPLES OF CANADA
www.firstperspective.ca

WINDSPEAKER, CANADA'S NATIONAL ABORIGINAL NEWS SOURCE
www.ammsa.com/ windspeaker/

SASKATCHEWAN SAGE, THE ABORIGINAL NEWSPAPER OF SASKATCHEWAN
www.ammsa.com/sage/index. htm

Second, to help children develop as citizens of Aboriginal nations, with the knowledge of their languages and traditions necessary for cultural continuity.

"The source of traditional knowledge and teaching is dying with the Elders … Language retention is critical to the ongoing existence of the distinct cultures of Aboriginal peoples" (Western Canadian Protocol for Collaboration in Basic

TIMELINE HISTORY OF ABORIGINAL PEOPLES IN CANADA

Pre-contact
- Aboriginal nations with distinct cultures and languages in all areas of Canada.

1400s
- European settlement in North America begins.

1763
- Royal Proclamation of 1763 proclaims Aboriginal peoples as "nations or tribes" and acknowledges that they possess traditional territories until "ceded to or purchased by" the Crown. Recognized in section 25 of Constitution Act of 1982; still has force of law in Canada.

1849
- Removal of Aboriginal children from home and family for education and "civilization" begins with opening of first residential school in Alderville, Ontario.

1867
- The British North America Act creates the Dominion of Canada. Confederation, a new partnership between English and French colonists to manage lands and resources, is negotiated without reference to Aboriginal nations. Macdonald announces his government's goal to "do away with the tribal system, and assimilate the Indian people in all respects."

1876
- Indian Act is created and consolidates all previous Indian legislation; defines Indian status and superintendent general is given administrative powers over many aspects of Indian life.

1884
- Potlatch ceremony central to cultures of west coast Aboriginal nations is outlawed. Participation is a criminal offence. Law is rescinded in 1951.

1885
- Sundance ceremony central to cultures of prairie Aboriginal nations is outlawed. Participation is a criminal offence. Law is rescinded in 1951.

- Department of Indian Affairs institutes a pass system for entering and leaving reserves.

1906
- Delegations from several Aboriginal nations in British Columbia travel to London, England, about land rights.

1927
- Joint parliamentary committee in Ottawa finds that land claims have no legal bases. Committee recommends prohibition on raising money for land claims.

1951
- Indian Act is amended and laws prohibiting potlatch, sundance, and land claims activities are repealed.

1960
- Aboriginal people receive right to vote in federal elections.

- Phasing out of Indian residential schools begins.

1969
- Ottawa introduces "White Paper" that seeks to abolish certain "privileges" of Aboriginal people by abolishing the Indian Act and federal obligations to Aboriginal people.

1974
- Federal government starts negotiations with Nisga'a peoples.

1982
- New Canadian Constitution guarantees Aboriginal and treaty rights.

1985
- Bill C-31 is enacted by parliament, restoring status and band membership to native women, lost under section 12(1)(b) of the Indian Act. The bill also restores status to their children.

- Bands gain control over membership.

1994
- Landmark Nisga'a Agreement in Principle is initialled and signed by representatives of the Nisga'a Tribal Council and the federal and B.C. governments.

1996
- Report of the Royal Commission on Aboriginal Peoples released.

1998
- Statement of apology from the federal government for its treatment of Aboriginal peoples, based on the recommendations of the Royal Commission on Aboriginal Peoples.

Education, 1996, p. 1). Of the approximately 50 Aboriginal languages spoken at the time of contact, three are extinct and most others are endangered (Dickason, 1992). Only 15 **Aboriginal languages** are in "vigorous use" (Grimes, 1996–1999, http://www.sil.org/ethnologue/). Of 51 778 Aboriginal people surveyed in southern Ontario, 1601 (3.09 percent) spoke an Aboriginal language, and 90 percent of those individuals were over 40 years of age (Sweetgrass First Nations Language Council, 1995, http://woodland-centre.on.ca/Sgpage.html).

Working with the Community

Both the Assembly of First Nations (http://afn.ca/) and the Report (1996) emphasize that First Nations must assume responsibility for reserve schools. However, almost 70 percent of Aboriginal children attend neighbourhood schools, not reserve schools. Thus neighbourhood schools face challenges in developing community-based programming with Aboriginal parents and communities. The experiences of those engaged in this process suggest that educators must be respectful listeners. Tracy Friedel (1998) of the University of Alberta studied a parents' council in which Aboriginal parents took an active role. She recommends the participation of Aboriginal community organizations as well as individuals. Others also highlight the role of Aboriginal communities.

The University of Northern British Columbia (UNBC) has an institutional mandate to partner with both rural and urban Aboriginal communities. Evans, McDonald, and Nyce (1998) recommend mutual autonomy, a respectful approach, and inclusion of Aboriginal individuals and communities. They describe the three parts of the UNBC approach:

- A culturally relevant education and opportunities for students to learn directly from Aboriginal people, including teaching in Aboriginal communities.

- Aboriginal studies infused throughout the curricula for all students.

- Direct support to Aboriginal students, and a sense of community through the First Nations Centre.

- The UNBC approach reflects other recent developments in Aboriginal education.

Strategies and Approaches: Putting Community at the Heart

Much has been written about Aboriginal education and the importance of knowing about individual First Nations. It is also generally true that Aboriginal peoples have a holistic perspective and view education, culture, and language as being intimately related (e.g., Calliou, 1995; Hampton, 1995). Recent curriculum documents provide guidance for strengthening education, culture, and language simultaneously while focusing on community. The next sections elaborate on the three strategies apparent in the UNBC experience.

CULTURALLY RELEVANT CURRICULUM AND OPPORTUNITIES TO LEARN DIRECTLY FROM ABORIGINAL PEOPLE

Many who teach Aboriginal students neither are of Aboriginal heritage nor are knowledgeable about Aboriginal cultures and have to learn to develop **culturally**

Further Reading

About the maintenance and renewal of Aboriginal languages: Assemby of First Nations (1990). *Towards linguistic justice for First Nations.* Ottawa: Assembly of First Nations, Education Secretariat.

K. Freeman, A. Stairs, & E. Corbiere (1995). Ojibwe, Mohawk, and Inuktitut alive and well? *Bilingual Research Journal, 19*(1), 39–71.

L. McAlpine & D. Herodier (1994). Schooling as a vehicle for Aboriginal language maintenance. *Canadian Journal of Education, 19*, 128–42.

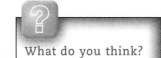

What do you think?

Preview some of the nine videotapes in the series *First Nations: The Circle Unbroken* (1993, 1998). Do they help you understand the perspectives of Aboriginal peoples? If you are Aboriginal, do these videotapes represent your perspective?

Put Into Practice

Develop an annotated bib-liography of references for teaching and learning materials on Aboriginal education. To begin, con-sult: J. Van Etten (1996). *Resource reading list: An annotated bibliography of recommended works by and about Native peoples.* Toronto: Canadian Alliance in Solidarity with Native Peoples.

Inuit: People Under the Great Bear (1998). Interactive CD-ROM by the Canadian Museum of Civilization.

Totem Poles: Myths, Magic, and Monumental Art on the Pacific Northwest Coast. (1996). Interactive CD-ROM by the Canadian Museum of Civilization.

Further Reading

F. BooksPlain (1989). *Eagle feather: An honour.* Winnipeg: Pemmican Publications. A story of an Ojibwe boy. Primary grades.

Sheila Thompson (1991). *Cheryl Bibalhats/Cheryl's Potlatch.* Vanderhoof, BC: Yinka Dene Language Institute. Carrier and English, story of a potlatch. Primary grades.

P. Monture-Angus (1995). *Thunder in My Soul: A Mohawk Woman Speaks.* Halifax: Fernwood Press. Autobiography. Grades 10–12.

relevant curriculum. Ann Pohl (1997), a non-Aboriginal, advises teachers like her to become informed about the local Aboriginal community through reading and by talking with Aboriginal people. A Friendship Centre or Band Office can help you contact chiefs, elders, and tribal or band councils. First, focus on the First Nation on whose traditional territory your school is located. "It is a respectful protocol, when working with Aboriginal people, to acknowledge the traditional territory on which you are living and working" (*Shared Learnings*, 1998, p. 17). After learning about local Aboriginal culture, focus on the territories and cultures from which your students and their families originate.

Carol Butler (2000), a teacher in eastern Ontario, describes the process of col-laborating with local Aboriginal leaders to develop and teach an arts-based unit on Aboriginal peoples. Mohawk elders, artists, storytellers, and dancers taught in the unit, *Cultural Awareness Through the Arts* (Butler & Swain, 1996). (Aboriginal pro-tocol also suggests that you ask permission before telling another culture's sacred tales; see Benton-Benai, 1988.)

Teaching materials such as the videotape series *First Nations: The Circle Unbroken* (Bob et al., 1993; Williams et al., 1998), books (e.g., Reed, 1999) and Web sites (e.g., www.innu.ca) will help you to bring Aboriginal voices into the classroom. Angela Ward (1996) of the University of Saskatchewan describes an Aboriginal teacher learning the stories and cultures of many First Nations to help the Aboriginal children in her classroom feel proud of their heritages and feel a con-nection to her teaching. There were posters to celebrate traditional values (respect yourself, your elders, and the land), children's illustrations of legends, and many books with a connection to Aboriginal life.

"Non-Native teachers who are the most successful [teaching Aboriginal stu-dents] are those who are continually learning, who understand and accept Native ways, and who can then transmit values, beliefs, and behavioral norms which are consistent with those of the community" (Gilliland, 1995, p. 8). In this process, question your taken-for-granted assumptions; begin with the strategies of critical analysis, adapted from the guide for *First Nations: The Circle Unbroken* (Williams et al., 1998, p. 8):

- Ask how you know what you know.

- Search for the biases in your socialization and in what you have been told about Aboriginal peoples.

- Consider the competing interests and powers that might have influenced your learning.

- Hunt your assumptions—they may be buried deeply under your positions; question them.

- Ask whose interests are served by what you have learned about Aboriginal peoples.

- Identify social and political problems; look for systemic sources of these problems.

You can show respect by adopting teaching approaches consistent with tradi-tional, Aboriginal, experiential learning. Arlene Stairs (1991) of Queen's University provides a poignant description of Aboriginal children learning to sew garments by watching. This suggests that replacing the verbal with the visual is a good place to begin. **Experiential learning** includes field trips, role-playing, designing, and making. Oral presentations reflect the oral tradition of Aboriginal cultures. Do not assume that Aboriginal students are knowledgeable about the traditions of their people. Aboriginal students in Butler's (2000) class appreciated learning directly from **Aboriginal elders** and artists, and some reported that the experience made them proud to be Mohawk. Table 5.1 presents strategies for Aboriginal education.

INFUSION OF ABORIGINAL STUDIES THROUGHOUT THE CURRICULUM FOR ALL

The second approach overlaps with and strengthens the first. Learning about Aboriginal cultures, developing respectful teaching, and involving the local Aboriginal community will ensure **infusion** of Aboriginal studies throughout the curriculum for all students. For the relations between Aboriginals and non-Aboriginals to change in Canada, all of us must become more aware of our shared history. Resources have been developed recently to guide schools in this process:

- *Planning Guide and Framework for the Development of Aboriginal Learning Resources* (B.C. Ministry of Education, 1999) (http://www.bced.gov.bc.ca/abed/planguide/toc.htm).

What do you think?

Why is it important for teachers to "hunt their assumptions" and cultural stereotypes? Discuss with your peers what makes these undertakings so challenging. Write an action plan for yourself to work toward these professional goals.

Table 5.1

STRATEGIES FOR ABORIGINAL EDUCATION

Strategy	Examples
Break down stereotypes	Start with the present; provide examples of Aboriginal Web sites, musicians, artists, professionals, urban and northern dwellers (*Shared Learnings*, 1998).
Engage students in Aboriginal culture through the arts	Invite storytellers, singers, dancers, painters, weavers, and other artists from the Aboriginal community to collaborate (Butler, 2000).
Help students to understand Aboriginal perspectives	Provide readings, etc., at the students' developmental level: fiction, reports, films from an Aboriginal point of view (Reed, 1999).
	Invite speakers who are comfortable telling their stories and providing their perspectives (*Shared Learnings*, 1998).
Use Aboriginal communication and participant structures	The talking circle, where the right to speak is indicated by passing a concrete object such as a feather (Ward, 1996).
Explicitly discuss Aboriginal values	Teach environmental education through an Aboriginal perspective, "caring for the earth" (Caduto & Bruchac, 1988; Pohl, 1997).
Help students to think critically about complex issues such as racism, cultural identity	Deal with sensitive issues and controversial topics in a caring and proactive way (*Shared Learnings*, 1998).
	Use video series like *First Nations: The Circle Unbroken* to teach about current issues (Williams & Marcuse, 1998).

- *Shared Learnings: Integrating B.C. Aboriginal Content, K–10* (B.C. Ministry of Education, 1998) (http://www.bced.gov.bc.ca/abed/shared.htm).
- Coalition for the Advancement of Aboriginal Studies (http://edu.yorku.ca/ caas).

There are also teaching materials for infusing Aboriginal studies throughout the curriculum at all levels. Indian and Northern Affairs Canada (1999, 2000a, 2000b) publishes *The Learning Circle* in three volumes (activities for ages 4 to 7, 8 to 11, and 12 to 14). For example, Unit 6 in the volume for students ages 8 to 11 is titled "First Nations and the Environment." The two objectives are to learn how First Nations viewed their responsibilities to the land and to explore how students' behaviour and actions affect the environment. The activities range from writing poetry through planning sustainable development in an expanding community. Each is debriefed to communicate First Nations' perspectives as the Earth's stewards. *Shared Learnings* (http://www.bced.gov.bc.ca/abed/shared.htmz) is also made up of activities to integrate Aboriginal content into K–10 curricula. The document for grades 8 to 10 includes activities in 15 subject areas from business education to visual arts. One activity is titled "Using the Internet to Learn about Aboriginal Peoples." It challenges secondary students to visit Web sites to learn about traditional stories, legends, and artwork and to answer questions about Aboriginal people in modern society.

DIRECT SUPPORT TO ABORIGINAL STUDENTS

The third approach, focused on providing direct services to Aboriginal students, should include much more than the remedial strategies used in the past. Providing opportunities to learn or strengthen **heritage languages** will be vital, as will a sense of community. You can view the *Common Curriculum Framework for Aboriginal Language and Culture Programs, Kindergarten to Grade 12* (Western Canada Protocol for Collaboration in Basic Education, 2000) at http://www.wcp.ca/languages/ abor.pdf.

These are school-based approaches that demand that we be knowledgeable about, sensitive to, and respectful of the cultures of individual Aboriginal students. Each of us can do this by learning about our students and their heritages—from them, their parents, and the community.

At UNBC, a **sense of community** was fostered through the First Nations Centre. Similar to a Friendship Centre, it provides a place where Aboriginal is the norm, not a minority. Counselling, tutoring, and socializing can be provided in such a context. In an elementary classroom, one could create a place where Aboriginal symbols and ways are dominant, perhaps a "circle" for reflection and quiet talk. Secondary schools with Aboriginal counsellors can create a First Nations Centre. *Aboriginal Education: Counselling of First Nations Students* (http://www.bced.gov.bc.ca/abed/reports/ welcome.htm) gives advice on providing direct services, especially counselling, to Aboriginal students. Students who find their culture accepted and valued seek safe places to talk and learn through counselling and tutoring.

Teaching Students from Culturally Diverse Backgrounds

Canadian classrooms have been increasing in racial, cultural, and linguistic diversity, and this trend is expected to continue (Canadian Council on Social Development, 1998). The reasons that students from **culturally diverse backgrounds** encounter difficulties in school are complex. These students often experience discrimination in society and lack role models because most teachers are from the majority Anglo-European culture. Societal expectations and realities for these students are often contradictory. Although they are told to aim high, low teacher expectations can influence their effort and participation. Schools may use discriminatory assessment practices and textbooks that promote stereotypes and omit culturally important information. This section describes cultural awareness, high teacher expectations, culturally relevant curriculum, cooperative learning, and teachers as role models.

Being Culturally Aware and Questioning Assumptions

Understanding students who are members of diverse groups involves us in recognizing the nature of their experiences in Canada. In a book with the poignant title *...But Where Are You Really From?* Hazelle Palmer (1997) describes how this question "keeps us forever foreign, forever immigrants to Canada" (p. vi). Sometimes teachers' cultural insensitivity can contribute to miscommunication, distrust, and negative school experiences. Keren Brethwaite (1996) writes about a teacher who had not heard a grade 5 girl from the Caribbean read in class. She assessed the student as unable to read and told the mother about her concerns at a parent–teacher conference. The mother protested that the girl read fluently at home. "So she brought a Bible to the school, and to the amazement of the teacher, the student read from it fluently. The teacher later recalled that she learned a very important lesson ... that parent and teacher often see students from different perspectives" (p. 109). Because the student had not shown her reading ability at school, the teacher assumed she could not read—a powerful reminder of the need for **cultural awareness**.

The prospect of learning about many cultures can be intimidating. However, we are responsible for understanding the characteristics students might have because of their backgrounds. For example, some students don't ask questions of the teacher, an authority figure, and some students don't participate in the classroom until they feel very comfortable. A teacher who came to Canada from Hong Kong when she was a child describes why she rarely answered questions in class: "We were constantly being asked for our opinion and I was never taught [to give my opinion] ... and I would always fear that question" (Lam, 1996, p. 33). If you understand this reticence in a student, you can make a special effort to initiate conversation with her, to make her feel comfortable.

All students from a similar cultural background will not have similar characteristics. Joyce Barakett (1986) of Concordia University interviewed and observed teachers and students in an inner-city school in Montreal. She reported that, when interviewed, teachers appeared "to call upon cultural differences" (p. 98); for example, they reported that Yugoslavian children "posed problems of control," and Greek children were "generally more motivated" (p. 99). When Barakett probed more deeply, she observed that teachers assembled extensive information with the help of speech therapists, volunteers, and specialized services to make informed, culturally aware decisions about individuals. We need to be aware of the cultural backgrounds of our students while still regarding them as individuals.

High Expectations and Respectful Treatment

What does it feel like to be a student from a visible minority? In interviews, Black youth told George Dei (1996) of the University of Toronto about three main perceptions of their school experiences. These three perceptions are also reported in other Canadian research: differential treatment by race, inadequate curriculum and teaching approaches, and absence of minority teachers. Students described feeling that teachers had low expectations, and some described racist incidents: "... I mean the way they treat you the way they talk to you it's just different than how they talk to white students" (p. 49). An Asian teacher described a racist experience when she was a student with a teacher who assumed from her appearance that she could not speak English (Lam, 1996, p. 22). Patrick Solomon (1992) of York University found that dominant-group teachers reported differential expectations for students from different racial backgrounds. Such expectations can influence curriculum, teaching approaches, and student–teacher relations.

If we teach to low expectations and students are unchallenged, they are unlikely to learn. Enid Lee (1985) of Toronto describes how students sometimes accept these limited visions of themselves, perform accordingly, and describe themselves as incapable. Students from some racial backgrounds are more likely to be streamed into less-challenging courses (Lewis, 1992) or into particular subject areas, but denied opportunities to develop in other important areas. In an articulate letter to his teachers, Kai James suggests: "Like all other students, Black students come to school with expectations that they will do well," but teachers believe "... we are more likely to succeed in sports than in academics" (1996, p. 303). Kai asks to be taken seriously as a student and asks for teachers who "will allow us to practice our culture without being ridiculed" (p. 304). Figure 5.3 includes a checklist for teachers in culturally diverse classrooms.

Culturally Relevant Curriculum

Minority students in Dei's (1996) interviews expressed concerns about not seeing themselves portrayed in Canadian history or literature. Nancy Hoo Kong (1996) also wrote about "... the history curriculum that rendered my racial group invisible" (p. 59). Black History Month (February) has offered schools an opportunity to highlight the accomplishments, contributions, and cultures of Black Canadians. In some Canadian schools, May has become South Asian History Month; but what about all the cultures that don't have a special month? This kind of band-aid measure is not enough (Coelho, 1998; Prince, 1996). Kai James suggested in his letter, "Our curriculum breeds stereotypes and does not address the issues that affect our

Further Reading

About multiculturalism and science teaching: E. Krugly-Smolska (1996). Scientific culture, multiculturalism and the science classroom. *Science and Education, 5*(1), 21–29.

E. Krugly-Smolska (1994). An examination of some difficulties in integrating Western science into societies with an indigenous scientific tradition. *Interchange, 25*(4), 325–34.

R.H. Barba (1998). *Science in the multicultural classroom.* Toronto: Allyn and Bacon.

Figure 5.3

CHECKLIST FOR TEACHERS IN CLASSES WITH HIGH DIVERSITY

- Can every student see himself or herself in the posters and adornments on my classroom walls?

- Do I have the autonomy to incorporate my students' cultures into the learning environment?

- Have I learned enough about my students' cultures to accommodate cultural diversity and ensure that my teaching is meaningful for my students?

- Do I know how prepared my students are for the topics that I teach?

- Do I practice antiracist education?

- Do I respond quickly and firmly when I see or hear racist behaviour in the school?

- Have I come to understand my own stereotypes that might interfere with my teaching equitably in a culturally diverse school?

- Am I aware of the language proficiencies and language needs of ESL students?

- Have I examined my topics, materials, and teaching methods for bias?

- Have I established legitimate standards for classroom work, but also made special efforts to ensure that all students reach these standards?

- Have I provided means by which students can relate their lives and issues to classroom learning?

Source: N.L. Hutchinson (1999). *Teaching Exceptional Children and Adolescents: A Canadian Casebook*, p. 104. Toronto: Allyn and Bacon Canada. Reprinted with permission of Pearson Education Canada, Inc.

lives every day." He continued, "What we need is a curriculum that all students can relate to and that will motivate us to be the best we can be by introducing us to people like us" (1996, p. 302).

Strategically applying cultural resources in your classroom curriculum is appropriate whether you teach elementary students or specialize in secondary science and whether you teach predominantly one social group or many distinct social groups of students. All students need to appreciate the role in history of the groups that make up our diverse country. Change of this magnitude calls for inclusive provincial curricula in addition to teachers making the classroom curriculum culturally diverse.

Cultural relevance may seem obvious in some subjects, such as social studies and literature. Exemplary curricula in social studies include *Coming to Gum San: The Story of Chinese Canadians* by Shehla Burney (1995) of Queen's University. For language arts, consider books like *Lights for Gita* (Gilmore, 1994), a story about Divali, the Hindu festival of lights. Continual underrepresentation of some cultural groups in science and mathematics, both in schools and in careers, suggests that culturally relevant curricula are just as necessary in these subject areas.

Introducing curricula that contain representations of the cultural backgrounds of your students requires sensitivity. Andrew Allen (1996) introduced picture books with multicultural characters into his grade 2 classroom in Toronto—with students whose families had immigrated from the Caribbean, East Africa, and South and East Asia. When he used books with bright, colourful illustrations of children engaging in familiar activities, the children's responses were positive. When he used books with pictures that the children thought showed them "with exaggerated features," looking "unhappy," or in unfamiliar scenes, they "acted out" (pp. 162–63). Allen recommends that teachers:

- involve students of every age in selecting and critiquing books for the classroom
- teach students of every age to detect bias in reading materials
- examine their own biases
- choose materials that show familiar scenes and people
- obtain a balance between materials that provide cultural information and those that entertain
- be attentive to students' reactions

Using Cooperative and Collaborative Learning

In *Teaching to Diversity*, Mary Meyers (1993) of North York recommends using cooperative learning so that all students develop social, group, and language skills. Research demonstrates that cooperative learning improves student attitudes and behaviours toward diversity and boosts self-esteem in elementary and secondary classrooms (Kagan, 1985; Aronson et al., 1978). The principles of **cooperative learning** are:

- tasks are structured so no one can complete the learning task alone
- positive interdependence is fostered and developed
- students work in different teams
- students learn both language and social skills necessary for cooperation while learning content

Begin with team-building activities such as brainstorming in triads, interviews in pairs, or assembly-line craft projects (or writing activities) in which each person does one step (or writes one sentence) and passes the project along to the next person. Figure 5.4 provides step-by-step instructions for a number of cooperative learning activities.

Teachers as Role Models

Many have argued that teachers who are members of visible minorities serve as **role models** for students of diverse cultures (e.g., Thiessen et al., 1996). Patrick Solomon (1996) suggests that dominant-group students also benefit from experience with teachers of colour because it helps to modify their stereotypes about minorities. Stephen Lewis (1992, p. 20) asked the same question that high-school students asked of George Dei (1996): "Where are the visible minority teachers?"

Put Into Practice

Develop lesson plans to introduce your students to cooperative activities on the first day. See the following books: P.J. Vermette (1998). *Making cooperative learning work: Student teams in K–12 classrooms.* Upper Saddle River, NJ: Allyn and Bacon.

E. Cohen & R. Lotan (1997). *Working for equity in heterogeneous classrooms.* New York: Teachers College Press.

Figure 5.4

COOPERATIVE LEARNING STRUCTURES

Brainstorming
Can be done in any subject
- to find a solution to school litter, or a story character's dilemma;
- to suggest cause-and-effect relationships (if trees grew dollars instead of leaves...);
- to decide on a class trip or fundraising project.

Think-Pair-Share
Everybody gets a say.
- The teacher asks a question of the whole group.
- Everybody has time to think of his/her own answer.
- Students then pair up and discuss their answers.
- After a signal for silence, students have a chance to share their ideas with the whole group.

Numbered Heads
Speak on behalf of the team.
- Students number themselves from one to four.
- The teacher then asks a question for discussion, e.g., "What do you think...?" or "Why would...?" Try to frame questions that elicit discussion about current studies.
- Students talk together in their groups to contribute to a team answer.
- After the silent signal is given, the teacher calls out a number. Only those students designated by that number raise their hands to respond.

Listening Triads
Everybody is a specialist.
- In groups of three, students take on the roles of talker, questioner, or recorder.
- The talker explains or comments on a brief task.
- The questioner prompts and clarifies.
- The recorder takes notes and reports for the group.
- Next time, the students change roles.

Jigsaw (also called expert groups)
Jigsaw is a four-step structure:
Step 1   Students form a "home" group.
Step 2   Each student is assigned a number, colour, or letter. The topic overview is presented.
Step 3   Students now move to form an "expert group" with other students who have same number or colour, etc. Each "expert group" works on one part of the larger topic.
Step 4   When time is up, the experts regroup with their original home groups. Each expert now teaches the skills or content learned in his/her subtopic to the home group.
- All members contribute something to the topic, so everybody is an expert.
- Team members depend on one another to complete the overall task.
- Each team member must learn skills or content from the others.
- Evaluation depends on both an individual mark and a team effort mark.

Source: Adapted from M. Meyers (1993). *Teaching to Diversity*. Toronto: Irwin Publishing. Reprinted by permission of Stoddart Publishing Co. Limited.

Teachers can serve as role models for students from minority cultures.

Jean-Brenda, interviewed by Dei, said: "I've never had a black teacher and I've been able to make it. But I think it would really help ... having someone who's Black up there [and] can share some of my experiences" (p. 52). Few minority Canadians choose teaching as a career. June Beynon and Kelleen Toohey (1995) of Simon Fraser University interviewed university students of Chinese and Punjabi-Sikh heritage. They found that the reasons given for not entering the teaching profession included parental influence, lack of proficiency in English, and discrimination. In a book subtitled *The Lives and Careers of Racial Minority Immigrant Teachers* (Thiessen, Bascia, & Goodson, 1996), a teacher of Chinese heritage describes her ease in communicating with Chinese parents. "Chinese parents tend to tell me at the outset that their children are very 'naughty' and express their gratitude towards me for dealing with their naughty children. I, in turn, disagree with them, easing their minds, while at the same time taking advantage of this opening to be honest with them." She continues, "This cultural practice is a required ritual for a successful interview between Chinese parents and their child's teacher" (p. 72).

Multicultural and Anti-Racist Education

What do you think?

Are anti-racist education and multicultural education different in substance or only in degree? Discuss with your peers.

Multicultural education involves creating a classroom in which students' cultures are acknowledged and valued. Many resources are available from teachers' federations and other groups (e.g., *Multicultural Education: A Place to Start* by Keith McLeod and Eva Krugly-Smolska, 1997). Canadian educators are being encouraged to move beyond multicultural education to anti-racist education (e.g., Allingham, 1992; Dei, 1994; Lee, 1985). **Anti-racist education** assumes that existing policies and practices are racist in their impact if not in their intent. It provides "teachers and students with the knowledge and skills to examine racism critically in order to understand how it originates and to identify and challenge it" (Ontario Ministry of Education and Training, 1993, p. 42). This approach remains controversial.

Teaching ESL Students

Some students from diverse cultures also speak **English as their second language (ESL)**. Some are born in Canada to parents who speak limited English and others arrive in Canada as refugees or immigrants. About 200 000 immigrants arrive in Canada each year, over 80 percent have a first language other than English, and half of those have no English proficiency (Bosetti & Watt, 1995). In spring of 1999, the percentage of grade 3 students enrolled in English Second Language (ESL) programs in district school boards in Ontario was 7 percent in Ottawa-Carleton, 11 percent in Toronto, and 17 percent in Peel (Education Quality and Accountability Office, http://eqaoweb.eqao.com). Canadian schools report that ESL students take between four and six years to match the achievement levels of first-language English students on achievement tests (Cummins, 1981; Klesmer, 1994).

Research shows that ESL students experience many learning difficulties in school. On the Education Quality and Accountability Office (EQAO) of Ontario 1999 grade 3 tests for the three district school boards of Ottawa-Carleton, Toronto, and Peel, the average percentage of students achieving at grade level or better (levels 3 and 4) was (http://eqaoweb.eqao.com):

- Reading: 24 percent of ESL students; 53 percent of non-ESL students
- Writing: 41 percent of ESL students; 60 percent of non-ESL students
- Mathematics: 43 percent of ESL students; 65 percent of non-ESL students

A Calgary study found that 74 percent of the ESL students in one secondary school dropped out, while the dropout rate for all Canadian students is reported to range between 18 percent (Gidney, 1999) and 30 percent (Human Resources and Labour Canada, 1993).

Teaching Students Who Are Immigrants and Refugees

On arrival in a new country, **immigrants** begin a period of adjustment thought to consist of four stages, although again we must be careful not to overgeneralize. These stages are (1) arrival and first impressions; (2) culture shock; (3) recovery and optimism; and (4) acculturation (Kim, 1988). Joining a welcoming classroom may help students feel comfortable at school before they feel comfortable in other contexts; thus our actions can make a difference. Many factors contribute to adjustment and acculturation. These include whether the family immigrated by choice, family separation, emotional preparation, and environmental factors such as the climate and size of the community (Coelho, 1998). Some family characteristics such as English proficiency, socioeconomic status, and cultural conflict between home and school are also influential.

Those who arrive as **refugees** have often lived through traumatic experiences that include war, violence, oppression, and flight. Mental health researchers have described typical early stages in the adjustment of refugees to life in a new country. These include (1) relief to be alive; (2) guilt about surviving when others did not; (3) recognition they may not be able to return home; and (4) stress associated with waiting for their refugee claims to be heard (Canadian Task Force on Mental Health Issues Affecting Immigrants and Refugees, 1988).

Canadian teachers describe refugee students as often withdrawn, restless, inattentive, and fearful of noises. Their drawings may depict war, violence, bombs, guns, and soldiers (Coelho, 1998). Some show symptoms of post-traumatic stress disorder, including nightmares, disturbed sleep, crying, and depression (Carter & Mok, 1992). In a study of refugee students in Toronto, Yau (1995) found that many were still afraid of the government they had fled, and suspected that someone was spying on them. Yau reported students who could not focus on their schoolwork due to a sibling dying in the home country or to impending return to the home country. Another Canadian study concluded that "the impact of incarceration in a [refugee] camp is dehumanizing" (Kaprielian-Churchill & Churchill, 1994, p. 11). These students may need psychological support beyond a sensitive and aware teacher, but most immigrant families are resilient and successful in their new lives.

Welcoming Students

Establish a procedure for welcoming ESL students and parents to your classroom. Elementary schools often involve the principal and ESL teacher, while secondary schools may include a counsellor. Whenever possible, an ESL student should be placed in a class where another student speaks the same first language. Many schools hold an informal interview with the student, parents, and an interpreter in the home language (Coelho, 1998). If you sense reluctance to answer particular questions, delay these questions until a later interview. Provide the family with information in a language that they can understand. Meyers suggests: "School information (hours, availability of dental care and special days, etc.) and community information (about adult ESL classes, daycare facilities, ethnic associations, and the Red Cross telephone number) is given to the family" (1993, p. 84). Teachers can collect relevant information about the student's linguistic and academic background through the interview and through assessment.

Teaching Strategies

Most ESL students are quiet, even silent, in their early days in your classroom. They are adjusting and may be figuring out how to fit in. Remain warm and accepting, even if they are silent for a few months. Observe how the student interacts with someone who understands his or her first language—a buddy in the class, an older or younger student, or a translator. When ESL students understand little of what you are teaching, you can feel unsure about how to begin. The following list highlights what to focus on in the early weeks:

- Make the student feel comfortable; use nonverbal communication to show warmth.
- Seat the student with a classmate who speaks the same language, if possible.
- Seat the student with classmates you know will be welcoming.
- Teach frequently used vocabulary first.
- Speak in short simple sentences.
- Stress the use of first-language skills.
- Use student translators in teaching content areas.
- If a large number of students speak the same second language, place them in pairs (later singly) into cooperative learning groups so they interact with English speakers.

Peer-Mediated Instruction

Research suggests that cooperative **peer-mediated strategies** promote high levels of language and academic learning and social interactions (e.g., Flanigan, 1991). Students of varied academic abilities and language-proficiency levels work together in pairs and small groups toward a common goal. In such groups, the success of one student depends on the help of others. Earlier in this chapter, many examples were given of cooperative learning strategies for teaching students from diverse cultures. A peer-mediated learning strategy is described in Focus on Research.

FOCUS ON | RESEARCH

Classwide Peer Tutoring (CWPT)

What Is CWPT?

CWPT involves the entire class in tutoring. Students are paired each week. ESL students are initially paired with students who speak their native language but have a higher level of English proficiency. Pairs are assigned to one of two teams that compete for the highest point total resulting from daily scheduled tutoring sessions. Students' roles are switched during the daily tutoring session, allowing each child to be both the tutor/teacher and the tutee/student. New content to be learned, teams, and tutoring pairs are changed on a weekly basis. Students are trained in the procedures necessary to act as tutors and tutees. In a given session, the students know their partner, the material to be covered, how to correct errors, how to award points for correct responses, and how to provide positive feedback. Teachers organize the academic content to be tutored into daily and weekly units and prepare materials to be used in CWPT. Teacher-prepared tests at the end of the week provide feedback to the students. Tutoring occurs simultaneously for all tutor–tutee pairs, involving the entire class at the same time. This leaves the teacher free to supervise and monitor students' tutoring sessions.

What Are the Basic Components?

- Weekly competing teams (heterogeneous grouping by cultural group, language, ability)
- Highly structured teaching procedure (content material, teams, pairing, error correction, system of rewards)
- Daily, contingent, individual tutee point earning and public posting of individual and team scores
- Direct practice of functional academic and language skills to mastery

How Do ESL Students Know What to Do?

Training of ESL students as tutors requires the teacher or a bilingual student to simply and clearly explain the procedure to them individually and, if possible, bilingually. At the beginning of each week, the new content should be introduced to them by the teacher or a bilingual student, individually or as a group, prior to the CWPT session. They should be encouraged to access knowledge and skills they have in their native language to assist them with the new academic content. In addition, the teacher should provide support by thinking aloud, using visual organizers or other aids to help students organize and relate information, and building on and clarifying the input of the students.

What Does the Research Say About CWPT?

CWPT was developed by researchers at the Juniper Gardens Children's Project, University of Kansas (Greenwood, Delquadri, & Carta, 1988). It has been successfully applied to passage reading, reading comprehension, mathematics, vocabulary development, spelling, social studies, and science instruction with culturally and linguistically diverse learners and with regular, special education, and low-achieving students. Studies have been conducted across grades K to 12. The most comprehensive study included more than 400 low-achieving minority and majority students enrolled in four schools across four years of implementation (grades 1–4) and a follow-up of these students in junior high and high schools. Results showed significantly greater gains in spelling, reading, and math for the CWPT students than for students in whole-class instruction. Furthermore, the CWPT students exceeded or approached national norms in all three academic domains, as measured by the Metropolitan Achievement Test (Greenwood, Delquadri, & Hall, 1989). Students and teachers consistently rated all CWPT components highly. Teachers have consistently reported higher levels of peer social interaction during the remainder of the school day and positive self-esteem outcomes as a result of CWPT.

The classroom procedures for CWPT are described in R.M. Gersten & R.T. Jimenez (1998). *Promoting/Learning for Culturally and Linguistically Diverse Students*. Scarborough, ON: ITP Nelson Canada. Also see Greenwood 1988, 1989 in the reference list.

Communicating High Expectations

You can communicate high expectations in many ways. Encourage group rehearsal before selecting individuals to respond to questions. Wait long enough for a response so students can ask peers for help with translation. Provide supportive feedback. Pay attention to and interact with all students. Group students heterogeneously for activities. Ensure that your expectations do not remain static and that students have to stretch a bit more on each new assignment. Never provide more assistance than students need.

Adapting Assessment

Cross-Reference
Chapter 8 focuses on adapting assessment to meet the needs of all students in your classroom.

Because language plays a large role in most means of assessment, this creates challenges for assessing ESL students equitably. Students may know what you have taught, but not be able to verbalize their understanding. You can observe them or conference one-to-one so you can use instructions such as "point to," "draw," and "find the page about." A peer may be able to translate, or a translator may be able to tell you the contents of an assignment written in the student's first language. Use performance-based assessment or portfolio assessment and provide models of what is expected. In the early days, you can implement a simple system of grades such as: = (meets expectations), + (exceeds expectations), and – (does not meet expectations). Ensure that the student understands your feedback about what was done well and poorly. Generally, ask students how they prefer to learn and ask an ESL teacher or consultant when you have questions.

Other Issues of Equity in the Classroom

Responding to Incidents in Your Classroom

Cross-Reference
Chapters 6 and 9 provide strategies for enhancing social relationships in the classroom.

In classrooms characterized by diversity, you may see incidents that could be described as racist, sexist, or bullying. When you are setting the class rules and procedures, be clear that such behaviours are unacceptable in your classroom. This means that when students fail to meet your expectations for respectful and equitable treatment, you must act. If you do not have effective procedures for deciding how to respond and for responding to such incidents, you will not have the safe community necessary for inclusive education. Figure 5.5 describes a problem-solving approach for responding to such incidents.

Proactive Teaching to Minimize Incidents in Your Classroom

It is important that you take actions from the first day that set the tone of community and that establish how students are to treat one another. Besides modelling respectful and equitable treatment, you will probably have to teach such ways of

FRAMEWORK FOR ANALYZING EQUITY INCIDENTS IN THE CLASSROOM

Ask yourself:

1. Is _____ part of what is happening here?
   (put in racism, sexism, etc.)

2. Who was present and/or involved in the situation?
   Who must be included in the intervention/response?
   (all who witnessed must see support and see that the actions were not condoned)

3. Who does this situation affect? How does it affect them?
   (support the victims; teach all who witnessed; punishment may be required)

4. Was the behaviour conscious or unconscious? Was malice involved?
   (intervention should address intent, carelessness, or both)

5. What can you achieve with an intervention?
   (teach students what is unacceptable, acceptable, and reasons)

6. What *actions* must be taken and *why*?
   (immediately support victim, address perpetrator; over time teach for prevention)

Equity education means tailoring teaching to challenge inequities and discrimination.

behaving and thinking. Students act differently in different situations depending on what is expected of them. That is why you may find a class to be cooperative and eager learners while another teacher may describe the same students as unmanageable. There are many effective proactive programs that will be discussed in Chapters 6 and 9. These include Tribes (Gibbs, 1990); Children as Peacemakers (Fine, Lacey, & Baer, 1995), which describes a program implemented in inner city Toronto; and Teaching Young Children in Violent Times (Levin, 1994). Many suggest that implementing cooperative learning (e.g., Vermette, 1998) is the most effective proactive approach for secondary classes (see Edwards, 2000; Hutchinson, 1996).

Issues of Gender Equity

INEQUITABLE TREATMENT OF MEN AND WOMEN

Sexual harassment is a problem throughout our society, but particularly so in schools (American Association of University Women, 1993; Larkin, 1994). Both males and females can be stereotyped and can experience sexual harassment. I often ask pre-service teachers to complete a questionnaire about sexual harassment. Almost as many males as females report that they have experienced sexual harassment in a school context. The researchers in a large study in Ontario concluded that:

Put Into Practice

Develop a classroom activity for your students after reading one of the following: J. Robertson, B. Andrews, S.A Cook, & T. Stanley (1998). *Words can change the world.* Toronto: OADE/OWD.

J. Wallace & H. Harper (1998). *Taking action: Reworking gender in school contexts.* Toronto: OADE/OWD. (Includes video)

The young women involved in this project experienced strong feelings of humiliation, fear, and suffering as a result of sexual harassment. The intensity of their anger, outrage, denial and pain was overwhelming. They came together as young women to examine their lives and express their helplessness regarding sexual harassment, and their anger that schools had done nothing to effectively prevent or penalize it (Ontario Secondary School Teacher's Federation, 1995, p. 3).

Sexual harassment includes put-downs and negative comments made about gender or sexual preference, sexist jokes, and calling someone gay or lesbian. Other examples of sexual harassment include inappropriate staring, bragging about sexual ability, demands for dates or sexual favours, questions or discussions about sexual activities, rating people on a scale, displaying sexually offensive pictures or graffiti, and intimidating hallway behaviour such as blocking a person's way. Students say they don't report incidents because most teachers never do anything about them. Ensure that you are a teacher who acts. Urge your school and school district to develop, display, and enforce anti-harassment policies.

Curriculum materials have tended to show men and women in stereotyped roles and occupations. You and your students can complete activities to collect data on the books you use in your classroom. These activities answer questions about the suitability of instructional materials and enable you to teach your students about gender equity issues. Figure 5.6 provides an example of such an activity.

Further Reading

On teaching gay and lesbian students: A. Lipkin (1999). *Understanding homosexuality, changing schools: A text for teachers, counselors and adminstrators.* Boulder, CO: Westview Press.

Students who are gay and lesbian are at risk for identity confusion, bullying, and suicide. They need teacher support and safe spaces.

INEQUITABLE TREATMENT OF GAY AND LESBIAN YOUTH

Gay and lesbian youth who are questioning and exploring their sexual identity are also targets of discrimination (Anderson, 1994). **Homophobia** takes the form of taunts, ridicule, and physical assaults. Seeing the way others are treated causes many gay and lesbian youth to hide their sexual orientation. This can cause feelings of alienation, depression, self-abuse, and confusion about sexual identity. These factors put them at greater risk for poor school performance, criminality, substance abuse, dropping out, and suicide. Misunderstanding and rejection by their families can lead to homelessness. Attempted suicide rates are three times higher for gay and lesbian students than for their heterosexual peers. Do not tolerate teasing, bullying, or harassment based on sexual orientation.

The rainbow is a symbol understood by gay and lesbian students to indicate support for them. Many school boards offer "Safe Spaces" programs that teach teachers how to communicate that their classrooms are safe spaces for gay and lesbian students and to ensure the safety of their classrooms. If your school district does not have such a program, you might talk with the youth officer in your police force to learn about com-

Figure 5.6

ASSESSING THE GENDER STEREOTYPES IN TEXTBOOKS

To be used to analyze school books that contain numerous illustrations

For *each book*, record the summaries below:

Title: _____

Chapter: _____

Number of women portrayed: _____

Number of men portrayed: _____

Number of boys portrayed: _____

Number of girls portrayed: _____

_____

Girls are represented doing: _____

_____

Boys are represented doing: _____

_____

Women are represented doing: _____

_____

Men are represented doing: _____

_____

Source: H. Beaudoin (1998). *Equality in Education: Student Manual.* Toronto: OADE/OWD, p. 41. (One of several publications developed through a Partners for Change Project of the Ontario Associate of Deans of Education, the Faculties of Education at Laurentian University, the University of Western Ontario, the University of Ottawa, and Ontario Women's Directorate.) Used by permission.

Weblinks

THE RAINBOW CLASSROOM NETWORK
http://www.dezines.com/rainbow

munity supports. See Figure 5.7 for ways you can support gay and lesbian students. Our goal is to remove the stigma so it is no longer a slight when students are called gay or lesbian.

Teaching Students Who Are at Risk Due to Poverty, Homelessness, and Abuse

Students are at risk for school failure for a number of reasons. In this section, the characteristics and needs of these students are described. Poverty, homelessness, and abuse are explored for their impact on learning and classroom participation.

Figure 5.7

SUPPORTING GAY AND LESBIAN STUDENTS

- Provide safe, nondiscriminatory environments in which all students are valued.

- Learn about the social, psychological, and educational needs of gay and lesbian youth.

- Don't assume heterosexuality. Use language that is broad, inclusive, and gender neutral.

- Provide all students with confidential access to materials that address their needs.

- Challenge homophobia, heterosexism, and stereotyping in school and society.

- Help students obtain appropriate services from agencies and professionals who are sensitive and trained to deal with gay, lesbian, and bisexual issues.

- Make it clear that language has power and that abusive language will not be tolerated.

- Offer a range of academic, extracurricular, and mentoring activities for all students.

- Examine the curriculum for bias against gay and lesbian issues and individuals.

- Discuss diversity in families and family structures.

- Enforce sexual harassment, anti-violence, and anti-discrimination policies in your school.

Source: Adapted from S.J. Salend (1998). *Effective mainstreaming: Creating inclusive classrooms*, Third edition. Toronto: Prentice Hall. Used by permission.

Teaching Students Who Live in Poverty

In Canada, **poverty** means insufficient access to the basic goods, services, and opportunities accepted as necessary for a decent standard of living (Ross & Roberts, 1999). Statistics Canada sets low-income cut-off (LICO) levels that vary according to the size of family and community. For a four-person household living in a city, the cut-off would be $34 226. For the same family living in a rural area, the cut-off would be $23 653 (Canadian Council on Social Development, 2000, http://www.ccsd.ca/briefs.html). The incomes of most low-income Canadians are substantially below the LICO levels.

Poverty is strongly associated with poor academic performance. In turn, students who perform poorly in school, many of whom will eventually drop out, will have difficulty changing their economic status and that of their children. In summarizing Canadian research, Hess (1991) wrote that "many [children of poverty] experience less motivation to learn, delayed cognitive development, lower achievement, less participation in extra-curricular activities, different types of teacher-

Weblinks

CANADIAN COUNCIL ON SOCIAL DEVELOPMENT
http://www.ccsd.ca

NATIONAL ANTI-POVERTY ORGANIZATION
http://www.napo-onap.ca/

student interactions, ... an increased risk of illiteracy and higher dropout rates" (p. 1).

The Canadian Council on Social Development (Ross, Scott, & Kelly, 1996) reported that one in five children lives in poverty. You are likely to be teaching the children of the poor at some time in your career. They are more likely than advantaged students to experience parental neglect, to witness violence, and to change schools and residences frequently. These disruptions in personal life can show up as behaviour problems at school. Poor children often come to school tired and stressed. They may lack nutritious meals, a safe place to play, a quiet place to do homework, or basic school supplies. They may lack warm clothes in winter and the footwear needed for gym class. Healthy snacks such as apples and granola bars (beware of allergies) and pencils and erasers can be kept in the classroom for children who need them. Some elementary schools collect winter clothing and teachers invite children to stay after school to choose mittens or a warm hat. Sometimes students may be preoccupied about their families' circumstances. Older students may be expected to work weekends and evenings to support the family or miss school to babysit younger siblings.

Children of poor families are less likely to participate in community sports. Regina has a hockey league that supplies equipment and registration to children who couldn't normally afford to play.

David Ross and Paul Roberts of the Canadian Council on Social Development reported on the relationships between family income and child well-being (1999). Poverty makes it more likely that children will be at risk for health problems, inattention, friends who are poor role models, low achievement in math and vocabulary, not participating in organized sports, and more likely that as adolescents they will drop out of school without employment. However, research by Genevieve Johnson (1997) of the University of Alberta and others (Scales, 1992) suggests that some students are resilient—they have risk factors but do not manifest risk outcomes. **Resilient students** tend to possess four attributes: social competence, problem-solving skills, autonomy, and a sense of purpose and future (Connell, Spencer, & Aber, 1994; Reed, McMillan, & McBee, 1995). Families, schools, and communities that protect at-risk children and adolescents tend to be caring and supportive, have positive expectations, and provide opportunities for participation (Phelan, Davidson, & Cao, 1992; Taylor & Reeves, 1993).

While it is not the ultimate solution to poverty, education has always been part of the solution, because good teaching raises achievement for all students, including those at risk due to poverty. Good teaching includes targeted interventions, high expectations, programs that enhance family–school teamwork, collaborative learning, and effective teams of community professionals as well as educators (Levin, 1994; McLaughlin & Vacha, 1993).

> **Further Reading**
>
> An analysis by J. Kirby, J. Parrila, & R. Parrila of the report by Statistics Canada, *Growing Up in Canada*, in the *Canadian Journal of Education* (1998).

At-Risk Students: Breakfast Club Eases Transition to High School

In British Columbia, Mission Secondary School has developed a "Breakfast Club" to help moderately at-risk students. The Breakfast Club is designed for younger students, usually in grade 8, who are having difficulty adjusting to secondary school. Students and parents who commit to the program have recognized a need to change their approach to schooling if they wish to avoid failure.

In the Breakfast Club program, small groups of grade 8 students meet three times per week for four weeks, with the aim of improving study skills and setting personal goals. The program operates from 7:00 to 7:45 a.m. To provide motivation, students are provided an opportunity to "job shadow" a potential employer for a day and promised a breakfast at a restaurant upon completion of the program.

The first eight students in the program were failing a total of 58 out of 64 courses when they enrolled. At the end of the year, the students failed only 18 courses.

Vice-principal Bill Dickson teaches the program. At 6:50 a.m. on Tuesday, Wednesday, and Thursday mornings the students gather in the main foyer and receive a can of fruit juice. The students and teacher then go to a classroom, armed with juice, student handbooks, and pens. Vic Hollister (from the community) often joins the group.

The students receive instruction on study skills, reading, spelling, math patterns, test taking, memory, and term papers. They keep notes in the back of the handbook and use the handbooks to set up their school day and to ensure that homework is completed.

Mr. Hollister informs the students of job-shadowing opportunities. Often students are released from regular classes for these opportunities. Mr. Hollister or an "employer" provides transportation to the work site. Each student spends an entire day shadowing a person who works at a job that interests the student. Job placements have occurred in horticulture, computer-assisted drafting, electrical engineering, water sprinkler manufacturing, policing, marine biology, medicine, computer programming, cartooning, secretarial work, and others. Dickson, Hollister, and "employers" stress the importance of using school to work toward personal goals.

Upon successful completion, Dickson and Hollister treat the students to a breakfast of their choice. Letters are sent to parents to acknowledge the students' and families' efforts. Students and parents are invited to an evening meeting to provide feedback on the program and help shape its future. Student performance is monitored for the remainder of the year.

Source: Adapted from W.W. Dickson (1993). Breakfast club eases transition to high school. *The Canadian School Executive, 12*(9), pp. 28–29.

Homelessness

Some children and adolescents in our schools are not only poor, but also **homeless**; the loss of the home is usually sudden, unexpected, and traumatic. The family is thrust away from its community, friends, and support system. The effects can be devastating (Rafferty, 1998). The Canadian Council on Social Development estimates that 1 percent of Canadians are homeless at some point over the course of a year, and more than 25 percent of Canada's homeless are children (http://www.napo-onap.ca/nf-child.htm). There is increasing concern that homeless children do not attend school regularly (Salend, 1998). They move from shelter to shelter and eventually some families move to the street. Obstacles to school attendance include health problems, hunger, transportation, and lack of school clothes and supplies. When homeless children are at school, you may see socialization and behavioural problems, language delays, and self-esteem problems.

Gracenin (1993) also noted that some homeless children show a behavioural pattern resembling that of abused children—they act out, are distrustful of others, and feel incompetent. Homeless children also confront stigmatization, insensitivity, and rejection by classmates and teachers.

Teachers can be a powerful force in the lives of homeless students, helping them both academically and emotionally. Be sensitive and accepting. When a student transfers into your class, communicate with the previous teacher and when a student transfers out, try to contact the next teacher. Refer students to counsellors and ADAPT teaching to help students keep up in spite of absences; academic achievement drops as a result of homelessness (Rubin et al., 1996). Help homeless students to make friends and do not tolerate bullying or victimization of vulnerable students.

Homeless adolescents have become a feature of life in Canada in the past two decades. Some, like April, described in *Education Today* (Arnott, 1998), live a **transient lifestyle**, moving from shelter to shelter. When April was interviewed, she lived in a women's shelter and was planning to return to her Hamilton high school. These youth live in unstable conditions without adult guidance, except that of a concerned teacher. Others live on the streets and are vulnerable to using and pushing drugs. Some return to secondary school only to leave before obtaining credits for their courses. They need encouragement, support, and ADAPTed teaching. Often if they can connect with one teacher and one other adolescent, they have enough support to persevere.

Teaching Students Who Have Experienced Abuse

Reports of **child abuse**, **neglect**, psychological harm, sexual abuse, and children observing violence have increased (National Clearinghouse on Family Violence, http://www.hc-sc.gc.ca/hppb/familyviolence/index.html). Contributing factors are thought to be unemployment, poverty, unwanted pregnancy, substance abuse, and history of abuse as a child. Being abused may lead to higher rates of sexual promiscuity, alcohol use, other risky behaviours, and impaired intellectual functioning. Figure 5.8 lists signs that may suggest a student is being abused. If you suspect child abuse or neglect, it is your responsibility to report your concerns to the child welfare agency in your community. When a child tells you about or discloses abuse, listen calmly. Tell the child that you believe him, that you will do your best to find help, and that you cannot keep this a secret because the law says you must report it. Report the disclosure to the child protection services immediately. Consider that there may be emotional and behavioural repercussions and such children may need the support and teaching adaptations usually provided for children with behavioural and emotional exceptionalities.

Put Into Practice

Develop a handout for your peers about another factor that puts students at risk, such as substance abuse: D. Hodson (1991). Substance abuse resource teachers. *OPSTF News, 5*(3), 22–23.

A. Mainous, C. Martin, M. Oler, E. Richardson, & A. Haney (1996). Substance use among adolescents: Fulfilling a need state. *Adolescence, 31,* 807–815.

Weblinks

CANADIAN CENTRE ON SUBSTANCE ABUSE
http://www.ccsa.ca

Figure 5.8

SIGNS OF CHILD ABUSE

Signs of Physical Abuse

- Bruises, welts, abrasions
- Burns
- Fractures and dislocations
- Delays in seeking medical attention

Signs of Neglect

- Attending school hungry or fatigued
- Poor hygiene and inappropriate dress
- Inadequate supervision
- Medical needs that go unattended
- Frequent absence from school

Signs of Sexual Abuse

- Problems in walking or sitting
- Bloody, stained, or ripped clothing
- Pain in or scratching of genital area
- Evidence of sexually transmitted diseases
- Pregnancy
- Painful discharges
- Frequent urinary infections
- Talking about bizarre, sophisticated, or unusual sexual acts
- Running away from home
- Engaging in seductive behaviours with others
- Fear of being touched by others
- Absent from school frequently
- Frequent self-injurious acts and suicide attempts

Developed after reading Health Canada (1995). *Child Abuse: Awareness Information for People in the Workplace.* Information is available from the National Clearinghouse on Family Violence, http://www.hc-sc.gc.ca/hppb/familyviolence/index.html.

Summary

This chapter has dealt with many aspects of teaching for diversity. Aboriginal education has become a greater priority in Canada since the *Report of the Royal Commission on Aboriginal Peoples* (1996). Because of issues like the preservation of almost-extinct languages and cultures, the issues are distinct from those in multicultural education. As well, students from diverse cultures and students with English as a second language require ADAPTed teaching. For all of these students, high expectations, cooperative learning, culturally relevant curricula, and sensitive teaching are appropriate. Other equity issues that arise in classrooms concern gender and students who are gay and lesbian. You can teach proactively to reduce the occurrence of inequitable incidents. We teach students who are at risk for a range of reasons, including poverty, homelessness, and abuse. However, many of these students are resilient and, with the support of a caring teacher and the friendship of a classmate, can overcome what appear to be impossible risks. We are challenged to create classrooms that respect diversity and foster learning for *all* students. ■

Key Terms

diversity (p. 142)

equity (p. 143)

Aboriginal cultures (p. 143)

Report of the Royal Commission on Aboriginal Peoples (p. 143)

Aboriginal languages (p. 147)

culturally relevant curriculum (p. 147)

experiential learning (p. 149)

Aboriginal elders (p. 149)

infusion (p. 149)

heritage languages (p. 150)

sense of community (p. 150)

culturally diverse backgrounds (p. 151)

cultural awareness (p. 151)

cultural relevance (p. 153)

cooperative learning (p. 154)

role models (p. 154)

multicultural education (p. 156)

anti-racist education (p. 156)

English as a second language (ESL) (p. 156)

immigraants (p. 157)

refugees (p. 157)

peer-mediated strategies (p. 159)

sexual harassment (p. 162)

homophobia (p. 162)

poverty (p. 164)

resilient students (p. 165)

homeless (p. 166)

transient lifestyle (p. 167)

child abuse (p. 167)

neglect (p. 167)

LEARNER OBJECTIVES

After you have read this chapter, you will be able to:

1. Identify and describe the key elements of creating a classroom community.

2. Describe developing an inclusive climate: physical layout and norms for interaction.

3. Identify and describe the major parts of negotiating and enforcing classroom rules and procedures.

4. Describe the major components of managing behaviour in an inclusive classroom and explain how they can be adapted to meet the needs of exceptional students.

Chapter 6

Climate, Community, and Classroom Management

Mandy has been at Bayside since September. She is in Ms. Turner's grade 6 classroom. Ms. Turner tells visitors to her classroom how Mandy invited another student who has few close friends to play basketball on the schoolyard. This act of kindness assumes significance when you know the rest of the story. If you had visited Mandy's grade 5 class at another school the previous June, you might have seen Mandy scream at her teacher, punch another student, or storm out of the classroom. It was terrible for Mandy and for her previous teacher. What has changed? Mandy moved to a small school with a caring and involved principal and to Ms. Turner's classroom. Ms. Turner is described as an exemplary teacher—every year children hope they will be in her class. Pre-service teachers love interning with her. They say, "All the kids treat each other so well. There is never any bullying. She won't have it. Everyone belongs." Mandy says, "I like Ms. Turner. She always says 'good morning' to me and makes me feel important. I don't want her to be disappointed in me. So I try my best. She never lets anyone hurt me and I don't have to hurt anyone back." At her last school, Mandy had been identified as having a behaviour exceptionality. Her principal thought that she needed a fresh start where the students and teachers were unaware of her reputation, with a teacher known for valuing and respecting every student, a teacher like Ms. Turner.

Jacob is in grade 10. He has cerebral palsy and a learning disability. He uses arm crutches to move around the school. To keep his energy up, Jacob has permission to eat healthy snacks in class. Recently he has been bringing chocolate bars and candy to his history class and has become very popular by handing out treats. Mr. Chan knows he will have to tackle this threat to his orderly classroom. Every day when the grade 10 students enter class, they find a "challenge" on their desks and have four minutes to determine, with a partner, which historical figure made the quoted statement. Recently some students have been too busy seeking a treat from Jacob to seek solutions to the "challenge." Mr. Chan does not approve of bribery, but he has noticed that more students talk with Jacob and invite him to join their groups for collaborative activities. Perhaps talking with the resource teacher who tutors Jacob will help Mr. Chan develop a response to the actions of Jacob and his classmates.

1. Under what circumstances could Mandy and Jacob be considered a challenge to the climate, organization, and management of their inclusive classrooms?

2. How can teachers develop classrooms that feel like communities, where all students are respected?

3. How can teachers discuss their approaches to classroom management with their classes and later refer to these discussions when responding to students who challenge order and learning in the classroom?

4. Who might teachers like Ms. Turner and Mr. Chan turn to for assistance in teaching students to change their actions in the classroom?

5. How can Mr. Chan enable Jacob to eat a healthy snack when he needs it and to maintain his improved peer relations, but prevent bribery and chaos in the classroom?

Mandy and Jacob are two of the approximately 600 000 exceptional students in Canadian schools. You already know that you can expect to meet exceptional students in almost every class you teach, which means you will meet challenges like those described above. The purpose of this chapter is to introduce you to ways of creating positive classroom climate and to negotiation and management as aspects of teaching. The goal is to create a community in which diversity is encouraged and all students feel they belong and their contributions are valued.

Creating a Community

You know to expect diversity in any Canadian classroom at the beginning of the twenty-first century. You will be teaching students with a wide array of high-incidence and low-incidence exceptionalities and health conditions, as well as students who are at risk. Your classes may include Aboriginal students, students who speak English as a second language, and students with many cultural and ethnic heritages. This diversity reflects our country, and as teachers we must shape an inclusive classroom community in which everyone belongs. The spirit of community doesn't happen by occasionally using cooperative learning activities. Building community is a deliberate process that you lead over a period of time.

Community involves sharing, participation, and fellowship according to the Working Forum on Inclusive Schools (1994), which documented successful inclusive schools in Canada and the United States. These schools were characterized by a common vision within each school; problem-solving teams; parents, teachers, students, and others functioning as partners; time for planning and collaboration; little jargon; and flexible scheduling. These characteristics may help us describe community at the classroom level.

Common Vision and Problem-Solving Teams

In order to help students feel that they have contributed and that they must take responsibility for classroom conduct, it helps to involve them meaningfully in setting classroom rules and the consequences for not following these rules. Students have a plethora of ideas about what classrooms can and should be like and great energy to work toward their own goals (Kohn, 1996). Harnessing this energy requires that you provide leadership and a structure for productive student discussion as well as that you listen and model behaviour that includes everyone. Emphasize the importance of **climate**, that is, the general feeling we create when we treat each other respectfully. Table 6.1 provides a set of norms for communication that creates community.

Making groups of students responsible for recommending possible solutions to classroom challenges uses problem-solving teams, teaches students to handle real-world problems, and creates a sense of belonging. In elementary classrooms, this problem solving may focus on devising efficient ways to ensure that all students have computer time or to study pond-ecology in the community on a realistic

Cross-Reference
Chapter 1 focuses on the general context for inclusion in Canadian society, while Chapter 5 emphasizes diversity arising from sources other than exceptionality.

Put Into Practice

Read about creating an inclusive climate. Develop an approach you might use from the first day of school: J.W. Putnam (1993). *Cooperative Learning and Strategies for Inclusion: Celebrating Diversity in the Classroom.* Toronto: Brookes.

M. Meyers (1993). *Teaching to Diversity: Teaching and Learning in the Multi-Ethnic Classroom.* Toronto: Irwin Publishers.

Table 6.1

COMMUNICATION AND COMMUNITY BUILDING

Norms for Communities	What to Do
Negotiation	Replace hostility and confrontation with give-and-take discussion. Don't assume all students know how to negotiate.
Cooperation	Increase the role of cooperation. Create situations that enable individuals to share goals, efforts, and outcomes.
Consensus	Use consensus to build community. Find areas of agreement. Use these to work toward consensus in new areas.
Decentralized management	Share decision making when that is feasible rather than practising authoritarian management.
Work teams	Use work teams to accomplish shared goals. Make work into fun by enjoying one another's company.
Shared responsibility	More ideas, better ideas, strength, and continuity. No one has to feel overwhelmed when people work together.

Adapted from Jeanne Gibbs (1995). *Tribes.* Sausalito, CA: Center Source Systems.

timeline and budget. In secondary settings, student committees can organize sports tournaments, orchestrate classroom debates, invite community leaders to help stage a simulated election, and much more.

Parents, Teachers, and Students as Partners

There are many resources about team building. Some focus on parents and extended families as partners (e.g., McCaleb, 1994) and recommend sending letters to parents early in the year and meeting to talk about their priorities for their children's learning. Other strategies include inviting a parent to observe his or her child who is disrupting the class to devise joint approaches for home and school (Krogness, 1995). McCaleb (1994) described involving parents in working collaboratively with their young children. Together each parent and child chooses a story to tell and make a book, while the teacher leads the activity for the group. The parent sees the child following instructions in a group setting, has a realistic idea of his or her classroom participation, and comes to know the teacher better. Three educators from Toronto suggest student-led parent–teacher conferences and students as peer negotiators or peacemakers (Fine, Lacey, & Baer, 1995). Whatever strategies you choose, focus on creating an equitable community (Levin, 1994) with high-quality communication among all partners (Faltis, 1993).

> **Further Reading**
>
> About creating community in the classroom: S.P. McCaleb (1994). *Building Communities of Learners: A Collaboration Among Teachers, Students, Families, and Community.* New York: St. Martin's Press.
>
> E.S. Fine, A. Lacey, & J. Baer (1995). *Children as Peacemakers.* Portsmouth, NH: Heinemann.

Time for Collaboration and Joint Planning

Set small amounts of scheduled time aside for your students to learn and practise collaboration and joint planning. Always include learning outcomes listed in your curricula, such as effective oral communication, setting priorities, planning and cooperating, and development of self-awareness. Write plans for these times, list them in your term's teaching plans, and be prepared to explain their role in creating community.

Little Jargon and Flexible Scheduling

Model clear use of language that is understood by all members of the extended classroom community. Listen to the language of classroom partners and point out when people are referring to the same phenomenon with different names. Make schedules as flexible as possible so students can work with volunteers and each other at strategic times. Building community should complement, rather than replace, the mandated curriculum and should enhance collaborative learning. Include multiple learning outcomes and community goals in your lesson plans and activities.

Developing an Inclusive Climate

The physical space can be inviting and inclusive for all students, including exceptional students, as well as work efficiently for learning. Classroom norms for interaction and discussion can also contribute to an inclusive climate.

Making the Physical Space Efficient, Inviting, and Accessible

The social environment you are creating should be supported by a physical arrangement that allows students to talk and collaborate for part of each day or part of each period as well as learning in a whole-class setting and individually. Arranging the **physical space** to make it inviting as well as accessible and efficient is something you should do before the school year begins and revisit frequently (Martin, Dworet, & Davis, 1996). Consider furniture (including desks for the students and yourself), audiovisual equipment (e.g., overhead projector), visual aids (such as bulletin boards), and any extra items you bring (such as plants). Think proactively about the physical needs of exceptional students for space, adapted desks, computers, and other specialized equipment.

ARRANGING FOR EFFICIENCY AND ACCESSIBILITY

The classroom is a small workspace for 30 or so students and yourself, myriad learning materials, and a variety of activities using different structures and different parts of the room. There may be exceptional students who need a predictable physical layout because of visual impairments and students who need wide aisles to manoeuvre their wheelchairs. Your goals should be to keep pathways clear to permit orderly movement, keep distractions to a minimum, and make efficient use of the available space. Table 6.2 contains guidelines for arranging the physical features of the classroom.

After your teaching is underway and patterns of use of time and space emerge, make a floor plan showing the size and location of built-in features. Make scale representations of the furniture and consider spaces, pathways, and room for activities. Ask yourself the following questions (Faltis, 1992):

- What learning spaces are available for students, both small and large activity spaces?
- Which spaces are used frequently by students, used occasionally, never used?
- What are the crowded areas?
- Which spaces are the pathways for movement?
- Which spaces are used for quiet activities, for noisy activities?

Making the class inviting is part of your work as a teacher.

Use this information to rearrange the room to support all of the learning activities you value and to make access as easy for exceptional students as it is for everyone else.

Table 6.2

GUIDELINES FOR ARRANGING PHYSICAL FEATURES OF THE CLASSROOM

Features	Guidelines
High traffic areas	Avoid congestion near doorways, the teacher's desk, pencil sharpeners, and storage areas that are used regularly.
	Separate high traffic areas.
	Ensure that you can reach everyone in the room with ease.
Sightlines	Make certain you can see all of your students easily so you can monitor their activities and prevent disruptions and distractions.
Teaching materials	Arrange the teaching materials you use regularly so you can access them and put them away easily without disrupting your teaching.
	Arrange materials that students access frequently in decentralized locations, where they are needed.
Seating arrangements	Use seating arrangements that allow students to see the chalkboard, overhead projector, video screen, and demonstrations, as well as work with peers collaboratively.

Adapted from Carolyn M. Evertson, Ed T. Emmer, & Murray Worsham (2000). *Classroom Management for Elementary Teachers.* Boston: Allyn and Bacon.

Ask yourself what would make each student feel that he or she is a valued part of your classroom. For students who speak English as a second language, perhaps it is a sign in their first language. For a student in a wheelchair, it might it be a poster that includes someone in a wheelchair. For a student with learning difficulties, it might be feeling that he or she knows exactly what is expected. Write an agenda on the board or on chart paper to ensure that all students find the day predictable. For preliterate students, use symbols such as a book to show story time and a sun to show when the weather chart will be completed. If there is one preliterate student in a literate class, tape a daily schedule in symbols to that student's desk to reduce embarrassment. Students with behaviour disabilities, AD/HD, or other exceptionalities may also benefit from a schedule taped to their desks.

Bulletin boards hold relatively permanent displays. Use inspirational posters and generate interest in an upcoming unit by connecting the topic to current events or popular culture. Post student work or seasonal art. Students can design collaborative displays on curriculum topics or murals about their novel study. Change displays frequently, post classroom rules (discussed in the next section), and ask students for suggestions to enhance bulletin boards. Use colour, but avoid distracting students. Ensure that before the first day of school, you post a welcome message for the students.

Desktops and tabletops should be clean and the room free of clutter. The appearance of order and organization in the physical environment communicates that you expect students to behave in an organized way. Place relevant materials at a level where they can be reached independently by a student in a wheelchair to communicate that you value independence. Look at the classroom from the perspective of the students and of a parent who comes to visit, as well as from your own perspective. Ensure that it is inviting.

Put Into Practice

Visit classrooms at your grade level. Observe the physical organization and consider how to ensure that the physical organization supports the classroom community you want to create.

Teaching Norms for Classroom Interaction and Learning

Teaching **norms for classroom interaction** and learning is complex. First, be a model of effective communication and respectful interaction in all your dealings with students. You also need to establish norms for discussion and lead discussions effectively.

MODELLING COMMUNICATION AND LEADING DISCUSSION

You are responsible for making it safe for people to share ideas and for affirming them as part of the community. This means teaching students to engage in give-and-take dialogues. If you are teaching young children, you might consult Levin's (1994) book, *Teaching Young Children in Violent Times: Building a Peaceable Classroom*. For students of any age, lead **give-and-take dialogues** from the first day to deal with problems that arise. When leading such brainstorming sessions, listen to all ideas, ask students to "tell us more" if their ideas are not clear, write all suggestions briefly on chart paper, and encourage a range of solutions. Don't evaluate during this stage. Model combining suggestions. Stop before everyone tires of the discussion and acknowledge the group's accomplishments in specific terms: "Thanks for listening to one another," etc. Before you leave the topic, suggest what the class will do to complete the task and when this will happen. Make "discussion rules" one of the earliest topics for discussion. Figure 6.1 contains guidelines for leading a successful discussion. Although these guidelines were designed for children, many apply to adolescent discussions, especially early in the school year.

LEADING A SUCCESSFUL GIVE-AND-TAKE DISCUSSION

Prepare in advance for the discussion:

- choose topics in advance and decide how you will introduce them to the children;
- identify the children's likely key issues and ways of understanding the topic;
- plan questions that will get children to express their diverse ideas and will stretch their thinking;
- identify a variety of possible outcomes, so you can guide the children toward them, but also be ready for ideas you never anticipated.

Expect to make constant decisions about such issues as:

- what question to ask next and how to ask it;
- how to balance the needs of individual children with the needs of the group;
- how far afield to let comments go before bringing things back to the main topic;
- how to pace the discussion to keep all the children interested and invested;
- when to let "wrong" answers and values you do not want to promote go uncorrected in the service of promoting give-and-take;
- how to incorporate new ideas and information that extend the children's thinking while acknowledging and accepting what they have to say;
- when to end the discussion and with what group conclusions.

Offer children a lot of help (especially at the beginning of the year):

- learning how to participate in give-and-take dialogues;
- feeling safe contributing their ideas;
- staying task-focused in their comments;
- filling in the words and information others need to fully understand what they are saying;
- applying the ideas they get from the discussions to their everyday actions and experiences.

Source: Diane E. Levin (1994). *Teaching Young Children in Violent Times: Building a Peaceable Classroom.* Cambridge, MA: Educators for Social Responsibility. Copyright © 1994 by Educators for Social Responsibility. Used by permission.

ESTABLISHING NORMS FOR DISCUSSION

The *Tribes* program is proactive in teaching discussion and community participation (Gibbs, 1995). The two groupings in *Tribes* are the community circle (all members of the class) and the small groups or tribes that are introduced gradually. For secondary students, you can refer to whole-class discussion and small-group discussion and use the *Tribes* approach flexibly. Explain that "This year we will work together in new ways. There will be small groups so people can help each other learn and can learn together. We will also talk as a whole class like this." During the introductory session, introduce the **signal** you will use to get attention. *Tribes* recommends raising your hand, but some teachers flick the lights, play a few notes on the piano, or start rhythmic clapping and invite everyone to join in. Explain that at this signal, everyone stops talking and raises his or her hand, etc. With young students, practise the signal. Tell older students that if they are not successful on the first few occasions, you will practise the signal with them.

Tribes begins with the whole group or **community circle**. There are about 175 activities with detailed lesson plans, many of which are appropriate to the community circle. You might start with "Five Tribles" (faces ranging from very sad to joyous), in which you ask everyone to report how they feel today, or with "Introductions." One of the earliest discussions should be about what we need in order to feel safe in a group. From this discussion, pull out a maximum of four or five statements. Gibbs (1995) suggests the four "**community agreements**" below:

- attentive listening
- appreciation/no put-downs
- right to pass
- mutual respect

TEACHING AND PRACTISING CLASSROOM NORMS

These agreements express norms for how students interact in the classroom, distinct from the classroom rules discussed in the next section of this chapter. Attentive listening can be taught and practised with activities in paraphrasing and reflecting the feelings of the speaker. Look at *Tribes* and other similar programs for activities. Students can practise appreciating others by saying something positive about another student's role in the activity—model this yourself, because it is not practised much in our society. Be specific: "I admire you for [the way you can work so patiently with your reading buddy]." Enforce no put-downs vigorously. The **right to pass** means that students have the right to choose the extent to which they will participate in a group activity that requires sharing personal information. Acknowledge a pass by saying, "That is fine," but do not allow students to avoid doing class assignments by saying, "Pass." You can offer a second chance to those who passed. Finally, mutual respect means that everyone's beliefs, values, and needs are honoured. Students' property should be respected, as well as their confidentiality. What is said during community circle and small groups should be treated in confidence and not become the basis for gossip.

The skills for working together need to be taught and practised regularly. You can make these skills explicit. Consider the example of listening. Discuss and come

What do you think?

Is it sound to allow students to pass when discussing personal feelings or information? How can you ensure that this privilege is not abused? What reading informs your thinking on this issue?

to agreement on what listening *looks like* (e.g., eyes looking, leaning forward), *sounds like* (one person talking at a time, sounds of "good idea"), and *feels like* (people care, "I'm being heard"). Post the four community agreements in a prominent place. Affirm students when you see them upholding the agreements, and refer to the agreements when you notice infringements.

Negotiating and Enforcing Classroom Rules and Procedures

Rules and procedures enable the classroom to function smoothly and predictably. After negotiating and teaching rules and procedures, you must monitor students to ensure they are followed. Consistent application of consequences is critical.

Negotiating Rules

What classroom rules do you intend to establish? Rules help create a sense of order and predictability and enable you to be proactive in preventing difficulties. Teachers who are effective at managing their classrooms engage in community building but also have well-defined rules (e.g., Bullara, 1993; Smith & Mirsa, 1992). Effective classroom **rules** are brief and specific, positively worded, and clearly understood by students (Doyle, 1990). They should be consistent with school rules, so become aware of the school code of conduct before the term begins. Then think about the general rules you hope to enforce for an orderly and predictable classroom.

Although there is disagreement on this issue, with research supporting both sides (see Emmer et al., 2000), I recommend involving the students in the discussion about rules rather than deciding the rules alone. You might ask students to think of reasons for having rules and reasons for dispensing with rules, and ask what kind of class they want to have. Then, ask students to talk in small groups to come up with three rules they think are important. It will help if you provide a general model—short, clear, and positively stated—such as "Respect and be polite to all people." Each group, in turn, states a rule it thinks is important that has not already been stated. Continue eliciting suggestions until no new ones emerge. To prevent key issues being overlooked, you could take a turn. After writing the suggestions on the board, group them into about five specific but broad rules and use other student suggestions as examples of the rules. Table 6.3 contains five rules with examples.

As soon as possible, write the rules on a poster and mount it in the classroom. Then you can point to them from the first day of class. Student input usually helps enhance classroom climate, build community, develop student understanding of the need and rationale for rules, and enhance the quality of your relationship with students. The standard to aim for is that there is no difference in student conduct when you leave the classroom briefly. This means that students must be enforcing the rules, reminding one another, and growing in self-discipline and respect for the rules. Before discussing the procedures that govern daily routines, I focus on how you can teach rules so they are integral to the life of the classroom.

Weblinks

CANADA'S SCHOOL NET
http://www.schoolnet.ca/

UNIVERSITY OF ALBERTA FACULTY OF EDUCATION
http://www.quasar.ualberta. ca

EDUCATION NETWORK OF ONTARIO
http://www.enoreo.on.ca

COMMUNITY LEARNING NETWORK COLLECTION OF LESSON PLANS
http://www.cln.org/subjects/ general_inst.html

Further Reading

On classroom management: E.T. Emmer, C.M. Evertson, & M.E. Worsham (2000). *Classroom Management for Secondary Teachers*, Fifth edition. Boston: Allyn and Bacon.

T. McQueen (1992). *Essentials of Classroom Management and Discipline*. New York: HarperCollins.

A. Kohn (1996). *Beyond Discipline: From Compliance to Community*. Alexandria, VA: Association for Supervision and Curriculum Development.

Table 6.3

CLASSROOM RULES AND EXAMPLES

Rules	Examples
1. **Be polite and helpful.**	• wait your turn, say please and thank you
	• ask the teacher for help only after asking your group; offer help in your group
	• behave well for a substitute teacher
2. **Respect other people's property.**	• keep the room clean
	• do not borrow without asking
	• return borrowed property
3. **Listen quietly while others are speaking.**	• raise your hand during whole-class discussion
	• speak when the previous person is finished in small groups
	• don't call out
4. **Respect and be polite to all people.**	• never call anyone a name or bully anyone
	• don't allow anyone to do these things to you or to another person
	• treat the teacher respectfully
5. **Obey all school rules.**	• follow rules for the schoolyard, cafeteria, etc.
	• remember that all teachers and students are expected to help with enforcement of school rules

Many researchers and educators agree that there are three key aspects of teaching rules: demonstration, practice, and feedback (e.g., Martin & Sugarman, 1993). First, teaching is much more than telling. Describe and then demonstrate the desired behaviours. Be specific. If students may talk to one another in quiet voices while working in small groups, then ask a student to converse in a quiet voice. Give feedback about the volume; if it was too loud, repeat the procedure. With adolescents, engage in teaching the rules with sensitivity to their age; perhaps ask each group to teach a rule to the class. Second, rehearsal means asking students to show that they understand. Younger students may need to practise standing up to a bully. Never have a student enact the role of the bully, because that amounts to you teaching someone to be a bully. Rather, ask students to imagine seeing a bully push their friend. Then have them practise asking the bully to stop and helping their friend report the incident to an adult (including asking the adult when they can expect a report on action taken). Again, feedback is important. Develop the habit of giving feedback after students have followed a rule. Make specific comments: "I like the way you were raising your hands in the large group and taking turns talking in your small groups."

If one student violates a rule, take him aside and say privately, "I saw you call John an unpleasant name. Next time that happens, I will call your name, and you will stand beside the door until I discuss this with you. I will not tolerate bullying. We agreed that we will not treat one another that way. Do you understand what I am saying? Do you need to practise following the rules?" This kind of follow-up is called **enforcing a rule**.

Monitoring is important to ensure that students engage in learning activities and internalize classroom rules and procedures. A discussion of monitoring follows the section on establishing procedures.

Establishing Procedures

Teachers usually develop classroom procedures for areas of classroom space, seat work and teacher-led activities, transitions into and out of the room, small-group activities, and general procedures. Figure 6.2 contains examples of procedures. **Classroom procedures** are efficient ways of moving everyone through the day or the period that are consistent with your goals for the classroom. Because procedures usually follow from the rules, making this connection will help most students understand them. Teach the most critical procedures first, introduce them as the need arises during the first few days, and introduce only as many in a day as the class can handle.

Monitoring Student Actions

Monitoring refers to being alert and responsive to student action. When you present information to the class, position yourself so you can see every student's face. Move around the classroom so you come close to all students. Ensure that a student who speech-reads can see your face straight on; you will not be able to move around the classroom while presenting. Scan the whole class; some teachers tend to focus on the middle front rows; however, you should be aware of the reactions of students on the periphery.

If you teach one small group while others are working independently, position yourself so you can see all students, and move around the room between working with one group and the next. When you circulate, look closely to see that the students are completing the assigned work. Ask if anyone has a question that could not be answered by a classmate; offer to give a brief reply. After one minute of helping, name a peer for the student to ask, and call for the next small group to assemble. While you are engaged with a small group, keep monitoring; look up frequently and be alert for disruptions.

Students learn to work collaboratively in small groups, enhancing social skills and social acceptance while meeting learning goals.

Figure 6.2

PROCEDURES FOR THE CLASSROOM

Procedures to Organize Use of the Room

Teacher's Desk and Storage Areas

- normally students remove items only with your permission

Student Desks and Other Student Storage Areas

- normally students remove items from others' desks only with permission

Storage for Common Materials

- tell students if and when they may remove texts, paper, rulers, etc.

Drinking Fountain, Pencil Sharpener

- normally one student at a time, and not during large group presentations

Centres, Stations, Equipment Areas

- tell students when they may use these areas, how many at a time, and post instructions for the use of any equipment

Transitions into and Out of the Room

Beginning of the School Day

- establish a routine that you supervise; with young children, it may be a "sharing" time; with older students, it may be a "challenge" that they work on for a few minutes alone, in pairs, or in groups

Leaving the Classroom

- quietly, in line, and when you give the signal for young children
- quietly and when you give the signal (not just when the bell rings) for older students

Returning to the Classroom

- from a noisy activity, allow quiet talking and then request silence before you begin an activity
- from a quiet activity, provide a challenge to focus students and request silence before you begin an activity

Ending the Day or Period

- review what was learned and look ahead to any homework, upcoming activities; end on a positive note
- tidy the room with all students doing their part; use procedures for leaving

General Procedures

Distributing Materials

- make it efficient; assign a student to this task for each group each week

Interruptions or Delays

- teach students that after an announcement on the public address system, they are to return immediately, without comment, to their work
- if you leave the room, remind them you expect them to act the same as when you are present; leave them working

Bathrooms

- tell students how many can leave class at a time and whether they need your permission

Library, Resource Room, School Office, Cafeteria

- review school rules

Schoolyard

- review school rules, prevent bullying, and help students include everyone

Fire Drills

- learn school procedures; practise with your class prior to the first drill (October is fire prevention month in Canada)
- arrange to assist students with physical, visual, hearing, or developmental disabilities

Classroom Helpers

- share these privileges systematically; identify helpers (or pairs of helpers) at the beginning of the week
- demonstrate how helpers are to fulfil their roles; don't accept shoddy work

When all students are working on independent assignments, circulate and check each student's progress. Avoid prolonged discussion with one student that interferes with alert monitoring. Remind students that they should ask you for help only after they have tried to obtain the assistance of a peer. If a student requires sustained assistance, the two of you should move to a location from which you can monitor the entire class. If you move to your desk, do not let students congregate there and block your monitoring of the room or distract students seated nearby.

After introducing a new lesson to the whole class, instruct students to take out the appropriate materials. Scan the class to ensure that every desktop has what is needed. Then you may want to have all students try the first example under your direction and take this example up with the group. Scan the class to see that everyone is writing. Check on exceptional students to ensure that they understand the instructions. Keep checking when students move to the next example. Quietly and individually ask the students experiencing difficulty to join you for reteaching at an area from which you can monitor the rest of the class. To prevent these invitations being seen as punishment, also ask the advanced students to join you at the reteaching area for challenge activities after they have completed the assigned work. Ensure that all students have opportunities to work with you at this location.

You will find it helpful to monitor student work by collecting assignments frequently, even if you have asked students to check their own work in class. Write brief comments so students see you have read their work, and keep your mark book current. You will see patterns of students who do not attempt assignments, leave assignments incomplete, or complete assignments only with assistance. When teaching students to do long-term assignments, set quarter- and halfway **checkpoints**. Devise a checklist for students to complete that shows what they have finished, and write brief, specific, and encouraging feedback on the checklist. It will be necessary to conference with students who need guidance or **scaffolding** (support that can gradually be removed) to ensure that the adapted outcomes of exceptional students are appropriate.

Applying Consequences Consistently

You know how important it is for teachers to be consistent. **Consistency** and equity should be discussed together to eliminate any misunderstanding on this important matter. Be consistent in your expectations from day to day. Also apply consequences consistently. For example, if you say students must move to the door and await a conversation with you for being disrespectful to a peer, then apply this consequence to all students; don't excuse one student because he begs or suspend another because he annoyed you earlier. Obvious inconsistencies confuse students about what is acceptable behaviour, and they may test you to find the limits.

However, there are occasions when circumstances justify making exceptions. Consider the student who was ill between when the assignment was set and the halfway checkpoint. It makes sense to compare his work to the quarter-way checkpoint and ensure that he understands the assignment. Then renegotiate the date for his halfway checkpoint. His participation in setting a new timeline increases the likelihood he will stay on schedule. Students with IEPs, second-language speakers of English, and those at risk for other reasons may need adapted outcomes and more scaffolding. Lead discussions that help students value diversity and understand that fairness does not necessarily mean sameness.

Managing Behaviour in the Inclusive Classroom

Managing student behaviour contributes to learning in the inclusive classroom. We focus on increasing appropriate behaviour, decreasing undesirable behaviour, and enhancing self-management. The section ends with a discussion of harsh and inappropriate punishments.

Increasing Appropriate Behaviour

In effective classrooms, teachers and students respect each other and students are engaged in learning. There are many actions you can take to increase students' appropriate behaviour. George Foster (1995), a principal in New Brunswick, describes it simply—give positive attention to the behaviour you want to maintain or increase. Provide verbal cues, prompts, and praise to indicate the behaviour you expect. And recognize social and academic achievement and qualities unique to individual students. Two Canadian educators, Barrie Bennett and Peter Smilanich (1994), describe teachers who are effective and increase students' appropriate behaviour as having **"invisible" classroom management** techniques. Sometimes it is difficult for students, administrators, and even these teachers, themselves, to describe what effective teachers do, because they make it look easy. Focus on Schools describes a program in which teachers clearly concentrate on students' appropriate behaviours, especially respectful behaviour.

In recent research, students describe "good" teachers in the following ways: "he likes teaching," "she is interested in us as people," and "they treat us fairly." Shelly Gauthier-McMahon, a graduate student at Queen's University, found that adolescent female students also refer to good teachers making them "feel safe" (Gauthier-McMahon & Hutchinson, 1998). In one of the cases at the beginning of this chapter, Mandy described Ms. Turner this way: "She never lets anyone hurt me and I don't have to hurt anyone back." Bennett and Smilanich (1994) describe effective teachers as realists who predict how students could misbehave in a particular situation and prevent this from happening, so that students are more engaged with learning and feel safe and valued.

CATCH 'EM BEING GOOD

Catch 'em being good is a strategy that was developed many years ago and is exemplified in Focus on Schools. When a student's behaviour is consistent with expectations, you acknowledge and reward the behaviour. If a student enters the classroom and immediately focuses on the challenge you have placed on her desk, you might say, "Mandy, I like the way you went straight to your desk and started on today's challenge. That's exactly what you are supposed to do." This comment

What do you think?

What would you say if asked to describe a good teacher? What do you think are the similarities and differences between teachers' and students' views of good teachers? Why might they be different?

The Three Rs Plus Respect Equals Results

The project called Together We Light the Way at Holy Cross Catholic School in Oshawa is an attempt to replicate the remarkable success one principal achieved in a decaying school, South Simcoe Public School, in Oshawa, Ont., over the past decade.

Early in Sandra Dean's tenure at South Simcoe Public School, the students scored the worst out of 89 schools in the Durham District School Board on board-wide tests in reading, writing, and math. But within five years, the school sat among the top performers in the region, just east of Toronto, and won a national award for excellence from the Conference Board of Canada.

Ms. Dean's approach, an attempt to recreate the village environment of her childhood in Trinidad, is hardly revolutionary. If anything, it seems old-fashioned: A teacher at the door, smiling, and greeting children by name. Flowers planted in the school yard. Neighbourhood business people reading to children. Regular phone calls filled with good news to parents from teachers. And a concerted focus on values such as respect and interdependence, using them as a foundation for better students and more resilient human beings. Students receive a "respect ticket" each time they say or do something that demonstrates good behaviour. A certain number of tickets qualifies them for gifts, the ultimate being a free dinner at Swiss Chalet served by teachers and community leaders such as the police chief.

Nothing in her upper-middle-class background prepared Ms. Dean for South Simcoe Public School, which she joined as principal in February 1991. Her first task was to make the school a "home away from home." If the students were to show respect for themselves and others, they would also have to be respected. Teachers were forbidden to yell at children or use the S word: shut up. "When a child walks into a room and you like that child, your eyes light up. Then the whole tone and atmosphere is set for learning," Ms. Dean said.

The word "respect" is everywhere at Holy Cross, a lower-middle-class downtown Oshawa school of just 215 students, one-third of them from single-parent homes. On the morning a reporter visited, the school held a "respect assembly" in the gymnasium. Each class presented a song or banner about respect. In the hallway a Respect Tree holds the pictures of every student who collected at least 75 respect tickets. And in the grade 4 classroom, students stand at the front of the class explaining how they earned respect tickets at recess. "I earned a respect ticket for grabbing a ball and giving it to the teacher, instead of just kicking it," a boy said. On the blackboard is the classroom's goal for the week: "I will walk respectfully in the corridors."

Teaching respect might seem to be the very stock-in-trade of schools, but the truth is it got lost somewhere along the way, Ms. MacInnis, the Holy Cross principal said. "Has respect always been a part of our curriculum? Truly, we've always expected that it's there, but have we ever taught it?"

When the program started a year ago, she wondered how staff would respond to the challenge of treating students more respectfully. "It's a total shift in philosophy," she said. "Instead of looking for things going wrong, you're looking for ways to support things going right for the child."

Teaching respect starts with acts as small as encouraging a student to push her chair in at the end of the day, Ms. MacInnis said. "You can't minimize the most minimal change in behaviour with some of these children." From such a seemingly small foundation, she says, self-awareness can be built. "They gain a strong sense of self, a respect for themselves, each other, and it extends out into the community. It's no longer a self-centredness. It's a true meaning of who they might be, what their potentials might be."

Grade 7 teacher Andrea Cannon believes the program is working and says praise has played a big part in its success. "A lot of children in this area aren't used to being praised by an adult," she said. "You can see them shine, almost."

[Read about Sandra Dean's program at South Simcoe Public School in her book *Hearts & Minds: A Public School Miracle* (Toronto: Penguin Books Canada, 2000).]

Source: Sean Fine (2000). The three Rs plus respect equals results. *The Globe and Mail*. October 10, p. A9. Used by permission.

rewards Mandy's behaviour. If she sometimes misbehaves to feel noticed, she receives the message that good behaviour gets your attention. If she sometimes misbehaves to gain control over some aspect of her situation, letting her know that she is positively in control may help to overcome this.

Sometimes students misbehave simply because you have not communicated effectively what is unacceptable and will not be tolerated. You know this is probably the case when you see Mandy behaving well in another class after she has just raised a ruckus in your class. Catching one student being good lets all the others know what you expect and value. However, I have found it more effective to speak privately to adolescents to let them know I appreciate their positive behaviour. You may also find that it is effective to speak privately to students for whom English is a second language, so you can discern the extent to which they have understood your comments.

THE GOOD BEHAVIOUR GAME

Another more formal version of the same strategy is the **good behaviour game**. Developed over 30 years ago (Barrish, Saunders, & Wolff, 1969), teachers still find it effective. Tell students that you will award points to teams within the class for positive behaviours; then describe these behaviours clearly. Points might be awarded for returning materials to their proper places at the end of an activity or for only one person speaking at a time in small-group discussions. Select only a couple of positive behaviours at a time and post them at the front of the classroom to remind all teams. Set a time period during the day when the game will be played. For a secondary class, it could be the first 20 minutes of the period; usually by then a positive tone has been set. Let the students know every time you see an appropriate behaviour and tally a point. At the end of the day, post the points.

You can give awards daily to young children and weekly or less frequently to older students. In a variation, you might set a target for all groups to reach, and provide a reward as long as all teams reach the minimum. For elementary children, extra time in the gym, computer room, or school library might be a suitable reward. For secondary students, viewing a video and debriefing the rest of the class might be a suitable group reward. Choose a reward that is meaningful for students of a particular age and for the particular class. Some teachers use a strategy like this early in the year and then only during the most stressful periods of the school year, such as before winter break. Others vary the reward or time of day.

REWARD SYSTEMS

Reward systems can also be effective. You can reward students as a group or as individuals with a token or point system (Foster, 1995). Token reinforcement is often called a "**token economy**." A teacher and a student select a *specific* appropriate target behaviour for which the student earns points or tokens to display. The behaviour could be social, such as raising a hand instead of blurting out answers, or academic, such as time spent on a task. The tokens or points are non-consumable items that are collected and then traded in for some kind of reward once the agreed-upon amount has been earned (Martin & Pear, 1992). This can help increase attention span and impulse control through a gradual training process. Remember to pair the reward with praise so the tokens can be gradually phased out and replaced with more natural reinforcers. The advantage to increasing positive behaviour is that you only have to go through one step with the students to arrive at your goal—appropriate behaviour.

Put Into Practice

Talk with students of the age you intend to teach. Ask individual students what they would find rewarding. Generate a list of rewards you think would be effective for students this age.

Decreasing Undesirable Behaviour

Your attempts to make everyone feel included and to increase positive behaviour will not be enough for some students. An alternate approach is to focus on decreasing undesirable behaviours. In this approach, you act to reduce behaviours you don't want to see and help students replace them with desirable actions. Often we assume that students know what to do and are simply refusing to do it. This is not always the case. Try using the steps of the ADAPT strategy described in Chapter 1 and minimal interventions or low-key responses. When a student exhibits problem behaviour, refer to the classroom rules that were established. Remind the student which rule is being violated. This can be done with a pre-arranged gesture or signal, by using humour (with good judgment), or by verbally confronting the student (but always in private). Try to identify environmental factors that could be altered. Consider changing the student's place in the classroom, or changing the student's task (Foster, 1995). A quick tension- or energy-releasing activity may allow the student to return to work.

LOW-KEY INTERVENTIONS

Effective teachers appear to respond to misbehaviour at a moment's notice; however, they actually anticipate and act or **"pro-act"** almost before the behaviour occurs. Such **low-key interventions** or minimal actions do not disrupt the flow of the class. They de-escalate rather than raise the stakes, and communicate to the student that you are "with it" and that they cannot get away with anything. Over time, effective teachers develop a repertoire and match their "proaction" to the action they anticipate. If you overuse a proaction, it loses its effectiveness. Low-key proactions or responses (recommended by Bennett & Smilanich, 1994) appear in Figure 6.3.

You may find it effective to combine these low-key responses. Imagine that one student is speaking to the class and a restless student catches your attention, although you are not certain why. You move silently toward this student, signalling to him to be quiet, touching him lightly and briefly on the shoulder to calm him, and smiling your appreciation when he begins to listen again. You did not disturb the flow of the class and prevented a distraction for the others. You can be "artful" in proactively noticing, selecting an effective response, and carrying it out to refocus the student who was venturing into undesirable behaviour.

TIME OUT

Inappropriate behaviour sometimes requires more than a low-key response. **Time out** is a consequence for inappropriate behaviour that should be planned ahead. Explain to the student what the misbehaviour was and why a time out is being imposed. It could be carried out away from the immediate setting that is reinforcing the behaviour. For example, a child who becomes too aggressive during a game in the classroom may be given a time out in the hall. However, if a student wants to leave a class she does not like, removing her will reinforce the inappropriate behaviour. In this case, have the student serve the time out in the classroom, but where her presence will not detract from the activity and she will

Further Reading

Learn about the root causes of anger and specific methods for responding to anger in the classroom: D. Leseho & D. Howard-Rose (1994). *Anger in the Classroom.* Calgary: Detsileg Enterprises.

LOW-KEY PROACTIVE RESPONSES TO DECREASE UNDESIRABLE BEHAVIOUR

Proximity: Move toward a misbehaving student immediately, but not so close that the student feels physically threatened; usually no verbal exchange

Touch: Check your school's policy; a quick, light non-threatening touch to the shoulder without eye contact or verbal exchange shows that you are aware and care

The look: Quickly and silently communicate to a student that a behaviour is inappropriate, as soon as attention seeking begins; this is not a glare

Student's name: Use positively to make student feel included, just before misbehaviour or as soon as misbehaviour occurs; use kind not nagging tone; don't overuse

Gesture: Communicate expected behaviour, e.g., a finger on the mouth to say "shh" or a shake of the head to say "no"; ensure meaning is understood by ESL students

The pause: At beginning of instructions, if a few are not listening, pause obviously; combine with moving toward them, catching their gazes, and gesturing for quiet

Ignore: Use with caution; best when the student's behaviour does not interfere with teaching or learning; if two students misbehave together, ignoring will be ineffective; don't show agitation or the students will have won the attention they sought

Signal to begin/signal for attention: To get or refocus the attention of the class; do not continue until you have their attention; make signal age-appropriate: a flick of the lights, a whistle, rhythmic handclapping, a sign you hold up; Bennett and Smilanich (1994) give the example of an elementary teacher who called out a word (baseball) and the students gave a choral response (Blue Jays); the students chose a new word/response each week

Deal with the problem, not the student: Quietly remove the object the student is tapping on her desk; if two students are fighting over a book, say "Book please," and extend your hand; say it as if you expect them to comply; if they do not, they have escalated the situation beyond a low-key proaction on your part.

Figure 6.3

Cross-Reference
In Chapters 3 and 4, you read descriptions of many exceptionalities. For which exceptionalities do you think time out might be suitable? For which personal characteristics might it be a bad match?

observe appropriate behaviour. Roberts et al. (1997) suggest that a one- to five-minute time out has the same effect as a longer one; try assigning one minute of time out per two years of age. For students with autism or developmental disabilities, you may want to use very short time outs with supervision. Sometimes a **verbal reprimand** is necessary if a behaviour continues. "If reprimands are to be used, the most effective ones are those that are prudent, in other words, immediate, unemotional, brief, and backed up with a time-out or loss of privileges" (Roberts et al., 1997, p. 81).

GIVING THE CHOICE TO BEHAVE APPROPRIATELY

Sometimes you want to provide a student or pair of students with a choice to behave appropriately. For example, two students are discussing hockey rather than

188 INCLUSION OF EXCEPTIONAL LEARNERS IN CANADIAN SCHOOLS geography. Say: "You can choose either to work quietly together on the map you are making or to have your seating arrangement changed until the end of this unit." If the pair does not choose to work quietly on the map, then you must follow through and seat them apart. Do not offer any choice that you are unwilling to apply. One of my favourite choices when students play with toys, hair accessories, etc., is, "In your pocket or mine—you choose." These choices are not ultimatums. They are effective in ending problem behaviour without escalating conflict. Often they involve **natural consequences**. Stay calm, speak in a private-conversation voice, and offer to conference with the student. Help the student to feel respected rather than humiliated or overpowered. If possible, thank the student sincerely as soon as the unacceptable behaviour stops

Engaging activities with peers help to decrease inappropriate behaviour.

(even smile or mouth your thanks). Keep your sense of humour; sometimes it is better to laugh and give a second chance than to prosecute, especially over small infractions.

HOLDING PATTERN

Sometimes you need to put a student in a **holding pattern**. Some teachers arrange to have a misbehaving student wait in an office until the teacher is free to meet and talk with the student. I find it simpler to have a student stand beside the door in the classroom or, if I think he will distract others, immediately outside the door until I come to talk to him. These talks are rare and are taken seriously by the students.

Mick had extreme difficulty controlling his temper; we used a holding pattern for him to get control. His psychologist's office was a block from the school. I arranged that Mick leave the school when he was losing control and cool down at the psychologist's office. I thought this was preferable to him striking a student or teacher. In the first week he left school four times, and I felt he might be abusing the privilege. However, in the third week he left only once. After that, Mick usually cooled off in the hall and returned to class as soon as I had spoken with him. The goal (related to his IEP) was to use the holding pattern less and less so it would be unnecessary by the end of the term. He met that goal; Mick was engaging in self-management.

Further Reading

Consult a recent paper on connecting behaviour interventions to IEPs: G.H. Buck, E.A. Polloway, M.A. Kirkpatrick, J. Patton, & K.M. Fad (2000). Developing behaviour intervention plans: A sequential approach. *Intervention in School and Clinic, 36*(1), 3–9.

Enhancing Self-Management

The goal of this chapter is that your class conduct themselves the same way whether you are in the classroom or have stepped into the hall. Similarly, you want to help individual students develop self-control or self-management.

PROBLEM-SOLVING APPROACHES

Some educators develop a **problem-solving approach** that asks a student to answer a set of questions after engaging in unacceptable behaviour. The questions usually ask the student what they think the problem was, what they did to contribute to the problem, how they can make amends, and how they can prevent the problem from recurring. Sometimes the student and the teacher sign the form. What makes this an effective strategy is the follow-through, in which the adult and the student decide "who is going to do what" about the situation. If the two can feel that they are on the same side and working together to overcome a common foe—such as an easily lost temper, peers who tease, or restless hands that poke—then the student may work hard to honour the problem-solving solution.

INFORMAL CONFERENCES

In a sincere offer to help, made in an informal conference, a teacher can often see that an exceptional student wants to change a troublesome behaviour, but cannot do it alone. Such conferences can be effective if there is follow-through. Bennett and Smilanich (1994) suggest the following steps for an **informal conference**:

- greet the student to set a positive tone
- define the problem clearly and ensure that you agree before going to the next step
- generate solutions together, so you solve the problem mutually
- choose the best solution(s) together (and perhaps prioritize the other solutions); agree on what each of you will do to implement the solution; be sure you have a role as well as the student
- ensure that you have a shared understanding of the solution(s) to be undertaken
- end positively by thanking the student

Improving self-management is not easy for students. Be prepared to provide moral support, encouragement, regular checks on progress, praise when you observe the student being good, and additional informal, positive chats. If the informal conference is no match for the problems that need to be solved, then provide a warning and try a formal contract the next time the problem occurs. Warnings are respectful ways to "raise the stakes" without students feeling attacked, and they remind students that what happens next is a consequence of what they do.

CONTRACTS

When raising the stakes from informal conferences, contracts can be effective. I found that young students enjoyed contracts and told their classmates about them, while adolescents appreciated private contracts. I informed parents so they would understand my rationale and the student's account of the consequences if the contract were broken. With a young child, a contract can be about a matter as straightforward as hanging her coat on a hook when she comes into the classroom instead of throwing it on the floor. This reflects the principle of starting with a series of easily and quickly met agreements that provide immediate evidence of success and provide you with a way to give genuine praise (privately or publicly).

After two easy and successful contracts, you can move to your real objective.

This might be the student starting the day and getting to her desk without touching, or having a verbal disagreement with, another student. A good start can make quite a difference to how a student conducts herself all day long. You may reap multiple benefits from start-of-day contracts. When they work well, the student avoids getting into "a funk," and you avoid the student disrupting others. As well, you can begin the day by praising the student sincerely instead of reprimanding her, and you can build on this success to tackle bigger unacceptable behaviours that sabotage learning throughout the day. I have seen adolescents thrive on contracts when they were private and highly individualized. Word the **contract** simply (not like a legal document), ensure that it states what both you and the student agree to do, and ensure that it specifies the positive reward and the consequence for failure to live up to the agreement. Figure 6.4 shows a simple form for behaviour contracts.

SELF-MONITORING

Self-monitoring is another strategy for transferring responsibility to the student. It is particularly applicable for students who are off-task and require help focusing attention. Students observe and collect data on their own behaviour. Marking down and keeping track of behaviour can change how frequently the behaviour

Figure 6.4

BEHAVIOUR CONTRACT

Contract between _____ and _____
             (student)   *(teacher)*

Date: _____
        (may specify period in which contract applies)

_____ agrees to _____
        (student)   *(describe behaviours)*

_____

and _____ agrees to _____
        (teacher)   *(describe behaviours)*

_____

Consequences: _____

Rewards: _____

_____

Dates for checking progress: _____

Completion date: _____

Signatures: _____ and _____
             (student)   *(teacher)*

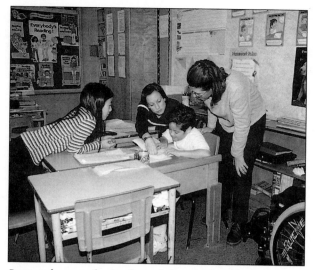

Peers and paraprofessionals can help to implement cognitive behaviour modification programs.

occurs. Students need an understanding of the behaviour they are to monitor, an easy recording system, and a reward. In the beginning, you should monitor closely and then give increasing responsibility to the student. Explain in advance: "Put a check on your tracking sheet when I say 'let's keep track'" or "Put a check at the end of every page." Dawn Reithaug (1998), a B.C. educator, has developed a book of attractive forms and guidelines for making clear behaviour plans. A simple self-monitoring card can be taped to the student's desk; the student makes a check mark at each signal or at the end of each task, etc. After some successful self-monitoring, you could move to checklists taped to the desk or to sticky-note reminders. These strategies work well with young students, but I have also seen exceptional adolescents inconspicuously use self-monitoring cards taped inside their notebooks to help them focus their attention. Figure 6.5 outlines SNAP, a cognitive behaviour modification (CBM) strategy with four steps.

Put Into Practice

Develop a tracking sheet for self-monitoring to be used by a student in grade 3 or in grade 10 who was trying to increase his focus in your class. Seek models in books and journals.

Harsh Punishments and Inappropriate Punishments

There are harsh punishments, such as suspension and expulsion, and there are inappropriate forms, such as corporal punishment and academic tasks. **Punishment** is usually defined as an unpleasant consequence aimed at reducing the likelihood of inappropriate behaviour. It is expected to work because it causes pain. The research indicates that punishment can control misbehaviour, but by itself it will not teach desirable behaviour (Good & Brophy, 1987). Harsh punishment also alienates students from you and tends to destroy the goodwill you have built up that enables the two of you to be on the same side in helping the student to change.

SUSPENSIONS AND EXPULSIONS

School policy may dictate that suspensions and even expulsions are used when a student's behaviour is so disruptive that the teacher cannot continue to meet the legal obligations to teach and keep the students safe. These are drastic measures, so try every other possible avenue first. **Suspension** means temporary removal from the classroom (for a day or more), while **expulsion** means permanent removal. For a number of reasons, these strategies do not enable us to teach a student or help her to change for the better. According to McQueen (1992), these reasons include:

- the student misses the content you are teaching
- the student does not receive assistance from school personnel, including teachers and counsellors
- those who want to be out of school are rewarded

Figure 6.5

IMPLEMENTING A COGNITIVE BEHAVIOUR MANAGEMENT PROGRAM

Cognitive behaviour modification (CBM) is a broad term. It describes a number of specific techniques that teach self-control. They all work by increasing a student's awareness of cognitive processes and knowledge of how behaviour affects learning.

CBM interventions require student evaluation of performance rather than teacher evaluation. This means that they are practical for busy teachers and parents.

Self-instruction is one technique that helps students to regulate their own behaviours—social and academic. It uses self-statements to help students recall the steps required to solve a problem—social or academic. Examples of problems include: rushing through assigned work, looking around instead of focusing on assigned work, talking out in class, eating or giving food to others in the classroom. Initially students say the steps out loud to a teacher or parent, then to a peer or themselves. Gradually they say the steps covertly.

The actions a teacher and student follow include:

1. They agree on a problem—social or academic—that is getting in the way of learning.

2. The teacher makes a cue card to prompt the student to use the steps of self-instruction.

3. The teacher models using the self-instruction steps to solve a problem like the one impeding the student.

4. The student practices using the self-instruction steps aloud with the teacher to solve the problem.

5. The student practices with a peer and then alone using the steps to solve the problem.

6. The teacher arranges booster practice regularly to review the strategy with the student. For booster practice, they use verbal rehearsal as well as practicing in familiar and new situations.

7. They arrange a signal for the teacher to let the student know this is a time to use the steps. This is phased out because the student is supposed to do the monitoring. For the SNAP strategy, snapping fingers may be a good signal.

Sample Cue Card to Tape to Student's Desk or Book

SNAP *out of it!*

See my problem.

Name my best plan.

Act on my best plan.

Pat myself on the back. I solved my problem!

Source: N.L. Hutchinson (1999). *Teaching Exceptional Children and Adolescents: A Canadian Casebook.* Toronto: Allyn and Bacon. Used by permission of Pearson Education Canada, pp. 87–88.

- some students who have been suspended or expelled come to school to "hang out," and school officials have little authority over them
- as a general rule, behaviour does not improve as a result of suspensions or expulsions

The exception to these drawbacks may be in-school suspension: a student is expected to attend school, complete assigned work, spend the day in a suspension room under supervision, and stay away from peers and social interactions. Some schools have developed a room that is supervised by the principal, vice-principal, or another member of the school staff at all times. A teacher can take a student to this room for a short-term in-school suspension, during which the student works independently but is supervised. Parents are notified, and the student and parent are asked to work with the school staff to improve the student's school behaviour. "Suspension" is not used in the name of this room; its function is to remove a student who disrupts the learning of others. Familiarize yourself with your school's policies and school-wide expectations for students. Ask questions about a school's policies about suspension during an employment interview. It is usually easier to teach in a school when you agree with the policies.

CORPORAL PUNISHMENT AND USING ACADEMIC TASKS AS PUNISHMENT

We are expected to conduct our classes without **corporal punishment**. In Canada, it is unacceptable to strike a student or threaten to strike a student. Corporal punishment violates students' rights and is ineffective in changing behaviour. It is likely to lead to hostility and retaliation, and it sends the message that it is acceptable for the strong to use might against the weak. As well, beware of assigning "lines" or mathematics problems as punishment. Educators are responsible for teaching students to practise written expression and mathematics to develop proficiency. The contradictory message sent by assigning **academic tasks as punishment** only makes our job more difficult. However, requiring students to complete work missed due to absence is defensible. Make your classes so well taught and interesting that students hate to miss anything. The challenge with having exceptional students included in every class is that each of their adapted programs also has to be so worthwhile that they hate to miss class.

What do you think?

Debate with your peers whether *harsh* and *inappropriate* are always apt descriptors for the punishments described in this chapter. Defend the position opposite to what you believe. Why is this a valuable experience for an educator?

Further Reading

Six 30-minute videotapes with classroom scenes: North York Board of Education with TVO (1993). *Managing Your Classroom: Tips, Techniques, Strategies to Focus on Learning, Reduce Distractions, Manage Misbehaviour.* Titles are (1) Getting Ready, (2) Planning for Prevention, (3) Connecting with Kids, (4) Teaching Social Skills, (5) Dealing with Misbehaviour, and (6) Supporting Kids at Risk.

Summary

It is important that classrooms in inclusive schools provide a sense of community wherein all members feel accepted and valued. Many elements contribute to developing an inclusive classroom climate, including the physical layout and the norms of classroom interaction. Teachers negotiate and enforce classroom rules and procedures to ensure that all students, including exceptional students, find the classroom predictable and safe. Managing behaviour in an inclusive classroom requires strategies for increasing appropriate behaviour, decreasing unacceptable behaviour, and enhancing self-management. The chapter ended with a discussion of harsh and inappropriate punishments. ■

Key Terms

community (p. 172)

climate (p. 172)

physical space (p. 174)

norms for classroom interaction (p. 176)

give-and-take dialogues (p. 176)

signal (p. 178)

community circle (p. 178)

community agreements (p. 178)

right to pass (p. 178)

rules (p. 179)

enforcing a rule (p. 181)

classroom procedures (p. 181)

monitoring (p. 181)

checkpoints (p. 183)

scaffolding (p. 183)

consistency (p. 183)

"invisible" classroom management (p. 184)

catch 'em being good (p. 184)

good behaviour game (p. 186)

reward systems (p. 186)

token economy (p. 186)

pro-act (p. 187)

low-key interventions (p. 187)

time out (p. 187)

verbal reprimand (p. 188)

natural consequences (p. 189)

holding pattern (p. 189)

problem-solving approach (p. 189)

informal conference (p. 190)

contract (p. 191)

self-monitoring (p. 191)

punishment (p. 192)

suspension (p. 192)

expulsion (p. 192)

corporal punishment (p. 194)

academic tasks as punishment (p. 194)

Adapting Teaching

Ms. Ash teaches mathematics at a large inner-city secondary school. She starts every class with an example of how the day's math can be used—perhaps by engineers to design a heating system or by the marketing department of Healthy Foods. When she teaches new mathematical content, she teaches to the whole class, with the students seated in pairs. First she reviews, pointing out explicitly how recent lessons relate to today's class. Next she hands out a partially completed outline and places the same outline on the overhead projector. She demonstrates, questions, and fills in the overhead transparency while she explains the new content. She stops every few minutes for students to ask questions and complete their outlines. She moves to guided practice by demonstrating an example on the overhead projector while students work in pairs on the same example. Then students complete two or three examples in pairs without Ms. Ash guiding them. She takes up these examples, guides students in practising another if necessary, and then asks students to work together on two or three examples and finally to complete two or three independently. She moves to the round table and invites students who want to review the steps to join her while the rest complete a challenge task in collaborative groups. Samuel has a learning disability and has always found math difficult. This term, Ms. Ash paired Samuel with a boy who answers his questions with explanations, and Samuel is learning. He likes to go to the round table to hear Ms. Ash explain the concepts and the steps again and to have her correct his work. Ms. Ash has taught him how to use a calculator and encourages him to use it, one of the adaptations listed on his IEP. Now he feels that he is learning to solve problems rather than spending all his time trying to do calculations.

Hema has developmental disabilities; she has a pacemaker, but it does not restrict her activities. She is included in a grade 5 class and learns best with visual materials, hands-on activities, and pre-teaching. Hema reads common signs in the neighbourhood, recognizes the written names of family and friends, and reads calendar words. She prints her name on forms or applications, draws simple pictures, and types a couple sentences on the computer with a model. Her annual goals (on her IEP) include sustaining a conversation; maintaining socially appropriate behaviour; using a telephone; describing events, interactions, etc.; using money; and reading to get information. For the weather unit in Hema's science class, the resource teacher and classroom teacher, Mr. Carvello, used the ADAPT strategy. While the other students completed a full-page chart on the weather each day using the class's weather station, Hema recorded only three aspects: she wrote the temperature, drew the cloud cover, and wrote the precipitation. To meet the IEP goals of using the telephone and relaying information, the two teachers designed a learning activity: In the company of a peer, Hema goes to the school office to telephone the regional weather office daily. Eleven peers volunteered to take turns accompanying Hema. Mr. Carvello demonstrated their role to the peer volunteers twice. Hema dialled the number, listened, and repeated what the meteorologist had said. Mr. Carvello printed it neatly and prompted Hema while she practised telling the class. Hema gradually used the telephone more independently, and the peer who had accompanied Hema provided any information she missed in her summary. Hema's daily goal was to give a full account, which she was soon able to do.

1. How have these two teachers compared the strengths and needs of each exceptional student—Samuel and Hema—to classroom demands?

2. What adaptations do these teachers make for each of these exceptional students? How do these adaptations relate to the students' IEPs?

3. How have these teachers considered the perspectives of and consequences for others as well as for Hema and Samuel?

4. Are these adaptations beneficial to students other than Hema and Samuel? How?

5. How have these teachers ADAPTed teaching without unduly increasing their own workloads?

Introduction

Effective teachers analyze their classroom environment and teaching in relation to students' academic and social needs and make adaptations to ensure success. This chapter provides explicit examples for using the ADAPT strategy introduced in Chapter 1. These examples represent many exceptionalities and many areas of the elementary and secondary curriculum. Individual teachers find some adaptations more acceptable and feasible than others, and students also find particular adaptations more helpful than others. For example, Ms. Ash finds it easy to model and provide guided practice, followed by independent practice, for the whole class. Samuel finds the partially completed outline helps him follow her teaching. He benefits from using a calculator and from thoughtful pairing of students. Receiving immediate feedback on his completed work motivates Samuel. These adaptations help other students as well. Hema is learning about weather at a level consistent with her strengths, prior knowledge, and needs, and meeting goals from her IEP: providing a reliable verbal account and using the telephone. She is also developing better social relationships with her peers, who are coming to appreciate the effort Hema puts into learning. Mr. Carvello is accommodating Hema's learning needs without undue effort.

Examples of elementary and secondary adaptations provide models for ADAPTing literacy instruction, textbook use, and teaching in specific content areas. I hope these examples help you extract patterns for action, ponder the perspectives of those experiencing the adaptations, and think about the consequences for all affected by adaptations. Making adaptations in teaching and assessment is the heart of exceptional education that honours diversity and strives for equity.

Using the ADAPT Strategy to Analyze Teaching for Individuals and Groups

You need strategies for adapting teaching that are effective for exceptional students, efficient for you, and become a regular part of your planning and teaching. Chapter 1 introduced ADAPT. This strategy is similar to others, but it includes considering the perspectives of many people, including classmates, on the adaptation and the consequences for them. The characteristics of the student (strengths *and* needs) and the demands of the classroom are important when devising adaptations to build on the student's strengths and either bypass areas of need or help the student strengthen these areas.

The ADAPT strategy has the following five steps:

- Step 1: <u>A</u>ccounts of student's strengths and needs
- Step 2: <u>D</u>emands of the classroom
- Step 3: <u>A</u>daptations
- Step 4: <u>P</u>erspectives and consequences
- Step 5: <u>T</u>each and assess the match

Further Reading

Two general resources on adapting teaching: E.J. Kame'enui & D.C. Simmons (1999). *Toward successful inclusion of students with disabilities.* Reston, VA: Council for Exceptional Children.

J.J. Hoover & J.R. Patton (1997). *Curriculum adaptations for students with learning and behaviour problems,* Second edition. Austin, TX: Pro-Ed.

Further Reading

Two specific resources on adapting teaching: J.S. Shumm (1999). *Adapting reading and math materials for the inclusive classroom (kindergarten through grade five).* Reston, VA: Council for Exceptional Children.

J. Schumaker & K. Lenz (eds.) (1999). *Adapting language arts, social studies, and science materials for the inclusive classroom (grades six through eight).* Reston, VA: Council for Exceptional Children.

These five steps constitute a procedure you can use with learners with a variety of exceptionalities in both elementary and secondary classrooms.

Step 1: Accounts of Students' Strengths and Needs

This first step requires that you know from the first day of school the content of the confidential file of each exceptional student you teach. Usually the file contains the student's IEP, test reports, comments from previous teachers, and medical information that could be critical to the student's well-being. The IEP includes specific statements about both strengths and needs, usually in three general areas: social, emotional, and behavioural; physical; and academic.

Social, emotional, and behavioural strengths include engaging in conversation, responding positively to suggestions, and controlling anger. You can use a strength such as engaging in conversation to help the student learn in a collaborative group. On the other hand, social, emotional, and behavioural needs could mean that a student requires significant instruction and support because she fights when unsupervised. Physical strengths and needs include motor skills, neurological functioning, and sight and hearing. One child may have a strength in that she can print neatly and

Talking with your students will help you know their strengths and needs and enable them to trust you. This boy's father will be out of the country for the next six months.

quickly, while another may need significant instruction and support to enter assignments into a computer. Academic strengths and needs include the basic skills of reading, writing, mathematics, and learning strategies for test taking, studying, and problem solving. Students like Samuel have strengths such as completing calculations with a calculator. Students like Hema have needs such as requiring significant instruction and support to develop beginning reading skills. It is helpful to prepare a brief description of the strengths and needs of each exceptional student and tape it into your daybook so you see it while planning and teaching.

Step 2: Demands of the Classroom

Next consider the social, emotional, and behavioural demands of your classroom. Do students learn individually, work with peers, or both? How long is the lecture portion of each lesson? Do you model positive interactions with and respect for all students? For physical demands, consider the frequency with which you move classroom furniture. Do you rely on an overhead projector and can everyone see it clearly? The academic demands are manifested in the instructional materials you use (e.g., textbooks, computer programs) and in the instructional approaches. Direct instruction followed by guided and independent practice benefits students with learning disabilities while open-ended assignments challenge gifted students. Academic demands also appear in assessment methods. Devise assessments that enable exceptional learners to show what they know and that challenge advanced students.

Step 3: Adaptations

Put into Practice

Informally ask parents, teachers, and students how they feel about adaptations to meet the learning needs of exceptional students. What "hard questions" might you be asked by students without exceptionalities and their parents?

In this step you compare a student's learning needs to the demands of the classroom and identify potential mismatches and adaptations that eliminate these mismatches. You can make adaptations—when planning and then carry out these adaptations when teaching—in the fundamental organization and instruction that goes on in the classroom. You can bypass a mismatch between student and curriculum demands and you can teach through the mismatch. These strategies are discussed in the next section of this chapter.

Step 4: Perspectives and Consequences

Take time to reflect on adaptations from many perspectives. What was your experience? If you are uncomfortable with an adaptation, it is unlikely that you will continue to use it. To get the most return for your effort, choose adaptations that are beneficial for many students and that have demonstrated effectiveness. Use observation to learn about the exceptional student's experience of the adaptation. How did the rest of the class view the adaptation? How would the parents of the exceptional student view the adaptations you used? And how would the community look on these adaptations? Next consider the consequences, intended and unintended, for the exceptional student—participation, learning, drawbacks—and for others affected by the adaptation.

Step 5: Teach and Assess the Match

During and following the teaching, assess how well the adaptation overcame the mismatch between student strengths and needs and classroom demands. This analysis will help you decide about altering the adaptation while it takes place and about continuing the adaptation. Persevere and give the adaptation time to be effective. You can observe how engaged the student is, ask the student how she finds the changes, chart marks and analyze errors, and talk with parents.

Choosing and Combining Strategies for Adapting

Make the effort to adapt only when there is a mismatch. Providing more adaptations than students need gives them a crutch that may limit independence. Sometimes a student *can't* do what you ask, even if highly motivated. Sometimes a student *won't* do what you ask, and lack of motivation is the issue (Blankenship & Lily, 1981). Distinguishing between the two is important. Generally, keep adaptations as simple as possible. Types of adaptations to choose from and combine include teaching around the mismatch, remediating or accelerating in hopes of overcoming the mismatch, and teaching through the mismatch.

Teaching Around the Mismatch

This section addresses teaching around the problem, which is helpful for *can't* after trying concertedly for some time. (Behaviour management and encouragement are usually more appropriate for *won't*.) Teaching-around strategies are sometimes called **bypass strategies** (Friend et al., 1998), because they allow students to succeed in the classroom using alternative means. Samuel bypassed his lack of computation skills with a calculator so he could concentrate on solving problems. Like most bypass strategies, it was successful because he was taught to use the calculator proficiently. To teach around a spelling disability, one can use a spell checker or a peer editor, and Braille bypasses sight to enable reading. Bypass strategies that enhance independence are usually preferable (e.g., a spell checker rather than a peer editor).

Remediating or Accelerating to Overcome the Mismatch

A second strategy for overcoming a mismatch is intensive remediation or acceleration. Intensive instruction or **remediation** is designed to address basic skills or learning strategies that the student needs and that you believe the student can acquire. A resource teacher may do unison reading with a slow reader in grade 9 to help him increase his reading speed and comprehend his textbooks. You could tutor four students who have difficulty printing while the class writes daily journal entries. An example of **acceleration** (used to move academically advanced students into challenging learning) is teaching two adolescents in your geography class to run a statistical program and analyze Statistics Canada data. They are bored by your unit on immigration, well prepared to take the unit test, and eager to meet this challenge.

Weblinks

STATISTICS CANADA LESSON PLANS FOR SENIOR COURSES
http://www.statcan.ca/ english/kits/senior.htm

LESSON PLAN FOR "CANADA'S IMMIGRATION PATTERNS, 1955 TO PRESENT"
http://www.statcan.ca/ english/kits/immig1.htm

Teaching Through the Mismatch

A third strategy for overcoming a mismatch is teaching through the mismatch. You can make adaptations—when planning and then carry out these adaptations when teaching—in the fundamental organization and instruction that goes on in the classroom. In the planning process, try using these four steps (Collicott, 1994):

1. Identify the underlying concepts and learning outcomes of the lesson and adapt these for exceptional students when necessary. (Why do I teach this?)

2. Identify the methods of presentation and adapt these for exceptional students when necessary. (How do I teach this?)

3. Identify the means of students' gaining understanding of the concepts or the means of student practice and adapt these for exceptional students when necessary. (How do students learn this?)

4. Identify the means of student evaluation and adapt these for exceptional students when necessary. (How do students show they have learned this?)

Sometimes exceptional students participate fully and sometimes they engage in partial participation. They complete part of a task or a different task to achieve the same outcome—drawing instead of writing to enhance communication and self-awareness. The many aspects of the classroom that can be adapted are the focus of the next section.

Analyzing Teaching: What You Can Adapt

When you use the ADAPT strategy to analyze teaching, you may be struck by how many ways there are to make changes that meet student needs. For example, you can adapt the substance of your teaching (e.g., outcomes, content, cognitive complexity, authenticity, and interest of the task). Or you may find that it makes more sense to change the environment (e.g., seating). You may want to enhance student engagement by changing the method of instruction—through activity-based learning or by changing the form of practice. All these aspects of teaching are closely related; however, looking at the components that make up teaching enables us to see myriad ways of adapting for exceptional students. Because the aspects of teaching are so interconnected, a change in one may have implications for many others. A new concept, universal design for curriculum access, has emerged in the past few years. Focus on Curriculum Concepts shows how this concept may change the way we think about adapting teaching.

Outcomes, Content, Cognitive Complexity, Authenticity, and Interest of Task

Outcomes and these other aspects of teaching are all related to the substance and intent of what is taught. You remember, from Chapter 1, that when you change the learning outcomes to something radically different from those in the grade-level curriculum you teach the class, you are modifying curriculum. This occurs when 14-year-old Adam, who has autism, needs to learn to make a sandwich. While Adam and a paraprofessional work toward this outcome, you and the rest of the class study the geography of your province. However, a student who is blind may have the geography curriculum adapted. Using raised maps of the province and the guidance of a peer tutor, she learns to identify only the most obvious landforms and the major cities and towns. She focuses on the demographics of the province, which she can access on her computer in an auditory form and print in Braille. Her outcomes are based on but changed from those in the curriculum. Adapting outcomes for a gifted student may include a critical analysis of the declining role of landforms in demographic patterns (population and economics). Changes range from mild (adaptations) to massive (modifications) depending on the students' strengths and needs and on classroom demands. The changes should ensure that the student continues to learn.

Cognitive complexity refers to the cognitive demands made of the learner. **Authentic tasks** tend to be complex when they are presented to students in the

Cross-Reference
Chapter 1 defined modifying teaching and adapting teaching. Consult your local and provincial documents to see if this distinction is made.

What Is "Universal Design" for Curriculum Access?

The concept of universal design originated in architectural studies, where considerations of physical access led to designs that incorporated assistive technologies and adaptations (e.g., curb cuts and automatic doors). One essential quality of universal design of physical space is that the adaptations not only allow access to those who have disabilities but also make it easier for *everyone* to use the space. For example, a ramp allows people to enter a building easily when using a wheelchair or when pushing a cart or a stroller.

Researchers in education have expanded inclusive accommodations from architectural space to the educational experience, first in designing physical and sensory means of access to the curriculum for children with disabilities (e.g., screen readers and preprogrammed "hot" or "sticky" keys). More recently this research has moved into considering cognitive disabilities and curriculum design.

A Definition of Universal Design for Learning

Universal design for learning means the design of instructional materials and activities that allows the learning goals to be achievable by individuals with wide differences in abilities to see, hear, speak, move, read, write, understand English, attend, organize, engage, and remember. Universal design for learning is achieved by means of flexible curricular materials and activities that provide alternatives for students with disparities in abilities and backgrounds. These alternatives should be built into the instructional design and operating systems of educational materials—they should not have to be added on later. Using universally designed materials, both print and electronic, teachers only need to teach one flexible curriculum and become familiar with its variations in order to reach all students.

Three Essential Qualities of Universal Design for Learning

1. Curriculum Provides Multiple Means of Representation
   - Alternative modes of presentation reduce perceptual/learning barriers
   - Can adjust to different ways students recognize things
2. Curriculum Provides Multiple Means of Expression
   - Students can respond with preferred means of control
   - Can accommodate different strategic and motor systems of students
3. Curriculum Provides Multiple Means of Engagement
   - Students' interests in learning matched with mode of presentation/response
   - Can better motivate more students
   - Digital format is the most flexible means for presenting curricular materials:
   - Transformable (easily changed from one medium of presentation to another)
   - Transportable (customizable for individual needs)
   - Recordable ("learns" and "remembers" user patterns; tracks progress, areas of difficulty)

Web Sites about Universal Design and Curriculum Access

- CAST (Center for Applied Special Technology), http://www.cast.org
- National Center to Improve the Tools of Educators (NCITE), http://idea.uoregon.edu/~ncite/

Two Examples That Use Universal Design Principles

- Wiggle-Works, an early literacy program from Scholastic, builds in design features that allow children with many different abilities and disabilities to learn together: http://www.scholastic.ca/education/wiggle.htm.
- Encarta '98 for Windows uses audio and video to make concepts clearer than text alone could do and uses captioning: http://www.encarta.msn.com/products.

Source: Based on information available in R. Orkwis and K. McLane (1998). *A Curriculum Every Student Can Use: Design Principles for Student Access.* CEC.

Weblinks

ELECTIONS CANADA
http://www.elections.ca

HOW TO ORGANIZE AN ELECTION
SIMULATION (IN CANADA AT THE
POLLS!):
**http://www.elections.ca/youth/
english/getkit.html**

form in which they appear in society. A class of students could stage a mock municipal election for their school. This would involve them in researching how to nominate municipal candidates, hold press conferences, produce brochures, and cast and count votes. They would also learn about the issues. A student could work toward the goal of improving cooperation with peers (on his IEP) by becoming a member of a campaign team. A gifted student challenged by the demands of leadership might be an ideal candidate to run for mayor. These students are experiencing high cognitive complexity. However, students from other classes who listen to speeches, read newspapers to learn the issues, and cast a ballot may be learning about democracy in a concrete way. Some authentic tasks are valuable because they provide concrete experiences of abstract ideas such as democracy.

Interest refers to an affective interaction between students and tasks. It is often suggested that gifted students need to follow their interests (Coleman, Gallagher, & Nelson, 1997). However, interest also plays an important role in engaging students who are not largely interested in learning for its own sake—those with learning disabilities, AD/HD, and other exceptionalities. John Freeman (1998) of Queen's University showed that, for these students, developing curriculum around interests (in trucks, pets, etc.) can produce focused attention and learning. For students unwilling to learn, try adapting by creating activities around their interests for curriculum goals. I taught a reading comprehension unit that included all of my curriculum goals (identifying main idea and supporting details, reading captions of figures, etc.) and was based on Saskatchewan's driver handbook. The idea came to me as I watched my students struggle to read the content they needed to pass the test for a learner's driving permit. I capitalized on their interest in learning to drive to improve their reading comprehension, and they all secured the coveted permit.

Environment, Method of Presentation, Pace, and Quantity

Environment has to do with classroom climate and physical layout, both of which are addressed in Chapter 6. High expectations accompanied by high support makes for the best learning environment. You can increase your support and encouragement simply by being alert to signs of discouragement and reminding students of their accomplishments. You can also adapt the environment by changing seating, often a useful strategy but rarely intense enough to make big changes in learning. Remove distractions, glare, and clutter if such actions meet the needs of exceptional students. Consider keeping exceptional students near you so they can focus.

Cross-Reference
Chapter 6 focuses on classroom climate, community, and management—including strategies for creating an environment in which to ADAPT.

You can vary **method of presentation** to the advantage of your whole class. When you present ideas orally, you may choose to use an approach similar to that of Ms. Ash (described in the case study at the beginning of this chapter). She gave students a partially completed outline, modelled how to complete the outline, stopped to allow students to write on their outline, and used methods of direct instruction. Research suggests that most exceptional students, with the exception of some gifted students, benefit from having been directly shown with clear explanations, models, guided practice, sufficient independent practice, and feedback

(Friend, Bursuck, & Hutchinson, 1998). Videotaped presentations allow all students to learn about atoms, for example, before tackling the textbook on the subject. Guest speakers may capture students' interests. Hands-on learning is often necessary for exceptional learners and helpful for other students. When planning a presentation, run down your list of exceptional students and ask what you expect each of them to get from the presentation. Then ask what you can ADAPT to ensure they learn as much as possible. This does not mean planning separate lessons; rather, it means making small changes to the lesson presentation while planning it and again while teaching it.

Pace refers to the rate of presentation of new information or to the rate of introduction of new skills. Generally, exceptional students need new skills introduced in small steps and slowly to ensure mastery, and need concepts introduced slowly with opportunity and time to develop understanding before the next concept. This may mean setting priorities and deleting some concepts or skills for exceptional students. While Ms. Krugly introduced three reading comprehension strategies to her class, the resource teacher taught one comprehension strategy to a group of three exceptional students. Their follow-up activities contained only sequencing exercises. Instead of learning three strategies to a small extent, these three students learned one reading comprehension strategy well and were able to use it when they read. Introducing skills slowly is a helpful and easy adaptation—use fewer new spelling words, etc., and expect learning to the same standard as the others in the class. Over time, the volume learned is reduced, and given the hierarchical nature of the curriculum in areas like math and science, this can have long-term impact.

Student Engagement and Activities, Amount of Practice, and Form of Practice

Student **engagement** has to do with the extent to which students embrace learning and throw themselves into the activities of the classroom. Students who are disengaged from learning and from the social life of the classroom have little reason to go to school or to cooperate with those around them. It is critical that we engage every student and ensure that every student learns, even if what they learn is not the same as their peers. A danger of poorly implemented inclusion is that students are only physically present in the classroom without being part of the community or engaged in learning. Students must be cognitively active to be engaged (Blumenfeld, Puro, & Mergendoller, 1992); without engagement, expect behaviour problems and alienation (Seidel & Vaughn, 1991). Use three novels of varying levels of difficulty if that means that every student will engage with a book, or place a few students with LD at a listening station with a book on tape and expect them to demonstrate comprehension.

Additional practice is often critical to the learning of exceptional students. Brief reviews of key information or skills may help exceptional students' retention. Don't be afraid to use different follow-up activities after your presentation of new information. For example, the follow-up activity on blue paper may place triads at a centre in the classroom after they have completed the practice examples. The yellow follow-up may require students to independently develop challenge questions, and the green follow-up may place students with you for review and practice. Change the colours so that green is not always the "easiest," change the groups so they don't become the stereotyped "buzzards, bluebirds, and owls," and change the group that receives your attention. There are many ways to vary the rate and quantity of practice. Adapting the **form of practice** means accepting oral or written practice or whatever advances the students' learning.

Scaffolding, Grouping, Collaboration, Independence, and Assessment

Cross-Reference
Ways to enhance social relations and use cooperative and collaborative learning are elaborated in Chapter 9.

Scaffolding refers to the support that may enable a student to do more with the assistance of a peer or the teacher than she can do on her own. **Zone of proximal development (ZPD)** refers to the learning the student is about to undertake that they can already understand with support. This comes from the work of Vygotskty (1986), who hypothesized that students learned things socially first and later appropriated them as their own understanding. Exceptional students often benefit from gradually decreasing scaffolding. This is why **grouping** as seen as such an important strategy in inclusive classrooms. As well, collaborative and cooperative learning have appeared as teaching strategies throughout the chapters of this book.

Adapting Teaching of Listening, Reading, and Writing

Building Listening Skills, Story Telling, and the Use of Environmental Print

We may assume that our students know how to listen and that they choose to misbehave when they aren't listening. Some exceptional students may not know how to listen; other students may also benefit from activities that build listening skills. When you teach students to listen, ensure that you have everyone's attention.

The following strategy is effective in elementary classrooms (Evans & Strong, 1996) and can be adapted for secondary classes in literature and content areas. Create a brief, narrative account that you think will interest your students. Remind them of three skills for *paying attention*:

1. Look at the person reading or speaking.
2. Sit still.
3. Keep your hands in your lap.

Then focus on *listening skills* by giving a purpose for listening:

1. With younger students, show three pictures of an event in the story, such as the ending. Ask them to listen so they can choose the correct picture of the ending.
2. With older students, replace the pictures with three brief sentences or passages. Ask them to listen so they can choose the passage with the viewpoint of a particular character, etc.

Teach students both to recount personal experiences and to listen to each other's accounts. Find another adult to form a pair with you. Model telling a brief personal-experience story while the other adult models active listening followed by a genuine question. Model restating the question and responding. Switch roles. Model a realistic exchange for your students to emulate. Next have students in pairs follow your model, switching roles. For young children, you could put an older student in charge of small groups. Provide additional days of practice for those still learning to listen.

Environmental print refers to the common words and symbols of our environment—that represent fast food restaurants, soft drink products, toy companies, and car makers. With a bit of practice, children recognize these familiar words in manuscript printing as well as in symbols. Parents can post the child's name and the names of other family members to promote recognition. At school, children with developmental disabilities often recognize environmental print, the names of classmates, and classroom signs. This is a step toward becoming a reader that you can capitalize on with children who acquire literacy slowly and with effort. Strategies to take advantage of environmental print:

Further Reading

D.D. Evans & C.J. Strong (1996). What's the story: Attending, listening, telling in middle school. *Teaching Exceptional Children, 28*(3), 58–61.

K.M. Arnold & D. Hornett (1990). Teaching idioms to children who are deaf. *Teaching Exceptional Children, 22*(4), 14–17.

- encourage cutting and pasting of symbols from magazines until the child can print the words in her journal
- use manuscript print under the environmental print symbol to promote recognition of the printed form
- post printed signs around the classroom on the window, door, desk, etc.
- post children's names on their desks so the child with developmental disabilities can match names on books to names on desks and distribute books, etc.
- enlist parents to help their child in using environmental print at home as well as at school.

Adapting to Promote Learning to Read: Phonological Processing and Balanced Reading Programs

The past 15 years have seen the so-called "**reading wars**," controversies over the whole language versus phonics emphases in early reading (Stanovich & Stanovich, 1995). Research indicates that the most critical factor beneath fluent word reading is the ability to recognize letters, spelling patterns, and whole words effortlessly and automatically on sight (Adams, 1990). In a recent paper, Keith Stanovich (1994) of the University of Toronto discussed the nature of effective programs for developing word recognition skills and phonemic awareness (early reading) and for developing comprehension, the topics of this and the next section.

Research shows that the best way to develop early reading skills is with explicit instruction and teacher-directed strategy training, especially for at-risk children and children with learning disabilities (Stanovich, 1994). Many researchers like Dale Willows (1999) of the University of Toronto (see Focus on Schools) suggest balancing explicit instruction of word recognition skills (e.g., phonemic awareness) with meaningful reading activities (e.g., Collins-Williams & Willows, 1998; Jackett & Willows, 1998).

To teach phonemic awareness, it is important that teachers understand what is involved. **Phonemic awareness**:

- is sensitivity to and explicit awareness of individual sounds that make up words
- demands that children analyze or manipulate the sounds rather than focus on the meaning
- includes early skills such as recognizing rhyming, and later skills such as segmenting the sounds in words and synthesizing the sounds in words

Use the following general teaching ideas to introduce phonemic awareness into your primary reading program:

- read widely about phonemic awareness
- start with easy tasks and build up gradually
- teach explicitly, because children who lack phonemic awareness do not usually generalize well and are at risk of developing reading disabilities
- develop 15- to 20-minute daily activities for a group that supplement and are a natural extension of shared reading activities
- use literature and play with the sounds in language; make it fun!

Figures 7.1 and 7.2 demonstrate how to teach phonemic awareness.

Put Into Practice

Develop a plan for teaching phonemic awareness to all grade 1 students with more regular practice for those at risk for learning disabilities: M.J. Adams, B.R. Foorman, I. Lundberg, & T. Beeler (1998). *Phonemic Awareness in Young Children: A Classroom Curriculum.* Toronto: Irwin Publishing.

Figure 7.1

TEACHING PHONEMIC AWARENESS

Instructional Guidelines for Planning Phoneme Awareness Activities

1. Identify the precise phonemic awareness task on which you wish to focus and select developmentally appropriate activities for engaging children in the task. Activities should be fun and exciting—"play" with sounds, don't "drill" them.

2. Be sure to use phoneme sounds (represented by / /) and *not* letter names when doing the activities. Likewise, remember that one sound may be represented by two or more letters. There are only three sounds in the word *cheese:* /ch/-/ee/-/z/. You may want to target specific sounds/words at first and "practice" beforehand until you are comfortable making them.

3. Continuant sounds (e.g., /m/, /s/, /l/) are easier to manipulate and hear than stop consonants (e.g., /t/, /g/, /p/). When introducing continuants, exaggerate by holding on to them: rrrrrring; for stop consonants, use iteration (rapid repetition): /k/-/k/-/k/-/k/-/k/atie.

4. When identifying sounds in different positions, the *initial* position is easiest, followed by the *final* position, with the *medial* position being most difficult (e.g., top, pot, letter).

5. When identifying or combining sound sequences, a CV pattern should be used before a VC pattern, followed by a CVC pattern (e.g., pie, egg, red).

Note. CV = consonant-vowel; VC = vowel-consonant; CVC = consonant-vowel-consonant.

Source: P.J. Edelen-Smith (1997). How now brown cow: Phoneme awareness activities for collaborative classrooms. *Intervention in Clinic and School, 33*(2), 105. Used by permission.

Figure 7.2

PHONEMIC AWARENESS: AWARENESS OF ONSET AND RIME

Onset and Rime: In families of words (like lend, send, tend), the initial consonant (l, s, t) is the onset, and the following vowel/consonant combination (end) is the rime.

Word Families:

(1) Play games and put the resulting words on charts. For example, say /b/ + it = *bit*. Ask the children to name other words that sound like *bit*.

(2) Use literature. For example, *Tog the Dog* (Hawkins & Hawkins, 1986) places various onsets in front of the rime /og/. Many of the books recommended by Yopp could be used to create reference books of families of words. These could be used in making new rhymes. Remember to say the words and draw attention constantly to the sounds.

Literature:

Choose books with rhyme patterns (many by Dr. Seuss), and with alliteration (e.g., *Aster Aardvark's Alphabet Adventures* by Kellogg, 1987), and with assonance (e.g., *Moses Supposes His Toeses are Roses* by Patz, 1983). Raffi's tapes contain many songs with these patterns.

Direct Teaching:

- Say pairs of words and ask if they sound the same or different (e.g., run, sun and hit, pan).

- Say a list of words and ask which is the odd one out (e.g., kite, site, pen, right).

- Create card games, songs, and picture collections that provide opportunities for children to say words, attend to their sounds, and decide whether specific sounds are the same or different.

Simple Phonemic Awareness

Targeted Skill	Example
Isolated sound recognition	Sammy snake sound says _____. (/s/)
Word/syllable/phoneme counting	How many (words/syllables/sounds) do you hear in this (sentence/word)?
Sound synthesis	It starts with /l/ and ends with /ight/, put it together and it says _____. (*light*)
What word am I saying?	Put these sounds together to make a word—/f/-/i/-/sh/.
Sound-to-word matching	Is there a /k/ in *cat*?
	What is the first sound you hear in *dog*?
Identification of sound positions	Where do you hear the /g/ in *pig* (at the beginning, middle, or end of the word)?
Sound segmentation	What sounds do you hear in the word *ball*? Say each one.
Letter-sound association	What letter goes with the first sound in this word—*book*?

Source: P.J. Edelen-Smith (1997). How now brown cow: Phoneme awareness activities for collaborative classrooms. *Intervention in Clinic and School, 33*(2), 106. Used by permission.

Early Reading: A Delicate Balance

It's impossible to escape the sights and sounds of children learning to read at Ridgewood Public School. In Phyllis Trudeau's kindergarten class, the children follow her lead in sounding out—and shaping with their fingers—the letters and sounds of the alphabet. Swaying from side to side to make the letter T, the children chant out "tuh, tuh, tuh" to make the sound. In the school library, teacher-librarian Pat Brodie and a group of grade 3 students discuss a Judy Blume novel. The students take turns reading passages, eager to jump in when Ms. Brodie pauses to ask questions about what's happening in the book.

Throughout the school, the tools for learning to read are everywhere. Direct, systematic phonics (to figure out letter–sound relations) is in place from kindergarten. A wide range of books and other print materials are used in the older grades (one of the elements of whole language). Each of the classrooms has a "word wall" for high-frequency words to help build a child's vocabulary. The letters of the alphabet—and the sounds they make—ring the top of the walls in every room.

This is a school that takes reading very seriously. The results of that commitment show up in steady improvement in reading test scores by the school and the Peel District School Board. The data show students in the kindergarten to Grade 5 school who spend their entire time at Ridgewood do better than students who transfer in from other schools. For this school of 650 students, where 58% of the population speaks a language other than English, about the only thing missing from the picture is any controversy over reading.

Moving past the "reading wars" of the past decade, Ridgewood is one of a growing number of schools that have adopted a balanced approach to early reading. "There's a movement away from dogma to common sense," observed Prof. Dale Willows, a psychology professor at the Ontario Institute for Studies in Education at the University of Toronto, and a proponent of "balanced literacy." In addition to her work in coaching classroom teachers on how to put together a balanced literacy program, she has been selected to serve on the National Reading Panel, established last year by the United States Congress to assess the status of research-based knowledge on reading, including the effectiveness of various ways to teach children to read.

The balanced literacy approach at Ridgewood, where Prof. Willows has worked with teachers, has many components. It includes:

- explicit, systematic phonics so students learn letter–sound combinations that will help decode the words on the page.

- teaching of phonemic awareness, through rhymes and other tools, so students go a step beyond the letter–sound combinations. For example, the S sound in sand is about phonics, but the *and* portion of the word is about phonemic awareness.

- integrated use of the principles of whole language, with students drawing on a wide range of books—sometimes guided by the teacher, sometimes not—to do their own independent writing.

- school-based and board-wide testing to identify student weaknesses in spelling, writing and reading.

- informal grouping of students, by reading levels, to offer stimulation to the strong readers and extra help for those in need.

- parent contracts for reading, so those at home can support what is happening at school.

- daily and weekly book bags, with books selected on the basis of the child's reading ability, that go home with the child.

- after-school workshops for teachers and occasional release time during the school year for teachers to confer with each other on strategies to improve the children's reading performance.

- dedicated use of scarce school resources to buy test material, books and other resources to support what the teachers say they need for their reading programs.

For Ms. Awde, the Grade 1 teacher and a teacher for 33 years, the most positive part of the most recent reading trend is the focus on the individual child. In this way, she says, teachers know how to build on strengths and rectify weaknesses.

Source: Jennifer Lewington (1998). *Globe and Mail*. November 9, pp. C1, C7. Used by permission.

Adapting Reading to Learn: Using Textbooks by Adapting, Supplementing, and Bypassing

After most students have learned to read, classroom routines depend on students reading to learn. Many exceptional students are inefficient at getting meaning from text, while academically advanced students are proficient, fast readers. In reading to learn, students must comprehend new text, relate new ideas to prior knowledge, and create an elaborated understanding. Inefficient readers often require prompting to attend to their relevant prior knowledge and relate it to their new learning, and require assistance with vocabulary and word recognition.

You may be able to use scaffolding to help you adapt reading-to-learn tasks. Scaffolding allows us to provide the cueing, questioning, coaching, and corroboration that "allow students to complete a task before they are able to complete it independently and while they gradually gain control of it" (Pearson, 1996, p. 169). The **Scaffolded Reading Experience (SRE)** is designed for classes with students of varying abilities in reading to learn. It applies the steps of the ADAPT strategy, encouraging teachers to plan by considering (1) the students, (2) the reading selection, and (3) the purpose of the reading. SRE considers three steps in teaching: (1) pre-reading activities, (2) reading activities, and (3) post-reading activities. See Table 7.1 for examples.

Table 7.1

POSSIBLE COMPONENTS OF A SCAFFOLDED READING EXPERIENCE

Prereading activities	During-reading activities	Postreading activities
Relating the reading to students' lives	Silent reading	Questioning
Motivating	Reading to students	Discussion
Activating background knowledge	Guided reading	Writing
Building text specific knowledge	Oral reading by students	Drama
Preteaching vocabulary	Modifying the text	Artistic and nonverbal activities
Preteaching concepts		Application and outreach activities
Prequestioning, predicting, and direction setting		Reteaching
Suggesting strategies		

Source: M.F. Graves & S. Braaten. Scaffolded reading experiences: Building bridges to success. *Preventing School Failure, 40*(4), 169–73. Used by permission.

Graves and Braaten (1996) describe a grade 7 teacher using SRE with a class of 28 (16 typical, 6 better-than-average, and 6 below-average readers). The text used was "The King of Storms" (Flatow, 1985), an expository piece, 1500 words, in eight sections, about hurricanes. The **pre-reading activities** for the entire class included a discussion about the movie *Twister*, a video clip of tornadoes, a discussion of destructive weather the students and their families had experienced, a preview of the text by the teacher, and a contrast of hurricanes and tornadoes.

Then the groups participated in differing amounts of scaffolding. The strong readers received written instructions for **post-reading activities** and began silent reading. The average readers began a vocabulary- and concept-building assignment in small groups and then read. The less-skilled readers worked with the teacher on vocabulary and concepts and the teacher read half the article aloud. Then, two groups of three students each received instructions to become experts on a designated section of the article. The teacher served as a resource for all students. The skilled readers contrasted the destruction caused by hurricanes and tornadoes and made a chart to show the path hurricanes usually follow and the countries that can be struck by hurricanes. The average-readers groups wrote a summary of a section of the article and created a visual representation. The two groups of less-skilled readers had the same assignment with more scaffolding prior to and during the activity. A few classes later, each group presented its information, and the teacher corrected any misinformation and closed the unit with highlights and video clips of hurricanes. All students had been challenged to learn content and improve their reading comprehension.

Textbooks can be supplemented with guest speakers, videotapes, field trips, television programs, trade books, newspapers, and hands-on activities. Trips to art galleries, museums, nature reserves, symphonies, shops, parks, and the schoolyard can provide the same information as textbooks in an experiential mode. If this kind of supplement is valuable for all students, it may become part of any unit. Grouping children with similar exceptionalities and assigning these activities to paraprofessionals are two ways that inclusion teachers can ensure that these activities take place. Provide opportunities for gifted students to challenge one another (Coleman et al., 1997). To bypass the textbook, look for alternate texts that cover the same topics. Seek **high-interest low-vocabulary books** for novel study and general reading.

Put Into Practice

Adapt a lesson plan you have prepared, using one of the following sources: J. Ciborowski (1992). *Textbooks and the Students Who Can't Read Them: A Guide to Teaching Content.* Cambridge, MA: Brookline.

M.F. Graves & S. Braaten (1996). Scaffolded reading experience: Bridges to success. *Preventing School Failure, 40*(4),

Newspapers can supplement textbooks in many subjects.

Teaching Vocabulary and Comprehension Strategies

Teaching reading and teaching content classes involve teaching students new **vocabulary**. For many students, it is enough to introduce a new word and connect it to their existing language. However, you may need to do more to ensure that exceptional students acquire new vocabulary. Carnine and his colleagues (1990) developed an effective and direct way to teach vocabulary with five steps. You might use this adaptation to help students with limited vocabularies at the beginning of a unit, to review at the midpoint, and to reinforce shortly before the assessment at the end of a unit:

1. Choose a range of positive and negative examples to teach the new word or concept. For the concept of leisure, give examples of watching television, viewing movies, camping, fishing, attending art galleries, and playing tennis. Non-examples might include working at a part-time job and running errands for your parents. Use six examples of the concept and at least two non-examples.

2. Use synonyms that the students already know. For leisure, you could use play. State the definition simply and clearly. Leisure is time that is free from work, when you can choose what you want to do.

3. Model or point to positive and negative examples. For leisure, model telephoning a friend and arranging a game of tennis. Point to pictures of people at a sporting event, hiking in the mountains, viewing a painting in a gallery. For negative examples or non-examples, model going to work and point to pictures of people entering a factory, sitting at a desk, etc.

4. Ask a series of yes/no questions to help students discriminate examples from non-examples. Ask how they know whether to say yes or no. For the concept square, point to a rectangle and ask if it is a square. Ask the students why they answer no. Ask them to use the definition you have taught.

5. Find out whether students can discriminate this concept from others. Is leisure the same as rest? How might they be different? Explore features that are sometimes present in the concept. For example, leisure is sometimes done alone and sometimes done with friends.

Vocabulary development is important to reading and to understanding in content subjects. In mathematics, many students need direct teaching of vocabulary.

Enhancing Written Expression and Facilitating Note Taking

To adapt the writing of **narrative text**, you can use a series of scaffolded tasks. For those who write fluently and willingly, use only topic prompts. For students who cannot start with a topic prompt, introduce picture prompts and brainstorming about the pictures. Next time try only topic prompts, reintroducing picture prompts only for those who need them. For students who cannot begin from a picture prompt and brainstorming, add a **story planning sheet** with the following prompts:

Further Reading

Lists of books that are easy to read and high in interest: P. Phelan (ed.) (1996). *High Interest—Easy Reading: An Annotated Booklist for Middle School and Senior High School*, Seventh edition. Urbana, IL: National Council of Teachers of English.

R.J. Ryder, B.B. Graves, & M.F. Graves (1989). *Easy Reading Book Series and Periodicals for Less Able Readers*, Second edition. Newark, DE: International Reading Association.

- Setting—where and when the story took place
- Main character—the person or persons around whom the problem or conflict revolves
- Character clues—appearance, actions, dialogue, thoughts of character, comments of others
- Problem—conflicts
- Attempts—how the character tries to solve the problem
- Resolution—how the problem gets solved or does not get solved

Students can complete the prompts briefly on the story planning sheet while brainstorming with a partner and later independently. Those who don't need a planning sheet can use a checklist of these prompts, with the addition of theme, to check that all essential elements are in their narratives. This approach can be adapted to scaffold student writing of notes from a text, lecture, discussion, or videotape. The principles are to provide no more scaffolding than students need and to gradually move students from peer and teacher support to independence with self-checking. Keep records of the scaffolding students use each day so you can prompt for more independence. If you copy each degree of scaffolding onto a different colour of paper, you can encourage students to move from yellow to green, etc., and see at a glance who is using each degree of scaffolding (Simmons, Dickson, & Chard, 1993).

Adapting Teaching of Mathematics

In mathematics, as well, adaptations depend on the mismatch between the student's strengths and needs and the demands of the curriculum. Young children learn number sense as a foundation for all mathematical development. Then they learn computation and problem solving. In each area they may need changes in order to succeed.

Number Sense

Number sense is difficult to define. Teachers seem to recognize when children lack this essential sense of what numbers mean, how to compare numbers, and how to see and count quantities in the world around them. Most children acquire this conceptual structure informally through interactions with parents, siblings, and peers before kindergarten. Students with good number sense can move effortlessly between quantities in the real world and numbers and mathematical expressions in the world of mathematics. They can make up procedures and represent the same quantity in multiple ways depending on context and purpose. They see that when they have three cars and five trucks, they have more trucks without executing a precise numerical operation. Children who have not acquired this sense of number require formal instruction to do so (Bruer, 1993). Number sense may serve the same function for mathematics as phonological processing serves for beginning reading—it appears to be essential for later competence in mathematics. There is increasing empirical support relating inadequate development of number sense to learning disabilities (Geary, 1993; Gersten & Chard, 1999).

Robbie Case (1998), who was at the University of Toronto, and Sharon Griffin (Griffin & Case, 1997) developed an instructional program in number sense using three representational systems:

1. Conventional math symbols: digits, addition, subtraction, equal signs
2. A thermometer that shows the number line in a clear vertical direction, so bigger is higher and smaller is lower
3. A representational system that looks like the Candyland game

Students play games comparing quantities and adding one number to another using the three representational systems, and have frequent opportunities to verbalize their understandings and rationales for the strategies they use to solve problems.

Many teachers use a "**hundreds chart**" to help students explore number sense. Vacc (1995) modified the hundreds chart to align its vocabulary and format with the vocabulary and methods used when manipulating numbers. It includes the numbers 0 to 99 and progresses from right to left (Figure 7.3). It places the numerals 0 through 9 in the "ones" column, the numerals 10 through 19 in the "tens" column, and so on. Vacc recommends that teachers use clear, coloured counters so students can see the numeral under the counter and model using a restructured hundreds chart on an overhead transparency. Students manipulate clear, coloured markers on their own hundreds charts to count, match number words and numerals, identify numbers and numerical relationships, and place value. Students can use the chart for numerical patterns, addition, subtraction, multiplication, division, and prime numbers. For example, to teach place value, say: "Cover the number that is 2 'tens' and 4 'ones.' Next cover 5 'tens' and 7 'ones.'" For numerical patterns say, "Begin with 0, count by 2s, placing a marker on each number counted. Describe the pattern you have made." Next you can add a prediction component for counting by 2s, 3s, etc. This is a systematic way to develop and enhance number sense.

Computation

Often an effect of math learning disabilities is lack of fluency with **computation** and basic number facts. Teaching older students to use a calculator, a bypass strategy, is only justifiable after you have adapted teaching to increase number fact fluency. When young children are counting the objects in two sets, do not immediately expect them to memorize number facts. Teach them to count on, by naming one number and counting on the other. Model this strategy using fingers, number lines, objects, or the three representational systems suggested by Griffin and Case. For example, for 6 + 3, say "Six, put your finger on 6 on the number line and put one counter on each of 7, 8, and 9," saying each number as you put the counter on it. Throughout, keep strengthening basic counting skills. Later, teach the child to always start with the larger of the two numbers, remembering that it takes number sense to judge which is larger. This can be called "the trick." Teach the commutative principle by showing that 4 + 5 = 5 + 4. Encourage students to read num-

Further Reading

To learn more about the Rightstart program: S.A. Griffin, R. Case, & R.S. Siegler (1994). Rightstart. In K. McGilly (ed.), *Classroom Lessons: Integrating Cognitive Theory and Practice* (pp. 25–50). Cambridge, MA: MIT Press.

S.A. Griffin (1997). Re-thinking the primary school math curriculum. *Issues in Education, 3,* 1–49.

What do you think?

Why might this modified hundreds chart help children? Read the following paper and discuss with your peers: N.N. Vacc (1995). Gaining number sense through a restructured hundreds chart. *Teaching Exceptional Children,* 28(1), 50–55.

Figure 7.3

REVISED HUNDREDS CHART

90	80	70	60	50	40	30	20	10	0
91	81	71	61	51	41	31	21	11	1
92	82	72	62	52	42	32	22	12	2
93	83	73	63	53	43	33	23	13	3
94	84	74	64	54	44	34	24	14	4
95	85	75	65	55	45	35	25	15	5
96	86	76	66	56	46	36	26	16	6
97	87	77	67	57	47	37	27	17	7
98	88	78	68	58	48	38	28	18	8
99	89	79	69	59	49	39	29	19	9

Source: N.N. Vacc (1995). Gaining number sense through a restructured hundreds chart. *Teaching Exceptional Children, 28*(1), 51. Used by permission.

ber problems aloud and verbalize what they are thinking. Garnett (1992) suggests the order in which addition (and multiplication) facts should be learned (see Figure 7.4). As students become more mature in their strategies, teach them to ask, "Do I just know this one?" and use retrieval strategies whenever possible. Press for speed with a few facts at a time, following the order in Figure 7.4. When students are not using retrieval strategies, encourage them to think out loud and discuss the strategies children can use.

Problem Solving, Representation, Symbol Systems, and Application

Many exceptional students experience difficulty with problem solving. Recent curriculum reforms have highlighted problem solving. Number sense and computational fluency are both essential to problem solving. It is difficult to bypass number sense while calculators can be used to bypass lack of computational fluency. Research provides many reasons for using calculators as an adaptation for exceptional students:

- calculators provide all students with practice and success in calculating ratios and solving proportion problems (Mittag & Van Reusen, 1999);
- calculators encourage students to focus on advanced concepts, rather than number crunching (Gilchrist, 1986);
- calculators make calculations less tedious for exceptional students (Harvey, Waits, & Demana, 1995);

ALTERNATE TEACHING SEQUENCE FOR ADDITION FACTS

(1)	+1 and +0 principles Adding 1 or 0 to any number	
(2)	Ties	2+2 3+3 4+4 5+5 6+6 7+7 8+8 9+9
(3)	Ties +1	2+3 3+4 4+5 5+6 6+7 7+8 8+9
(4)	Ties +2	2+4 3+5 4+6 5+7 6+8 7+9
(5)	+ 10 Principle from 2+10 through 10+10	
(6)	+ 9 Facts from 2+9 through 9+9 Use the linking strategy (n+10) −1	
(7)	Remaining facts	2+5 2+6 2+7 2+8 3+6 3+7 3+8 4+7 4+8 5+8

Must include major emphasis on the commutative principle
(5+6 = 6+5)

ALTERNATE TEACHING SEQUENCE FOR MULTIPLICATION FACTS

(a)	$\times$ 1 and $\times$ 0 Principles Multiplying any number by 1 or 0
(b)	$\times$ 2/2 $\times$
(c)	$\times$ 3/3 $\times$
(d)	$\times$ 9/9 $\times$
(e)	Perfect squares $(1 \times 1, 2 \times 2, 3 \times 3, 4 \times 4, 5 \times 5, 6 \times 6, 7 \times 7, 8 \times 8, 9 \times 9, 10 \times 10)$
(f)	Remaining facts

$$3 \times 4 \quad 3 \times 6 \quad 3 \times 7 \quad 3 \times 8$$
$$4 \times 6 \quad 4 \times 7 \quad 4 \times 8$$
$$6 \times 7 \quad 6 \times 8$$
$$7 \times 8$$

Must include major emphasis on the commutative principle ($5 \times 6 = 6 \times 5$).

Source: K. Garnett (1992). Developing fluency with basic number facts: Intervention for students with learning disabilities. *Learning Disabilities: Research and Practice, 7*, 210–16. Used by permission.

- calculators allow for the use of real data sets (Durham & Dick, 1994);
- calculator use increases student confidence, enthusiasm, and number sense (Campbell & Stewart, 1993).

Strategies to help students solve problems include using authentic problems, demonstrating concrete examples, providing calculators, and making the reasoning used to represent the problem visible to the student. These strategies are apparent in the following example. Mittag and Van Reusen (1999) taught students about the capture-recapture estimation method used to estimate the population of a fish in a lake. The naturalist takes a sample of fish (120) from a lake, tags them, and

Put Into Practice

Find an example of strategy instruction for teaching solving of word problems. Follow the steps to teach a friend or student. Here are two resources: M. Montague, C. Warger, & T.H. Morgan (2000). Solve It! Strategy instruction to improve mathematical problem solving. *Learning Disabilities Research and Practice, 15*(2), 110–16.

D.H. Allsopp (1999). Using modeling, manipulatives, and mnemonics with eighth-grade math students. *Teaching Exceptional Children, 32*(2), 74–81.

releases them. Then, after the tagged sample has had time to mix with the unmarked fish, another sample of 65 is taken and the naturalist finds that only two of the 65 fish have tags. The naturalist writes an equation to solve this proportion problem:

$$\frac{\text{number of marked fish in the population}}{\text{total number of fish in the population (N)}} = \frac{\text{number of marked fish in the sample}}{\text{total number of fish in the sample}}$$

$$\frac{120}{N} = \frac{2}{65}$$

$$7800 = 2N$$

$$3900 = N$$

The teacher gave groups of students classroom representations of the fish problem using two kinds of snack food in the shapes of fish (cheddar fish and pretzel fish). Then the students solved other problems in the same form using samples to predict populations.

I developed a strategy to teach adolescents with learning disabilities to solve algebra word problems (Hutchinson, 1993). In this approach, students learned first to represent word problems and then to develop solutions. The teacher models by thinking out loud using a set of self-questions, students engage in guided practice with an adult or a peer, and then they engage in independent practice. I used this approach to teach individuals, pairs, small groups, and finally whole classes (Hutchinson, 1997). The self-questions appear below:

Self-Questions for Representing Algebra Word Problems

1. Have I read and understood each sentence? Are there any words whose meaning I have to ask?
2. Have I got the whole picture, a representation, for this problem?
3. Have I written down my representation on the worksheet? (goal; unknown(s); known(s); type of problem; equation)
4. What should I look for in a new problem to see if it is the same kind of problem?

Self-Questions for Solving Algebra Word Problems

1. Have I written an equation?
2. Have I expanded the terms?

Encourage students to think out loud to you and discuss the math strategies they are using.

3. Have I written out the steps of my solution on the worksheet? (collected like terms; isolated unknown(s); solved for unknown(s); checked my answer with the goal; highlighted my answer)

4. What should I look for in a new problem to see if it is the same kind of problem?

Students complete each problem on a structured worksheet designed to match the self-questions. In all seven studies I conducted, students learned to solve the algebra problems they were taught, could solve similar problems six weeks later, and transferred their problem solving to new kinds of problems. These results taken with the other strategies described in this section suggest that it is possible to adapt to teach strategies to exceptional children and adolescents.

Adapting Teaching in Content Areas: Science, Social Studies, Visual Arts, Music, Drama, and French

Adapting Science Teaching

Adapting the teaching of science can appear overwhelming. Issues of safety and supervision in the science laboratory (Chin, 1997) are intensified by the inclusion of exceptional students. For example, blind students and students with low vision require an orientation to the location of equipment and supplies and must be paired with a sighted peer; all members of the class must be reminded to return equipment to the same location. The visually impaired student can identify the contribution he can make to an activity after reading a Braille description of the activity or listening to an oral description. He can time phases of an experiment on his Braille watch, make sound observations, or take readings on a Braille thermometer or a talking thermometer. For students with low vision, a **CCTV** image magnifier can be set up so that experiments can be directly observed, and hand-outs can be copied at 129 or 156 percent to allow easier reading. For blind students, a listing of the steps of the experiment in Braille and a "blow-by-blow" description by the teacher or a student will be necessary. Only a small number of students have visual impairments, so it is unlikely that your school laboratory will be stocked with the materials described here. However, you may find that another school in your district or the district board office has the materials required by a blind student. Contact the nearest office of the Canadian National Institute for the Blind (CNIB) (http://www.cnib.ca/). There are many resources available to guide science teaching of students with disabilities such as visual impairment, hearing impairment, and physical disabilities (e.g., Riendl & Haworth, 1995; Weisgerber, 1993). Hema's case study at the opening of this chapter suggests how you might include a student with developmental disabilities in a science unit.

Because about half of exceptional students have learning disabilities and adaptations that help these students tend to be effective for all who read below grade level, consider the reading demands of your science text. The reading expected by

Weblinks

SCIENCE WORLD
http://www.scienceworld.bc.ca/

EDMONTON SPACE AND SCIENCE CENTRE
http://www.ee.ualberta.ca/essc

CALGARY SCIENCE CENTRE
http://www.calgaryscience.ca/

SCIENCE NORTH
http://sciencenorth.on.ca

ONTARIO SCIENCE CENTRE
http://www.osc.on.ca/

DISCOVERY CENTRE
http://www.discoverycentre.ns.ca

PHYSLINK (FOR TEACHING SECONDARY PHYSICS, INCLUDING LINKS TO SIMULATIONS)
http://www.physlink.com/reference_edu.cfm

YES MAGAZINE, A CANADIAN SCIENCE MAGAZINE FOR CHILDREN
http://www.yesmag.bc.ca

science texts has increased over the past few decades. Look for texts with a lower reading level that provide parallel information or a Web site that is more accessible to students who are poor readers. Other strategies include graphic organizers and study guides that help students pull the main ideas from complex text and see them in order, in a hierarchy, or connected to each other. Models help students understand complex science (Woodward, 1994). For example, Figure 7.5 shows applications of the convection cell model to a range of weather and earth science concepts.

Adapting Social Studies and Literature

Reciprocal teaching involves teaching students to teach one another by taking turns leading discussion in small groups. Usually the teacher models how to lead the discussion, and provides scaffolding for the groups as they begin. This teaching approach, developed by Anne Marie Palincsar and Ann Brown (1984) has been used from grades 2 to 10. Form groups of four or five students with one exceptional student in each group, two if necessary. Choose a discussion leader for each group each day, beginning with a confident but patient student who will understand the process and model it well for peers. Students read a selection from their textbook (usually three to four pages). With younger students, you might ask them to stop after each paragraph. Each student receives a worksheet until the class is familiar with reciprocal teaching. Allow students to choose to use the worksheet after you make blank paper available. On the worksheet, ask students to think of three good questions about what they have read. Prompt them to list the subheadings and three main points under each subheading. Then the group goes through the strategies of questioning, summarizing, predicting, and clarifying. For example, for the strategy of questioning, help the discussion leader to use who, what, where, when, and why questions to elicit the key ideas of the passage. Summarizing involves the leader asking the others to provide a summary of the passage, beginning with the early highlights. After one student has answered, the discussion leader can ask others to add or to correct. Clarifying refers to asking questions "whenever we don't understand something." Encourage students that anyone who doesn't understand should ask a question. Suggest that passages often leave readers wondering and that together the group can puzzle these things out and clarify them. Predicting involves students in considering what comes next. The leader should read out a subheading and ask students to engage in predicting what will appear under this subheading. Sometimes students expect one kind of information and find something quite different. Discussion of these issues leads to increased comprehension. A large body of research attests to the effectiveness of reciprocal teaching—for students in general, including those with learning disabilities and reluctant readers (Lederer, 2000; Palincsar & Brown, 1984).

Concept maps and other explicit structures can help students understand the key relationships between the big ideas in social studies texts (Harniss, Hollenbeck, Crawford, & Carnine, 1994). **Problem–solution–effect**, an expository text structure, is one way to organize expository content. The problems that people or governments encounter might be linked to issues such as economic,

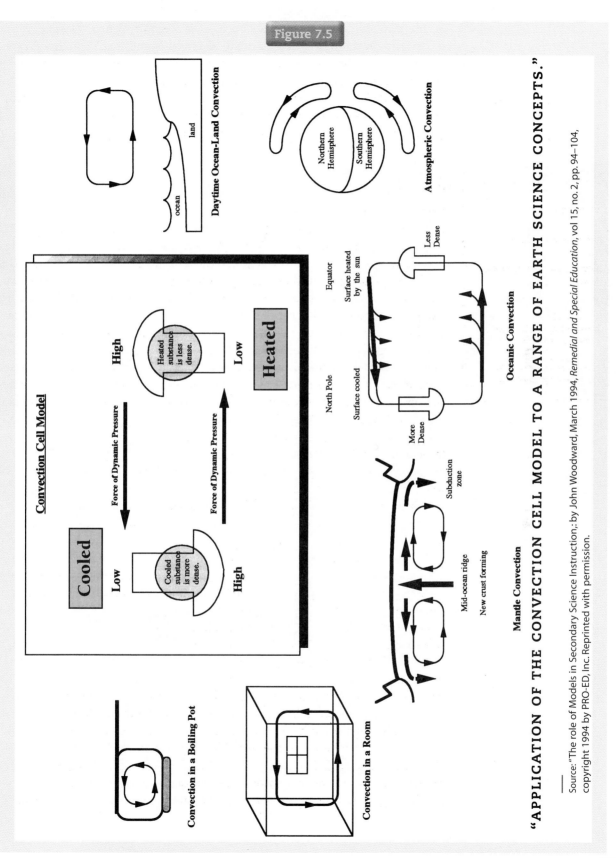

Figure 7.5

Daytime Ocean-Land Convection

Atmospheric Convection

Convection Cell Model

High

Cooled

Low

Force of Dynamic Pressure

Force of Dynamic Pressure

Heated substance is less dense.

Cooled substance is more dense.

Low

Heated

High

Equator

North Pole

Surface heated by the sun

Surface cooled

Less Dense

More Dense

Oceanic Convection

Subduction zone

Mid-ocean ridge

New crust forming

Mantle Convection

Convection in a Boiling Pot

Convection in a Room

"APPLICATION OF THE CONVECTION CELL MODEL TO A RANGE OF EARTH SCIENCE CONCEPTS."

Source: "The role of Models in Secondary Science Instruction,: by John Woodward, March 1994, *Remedial and Special Education*, vol 15, no. 2, pp. 94–104, copyright 1994 by PRO-ED, Inc. Reprinted with permission.

health, autonomy, or human rights issues. The solutions people generate can be described as inventing, fighting, accommodating, tolerating, etc., and the effects or outcomes could be new institutions, new problems, or changes in society. In *Her Story, Her Story II,* and *Her Story III,* Susan Merritt (1992, 1995, 1999) tells the stories of Canadian women who were pioneers in their fields. Applying the problem–solution–effect structure to the story of Adelaide Hunter Hoodless (1857–1910) in *Her Story II* takes the form shown in Figure 7.6.

Adapting Visual Art

A visual art program in which students work in small groups or individually on projects at an appropriate level of difficulty can be adapted for students. In an observational study, Guay (1993) found that teachers who successfully adapted visual art communicated regularly with resource teachers and other specialists, had clear classroom management systems, made rules and expectations explicit, and expected students to help one another. They also used clear instructions, repetition when needed by individual students, modelling, and motivation-creating openings to each class. Following the advice of resource teachers and others, they provided adapted tasks to students with physical, attentional, and other disabilities that allowed partial or full participation in the activities of the class.

Adapting Music

Music is often seen as a challenging area for exceptional students, especially those who are hard of hearing. Walczyk (1993) describes how included students who are deaf and hearing impaired can take part in music in elementary class-

Including exceptional students in art classes provides them with an outlet for expressing feelings and ideas and opportunities to develop appreciation as well as skill.

Figure 7.6

THE PROBLEM—SOLUTION—EFFECT MODEL FOR READING HISTORY

Problem ⟶	Solution ⟶	Effect
Unsanitary conditions caused disease and death in Canada in the late 1800s. Adelaide Hunter Hoodless' infant son died from drinking contaminated milk.	Adelaide learned everything she could about household management. She began teaching women about nutrition and sanitation. She started the Women's Institute, education and companionship for rural women.	Schools started teaching women domestic science. Women's Institutes spread around the world. Adelaide Hoodless changed the lives of women in Canada and beyond.

es. All children learn to sign the words while singing and portable electronic keyboards are used for children to learn to play keyboard duets. Walczyk found that the social atmosphere of the music classes motivated the hard of hearing children to participate fully.

Adapting Drama

Drama can provide an outlet for exceptional students to express themselves. Because drama includes many means of self-expression, including mime, monologue, tableau, and choral speaking, teachers can negotiate the forms of assignments and self-expression with exceptional students. Adaptations include replacing body movement with facial expression and hand gestures for students in wheelchairs, allowing mime for nonverbal or very shy students, and allowing students with learning disabilities to write and perform choral responses rather than monologues. Gifted students can negotiate open-ended and challenging assignments. The biggest challenge may be maintaining the attention of easily distracted exceptional students in the relatively unstructured classroom situation that often arises in drama. Principles of classroom management and approaches for teaching students with AD/HD may prove helpful in these circumstances.

Adapting the Teaching of French

Teachers of French as a second language often find that they have to make adaptations for exceptional students. They report that motivation is a key factor, especially when

- students have language acquisition and literacy difficulties (e.g., learning disabilities)
- the target language has no personal meaning for the student
- negative socio-political attitudes may be associated with the language
- students lack the basics from previous years' French classes

Some strategies that may reduce the need for adaptations are an assertive behaviour management plan, 20-minute blocks of time for activities, and a variety of activities to use the four skill areas of reading, writing, speaking, and listening. Figure 7.7 includes examples of how to increase student motivation, use pre-reading and reading strategies while teaching, and make adaptations for students who are disabled and for gifted students.

Adapting Homework

Most classroom teachers assign homework, and many report that students with learning disabilities and other high-incidence exceptionalities experience difficulties completing homework (Salend & Gajria, 1995). These students may have difficulty focusing their attention on homework, especially if they find the assignment difficult, and tend to show poor time management on long-term projects. The following guidelines are also relevant for students without exceptionalities and can be used to facilitate completion of homework by all students:

What do you think?

Some argue that exceptional students do not need or have time to learn music, visual art, French, etc. Construct both sides of this argument. Read: D.M. Guay (1993). Cross-site analysis of teaching practices: Visual art education with students experiencing disabilities. *Studies in Art Education, 34*, 233–43.

E.B. Walczyk (1993). Music instruction and the hearing impaired. *Music Educators Journal, 80*, 42–44.

Figure 7.7

SCAFFOLDING LEARNING AND MOTIVATION IN THE SECONDARY FRENCH CLASS

- Begin the year with a personal inventory sheet that includes students' interests, attitudes, likes, dislikes, parents' names and telephone numbers; use all of these
- Start with what students know: simple nouns, verbs, adjectives
- Teach the key building blocks: how to conjugate each type of verb, one at a time, with a quiz to follow; then students tend to have 3 strong quiz results at the start of term, which is motivating for those who have found French difficult in the past

Prereading, Teaching, and Assessment of a Chapter in the Text

- Build vocabulary understanding through activities and games
- Explain context of first reading in English or second language so students are prepared to relate new knowledge to prior knowledge
- Discuss the purpose, function, and construction of the grammar introduced in the chapter
- Paired treasure hunt of a grammar concept: pairs of students compete to find all examples of the concept in the reading selection
- Formal teaching of the grammar concept and cloze exercises or creation of examples
- Written/oral assignment: the grammar concept featured in the product
- Assessment through projects, assignments, games, dialogues, listening tests, quizzes, exams

Adaptations for Students with Disabilities

- Comprehension checks by the teacher; guidance from peer tutor
- Word cues on tests and quizzes
- Open-text exam with a textbook guide to key topics; guide could be created by students by predicting what will be on the exam

Adaptations for Developmentally Advanced Students

- Open-ended projects that allow them to be as creative as they can
- A bonus binder that all students can access when they finish assigned work and earn bonus points by completing challenging puzzles, crosswords, etc.
- Board games in French

Understanding the Learning Difficulties in French Class of Students with LD

- They require much support and encouragement
- The hardest part for them is understanding the comprehension questions
- Post a question-word list
- Teach them to use the words from the question in the answer
- Teach them to search for the words that appear in the question in the assigned readings in the text
- For writing, brainstorm sentence starters with the class so no one has a blank sheet

---

Developed by Nicole Lévesque, Barrie, Ontario. Used by permission.

- Assign work that students already understand and are practising, rather than assigning work they are likely to practise incorrectly. Assigning the latter will mean you will have to reteach.

- Vary the amount of work assigned or time for completion as you do for in-class assignments so the homework expectation is realistic.

- Consider the IEPs of exceptional students, and what is most important for them to learn. This may mean a different homework assignment, but it does not mean no homework assignment.

- Rather than using homework as a punishment, motivate students to become more independent through imaginative homework assignments; for students who cannot complete the assignment independently, offer the option of working in pairs.

- Comment on homework occasionally so students feel that you value it, give helpful feedback, and give the message that it is worth students' effort to complete homework.

- Discuss the reasons for assigning homework: consolidating classroom learning, increasing independent practice, thinking about and acting on an idea over time (e.g., a long-term project), showing progress to parents (young children reading books at home), etc.

- Use peer tutors, homework cooperative groups, or homework buddies, but develop some form of individual accountability.

- Develop predictable routines for homework early in the year, including a self-monitoring tracking system.

- Assign homework early enough in the period that students can try the assignment and ask for help before they leave if they do not understand what they are to do, or cannot complete the first few examples.

Some teachers involve parents in homework. Callahan, Rademacher, and Hildreth (1998) invited parents of grade 6 and 7 students to learn how to monitor their children's self-monitoring of their own math homework. The children recorded start and finish times and the number of correct and incorrect answers, and decided whether they needed more practice or were ready to move on to the next type of question (by the number correct). James Hendrikse (1999), an Ontario teacher, developed the **Parents as Tutors Program**, in which parents learned how to tutor their children from 5 to 11 years of age. Parents tutored in reading, math, writing, or spelling depending on the child's needs. Both these programs resulted in exceptional, at-risk, and ESL students learning with their parents and in parents feeling more confident about helping their children complete homework assignments.

Key Terms

bypass strategies (p. 201)

remediation (p. 201)

acceleration (p. 201)

cognitive complexity (p. 202)

authentic tasks (p. 202)

interest (p. 204)

environment (p. 204)

method of presentation (p. 204)

pace (p. 205)

engagement (p. 205)

additional practice (p. 205)

zone of proximal development (ZPD) (p. 206)

grouping (p. 206)

reading wars (p. 207)

phonemic awareness (p. 208)

Scaffolded Reading Experience (SRE) (p. 211)

pre-reading activities (p. 212)

post-reading activities (p. 212)

high-interest low-vocabulary books (p. 212)

vocabulary (p. 213

narrative text (p. 213)

story planning sheet (p. 213)

number sense (p. 214)

hundreds chart (p. 215)

computation (p. 215)

CCTV (p. 219)

reciprocal teaching (p. 220)

concept maps (p. 220)

problem–solution–effect (p. 220)

Parents as Tutors Program (p. 225)

Summary

This chapter has described how teachers can use the ADAPT strategy to analyze and adapt teaching for exceptional learners, choosing from and combining myriad strategies. You can ADAPT many aspects of teaching, including substance (outcomes, content, cognitive complexity, authenticity, and task interest), or you can focus on changing method of presentation, pace, and quantity for exceptional learners. Depending on the strengths and needs of exceptional students, it may be appropriate to ADAPT student engagement and activities, amount of practice, or the form of practice. Changing any of these aspects of teaching invariably affects other aspects because they are so closely linked. Many examples are drawn from practice and from research to illustrate adapting the teaching of listening, reading, writing, mathematics, and the content areas. Finally adapting homework is discussed. While it is necessary to ADAPT aspects of homework assignments, ensuring equity to exceptional students and to their peers suggests that as members of inclusive classrooms they should have homework assignments just as their classmates do. ∎

LEARNER OBJECTIVES

After you have read this chapter, you will be able to:

1. Describe how to use the ADAPT strategy to analyze assessment.

2. Describe large-scale assessment in Canada and the adaptations used for exceptional students.

3. Explain how teachers can carry out classroom assessments and the role of rubrics in classroom assessment.

4. Describe adaptations to classroom assessment, including tests, performance assessment, and portfolios.

5. Discuss adaptations and alternatives to report card marks.

Chapter 8

Adapting Assessment

Sasha is in grade 5 and has attention deficit disorder as well as a learning disability in reading. Sasha's teacher, Mr. Sinclair, has been adapting teaching with the assistance of the resource teacher and Sasha feels proud of being able to finish most assignments and understand what is being taught, especially in social studies and science. When Sasha receives his report card in October, he expects it to say he is doing well. He rips it open and sees low grades in every subject. Sasha doesn't understand. He asks the teacher, "Why do you say I am doing good work, and then give me Level 1, the lowest grade? I got 8 out of 10 on my science project." How can Mr. Sinclair explain to Sasha that his science project was only six pages long while those of the other students were eight pages long, and that Sasha was allowed to replace some paragraphs with drawings? These adaptations were consistent with Sasha's IEP, which had provided clear guidance for Mr. Sinclair in adapting teaching. Unfortunately the IEP contained no information about how to adapt assessment or grades and Mr. Sinclair had worried that Sasha would be crushed by his low marks.

Belle has hearing loss and uses an FM system and speech-reading to learn in the secondary classroom. She has an IEP that guides her teachers at Pacific Secondary School in adapting teaching and assessment. Belle's math teacher, Ms. Frost, knows that Belle tires easily and that although she is efficient at speech-reading, it only enables her to catch a fraction of what is said. Belle has math in the last period of the day. Her teacher uses a system of frequent oral tests to help students gauge their own learning and prepare for unit tests and term exams. Belle met with Ms. Frost after the first oral test to explain how difficult it was for her to understand the question and respond on paper quickly. The two of them reviewed Belle's IEP with the resource teacher. The decision was that Belle would take the tests and do her best, but that the oral quizzes would not contribute to Belle's final grade in the course. The weights of the other assessments—unit tests, homework completion, and term tests—would be increased. Belle felt that this was a fair resolution and was pleased that she could show Ms. Frost that she understood geometry and could use her graphing calculator effectively. However, she worried that other students who disliked the oral quizzes would think it was not fair for her to have different arrangements for calculating her grade.

1. What guidance do teachers need to adapt assessment for students who have disabilities that interfere with meeting the usual assessment expectations?

2. How can teachers match assessment to the adapted teaching they are providing for exceptional students?

3. How can teachers prevent students like Sasha and Belle from giving up because effort and improved work are not recognized and rewarded?

4. Why might parents object if schools adapt teaching and assignments and then penalize the students when they do well on what they are asked to do, which is not the same as what their peers are asked to do?

Introduction

The subject of this chapter is adapting assessment. **Assessment** is data collection. It refers to gathering information of many kinds about a student or a group of students, using a variety of tools and techniques. **Large-scale assessment** refers to nation-wide, province-wide, or district-wide efforts to provide information about student achievement, usually by means of paper and pencil tests. **Classroom assessment** refers to the day-to-day practices adopted by teachers to describe student learning, often through a variety of means, including portfolios, conferences with students, and other means, as well as paper and pencil tests. There is no judgment inherent in assessment. It is the act of describing student performance. **Testing** is one form of assessment, normally using a paper and pencil test (either designed by the teacher or commercially available) to gather information that describes a student's or a group's level of performance. **Evaluation** refers to making judgments about and making decisions based on the assessment data that have been gathered about a student or group of students. **Grading** refers to a symbolic representation of evaluation and **reporting** is the way in which evaluation results are communicated.

Using the ADAPT Strategy for Assessment

You need strategies for adapting assessment that are effective for exceptional students and efficient for you, and that become a regular part of your planning and teaching. Chapter 1 introduced ADAPT and Chapter 7 included examples of using ADAPT for adapting teaching. This strategy is similar to others, but it includes considering the perspectives of many people, including classmates, on the adaptation and the consequences for them. The characteristics of the student (strengths *and* needs) and the demands of the classroom are important when devising adaptations to use the student's strengths and either bypass areas of need or help the student to strengthen these areas.

The ADAPT strategy has the following five steps:

- Step 1: Accounts of students' strengths and needs
- Step 2: Demands of the classroom
- Step 3: Adaptations
- Step 4: Perspectives and consequences
- Step 5: Teach and assess the match

These five steps constitute a procedure for adapting assessment that you can use with learners with a variety of exceptionalities in both elementary and secondary classrooms for both large-scale and classroom assessment.

Large-Scale Assessment and Exceptional Students in Canada

In recent years, educators have experienced pressure from governments, parents, and the general public for evidence to show how well schools are preparing Canadian children to compete in the global economy (Government of Canada, 1991). We have already discussed the increasing diversity within communities, as well as the pressure, focused by the Charter of Rights and Freedoms (1982), for institutions including schools to ensure equity and respect the rights of individuals regardless of income, social class, disability, race, religion, age, or sex (Ignatieff, 2000). Other social trends that contribute to the pressure on educators to demonstrate their value through assessment results include the changing nature of families and the role they play in the education of youth (Leithwood, Begley, & Cousins, 1992). In a monograph on assessment, Lorna Earl of University of Toronto and Brad Cousins of University of Ottawa (1995) argue that assessment and evaluation practices are the concrete representation of the work of schools and of the values of societies. "What gets measured, how it gets measured, how it is reported and the significance of the decisions that get made give a vivid accounting of what is seen as important" (Earl & Cousins, 1995, p. xi).

Until recently, most schools in Canada were asked to demonstrate accountability by showing that they had conformed to the process that was expected, that is, that they had implemented new programs and methods of organization (Holmes, 1998). For example, in the education of exceptional students, schools were required to show that they had developed programs, identified exceptional students, and written IEPs for those students. However, in the most recent changes in Ontario, for example, schools have received standards to which IEPs must conform (Ontario Ministry of Education, 2000). Demands for accountability are increasingly focusing on whether the process is producing the desired outcomes at the provincial and national levels (Earl & Lemahieu, 1997; Mawhinney, 1998).

At the National Level

The Council of Ministers of Education, Canada (CMEC) was created in 1967 and provides a forum for the ministers responsible for education in the provinces and territories, although education remains a provincial responsibility. In 1989, CMEC initiated the School Achievement Indicators Program (SAIP), the first attempt by all the ministers of education to reach consensus on a national assessment. In 1991, they agreed to assess the achievement of 13- and 16-year-olds in reading, writing, and mathematics, and in 1993 they agreed to include assessment of science. The schedule for a cycle of assessments was set to cover the decade from 1993 to 2003. The first cycle of assessments took place in spring 1993 (mathematics), 1994 (reading and writing), and 1996 (science), and the reports were published the following winter in each case. The second cycle took place in 1997, 1998, and 1999. Descriptions of the instruments and the reports of the provincial outcomes are available in paper copies (e.g., CMEC, 1999) and on the CMEC Web site (http://www.cmec.ca/saip/indexe.stm).

Put Into Practice

Look for articles in local and national newspapers that reflect the recent demands for assessment to show that Canadian schools are delivering excellence.

Further Reading

Consult the provincial documents that guide IEPs in your jurisdiction to see if standards for IEPs have been released or are under development. Focus on standards related to adapting large-scale and classroom assessment.

Do exceptional students participate in the SAIP assessments? Samples are usually drawn and the majority of sampled students participate in the assessments. For example, the *1998 Report on Reading and Writing Assessment* (CMEC, 1999) provides percentages of students in the randomly selected samples who were declared exempt. For the 1994 SAIP reading sample, only 1.9 percent of 13-year-olds and 1.5 percent of 16-year-olds across Canada were declared exempt. For the 1994 SAIP writing sample, 1.4 percent of the 13-year-olds and 1.4 percent of the 16-year-olds were declared exempt. This suggests that only those students who have severe disabilities or who might be harmed by participating in the assessments were exempted. The accommodations for SAIP reading and writing assessments are described as including computers for students who normally use them for their composition work. Students are entitled to the accommodations usually made for them in the classroom. "For example, students who normally had a scribe to write were permitted a scribe for these assessments. Braille or large-print tests were also provided as needed. Students were given extra time to complete the assessments if they required it in the judgment of the school-based staff" (CMEC, 1999, p. 2). Some of the questions to ask when deciding what accommodations will make a large-scale assessment meaningful for an exceptional student appear in Table 8.1.

What do you think?

If provincial policies require that large-scale assessment generally adopt the adaptations used in classroom assessment, what are the implications for you, the classroom teacher, and the adaptations you are expected to make daily?

At the Provincial Level

There is great diversity in provincial large-scale student assessment. However, every province has some sort of program in place. For some time, Quebec (http://www.meq.gouv.qc.ca/GR-PUB/m_englis.htm), Alberta (http://www.learning.gov.ab.ca/k_12/testing/default.asp), and British Columbia (http://www.bced.gov.bc.ca/assessment) have had examinations for students finishing secondary school and have had provincial achievement tests at other grade levels. The latter are administered to all students or to samples of students in selected subjects (CMEC, 1999; Holmes, 1998). Other provinces have more recently developed assessment and provincial indicator programs. Saskatchewan (http://www.sasked.gov.sk.ca/k/pecs/ae/pub1.html) and Manitoba (http://www.edu.gov.mb.ca/metks4/curricul/assess/index.html) have provincially based programs. The Atlantic Provinces Education Foundation (Newfoundland, Prince Edward Island, Nova Scotia, and New Brunswick) has developed the Education Indicators for Atlantic Canada (http://apef-fepa.org). Ontario has recently implemented tests of mathematics, reading, and writing at grades 3, 6, and 9, and a grade 10 literacy test. While the other provinces house the evaluation or assessment office within the department or ministry of education, Ontario has developed an arm's-length organization, Education Quality and Accountability Office (EQAO) (http://www.eqao.com). Northwest Territories is currently developing culturally appropriate ways to measure the success of NWT students and programs; Yukon has some territorial examinations (e.g., at the grades 9 and 11 levels for English) (CMEC, 1999). Many provinces devote time to students working together to prepare for large-scale assessments.

Some Canadian provinces have well-publicized policies on accommodations on large-scale assessments. For example, Alberta's Web site describes how the province provides accommodations for exceptional students with "special diploma examina-

Table 8.1

ANALYZING THE TEST: QUESTIONS TO ASK

Requirement	Sampling of Questions to Ask
Setting	• Can the student focus on his or her own work with 25 to 30 other students in a quiet setting?
	• Does the student display behaviors that are distracting to other students?
	• Can the student take the test in the same way as it is administered to other students?
Timing	• Can the student work continuously for the entire length of a typically administered portion of the test (e.g., 20–30 minutes)?
	• Does the student use accommodations that require more time to complete individual test items?
Scheduling	• Does the student take a medication that dissipates over time so that optimal performance might occur at a certain time of the day?
	• Does the student's anxiety level increase dramatically when working in certain content areas, so that these should be administered after all other content areas are assessed?
Presentation	• Can the student listen to and follow oral directions given by an adult or an audiotape?
	• Can the student see and hear?
	• Can the student read?
Response	• Can the student track from a test booklet to a test response form?
	• Is the student able to manipulate a pencil or other writing instrument?
Other	• Is this the first time that the student will be taking a large-scale assessment?

Source: M.L. Thurlow, J.L. Elliott, & J.E. Ysseldyke (1998). *Testing Students with Disabilities: Practical Strategies for Complying with District and State Requirements.* Thousand Oaks, CA: Corwin Press. Reprinted with permission of Corwin Press.

tion writing needs" that are similar to the accommodations routinely provided by the school for examination writing and assignment completion (http://www.learning.gov.ab.ca/k_12/testing/diploma/dip_gib/sec11_policy_4.htm). A current IPP is required. The list of approved accommodations includes audiotape version, additional time, word processor, scribe, large-print version, Braille version, sign language interpreter, taped response, and miscellaneous accommodations as approved by the Special Cases Committee. For Alberta provincial achievement tests in grades 3, 6, and 9, superintendents may excuse a student when participation would be harmful to the student; however, students with IPPs and students in ESL programs will normally write the tests and may be granted accommodations. Detailed instructions are provided for accommodations such as using a Braille version of a test, a reader, additional time, etc. (http://www.learning.gov.ab.ca/k_12/testing/diploma/dip_gib/sec11_policy_3.htm).

Weblinks

COUNCIL OF MINISTERS OF EDUCATION, CANADA (CMEC)
http://www.cmec.ca/saip

CENTRE FOR RESEARCH IN APPLIED MEASUREMENT AND EVALUATION (CRAME) (AT THE UNIVERSITY OF ALBERTA)
http://www.education.ualberta.ca/educ/psych/crame/title.html

In Ontario, the policy on accommodations is spelled out on EQAO's Web site (http://www.eqao.com/eqao/home_page/information/1C1e.html). Educators must make every effort to enable exceptional students to participate in all aspects of the assessment to demonstrate their learning. "This may involve providing one or more accommodations." Accommodations that are suggested include giving extra time, helping students organize the activities in the test, assisting with pacing, providing a quiet workplace, allowing assistive devices (e.g., Bliss boards), and providing assessment tasks in a different format (e.g., Braille text) or allowing the use of technological resources (e.g., voice-activated computer). The policy states that a student may be granted full exemption only when the student would be unable to respond to the assessment instruments, even with the use of all possible accommodations, or when participation would be harmful to the student. Decisions for exemption are made on a case-by-case basis. Questions to ensure the fairness and validity of large-scale testing appear in Figure 8.1.

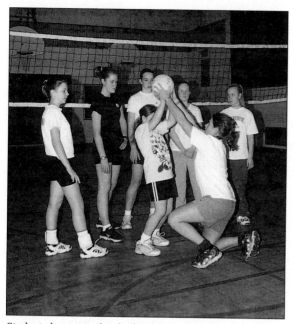

Students learn together in the classroom and on the volley-ball court.

Cross-Reference
Chapter 2 contains detailed information on IEPs and the role of the teacher in their development and implementation.

The recent standards for IEPs in Ontario (Ontario Ministry of Education, 2000) contain a section on "Accommodations for Participation in Provincial Assessments," which states that any testing accommodations recommended to facilitate the student's participation in provincial assessments must be identified in the IEP. These accommodations must be appropriate to the student's needs as identified in the IEP; included among the strategies, accommodations, and resources identified in the IEP as necessary or facilitating the student's learning and demonstration of learning in classroom assessments; and described specifically (e.g., use of a word processor). Another section addresses "Exemptions from Provincial Assessments" and states that only in rare cases will a student be exempted: essentially when, even with accommodations, the student would not be

---

Figure 8.1

ENSURING FAIRNESS AND VALIDITY

To help students take standardized assessments—and to ensure the validity of the results—answer these questions:

1. What test accommodations does the student need to take the test without the impediment of his or her disability?

2. Has the student had sufficient opportunity to learn what is on the test?

3. Does the student have the necessary test-taking skill?

Source: J. Elliott, J. Ysseldyke, M. Thurlow, & R. Erickson (1998). What about assessment and accountability? Practical implications for educators. *Teaching Exceptional Children, 31*(1), 25. Reprinted with permission.

able to provide evidence of learning on the assessment. A statement must appear in the IEP explaining why the assessment is not appropriate for the student and identifying the ministry or EQAO policy under which the exemption is applied.

Comparison with the United States

In the United States much has been written about adapting assessment for exceptional students on state and federal achievement tests, sometimes called "high stake" assessment (e.g., Elliott, Ysseldyke, Thurlow, & Erickson, 1998). Although the U.S. has had a national assessment program for some time, it lacked specific guidelines about who participated and what accommodations were allowed (Fitzsimmons, 1998). During the past decade, the National Center on Educational Outcomes (NCEO) at the University of Minnesota questioned the extent to which American national assessment included exceptional students. In 1994, they estimated that only half of students receiving special education services participated in the National Assessment of Educational Progress (NAEP) (Shriner, Spande, & Thurlow, 1994). SAIP exemption rates appear to be much lower (generally less than 2 percent). Recent changes to the Individuals with Disabilities Education Act (IDEA) require that, beginning in 2000, exceptional students in the U.S. be included in district and statewide assessment, with or without accommodations, or by using alternate assessments (Elliott et al., 1998). Recently NCEO has focused on the kinds of alternate assessments that might be appropriate for students with modified programs who cannot respond to large-scale assessment, even with adaptations. Ysseldyke and his colleagues (e.g., Ysseldyke & Olsen, 1999) recommend that alternate assessments focus on authentic skills and on assessing experience in community and other real-life environments, measure integrated skills across domains, use continuous documentation, and provide descriptions of needed and provided supports. Such alternate assessments have been pioneered in states like Kentucky and Maryland (Ysseldyke & Olsen, 1999).

Summary of Exceptional Students and Large-Scale Assessment in Canada

In summary, you can see that no matter where you teach in Canada, your students may be included in a sample for large-scale assessment. If you teach grade 3, 6, 9, or 12, all of your students are likely to be assessed. On the whole, exceptional students who have adapted programs are increasingly included in large-scale assessment, and the guidelines suggest they should receive the same adaptations that they experience day to day in the classroom. Those students whose goals are considerably different from their peers and whose IEPs recommend modified programs (estimated at less than 2 percent of the school population) are likely to be exempt from large-scale assessments. Being familiar with the IEPs of the students you teach will enable you to participate in school-based decisions about the adaptations or accommodations appropriate for your students on large-scale assessments.

Further Reading

On adapting large-scale assessment: L.S. Fuchs, D. Fuchs, S.B. Eaton, C. Hamlett, E. Binkley, & R. Crouch (2000). Using objective data sources to enhance teacher judgments about test accommodations. *Exceptional Children, 67*, 67–81.

G. Tindal, B. Heath, K. Hollenbeck, P. Almond, & M. Harniss (1998). Accommodating students with disabilities in large-scale tests: An experimental study. *Exceptional Children, 64*, 439–50.

What do you think?

Use the ADAPT strategy to recommend accommodations to large-scale testing for one of the students—Sasha or Belle—described in the cases that open this chapter. Which steps of the ADAPT strategy are most relevant for adapting large-scale assessment? Why?

Classroom Assessment

The Many Roles of Classroom Assessment in Teacher Decision Making

Bob Wilson of Queen's University (1995) suggests that classroom assessment plays many roles in teacher decision making. He describes a teacher as mentor to individual students, curriculum guide, marks accountant, reporter of the results of assessment, and program director for all the teaching that goes on in the classroom. Wilson provides examples of how teachers use assessment to make decisions in all these roles. Assessment provides the most valuable information about learning when there is consistency among the approaches used in teaching, learning, and assessment. Then teachers can use classroom assessment to guide decisions about what to teach, how to teach, and how to adapt teaching. Assessment helps teachers gauge student learning and decide who has learned to solve quadratic equations, for example. Before adapting assessment to provide each student with an opportunity to show what she knows rather than highlight her disability, it is necessary to prepare all students for the idea that equitable assessment does not mean same assessment. It is also necessary to prepare parents for the notion of equitable testing.

MAKING ASSESSMENT CONSISTENT WITH TEACHING

Assessment is most helpful when it is consistent with teaching. What does this mean for your daily practice? Assessment should be consistent in content with the learning outcomes or goals of the curriculum, unit, and activity. Thus if you undertook a particular spelling activity so students could spell common words in their daily journal writing, the assessment of that activity should reflect the words you taught and should ask students to produce those words in a context similar to that encountered in writing. For students who have strengths in spelling, the task might include spelling words (that were not taught) from the same word families to which these students can reasonably be expected to generalize. Other students who are not strong spellers may use and misspell simpler words in their journal writing and may need to learn these words; thus they may have a list of simpler words to learn and may be assessed on these words. In terms of task content, it would not make sense to ask students to identify the incorrectly spelled words in a list unless the goal was to help students to improve editing their written work. Given that written work is usually in sentence format, both the teaching and assessment of identifying incorrectly spelled words should probably occur with sentences rather than lists of words. The assessment should also be consistent with the teaching in that students should have access to the same adaptations during assessment that they used while learning. Jamie has cerebral palsy and cannot control a pencil so she practises by writing her words on the computer; thus she will use the computer to take her regular spelling tests. Similarly, Juan is blind and uses Braille for his spelling lessons from Monday to Thursday; he also uses Braille to complete his spelling test on Friday.

In their book *Assessment and Learning: The ICE Approach*, Sue Fostaty Young of St. Lawrence College and Bob Wilson of Queen's University (2000) describe a model that teachers can use to align assessment with teaching and learning. Much of assessment is usually a combination of **norm-referenced** data (in which a student's work is compared to the work of other students), and **criterion-referenced** data (in which a student's work is compared to expected outcomes). However, Fostaty and Wilson emphasize helping learners grow in their learning, that is, comparing a student's progress to where that student started from, regardless of whether that starting point is ahead of, even with, or behind others in the class. Such **self-referenced** data have long been recommended for assessment of exceptional students (e.g., Deno & Mirkin, 1977); however, Fostaty and Wilson recommend this kind of assessment of all students, thus making it much easier to adopt this approach for exceptional learners. The benefit is that teachers can give individual students the advice and tasks they need to extend learning, no matter where they are on the continuum.

In the **ICE model**, the first step is **Ideas**. These building blocks of learning include such things as the steps in a process, vocabulary, and facts and definitions in the textbook. Most fill-in-the-blanks and multiple-choice questions assess at the level of Ideas. **Connections** refers to the links or relationships that students make among the Ideas, and to the relationships that students establish between new learning and prior learning. In mathematics learning, students who memorize algorithms are learning Ideas, while those who use their new knowledge to solve new problems or apply new learning to figure out how many videos they can rent with their pocket money (that is, to solve an old problem) are making Connections. Making Connections enables students to combine steps, understand formulae, and explain one phenomenon in terms of another.

The third stage that Fostaty and Wilson describe is Extensions. **Extensions** can be seen in the ways students internalize the learning so that it becomes part of their perspective, that is, the way they view the world. Extensions are revealed when students use their learning in novel ways, distinct from the initial learning situation, and when they answer the hypothetical question, "So what does this mean for me and how I see things?" The ICE model suggests that assessment should match teaching, in that the level of assessment should match the level of your outcomes for the students. In classes with diversity, it is likely that students will be working at all these levels and some may be stimulated by your assessment to show that they are beginning to make Connections or establish Extensions that you were not anticipating. Because you are trying to move all your students along this continuum, you will probably use questions from all three levels, although some students may be encouraged to demonstrate their learning at a specific level. Table 8.2 contains examples of question starters you can use at the levels of Ideas, Connections, and Extensions.

USING ASSESSMENT TO GAUGE STUDENT LEARNING AND TO ADAPT TEACHING: RUBRICS

You can use classroom assessment to decide who has learned what and to guide decisions about what to teach, how to teach, and how to adapt teaching. By observing

Table 8.2

EXAMPLES OF QUESTION STARTERS AT THE LEVELS OF IDEAS, CONNECTIONS, AND EXTENSIONS

Ideas	Connections	Extensions
• List the…	• What effect does _____ have on…	• Predict how…
• Identify the main…	• Estimate…	• Propose solutions for…
• Give examples from the text of…	• What alternative methods…	#• What are the implications of…
• Paraphrase…	#• Of what value is…	#• In your opinion…
• Who was…	#• Explain the relationship between…	#• What did you learn from…
• When did…	#• How is _____ like…	
• According to…how is…	#• Compare…	
	#• Using an example from your own experience, illustrate…	

#Examples of questions that are accessible to all students, yet extendable.

Source: S.C. Fostaty & R.J. Wilson (2000). *Assessment and Learning: The ICE Approach*. Winnipeg: Portage & Main Press (Peguis Publishers). Reprinted with permission.

individuals and groups of learners and examining their assessments, you can decide to reteach concepts, supplement the text with an audiotape for some students, or ask an individual to write answers in individual words rather than in sentences. Assessment helps teachers gauge student learning and decide which students have met the curriculum outcomes and whether exceptional students have met their adapted or modified outcomes.

Developing a rubric may help you discern which outcomes have been met and what reteaching and changes to your teaching are needed. **Rubrics** are descriptions of learning at different levels of development. Many rubrics can be described as **quantitative rubrics**, that is, they identify that students with higher achievement have greater quantities of valued responses:

- Level 1: Includes some of the main ideas
- Level 2: Includes most of the main ideas
- Level 3: Includes all or almost all of the main ideas

Quantitative rubrics provide little guidance for teachers in adapting teaching. They imply that inadequacies are inherent in students, and fail to focus on the learning that students have accomplished and the challenges or steps that remain.

Qualitative rubrics describe the qualities that characterize learning at various levels and provide students with information about the steps they must tackle in

COMPONENTS OF A QUALITATIVE RUBRIC UNDER DEVELOPMENT

Elements	Ideas	Connections	Extensions
Legibility and visual appeal	• Forms recognizable letters	• Letters are grouped and spaced to form words	• Words follow in logical sequence
	• Initial draft is also the final draft	• Creates a final draft from the original	• Includes illustrations—used where appropriate
Planning	• Researches topic	• Sequences ideas	• Considers the readers' needs in the planning
	• Lists ideas	• Identifies sources	
Sentences	• Begins sentences with capital letters	• Sentences are linked in a coherent order	• Uses variety in sentence structure to create effects
	• Ends sentences with periods		

Source: S.C. Fostaty & R.J. Wilson (2000). *Assessment and Learning: The ICE Approach.* Winnipeg: Portage & Main Press (Peguis Publishers). Reprinted with permission.

order to improve. Table 8.3 shows the components of a qualitative rubric on written expression. Fostaty and Wilson suggest that when you undertake to develop a rubric, you place examples of student work in front of you and analyze the qualities of the work that you view as "okay," "average," and "wow!" These may be described as Levels 1, 2, and 3, although students may enjoy the more colourful titles, including "wow!" Fostaty and Wilson's qualitative rubrics embrace Ideas, Connections, and Extensions while breaking a learning outcome into elements. Qualitative rubrics tell you what has been demonstrated, not what is missing. You can continue the development of such rubrics, as you read or observe students' work and identify factors that influence your judgments about student work, until you are satisfied that you have an accurate map of the learning you hope to foster. For example, if an exceptional student's work demonstrates that he is working at the Ideas level for legibility and visual appeal, you would want to emphasize that he write words and focus on teaching him to leave "white spaces" between the words (see Table 8.3). At the same time, it might be helpful to encourage him to use illustrations to communicate his ideas. For a classmate who is writing full sentences with periods and capitals and whose initial draft is the only draft, you might want to focus on planning and sequencing. The student could practise listing her ideas and then putting numbers in front of them to improve the order or, if that proves too abstract, she could write each idea on a card and then try to sequence them in different orders until she decides on the best order. A group of academically advanced students who have reached the level of Extensions on legibility and planning might be taught to use variety in sentence structure to create effects like

Put Into Practice

Collect rubrics from the curricula you have taught, the textbooks you are studying, provincial documents from your ministry of education, fellow teachers, and other sources. Compare the quantitative and qualitative rubrics on the basis of thoroughness, guidance for adapting teaching, and utility to busy teachers.

surprise, suspense, or humour. Qualitative rubrics can help you see who has reached each level that you described and guide you in making decisions about adapting teaching and reteaching to enable students to reach the curriculum outcomes or the goals in their IEPs.

Preparing Students and Parents for Equitable, But Not Necessarily the Same, Assessment

Sometimes you will be able to set a test or task for all students and assess their learning by using a rubric. However, for students on adapted programs, you may be asking some to write sentences and others to write paragraphs. Or you may give some students 5 one-syllable spelling words and others 10 multi-syllable spelling words, depending on what they need to learn to spell. Suppose that while the class writes a history test in 45 minutes in the classroom, Jacob (who has learning disabilities) writes the same test in 90 minutes in the resource room. For students on modified programs, the differences in the history test may be even more visible. Bonita (who has developmental disabilities) may describe orally to a paraprofessional how to travel to the local sites that have historic significance. Two goals on Bonita's IEP are to learn to travel independently by bus (so far she has travelled with the paraprofessional) and to plan and carry out conversations with adults.

What do you say when students or parents ask you why Mandy has fewer spelling words, why Jacob has more time, or why Bonita has an oral test? You can do much to prevent these questions by planning ahead. From the first day with your students, refer to your commitment to meeting individual needs. Describe people as individuals with different strengths. From your first communication with parents, refer to inclusion. Explain that exceptional students are included in your classroom because this is school, school district, and provincial policy. Use examples with your students—and at your curriculum night or open house—that make it easy for students and parents to see your point. Students in wheelchairs are not tested on running. Fitness assessments are used that are meaningful for them and demonstrate their level of upper body physical fitness. Blind students are given tests in Braille, just as they are taught in Braille. This does not disadvantage other students because they don't need Braille tests. You can refer to research that demonstrates that students without learning disabilities are not disadvantaged when their learning disabled classmates are given appropriate accommodations on assessment. This research is reviewed in Focus on Research.

Fairness is a complex concept. Sometimes we treat everyone equally; all children deserve to be treated with respect. Sometimes we make equitable decisions based on merit or need. The child who sings brilliantly plays the lead in the school musical, and the laptop computer is provided to the child who cannot control a pencil to write her classroom work. Welch (2000) has studied student understanding of fairness. Student perceptions of fairness are influenced by many factors, including age, social and cognitive maturity, culture, and teaching. When students say, "It's not fair," try to reflect their feelings by saying something like "You don't think it's fair. Write me a note about your feelings and we will discuss your note at recess tomorrow morning." Then follow through. Welch suggests that the

Weblinks

FAMILY VILLAGE, A SOURCE OF ONLINE MAGAZINES FOR FAMILIES
http://www.familyvillage.wisc.edu/bookstore/onlineperiodicals.htm

Three Studies That Support Extended Time as an Effective and Equitable Accommodation for Students with Learning Disabilities

Research has shown that individuals with learning disabilities (LD) tend to process information more slowly than those without LD (Hayes, Hynd, & Wisenbaker, 1986; Zentall, 1990). This makes the provision of extended time on tests appear to be an appropriate adaptation or accommodation. However, many have asked whether this gives students with LD an unfair advantage over their peers without LD. Would students who do not have LD also benefit from more time on tests? The answer usually given is that on a power test, where the point is to give adequate time for students to show what they know, this adaptation will not be unfair if the instructor has provided adequate time for the typical students to show what they know. Poorly designed tests may be unfair to all students, and only more unfair to students who process information slowly. However, this argument would be more convincing if there were data to show that students with LD benefit from additional time while those without LD do not.

Centra (1986) compared timed and extended-time scores of students with LD on the Scholastic Aptitude Test (SAT) to determine the effect of extra time on those scores. The scores were drawn from SAT records of 1124 students with LD who took the test under both timed and extended-time conditions. With the unlimited-time test administration, students with LD scored an average of 30 to 38 points higher than they scored on the timed test. This result took into account practice effects and error of measurement. The more the time was increased, the more the scores increased. This suggests that additional time reduced the effects of LD on test scores. However, this study did not answer the question of whether students without LD would be similarly advantaged by more time.

Runyan (1991) also set out to answer the question about the benefit of extended time to students with LD. The students were attending the University of California at Berkley and a California community college. The scores were reading rate and comprehension scores on the Nelson Denny Reading Test. There were 55 students with LD and 52 without LD; groups were controlled for ethnicity, gender, age, and grade-point average. Reading rates were taken at the end of the first minute, and reading comprehension scores were obtained at the end of 20 minutes and upon test completion. The normally achieving students' reading rates were at the sixtieth percentile, whereas the reading rates of the students with LD were at the tenth percentile. The timed comprehension scores of the normally achieving students were higher than the timed comprehension scores of students with LD. However, the students with LD achieved scores on the untimed comprehension test that were not significantly different than students without LD on the timed test. Thus the extra time enabled students with LD to overcome their deficits in processing speed.

Alster (1997) set out to answer the question about the comparable benefits of untimed tests to students with and without LD. There were 88 community college students, 44 with LD and 44 without LD; the two groups were matched for age, gender, ethnicity, language background, and math achievement. All were given the ASSET Elementary Algebra Test, which had been divided into two comparable tests, A and B. The two groups took one test in 12 minutes and the other untimed, with 25 of each group taking the timed test first. In each of the four groups, thus formed, half took form A first and half took form B first. Under timed conditions, students with LD scored lower than peers without LD, showing that they were disadvantaged by too little time. There was no significant difference between the untimed scores of the two groups, showing that the disadvantage to students with LD was eliminated by the provision of extended time. However, while the scores of students with LD were greatly increased with additional time, the scores of students without LD increased only a small amount (significantly less) with additional time. The students with LD took significantly more time for the untimed test than those without LD. This suggests that the timed test may have provided slightly less than adequate time for students without LD to show all they knew. However, they benefited minimally from extended time while the benefits to students with LD were much greater. If teachers provide adequate time for students without LD, students with LD will benefit fairly from extended time. The average untimed test time for students with LD was double the original 12 minutes of the timed test. This suggests that the current practice of allowing up to double time may be appropriate to enable students with LD to show what they know.

While the results may not be as conclusive as one would like, they clearly show that individuals with LD process information slowly and are disadvantaged by timed tests. The benefits of extended time on assessment to students with LD are huge. There are no similar advantages to students who do not have LD.

act of writing often enhances a student's understanding. The note will help you know what the student means and how to respond. Welch suggests you consider whether this is a request for more of your attention; if so, you need to focus on this student's accomplishments or interests, rather than on justifications of your modifications.

Sometimes young students cannot put themselves into someone else's position, so they don't understand how difficult it is for Vianne, a child with AD/HD, to complete an activity. Welch suggests you ask the children who are objecting to Vianne getting stickers if they would like to "work on something that is hard" for them. This may also be a message that you are concentrating too much on external rewards with Vianne, and the solution may be to gradually reduce stickers as a reward for everyone.

There are other strategies for dealing with issues of fairness. Adopt a consistent approach (Welch, 2000). With older students, especially, remind them that you cannot discuss another student's work with them, that we are all different, and that the law provides for accommodations and fair treatment. Schools need to adopt consistent school-wide approaches to adaptations and modifications that are defensible and to teach about the equity issues that have arisen as a result of our Canadian Charter of Rights and Freedoms and the human rights laws in each province. Finally, remember that the students may be right and you may be providing a crutch to a child who can walk, that is, more adaptations than are necessary or fair. Be prepared to review your approach and reconsider the rate at which you are gradually increasing independence and decreasing scaffolding.

Cross-Reference
Chapter 1 contains information about teaching students about the Charter of Rights and Freedoms and about human rights in Canada.

Adapting Classroom Assessment

Adapting Learning Outcomes for Exceptional Students

This chapter contains many examples of adapting and modifying learning outcomes for exceptional students. Why is this such an important issue when considering how to adapt classroom assessment? In the past, many exceptional students spent part of their school day in a resource room, where the teaching and assessment might have been tailored quite precisely to their needs; this was known as individualized instruction (Espin, Deno, & Albayrak-Kaymak, 1998). In those days, the program they received in the regular classroom was often the program taught to the rest of the class, without much change—the outcomes might have been inappropriate, but the teacher could believe that their needs were being met in the resource room. Now that exceptional students are included in regular classrooms, you are not asked to individualize teaching and assessment. Rather, you are expected to adapt and modify your teaching and assessment of the class as a group, to meet the needs of exceptional learners as much as possible. However, the learning outcomes for exceptional students in the classroom are now guided by the contents of the IEP. Thus you need to consider what outcomes are appropriate for an exceptional student when you plan your teaching. These outcomes form the basis for the assessment following teaching for exceptional students, just as they do for students without exceptionalities. If Sasha, in the case study at the beginning of this chapter, is expected to produce less written work but work of a similar quality to his peers, then this outcome needs to be specified clearly. This adapted outcome can subsequently guide your construction and administration of tests for Sasha as well as your grading for his report card.

Preparing Students for Classroom Tests

What can you do to prepare all students, including exceptional students, for upcoming classroom tests? Creating a **study guide** that tells students what to study for the test can enable them to be more efficient in their preparation. While all students benefit, those who read slowly and who have memory problems can benefit most by focusing on the most important material. Some teachers use practice tests to prepare their students, especially to inform them about teacher expectations and test format. Tutoring by a peer, resource room teacher, or paraprofessional may also help. Study buddies or study groups are often acceptable to older students and may promote social relations while enhancing learning.

You can help students analyze their previous tests for typical errors and then group students in order to explain to each group how to overcome particular kinds of errors. Demonstrate on an overhead transparency the wrong way to answer and put a large stroke through it. Then demonstrate a correct strategy for tackling that type of question. If you solicit ideas from students, provide explicit feedback about whether they are correct or incorrect. If you are not clear, this kind of session can teach students poor approaches rather than tried-and-true strategies.

Teaching **study skills** and test-taking strategies can take the form of small-group or large-group instruction. Provide all students with a passage to study and have them work in pairs. Ask the pair to highlight what is most important in the passage. Then ask each pair to come up with a way to remember two parts they highlighted. On an overhead transparency, show which sections are most important and explain why. Then ask students to give their plans for how to remember the most important information—systematically go through the sections of the passage you highlighted asking for memory strategies from students. If they are focusing at the Ideas level, introduce elements of Connections and Extensions to make the content more meaningful. This should enhance their understanding as well as their memory.

Develop **chunking strategies** (ways of grouping information) as well as mnemonics for remembering important lists. A chunking strategy for remembering some of the key environmental milestones of the 1970s might be to focus on two clusters:

1. A cluster of three events that involved Aboriginal peoples:
   a. 1970: pollution of the English-Wabigoon River system and destruction of the native community's fishery
   b. 1975: the James Bay and northern Quebec agreement on hydroelectric development signed by governments of Canada and Quebec, and by the Cree and Innuit nations

c. 1977: the Berger report on the proposed Mackenzie Valley Pipeline was released and a moratorium was placed on pipeline development following Berger's consultation with Aboriginal people

2. A cluster of two events that involved anti-nuclear protests:
   a. 1971: the founding of Greenpeace by anti-nuclear activists in Vancouver
   b. 1971: the opening of the first CANDU nuclear power reactor by Ontario Hydro at Pickering, which began decades of anti-nuclear protests and controversy over disposal of nuclear waste (Kearney & Ray, 1999).

A **mnemonic** imposes an order on information to be remembered using poems, rhymes, jingles, funny sayings, or images. To remember the names, in order, of the five largest cities in Canada, you could teach your students the mnemonic, <u>T</u>eachers <u>M</u>ake <u>V</u>ery <u>O</u>dd <u>E</u>xams, for Toronto, Montreal, Vancouver, Ottawa, and Edmonton (*Canadian Global Almanac, 2000*).

Many students find it helpful to make **concept maps** when studying for tests. These are especially useful in prompting students to make Connections and Extensions. After teaching a unit about the Group of Seven and its role in enhancing Canadian nationalism, you might prepare students for a test by showing them a blank concept map with only the words in upper case filled in from Figure 8.2. Each student or pair of students completes their own concept map. Then you show yours on an overhead and ask students to discuss how their headings and details differed. Distribute copies of your concept map so students have a good model from which to study and develop concept maps on other topics.

Adapting Classroom Tests During Test Construction

All students are likely to benefit from tests that are clearly written. However, some test items that will present no difficulties for most students may create problems for exceptional students. When you use classroom tests, expect that exceptional

Students learn in many contexts including co-operative education workplaces and while doing community services.

Figure 8.2

CONCEPT MAP: STUDYING FOR TESTS

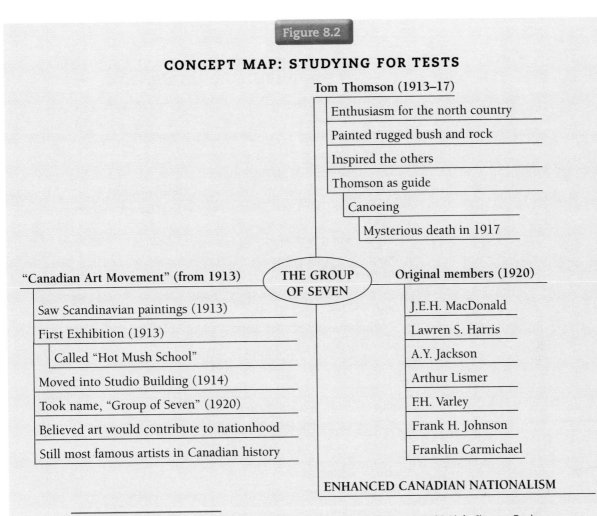

Tom Thomson (1913–17)
- Enthusiasm for the north country
- Painted rugged bush and rock
- Inspired the others
- Thomson as guide
  - Canoeing
    - Mysterious death in 1917

THE GROUP OF SEVEN

"Canadian Art Movement" (from 1913)
- Saw Scandinavian paintings (1913)
- First Exhibition (1913)
  - Called "Hot Mush School"
- Moved into Studio Building (1914)
- Took name, "Group of Seven" (1920)
- Believed art would contribute to nationhood
- Still most famous artists in Canadian history

Original members (1920)
- J.E.H. MacDonald
- Lawren S. Harris
- A.Y. Jackson
- Arthur Lismer
- F.H. Varley
- Frank H. Johnson
- Franklin Carmichael

ENHANCED CANADIAN NATIONALISM

Source: M. Friend, W. Bursuck, & N.L. Hutchinson (1998). *Including Exceptional Students: A Practical Guide for Classroom Teachers.* Scarborough: Allyn and Bacon Canada, p. 348. Reprinted with permission.

students may find the language and format of a test confusing and may be unable to recall information without an aid. They may need additional time due to slow processing, lack of motor control, or reading Braille. They may experience a variety of challenges that result from their reading and writing abilities. Figure 8.3 contains a number of suggestions for adapting a classroom test during its construction.

Some adaptations in Figure 8.3 may help all students and therefore you may incorporate them into the test you distribute to the entire class, or you may make an adapted version for a number of students when you construct the original test. You can mark small changes that only apply to one or two students on the student's copy just before you distribute the test or during the test. If you choose the latter option, take care not to confuse or distract students. Adaptations that can be made on the spot include changing the number of examples required in an answer or highlighting key words in a question. The next section focuses on adaptations made during the administration of tests.

What do you think?

How might cultural values influence parents' and children's views of fairness and adaptations in assessment? How could you learn about these influences and act on them in an effective and sensitive manner?

Figure 8.3

SUGGESTIONS FOR MODIFYING CLASSROOM TESTS DURING CONSTRUCTION

Suggestions for Modifying Objective Tests

- Pretape the questions so that a non-reader or poor reader can work from a tape recorder.
- Present questions in a familiar format (the way they were taught).
- Alter the reading level by eliminating difficult words (you could write in an easier word with the same meaning above the difficult word).
- For fill-in questions, provide the possible answers at the bottom of the page.
- Use simple direct statements in the stem of the question.
- Familiarize students with the format of the test by reviewing samples from previous tests.
- Use both oral and written directions (possibly with an example) for each section of a test.
- Consider an open-book test or allowing the use of a one-page summary.
- Make the print large enough to be read easily.
- Make the visual layout simple and clean.
- Underline, highlight, or bold key words.
- Arrange items in a logical sequence.
- Allow additional time for students who process or write slowly.
- Include or explain the marking scheme.

Suggestions for Modifying Essay Tests

- Use simple, direct phrases in the design of your essay questions.
- Underline, highlight, or bold key words in the questions.
- Suggest the number of key points that should be included and give the marking scheme.
- Provide a proofreading checklist.
- Provide an outline organization sheet.
- Alter the reading level by eliminating difficult words (you could write in an easier word with the same meaning above the difficult word).
- Allow additional time for students who process or write slowly.

Source: Adapted from Peel Board of Education (1990). *Looking at Assessment: More Than Just Marks.*

Adapted Administration of Classroom Tests

What problems would you anticipate might arise during administration when exceptional students are taking classroom tests? For an objective or short-answer test, they could require additional time to finish or fewer questions, oral administration, a scribe, interpretation of a question by you, a calculator for problem solving, relevant formulae or definitions, and other external memory aids (Peel Board of Education, 1990). For an essay test, extended time or fewer required points in answers may be critical for those slow to process information. A quiet, distraction-free environment may be necessary. A means of spell checking can improve the quality of written work. An open-book test may be appropriate so that you test use of knowledge rather than memory. Allow a student to use a tape recorder only if he has previously been taught how to use one in test conditions.

Remember that even a well-constructed test will fail to demonstrate the knowledge of exceptional students if it is administered inappropriately. Table 8.4 includes a wide range of adaptations. Those that you choose for exceptional students should depend on the students' areas of difficulty.

Adapting Scoring or Marking of Classroom Tests

Like other adaptations, adapted scoring or marking of classroom tests should be guided by the key information in the IEPs about students' areas of need. You may want to discuss the implications of the IEP for marking with the in-school team. When you mark objective tests or essay tests, students with disabilities in writing, spelling, or memory should not be penalized for spelling or grammatical errors. You could provide these students with an opportunity to edit their own work before you mark their tests, or you could ask them to indicate the places where they think they have made these types of errors. Providing adaptations does not mean that you and the students should not make efforts to improve skills in these areas, but don't confuse those efforts with classroom tests that should be a demonstration of learning on reasonable outcomes for exceptional students.

On essay tests, you may review written responses with students individually and allow students with disabilities in writing to elaborate orally on their written responses. You can also adapt the marking scheme for the test. Remember the case study of Belle at the beginning of this chapter. The marking scheme for her mathematics course was adapted because of her hearing loss; the oral quizzes did not count toward her grade. This serves as a model of the kind of reasonable adaptations that can be arranged—for students with disabilities in spelling, you could reduce the credit given on a test for spelling, style, and organization and increase the credit for content. It may be helpful to provide the exceptional student with feedback on how they would have scored both without and with the adapted scoring, so they can see the effects of the adaptations (Peel Board of Education, 1990). This kind of information should help individuals with disabilities to enhance their self-awareness and skills of self-advocacy.

Ensure that you know your own perspective on marking classroom tests and then work collaboratively with any others who teach the exceptional students in your class (Christiansen & Vogel, 1998). To grade classroom tests fairly, assess students frequently through a variety of means and make every effort to accurately convey achievement to parents and students. Give useful feedback that directs the students on how to improve and remember that successful classroom tests serve as motivators to students to continue to perform well or perform better (Bradley & Calvin, 1998).

Further Reading

D.F. Bradley & M.B. Calvin (1998). Grading modified assignments: Equity or compromise? *Teaching Exceptional Children, 31*(2), 24–29.

J. Christiansen & J.R. Vogel (1998). A decision model for grading students with disabilities. *Teaching Exceptional Children, 31*(2), 30–35.

ADAPTATIONS IN ADMINISTERING CLASSROOM TESTS

Area of Difficulty

Adaptation	Reading	Writing	Listening	Speaking	Organizing; Paying Attention
Oral explanation of directions	X				X
Repetition of directions; student repetition of directions	X		X		X
Oral, taped or dictated test; oral clarification of written answers by student	X	X			X
Written versus oral test; written versus oral directions			X	X	
Extra time	X	X		X	
Time checks during test					X
Segmented test with separate directions for each section	X		X		X
Peer or other assistance:					
to read directions	X				
to check comprehension	X				
to check spelling		X			
Technological aids:					
placemarks or markers	X				X
word processor		X			
tape recorder	X	X		X	
Visual aids and cues; verbal and visual prompts for word retrieval			X	X	
Use of outlines, diagrams, charts, tables, and webs to organize or answer	X	X			X
Permitted use of non-cursive writing		X			
Use of previously prepared notes or rehearsed answers				X	
Alternative sites:					
to minimize noise/distraction			X		X
for alternative testing	X	X			
Seating proximity to teacher			X		
Teacher paraphrase or summary of student answers in complete thoughts				X	
Checklist for materials needed and preparation					X
Allowing answering directly on test rather than answer sheet		X			

Source: M. Friend, W. Bursuck, & N.L. Hutchinson (1998). *Including Exceptional Students: A Practical Guide for Classroom Teachers.* Scarborough: Allyn and Bacon Canada, pp. 356–57. Reprinted with permission.

Using Adapted Performance Assessments

In using a wide range of classroom assessment approaches, consider performance assessment. **Performance assessment** is any assessment activity that provides opportunities for students to demonstrate directly their ability to combine and use their knowledge, skills, and habits of mind (Harper, O'Connor, & Simpson, 1999). In studying municipal government, your grade 5 students may read local newspapers, attend a meeting of the municipal council, invite a councillor to visit the classroom, and conduct library research. If you assess what they have learned by asking them to write a letter about a community issue to a local politician, the editor of the community newspaper, or a member of a service group, you will be using performance assessment. In your grade 11 course in career development and cooperative education, teach your students to answer interview questions by having them role-play interviewer and then interviewee. If you assess each student's interview skills while an unfamiliar adult volunteer is interviewing him or her, then you are using performance assessment.

Wiggins (1993) argued strongly that teachers should develop performance assessments that are also authentic. Both of these examples are also considered to be **authentic assessment** or close to real-world tasks. Characteristics of authentic assessment are:

- performance on engaging and important problems
- performance on contextualized tasks that represent those expected in the adult world
- real problems with a number of steps that require more than formulaic solutions
- tasks that demand students produce a quality product or performance

A set of steps is usually prescribed for educators who wish to develop and evaluate tasks for performance-based assessments. These steps appear in Figure 8.4.

Figure 8.4

STEPS NECESSARY FOR IMPLEMENTATION OF PERFORMANCE ASSESSMENT

1. Articulate the desired outcomes of a learning unit by defining the domain of content and identifying complex "authentic" performances and products.

2. State the specific requirements of performances, including the knowledge, skills, and processes that must be exemplified in a performance (or product) or collection of performances (or products). Develop rubrics for these requirements.

3. Develop tests of performances (and products) so central to learning that the test is valued and used to further as well as to demonstrate learning.

4. Educate educators and the community so they can work together and use performance assessments for students with and without exceptionalities.

Adapted from N.L. Hutchinson (1995). Performance assessments of career development. *ERIC Digest* ED414518.

For exceptional students, performance assessments can focus on lifeskills and leisure skills. These students are learning by building an airplane in a program designed to keep at-risk students in school.

Performance assessments often enable students to show what they know. They do not rely exclusively on reading and writing like pencil and paper tests, and they need not be subject to the same time constraints. Marlene has AD/HD. She is in the grade 5 class that wrote letters to municipal politicians. Marlene drafted her letter on a computer, read it aloud into a tape recorder, listened to it, and then reorganized the order of the paragraphs. By using a computer with a spell checker and grammar checker, she was able to correct most of the spelling and grammatical errors and produce a quality product. Because she knows that she speaks better than she writes, Marlene telephoned city hall, made an appointment with the councillor representing her district, and hand delivered her letter. Her teacher was able to assess Marlene taking action in an adult way and demonstrating what she had learned about municipal government. Because of the high level of motivation that accompanied this performance assessment, Marlene made many adaptations herself. The teacher had prepared a rubric against which she assessed each student's performance and product.

Sometimes students with disabilities miss the connections between assessments in school contexts and the real-world contexts to which they apply. That is why Marlene's teacher ensured that the letter was written to an adult in the local power structure rather than simply to the teacher. Well-designed performance assessments can help students see these connections. However, this assessment required that the students in Marlene's class were taught how to write a persuasive letter, to provide specific examples to support an argument, to sequence the parts of a letter, etc. They needed plenty of practice before they embarked on the culminating task. At the same time, Marlene's teacher recognized that if the process was drawn out or not engaging, then it would have become just another traditional test to exceptional students.

For students on modified programs, you will have to develop modified performance assessments. Bill, a nonverbal adolescent with autism, will have to learn to express his agreement or disagreement to unfamiliar adults if he is to find employment or volunteer work in the community. A modified performance assessment might require him to attend a meeting with the manager of a charity shop who requires a volunteer to sweep the floor, break up cardboard boxes, and unpack and sort donations. Bill has to show the manager how he would communicate agreement and disagreement, and that he can perform the tasks she assigns. Because he learns gradually in the real-world context, Bill practises the interview with the paraprofessional many times, sweeps the classroom daily, and practises breaking up boxes and sorting a box of housewares and clothing. The paraprofessional attends the workplace meeting with Bill and next term will accompany Bill to his two-hour-per-week on-the-job training at the charity shop. Performance assessments have great potential for assessing exceptional students in meaningful ways. For most students, you will use this relatively new method of assessment in combination with the other forms of assessment discussed in this chapter.

Portfolios as Classroom Assessments for Exceptional Learners

John Anderson and Dan Bachor (1998) of the University of Victoria describe a **portfolio** as a collection of student work that represents a sampling of the achievements of a student and provides evidence of learning over a period of time. If a student and teacher sample thoughtfully, the collection can become an integral part of learning. A portfolio should contain evidence of student reflection and self-evaluation that contribute to students' valuing their own work and themselves as learners (British Columbia Ministry of Education, 1992). The steps involved in portfolio assessment are (adapted from Harper, O'Connor, & Simpson, 1999):

- *collect* in a container that is efficient for your classroom organization
- *select* purposefully so the contents show students meeting outcomes and learning goals
- *reflect*; students can write on cover sheets or sticky notes, or teacher and student can summarize a conference together
- *inspect*; teacher, student, and parents should consider the accomplishments in light of the outcomes and goals that were set; use this event to close the year's or term's portfolio process

What should be placed in a portfolio? The kinds of content that might go into a portfolio in reading and writing (with adaptations for exceptional students in brackets) include:

- a log of books read with personal reactions to the books (for an exceptional student with limited writing ability, the personal reactions could be captioned drawings)
- an audiotape of the student reading showing best performance (for a student learning to read, audiotapes made monthly would show progress)
- representative assignments responding to pre- and post-reading questions (these could change gradually from multiple choice to fill in the blanks to written responses)
- scrapbook of representative writing samples (increasing in length and complexity)
- notes from conferences with the teacher (ranging from a checklist to a paragraph)

Put Into Practice

Consult a source on performance assessment, such as K.M. Hibbard (2000). *Performance-based learning and assessment in middle school science.* Larchmont, NY: Eye on Education, Inc. Develop a performance-based task and assessment with an accompanying rubric and make adaptations for an exceptional student (whom you describe in one paragraph).

A teacher-student conference provides an opportunity to reflect on a student's portfolio.

What do you think?

Read the paper by
Anderson and Bachor for
descriptions of the provincial directives on portfolio
assessment. Then consult
current documents and
Web sites of the ministry
of education in your
province. What do you
think of the use of portfolios in the assessment of
learning of exceptional
students?

Further Reading

H.L. Kleinert, J. Haig, J.F.
Kearns, & S. Kennedy (2000).
Alternate assessments:
Lessons learned and roads to
be taken. *Exceptional
Children, 67*, 51–66.

What do you think?

Read a paper on portfolio
assessment, such as C.L.
Wesson & R.P. King (1996).
Portfolio assessment and
special education students.
*Teaching Exceptional
Children, 28*(2), 44–48. What
do you see as the
strengths and limitations
of this innovative approach
to classroom assessment?

- student-selected best performance in writing of various genres (a limited range of genres)
- teacher-developed rubrics that show increasing accomplishments in written expression

While writers like Anderson and Bachor (1998) have observed considerable use of portfolios in elementary classrooms across Canada, there are also examples of secondary teachers adopting this approach to assessment. Focus on Teachers describes one secondary business studies teacher who uses both portfolio assessment and student-led conferences.

The kinds of adaptations you may have to make include teaching exceptional students how to select and reflect on portfolio pieces. You may need to provide more guidance in the efficient management and organization of so much information. And you may find that exceptional students cannot function as independently in student–parent conferences; you may wish to be present and participate in such conferences rather than be nearby and monitoring. The applicability of portfolio assessment for exceptional students has been convincingly demonstrated by U.S. states that have pioneered alternate assessments for students who cannot meaningfully complete large-scale assessments. Both of the states that led in this area (Kentucky and Maryland) developed portfolio assessment for student work with required entries that reflect performance across essential life areas. These include such things as a vocational resumé in grade 12, demonstrated promptness, management of a student's own schedule, engagement in hobbies, and working cooperatively with others. Both states viewed portfolios of student work as a more flexible and individualized approach to capture the learning outcomes of a heterogeneous group of students (Kleinert, Haig, Kearns, & Kennedy, 2000). Many have recommended electronic portfolios (e.g., Weidmer, 1998) and, while some school districts like the former North York School Board in Ontario embraced electronic portfolios to demonstrate career development, this still appears to be the exception rather than the rule in Canadian schools.

Adaptations and Alternatives to Report Card Marks

One of the most contentious issues in education is the question of how report card grades can and should be adapted for exceptional students. Assessments must not discriminate against students with disabilities. We do not want our grading practices to serve as disincentives to exceptional students like Sasha, described in the opening case study. Grades must speak to students, parents, post-secondary institutions, and employers. Teachers must also feel comfortable with the message they send to exceptional students and their classmates, and must feel they can "live with themselves." Given that adaptations are a relatively new phenomenon, we still have more questions than answers. What options do you have? Table 8.5 provides examples of grading adaptations. It is important to read the available information for your jurisdiction and school, so you understand which of these options are acceptable in the school in which you teach.

David Notman: The Effects of Portfolio Assessment and Student-Led Conferences on Ownership, Control, and Learning

David Notman describes himself as "a business teacher with 26 years' experience in the business classroom." He describes his course this way: "The Introduction to Business program is a survey course of business studies, offered at the grade 10 level to 15- and 16-year-old students in their second year of high school." After years of traditional assessment, he asked the question, "What would happen if the students had more ownership of the curriculum; more control of their own assessment? And what would happen if this was done in partnership with parents?"

He writes about ownership: "Ownership begins with the student's contribution to the classroom. The room is decorated with pop cans, cereal boxes, shopping bags, and other examples of interesting packaging. The students are encouraged to contribute to the collection if they can find something that is not already up. They will always point out their contributions to their parents during the student–parent interview. Many students return, even after graduation, to see if their 'stuff' is still there."

In describing his course, Notman said, "At the beginning of the semester, each student is required to select a company that he/she will profile throughout the semester. The only requirement is that the companies are traded on a stock exchange; that they are public companies and therefore have open and accessible records to facilitate research. As information is provided in class about business in general (how change affects business, for example) each student connects this information to the business he/she is profiling, and interprets the significance of the information in areas such as investment, expansion of markets, or the new methods of distribution."

Notman does not allow students to work in pairs and no two students can profile the same company. "The student begins to refer to the company as 'my' company. ('My company just sent me some information.') A list is posted in the classroom, matching students with companies, and students are encouraged to share information they find on other companies."

The students experience control through the student-led conference. "At mid-semester the students meet with their parent(s) or guardian(s) in the business classroom after school or in the evening. The student summarizes the curriculum to date and then presents his/her portfolio as a work in progress. The teacher is not present during the presentation but is available to answer questions. The mid-term mark is generated by the student and parent, and is based on both the effort shown up to that point as well as the plans that the student has made to finish the work. As this is a compulsory part of the course evaluation, the parent turnout is almost 100 percent."

The portfolio is the basis for the end-of-term assessment as well. "The final presentation is made one on one between the student and the teacher. The format is up to the student. The student is marked according to a rubric, which he/she has seen and studied throughout the semester. The rubric is based on the ICE model and provides opportunities for students to do well at various stages of the process. Not all students are expected to achieve the same level, but the student is given the opportunity to decide what level they are willing to accept. Passing grades are assigned if the student is working on the Information level, average grades are given for achievement at the Connections level, and honour grades are received by students who work at the Extension level."

Notman's assessment of his change to portfolio assessment and student-led conferences: "Students seem to have been able to do and submit much better work than before. The portfolios contain a thorough presentation of the course material, connected to the real world consistently, and often accompanied by analysis, criticism, suggestions, and other indications that students have gone beyond the course requirements. Their presentations, both to the parents and to me, require that they explain their work in a context; that they connect the course together, then tell about what they know. This experience leads to deeper knowledge than simple memorization. Active learning seems to involve students' taking ownership and control of their learning. I have noticed a marked decrease in the number of behaviour problems. The students say, 'This course is something you do for yourself.' I think [the success] has primarily to do with the amount of ownership and control the students have in directing their learning and assessment."

Source: Extracts from David Notman (2000). Another Way of Coming Downstairs: The Effects of Portfolio Assessment and Student-Led Conferences on Ownership, Control and Learning. Paper presented at the annual meeting of the Ontario Education Research Conference, Toronto. Used with permission.

Table 8.5

EXAMPLES OF GRADING ADAPTATIONS

Change Grading Criteria	Change to Letter and Number Grades	Use Alternatives to Letter and Number Grades
Vary grading weights.	Add written comments.	Use pass–fail grades.
Modify curricular expectations.	Add student activity logs.	Use competency checklists.
Grade on the basis of improvement.	Add information from portfolios and/or performance-based assessments.	Use contracts and modified syllabi.

Source: M. Friend, W. Bursuck, & N.L. Hutchinson (1998). *Including Exceptional Students: A Practical Guide for Classroom Teachers.* Scarborough: Allyn and Bacon Canada, p. 359. Reprinted with permission.

The first of these options is **changing grading criteria**. Belle's case demonstrates how you can vary grading weights so students are not disadvantaged by an impossible task—for example, students who are hard of hearing do not have part of their grade determined by their inability to hear during pop quizzes. Modifying curricular expectations must build on the IEP, and then it is critical to assess what is expected for the exceptional student. If you expect a student with developmental disabilities to learn to discuss the historical sites in the community, then assess her on this outcome with a high mark for excellence or a low mark for poor performance. Don't assign her a low grade because she cannot write an essay when this was never expected of her nor taught to her. **Grading contracts** or **modified course syllabi** *may* enable you to give students credit for attendance, promptness, effort, and cooperative behaviour. Make the criteria objective and consistent with the IEP, and ensure that the student and parents are aware of the criteria. Sometimes grading on the basis of improvement can motivate students to work hard, attend, and pay attention. This strategy complements the use of qualitative rubrics particularly well.

Changes to letter and number grades may mean clarifying them with a comment that explains the reading level of the books used in language arts or explaining that Billy is using the grade 3 math text although he is in grade 5. It may be better to make these explanations in a letter stapled to the report card and to also type on the report card that it is valid only if the explanatory letter is attached. This allows the child to show the report to peers without them reading the details of the clarification (a realistic strategy given that children are often under great pressure to allow peers to glance at their reports). What you write on the report about the adapted curriculum and the IEP may be limited by policy and by legislation regarding privacy of information. Learn the school policies well in advance of the first reporting period. A summary of student activities constitutes a **student activity log**. This may be particularly beneficial in reporting progress for students on modified programs. You may be able to include a summary that describes the key accomplishments shown in the portfolio or performance-based assessments. If this information cannot appear on the report, you can emphasize it in a conference with parents.

There are few alternatives to the letter and number grades that dominate North American reporting systems. However, some teachers have used **pass/fail** or **credit/no credit** designations to show that students have met the minimum requirements for a unit. Be sure to specify objectively what these requirements are and how you arrived at a judgment. Qualitative rubrics can be helpful in this task. Checklists for skills that are taught at the various grades may be available in the curricula or from the resource teacher. These can help you to communicate the skills that students have mastered, are working on, and have not yet begun to acquire. Often students and parents can understand how much progress the student has made and how the skills acquired compare to what is expected of other students by looking at a straightforward checklist. If this cannot replace a grade, perhaps it can help to explain a grade. Be sure to indicate the skills and knowledge attained compared to those listed in the IEP annual outcomes for the exceptional student.

Whatever forms of grading adaptations you use, be prepared to explain them to students and parents and collaborate with others who teach the exceptional students in your class. Remember that you may have to provide a written explanation for the receiving institution when students make the transition from elementary to secondary school, and for graduating secondary students. The section on fairness in this chapter raised issues that you must be prepared to address when you use grading adaptations. Finally, you have to feel proud of and comfortable with your grading practices. Be honest and avoid jargon. Think about how you would want a teacher to report on the progress of your exceptional child (if you were the parent of such a child); hold yourself to the standards you would expect of others.

Put Into Practice

If you are looking for an ongoing source of professional development, consider joining Council for Exceptional Children and receiving *Teaching Exceptional Children* **10 times annually. Visit the Web site at www.cec.sped.org.**

Key Terms

assessment (p. 230)

large-scale assessment (p. 230)

classroom assessment (p. 230)

testing (p. 230)

evaluation (p. 230)

grading (p. 230)

reporting (p. 230)

norm-referenced (p. 237)

criterion-referenced (p. 237)

self-referenced (p. 237)

ICE model (p. 237)

Ideas (p. 237)

Connections (p. 237)

Extensions (p. 237)

rubrics (p. 238)

quantitative rubrics (p. 238)

qualitative rubrics (p. 238)

study guide (p. 243)

study skills (p. 243)

chunking strategies (p. 243)

mnemonic (p. 244)

concept maps (p. 244)

performance assessment (p. 249)

authentic assessment (p. 249)

portfolio (p. 251)

changing grading criteria (p. 254)

grading contracts (p. 254)

modified course syllabi (p. 254)

student activity log (p. 254)

pass/fail (p. 255)

credit/no credit (p. 255)

Summary

This chapter focused on a contentious issue in exceptional education: adapting assessment to report fairly the learning of exceptional students. All teaching and assessment of exceptional students should be guided by the annual outcomes listed in their IEPs and by the descriptions of strengths and needs. This chapter reviewed how to use the ADAPT strategy to analyze assessment. It then described large-scale assessment in Canada and the adaptations used for exceptional students. This was followed by descriptions of how teachers conduct classroom assessment and the role of rubrics. There were descriptions of classroom assessment, including tests, performance assessment, and portfolios. The final topic was adaptations and alternatives to report card marks. ∎

Enhancing
Social Relations

Val started grade 1 in September with the children who had been in her kindergarten class and had attended preschool with her. Val participated in an early intervention program, was always encouraged to explore her environment, and is quite adventuresome once she is familiar with her surroundings. Because Val is blind, she does not play much on the equipment in the playground. Some days she asks the teacher on playground supervision to help her get onto a swing, but at recess she usually invites a classmate to stand with her under a tree or to sit with her on a bench outside the school entrance. One day, Val's teacher reminds the other children to play games at recess that can include Val. Peter and Francine pipe up that they like to play catch and that Val cannot play "because she can't see the ball." Peter says, "It just wouldn't be safe." On the way out to the playground later in the day, Francine tells the teacher, "It is kind of boring spending recess with Val. She can't do much. And I don't like when she doesn't look at me. Why does she look at my ear when I'm talking to her?"

Lynn rushes into the resource room with her friend Marcia. These two grade 11 students are almost inseparable. Both have learning disabilities and both are on the school cheerleading squad. When they aren't together, they are talking on the phone. Lynn has severe difficulties with written expression, and she has brought her latest English assignment to the resource room so she can edit it with a peer tutor from grade 12. When I ask Lynn how her day is going, she replies, "Great!" The girls part, promising to meet in the locker room after school. Marcia goes to her history class and Lynn sits down with her peer tutor. Few people know how severe Lynn's learning disability is— her closest friends, her peer tutor, her classroom teachers, and me. As Lynn's resource room teacher and counsellor, I know how hard it is for her to complete her written assignments without "blowing her cover." Lynn leaves class rather than read aloud in front of her peers, works hard with me and with her peer tutor to edit all written work before she submits it, and writes her tests in the resource room where it is quiet and she has extra time. When you ask Lynn why she comes to school, she will tell you, "To be with my friends!"

1. How would you describe the peer relations of Val and Lynn?

2. What should teachers be expected to do to meet the social and friendship needs of students like Val and Lynn?

3. How might the social characteristics and social relations of these students and other exceptional learners affect their learning in inclusive classrooms?

4. What teaching strategies are likely to help exceptional students be part of the social and academic life of the classroom?

5. What school and community resources can a teacher draw on to enhance the social relations of students like Lynn and Val?

The focus of this chapter is the **social relationships** of exceptional learners in inclusive classrooms. "Having and maintaining friends is an integral part of children's development" (Cooper, Griffith, & Filer, 1999, p. 110). Friendship is one of "the most prominent features of the social landscape during adolescence" (Hartup, 1993, p. 5). Much has been written about the need for friendship, social acceptance, and full participation if inclusion is to be more than a placement (e.g., Ballard, 1999; Hutchinson, Freeman, & Steiner-Bell, 2001). Recent research informs us of the perspectives of exceptional youth and of students without disabilities on friendship and belonging (e.g., Lévesque, 1997; MacCuspie, 1996). Considering the students' points of view may help you foster the kinds of friendships that are important for emotional well-being, and respond constructively when children and adolescents pull back from peers who, for example, don't look them in the eye. Social interactions are expected to foster learning in many approaches that are used extensively in schools and that are recommended to teachers (cooperative learning, collaborative learning, small groups, activity centres, etc.). You can use the ADAPT strategy to analyze the social demands of your classroom organization and of tasks and compare these demands to student strengths and needs. This chapter provides examples of some of the options for the social structure of learning, with examples drawn from current Canadian resources. The role of the community in social development is explored—for a society that is committed to inclusion.

Further Reading

Examples of books and articles available on topics like social relations and friendship: W.M. Bukowski, A.F. Newcomb, & W.W. Hartup (eds.) (1996). *The company they keep: Friendship in childhood and adolescence.* New York: Cambridge University Press.

M.J. Cooper, K.G. Griffith, & J. Filer (1999). School intervention for inclusion of students with and without disabilities. *Focus on Autism and Other Developmental Disabilities, 14*(2), 110–15.

The Importance of Social Development and Social Acceptance to Inclusion

Chapter 1 describes how participating in all facets of Canadian society, including educational institutions, is a fundamental right of all Canadians. The mandate of the Office of Disability Issues in the federal government is to "remove barriers and to improve the social and economic inclusion of Canadians with disabilities" (http://www.hrdc-drhc.gc.ca/hrib/sdd-dds/odi/content/about.shtml). In 1998, a review of educational policies across the country (Friend, Bursuck, & Hutchinson, 1998) showed two dominant themes in the education of exceptional learners: change and inclusion. Change refers to the emphasis on moving "from the goal of access for as many students as possible to success for as many as possible" (Gouvernement du Québec, Ministère de l'Éducation, 1999). Chapter 2 highlighted your role as a classroom teacher in fostering inclusion of exceptional learners. "Parents and students want a program which includes the [exceptional] student as part of the class" (Lennon, 1995, p. 24). We saw—in the descriptions of characteristics of students with both high-incidence (Chapter 3) and low-incidence (Chapter 4) exceptionalities and in the diverse groups of students described in Chapter 5—that social participation is often a key issue in their inclusion. In fact,

IEPs often include social (as well as physical and academic) strengths and needs. Chapter 6 focused on how you can foster a positive climate in the classroom through your organization and management strategies so students learn from your example, expectations, and follow-through that everyone is a valued member of the school and classroom communities.

Much has been written by Canadians (e.g., O'Brien, Forest, Snow, & Hasbury, 1989) and others (e.g., Ballard, 1999) about the need for friendship, social acceptance, and full participation if exceptional students are to be included in classrooms and not merely placed in them. If inclusion means full and valued participation in the life of the classroom, then we need to understand how important **social development** of exceptional students, **social acceptance** by peers, and **friendships** are to equity and inclusion (see Table 9.1 for definitions). In the next two sections, we focus on the perspectives of exceptional students on their peer relations and on the perspectives of their peers on social relations with exceptional students.

Cross-Reference
In describing the first two steps in the ADAPT strategy, Chapter 1 emphasizes students' social, emotional, and behavioural strengths and needs as well as the social, emotional, and behavioural demands of the classroom in the general area.

Perspectives of Exceptional Students on Their Peer Relations

What do exceptional students report about their views of their relationships, friendships, and feelings of belonging with their classmates? Do they think these relationships are important to their classroom learning? Only recently have researchers begun to focus on the voices of exceptional students on this issue, and there is great variability in the reports from children and adolescents.

"Friends are what gets me through school I guess you could say. They're always there to support me...friends you tell everything and they're always there, so they're very important." These are the words of Lynn, the grade 11 student with

Table 9.1

SOCIAL DEVELOPMENT, SOCIAL ACCEPTANCE, AND FRIENDSHIPS

Phenomenon	Source	Definition
Social development, social competence	Schneider (1993)	The ability to implement developmentally appropriate social behaviours that enhance one's interpersonal relationships without causing harm to anyone.
Social acceptance	Dodge (1985)	The response and evaluation, by peers, of students' social behaviours. Do peers approve of their behaviours, consider them to be members of the group, and include them in social and learning activities?
Friendships	Hartup (1996)	Close relationships characterized by reciprocity, that is, give and take, and by commitment between individuals who see themselves as equals.

Two 11-year-old girls with diabetes are best friends. They both enjoy skating and each understands what the other has to deal with—frequent finger-pricking, taking insulin, and a careful diet.

LD introduced in the case study at the beginning of this chapter. Lynn attends the same Canadian secondary school as Matt, a grade 11 student with LD and AD/HD. Here is what Matt said, when asked how important friends were to him: "Ah just sometimes I just don't know how to relate to a lot of the people anymore...It's not very important I don't think...Maybe they just don't like me or you know they find me annoying" (Lévesque, 1997).

These two adolescents with LD, who attend inclusive classes in the same school, have very different views of their social relations in these classes. Lynn is a popular cheerleader with close friends, while Matt is socially isolated and cannot find anyone to listen to him talk about Quake (his favourite computer game). Buhrmester (1996) developed a theory of adolescent friendship characterized by four elements of **interpersonal competence**: initiating and sustaining conversation, initiating plans to spend time with friends outside of school, disclosing personal thoughts and empathy, and managing conflict effectively. In interviews and observations, Nicole Lévesque of Queen's University found that Lynn demonstrated these four competencies, while all four posed a challenge for Matt.

Lynn's and Matt's social experiences differed radically; yet both cases exemplified the significance of peer relations in influencing thoughts about school and shaping psychosocial development. Lynn's close friendships and positive peer relationships enriched her educational experiences and enhanced her self-esteem. Her story is an uplifting illustration of how some exceptional students thrive academically, socially, and personally in supportive environments. Matt, on the other hand, stood alone in the halls, could not carry on a reciprocal conversation, and reported that he had nothing to look forward to when he returned to school after the winter break.

Karen, a blind woman who lives in New Zealand, described how she fit in during her adolescent years. "I really enjoyed the classes where I just went in and was treated like anyone else; and if I had not done my homework, I would get told off as well." Karen reported that she liked high school and had many of the same experiences as her peers. "I felt a bit out of it socially but I think that was because like most kids in their teenage years you want to be part of the popular group and I wasn't, and there was nothing I could have done about that." She described the groups or cliques and how she did not fit into "the sporty group, because I could not play team sports" or "the really academic group" who were "nerdy." Karen concluded, "I had a few close friends but I did not really fit into a group. This is not specifically [a problem] for disabled students, other students have the same problem" (Ballard & McDonald, 1999, p. 110).

Marilyn, a woman with a physical disability, was interviewed about her days in school. She talked about her relationships with other students and how important teachers are to the social experiences of students with disabilities. One of Marilyn's teachers, who meant well, created a roster of helpers who were forced to push Marilyn's wheelchair. That contributed to what she described as "the most miserable year I ever had at school" (Ballard & McDonald, 1999, p. 101). Marilyn contrasted this with another teacher who told the class about Marilyn, her disability, and her wheelchair and explained that Marilyn would be a full member of the class like everyone else. She urged them to be friendly and to make Marilyn feel welcome. In Marilyn's view, "This 'worked,' and I made some of my best friends and I have still got them. In that class I was included, I was allowed to sit at a desk, and everybody treated me really well." Marilyn suggests that, "The key to inclusion is making people without disability comfortable with disability, [but also] accept that they have got a responsibility to help remove the barriers" (p. 102). This points to the need for teachers to understand how students without disabilities view peer relations with their classmates with disabilities.

Perspectives of Peers on Social Relations with Exceptional Classmates

The research reports a wide array of **peer perspectives** on relationships with students with disabilities. The case study of Val at the opening of this chapter reflects some of the findings reported by Pat MacCuspie (1996) of Nova Scotia in an interview study about the inclusion of blind students. Classmates in elementary grades tended to describe their friendships with blind students as based on helping, rather than on shared interests or fun. Interests and fun were the basis for their relationships with non-disabled friends. When asked about joining in activities with their blind classmates, some children described the inconveniences of playing and learning with blind children. They saw play as problematic because blind classmates could not safely play catch or tag, and paired reading was problematic because a Braille reader is slower than a print reader and pages of Braille are large and awkward. Young children also seemed uncomfortable with classmates who did not make eye contact, and some did not understand that blind children could not see at all and rather thought they could see, just not as clearly as other people. Much like Marilyn's suggestion above, MacCuspie recommends that teachers be forthright in teaching classmates about the nature of the disability and, for example, explain why a blind child cannot maintain eye contact. Figure 9.1 contains information and resources for planning a **(dis)ability awareness program** for your classroom or school.

Many studies have reported that children and adolescents with learning disabilities and other disabilities tend to have low social status in regular classrooms (e.g., Haager & Vaughn, 1995; Conderman, 1995). Social status is based on **sociometric rating**, that is, whether classmates would choose these students as best friends, would choose them to play with, etc. Judith Wiener of University of Toronto and Nancy Heath of McGill University (e.g., Heath & Wiener, 1996; Wiener, Harris, & Shirer, 1990) have reported low **social status** in a number of studies of Canadian children with learning disabilities. Janet Chan (2000) of Queen's University observed the peer interactions (in a grade 5/6 class) of two grade 6 children

Further Reading

Adapt the recommendations for developing a (dis)ability awareness program appropriate for a secondary school environment. Consider a film festival. S.P. Safran (2000). Using movies to teach students about disabilities. *Teaching Exceptional Children, 32*(3), 44–47.

What do you think?

Why do you think parents of exceptional children might be concerned when classmates see their relationship with the exceptional student as primarily based on helping rather than on reciprocal enjoyment of each other's company? How can teachers encourage children (or adolescents) with and without disabilities to see themselves as equals in their relationships?

Figure 9.1

(DIS)ABILITY AWARENESS PROGRAMS

Purposes: To foster greater understanding of people with disabilities
To increase students' knowledge about specific disabilities
To increase students' sensitivity toward individuals with
disabilities

Develop a program that reflects your local school needs. Invite parents of children with disabilities, older students with disabilities, and adults with disabilities to take part in the planning and in the program.

Adults with disabilities may speak about their disabilities, share feelings, demonstrate how their adapted equipment (e.g., motorized wheelchair, hearing aid) works. Some adults are comfortable to eat lunch with a class of students or sit and talk in the schoolyard at recess as well.

Ask students with and without disabilities to be presenters. They can read from books about children with disabilities, show videos, and act as hosts for adult presenters. These students will benefit from a reflective component to their participation and will appreciate recognition as well.

Locate resources (videos, books, pamphlets, and other community resources). Consult the lists in this book, Web sites, and community organizations.

Take photographs to remember the occasion, invite the local press, and recognize participants in a school assembly.

Resources to consult:

Family Village Library, Disability Awareness
http://www.familyvillage.wisc.edu/general/disability-awareness.html

Center for Disability Information and Referral, University of Indiana
http://www.iidc.indiana.edu/~cedir/kidsweb/

New Brunswick Easter Seals
http://www.discribe.ca/crcd/dat1.htm

L.G. Denti & S. Meyers (1997). Successful ability awareness programs: The key is in the planning. *Teaching Exceptional Children, 29*(4), 52–54.

(Michael and Kelly) with learning disabilities over four months. She was interested in how often they initiated social interactions with classmates and responded to classmates. She also looked at the quality of their exchanges with their peers, trying to understand what might contribute to low social status with peers.

Chan observed Michael and Kelly in many contexts: during academic lessons in the morning, in classes such as physical education, and in the schoolyard. Michael's teacher seated him at the side of the classroom, away from the other grade 6 students. During academic lessons Michael initiated few social exchanges with peers, and they rarely spoke to him. For example, during the 11 mornings he was observed, Michael only made 12 initiations to peers and 4 responses. He rarely engaged with his peers during physical education; however, at recess Michael showed positive social skills in the schoolyard. He played "foot hockey" with grade 5 male classmates or played on a climbing structure with them. Michael seemed shy and was largely ignored in the classroom.

Kelly, on the other hand, made frequent overtures to her classmates (34 in 12 mornings), most of which were rebuffed. She also responded to her peers 17 times during these mornings. Other students usually answered Kelly with a single word; Kelly's responses were also brief. Outside the structured classroom setting, Kelly was socially isolated from her peers, especially at recess. She did not associate with the other grade 6 girls; occasionally, she played with one grade 5 student from her class, but their relationship diminished during the study. Usually, Kelly spent recess playing with the kindergarten children or standing alone.

Chan (2000) concluded that both children experienced difficulties with peer relations, although these difficulties manifested themselves in different ways. Michael had difficulty initiating and responding verbally; he was shy, sat in an isolated location, and was ignored by his classmates. Kelly tried to initiate many conversations unsuccessfully, often interrupting unresponsive classmates while they were engaged in work. Her peers frequently told her to leave them alone and reported to the researcher that Kelly annoyed them. She was more actively rejected than Michael and appeared to have no one to play with or in whom she could confide. Her classmates did not seem to value passing time with her.

In a recent study, Hall and McGregor (2000) reported on the peer relations of three boys with disabilities in an inclusive school in Australia. The school was described as "a school community where all children are viewed as individuals regardless of abilities" (p. 125). The three focal students were Nathan, Mike, and Manuel. Nathan had cerebral palsy, epilepsy, developmental disabilities, and limited verbal communication skills. He used a communication board. Mike had developmental disabilities, hyperactivity, and poor balance, while Manuel had Down syndrome. Data were collected at two points five years apart (kindergarten and grade 5) by a number of means, including interviews with peers who chose the boys as playmates in grade 5. One grade 5 peer suggested that Nathan was "fun to play with," and one said of Mike, "I've been with him since prep and I like him a lot. He's sort of a good friend. I like to help him." Of Manuel, a girl named Erica said, "He's my best friend. We go to each other's house sometimes." These three exceptional students were observed to participate in the same activities as their classmates, to be befriended by girls more than by boys, and to have long-term relationships (since kindergarten) with the children who chose them as playmates. In most cases, the children's families were friends in the community and encouraged the children to play together outside of school.

In an interview study in a British secondary school known for its inclusive practices, Ainscow, Booth, and Dyson (1999) learned through interviews what the students thought of the school. "Possibly the most significant and frequently mentioned factor relating to [their] positive feelings [was]…the school as a source of

Put Into Practice

Researchers have reported that some schools tend to be inclusive communities where there are many positive reports of friendships, social relations, and respect among students, including exceptional students. Look for a school that is developing such a reputation and make naturalistic observations of the students, teachers, and administrators in that school. What can you learn from such observations about how to create an inclusive community in your classroom and school?

social encounters" (p. 141). One student said, "It just seems a lot easier to make friends here—it happens in lessons and free time." Students described positive relationships with teachers and opportunities to pursue individual projects over extended time periods. They described coming into the school from "a close and supportive climate within their home districts," and the high number of supportive adult helpers (paraprofessionals) present because of the large number of students with disabilities. The researchers reported "relaxed relationships" between males and females, "little or no evidence of racism among the students," and that "students with disabilities are accepted as being just part of the 'normal' school community." They described a blind student who "talked openly about her own disability and, referred to the disability of others in a 'taken for granted' tone." She introduced one of her friends, Elaine, as follows: "She's special needs, not Down's [syndrome]."

These adolescents defended the practice of including exceptional students. One told the researchers, "I don't see why they shouldn't be in the school because they're just normal, just people same as all of us. They should all have the same chance as anyone else should have" (Ainscow et al., 1999, p. 148). Another student commented, "We have a laugh with them, treat them as normal people." One student explained that he had attended an athletics meet for students with disabilities. The students from his inclusive school behaved maturely, "so well balanced but the kids from the special school had the same disabilities but were so different...getting up and running all over the place and it was really dangerous" (p. 148).

These case studies, which provide the perspectives of students with and without disabilities on their social relations, suggest a number of implications for teachers and families of exceptional students. For teachers, these cases suggest that your role is critical. Teachers can make exceptional students into valued classmates and can teach so that everyone experiences the benefits of being included. Teachers can minimize students' sense that disabilities are foreign and exotic and can contribute to the kind of feeling that was prevalent in the school where disabilities were a common and accepted thing. Teachers can help make everyone comfortable with disability, as Marilyn suggested. Providing information and eliminating mystery about the exceptionality can go a long way. Treating exceptional students much as you treat everyone else is also essential. There are implications for parents, too. Long-term friendships appear to provide considerable benefits to exceptional students, as do family connections outside of school. Families of exceptional children may need to take an active role in initiating play opportunities in the early years so that children without disabilities, members of neighbourhood families, feel comfortable with the child with a disability. Figure 9.2 provides suggestions for parents (or teachers) to help their children or adolescents with severe disabilities to develop skills for interacting with peers and handling emotions. The next section describes the importance of friendship to development and elaborates on why teachers and parents should make the effort to foster such friendships.

Figure 9.2

STRATEGIES FOR PARENTS (AND TEACHERS) TO TEACH SOCIAL SKILLS FOR PEER INTERACTIONS

Incidental Teaching
This strategy means taking advantage of "teachable moments." During naturally occurring situations, parents (or teachers) remind or show children how to use social skills.

Example
Fiona is playing at Maggie's house. Fiona and Maggie reach for the green crayon at the same time. Maggie's mother takes this opportunity to remind Maggie to share, saying, "Maybe you can let Fiona use the green crayon now, and you can use the blue one until she is finished. Then you can use the green crayon. Remember: Fiona is our guest."

Analyzing an Incident
This strategy involves a parent (or teacher) in guiding a child through an analysis of what went wrong after a child has lost his or her temper or handled a social situation poorly. It usually helps to allow the child to cool down first.

Example
Marc was watching a video in the family room with two boys from his class. His father was reading the paper in the next room. When Marc did not understand what was happening in the plot of the movie, he started asking the other boys why the robbers were returning the money. When they didn't explain, Marc asked again and again. The other two boys became annoyed and decided to go home. Marc ejected the video and threw it across the room. Marc was sent to his room to cool down. When he returned to the family room, his father asked him, "What did you do?" "What happened next?" "Was this a good outcome?" "What will you do next time?" Marc's suggestion was to ask the other boys if he could stop the video, ask them to explain what the robbers were doing and why, then turn the video on again as soon as he understood.

Coaching Emotional Responses
This strategy describes parents (or teachers) leading children through steps to become more emotionally aware. It involves listening and being aware of the emotion, naming the emotion, and planning what to do next time.

Example
Vema tells her mother how another girl embarrassed her at school. Her mother asks Vema to explain what the other girl did, and how Vema felt. The girl had said she did not want Vema on her softball team because Vema's leg brace made her run too slowly. Vema's mother helped Vema find words to express her feelings. She said, "Oh, Vema, I bet you were embarrassed in front of your friends. I know you don't like your brace to be the centre of attention. Why don't you tell me about it?" Vema described feeling hot and knowing her face was red, and wishing she could fall into the ground. Her mother related a time when she felt like that and explained that this is called embarrassment. She told Vema what she had done in her embarrassing situation and reminded Vema that all people feel embarrassment at times. Vema's mother talked about what was not acceptable—throwing the softball bat or the ball at the girl. Then she and Vema discussed acceptable solutions. Vema laughed: "I won't even embarrass her next time. I will try to remember to suggest what you said—that they have a designated runner for me. Because I can hit the ball. But she's right: I am a slow runner."

Resources:
L.K. Elksnin & N. Elksnin (2000). Teaching parents to teach their children to be prosocial. *Intervention in School and Clinic, 36*(1), 27–35.

R.C. Richardson (1996). *Connecting with others: Lessons for teaching social and emotional competence, grades 3–5*. Champaign, IL: Research Press.

A. Vernon (1989). *Thinking, feeling, behaving: An emotional education curriculum for adolescents, grades 7–12*. Champaign, IL: Research Press.

The Role of Friendship in the Development of Exceptional Individuals

Both social development and social acceptance are important for all children and adolescents, in the classroom and beyond. "Affection, intimacy, and a sense of reliable alliance are primarily obtained in close friendships, particularly preadolescent and adolescent ones, whereas feelings of inclusion are likely to result from peer group relations" (Furman & Robbins, 1985, p. 45). Social skills and competencies are acquired in both close friendships and general peer group relationships. Intimacy skills are more likely to develop in friendships and skills like leadership are more likely to develop in peer relations.

Research suggests that children and adolescents with poor peer adjustment are at greater risk for criminality and dropping out of school (e.g., Parker & Asher, 1987). Social skills are also increasingly important to successful participation in the workplace (McLaughlin, 1992; Tennant, Hutchinson, & Freeman, 1992). Researchers have argued recently that social participation, especially cooperation among children and adolescents, also contributes to their cognitive development. Vygotsky (1978, p. 163) wrote that "social relations or relations among people...underlie all higher functions and their relationships." He argued that all learning is first carried out between the individual and others in the environment and then that the individual gradually internalizes what they have been doing, saying, and thinking in cooperation during these social interactions. Speech and dialogue are thought to be the most important mediators of internalization (Trent, Artiles, & Englert, 1998). Dialogues that lead to developmental change involve finely tuned coordinations between the child and another person, and occur within the "zone of proximal development" between the child's independent problem solving and what the child can do when problem solving with adult guidance or in collaboration with more capable peers. The most effective partners in these dialogues are thought to be two individuals who differ from one another in expertise, although two novices can contribute to each other's learning of problem solving (Azmitia, 1988). Conversation or modelling is necessary for internalization to occur (Hartup, 1996). Especially effective dialogues focus on strategies and on children or adolescents discussing one another's strategies and reasoning (Hutchinson, 1997; Kruger, 1992).

Do children cooperate better with friends than with non-friends? There is evidence that cooperation and friendship are linked in the thinking and behaviour of children and adolescents. For example, children cooperate to become and remain friends (Furman & Bierman, 1984). Children want to have their friends as cooperative partners at school, and cooperation increases children's liking for one another (Hartup, 1996; Johnson & Johnson, 1985). When children do school tasks with friends, they interact more, pay more attention to equity rules, and discuss mutually beneficial outcomes more—they cooperate and collaborate more (e.g., Hartup et al., 1993; Zajac & Hartup, 1997). There is also some evidence that they learn more, especially when they give differing points of view and discuss these differences cooperatively, trying to find the best solution or to combine elements of more than one perspective while staying task-focused (e.g., Azmitia & Montgomery, 1993). In some of our studies of adolescents working cooperatively, we have found that they say, "Two heads are better than one," and "Once you've worked in a group, you would never want to just learn alone" (Hutchinson, Freeman, & Quick, 1996). Researchers have shown that children's collaboratively written stories are more advanced than individually written stories. Furthermore the benefits of collaborative writing carry over into individual stories (Daiute & Dalton, 1991). When friends collaborated (compared to acquaintances) on writing stories, the dialogue was richer, more detailed, more task-oriented, and considered more possibilities for content and vocabulary. However, the immediately resulting stories were not of higher quality (Hartup, Daiute, Zajac, & Sholl, 1995). These findings suggest that children benefit from learning cooperatively and that they may benefit even more from learning cooperatively with friends.

Exceptional children who have not learned to socialize, who are not socially accepted in the classroom, or who do not have friends may be disadvantaged cognitively. Why might cooperation between friends be especially well suited to cognitive development? Think of exceptional students like Matt, who described himself as friendless, or Val, who did not have anyone to play with at recess. We are looking at individuals who have few opportunities to improve their interaction skills and thus to become better at learning with their peers.

Remember Kelly, whose questions to peers were answered with individual words or nods. These kinds of exchanges are not representative of the rich dialogue that contributes to cognitive development and learning, in which children give explanations, consider each other's solutions, and arrive at better outcomes than either could achieve alone. Friends usually show mutual understanding of one another's needs and capacities, and this probably helps them provide responses that are within each other's zone of proximal development, even if each is different in level of development (Berscheid, 1985). The reciprocity or "give and take" that characterizes friendships usually involves sharing and self-disclosure. This may foster open dialogue, willingness to exchange ideas, and constructive feedback. Companions who trust one another are freer to disagree, more readily believe the information they receive, and are more effective at communicating with one another (Collins & Repinski, 1994). These characteristics have been observed in friendships of both adolescents and children. All these characteristics are likely to contribute to the social interaction required for cognitive development. Thus friendships appear to contribute to the social and cognitive development of students.

Elementary and Secondary Schools as Social Environments

Schools are highly social environments in which students spend the day working and playing with their classmates. Research conducted by Tanis Bryan (1991) and Sharon Vaughn (1991) suggests that it is important to enhance both social development of youth with exceptionalities and social acceptance by peers, because neither alone is sufficient.

Social development and social acceptance require a context where cooperation, community, and peer support are a part of everything that happens. This means that teachers must engage in informal teaching of social development and acceptance of diversity with the entire class. Such informal teaching takes place in the way you conduct your classroom, express your expectations, and model social acceptance.

Informal Teaching: Climate and Role Models

Teachers create positive and inclusive climates in their classrooms by showing respect for all members of the class, and making all students feel that their presence counts. They interact with all students in ways that communicate caring and acceptance. McIntosh and Vaughn (1993) suggest, specifically, avoiding teasing and sarcasm. Teachers communicate high expectations—that they expect all students to be successful—and provide a high degree of adaptations and support to enable students to reach those high expectations. Students learn their manner of referring to and treating their fellow students from you, the teacher. This means that you must provide good models, and demand that students behave similarly. When there are difficulties, you can respond by "seizing the moment" and negotiating with the group. When you make your thinking apparent to students, you provide a model of deciding, acting, and explaining that promotes both social development and social acceptance, without patronizing (McIntosh & Vaughn, 1993). Chapter 6 provides many strategies for creating a community and inclusive classroom.

Cross-Reference
Chapter 6 contains considerable information on informal teaching of social expectations and social acceptance.

Facilitating Friendships

You may feel that it is beyond your responsibilities as a teacher to facilitate friendships among your students. However, social development and social acceptance contribute to learning by students and to positive classroom climate. This means that facilitating friendships may make the classroom a better place for everyone, including you.

During the early years at school, some children may lack the social skills expected by their classmates. Children who are aggressive or awkward may be ignored by others. A structured and supervised social program can help children practise relationships. In middle childhood, children choose friends on the basis of personality and interests and friendships become increasingly stable. Boys may form gangs, while girls tend to form small intimate groups. Some children can be excluded during the unstructured times of the day and it helps to provide activities for these students so they can do things with one another. During preadolescence, helping and confiding replace playing and many students need assistance with conversational skills. Using cooperative and collaborative activities throughout these elementary school years gives you an opportunity to teach social skills as part of curriculum activities (Roffey, Majors, & Tarrant, 1997). For adolescents, friendships are about trust, intimacy, and often the sharing of deeply personal thoughts. These close friendships are complemented by membership in larger groups identified by music, clothes, and slang expressions.

Research has been conducted and programs have been developed specific to enhancing the friendship and conversational skills of students with many of the exceptionalities described in Chapters 3 and 4:

- adolescents with behavioural exceptionalities or emotional disorders (Hartas & Patrikakou, 1997)
- young children with developmental disabilities (Rosenthal-Malek, 1997)
- children and adolescents with autism (Lord, 1995)
- adolescents with severe disabilities (including autism, developmental disabilities, physical disabilities, and communication disorders) (Hughes et al., 1999)
- children with AD/HD (Mervis, 1998)
- children with multiple disabilities (Hunt et al., 1996)

While intensive programs such as those listed above may require the participation of a resource teacher, occupational therapist, or social worker, there are also many teaching strategies that serve as friendship interventions. For example, provide activities, especially early in the year, to ensure that all students know each other's names. These can involve games, memory challenges, name tags, and name signs on desks. Use literature with friendship themes and integrate friendship into the curriculum whenever possible. This can range from discussions of alliances in history to discussing ways to express emotions. Use modelling, guided practice, and independent practice to teach the social skills needed for students to conduct themselves appropriately in your classroom, in assembly, or in an upcoming field trip. Take advantage of these occasions to promote pairs of students learning together who might form friendships. Be vigilant and when you see friendships developing and appropriate social behaviour occurring, provide acknowledgement and support. Give gentle praise and approval.

For students who have behaviour problems or who are lonely, set friendship goals. With young children, meet individually and ask who the student would like to get to know. Goals might include learning the other child's name, sharing a toy or game, or working together at an activity centre. With older students, you may be able to set goals for participation in an extra-curricular activity or group. Teach these students to handle rejection by considering what they should say if the peer they approach rejects them. Structure social times like recess and lunch periods by forming groups that include isolated students, creating peer buddy programs, or asking socially able students to include a shy child in their conversation. Provide assignments that require pairs of students to visit the community library or another location together as well as work together in class. Use activities with a friend as a reinforcer. Ensure that adult presence does not interfere in fledgling conversations or friendships. Help parents be aware of opportunities for their child to interact with children outside of school. For many more ideas for friendship interventions, read Searcy (1996) and Turnbull, Pereira, and Blue-Banning (2000).

Schoolwide Approaches and Teachers' Roles

The social climate of the school contributes a great deal to the social climate of your classroom. Important aspects of the social environment in a school can be influenced by **schoolwide approaches**. For example, your school may have adopted a code of conduct that is to be applied in every part of the school, including your classroom. The most effective violence-reduction programs involve students in many ways. Some schools adopt schoolwide anti-bullying programs that guide teachers, foster consistency, and ensure a high rate of teacher and peer response to bullying incidents. Research suggests this is necessary to make a school safe for all, including the most vulnerable students.

CODE OF CONDUCT

A **discipline code** or **code of conduct** clearly identifies school rules and acceptable student behaviours. The best ones are short and easy to understand, with clearly stated consequences for actions. Many schools involve students and the community in designing and committing to the code (Hendrickson et al., 1995). The code should include only rules that will be enforced. Research on school violence emphasizes the need for enforcing the code consistently (Bullock & Gable, 1995). It is not only a set of rules for students to follow; it also informs teachers, parents, and others what kind of behaviour is expected of students at a particular school. A copy should be sent to parents at the start of every school year and distributed to students and staff. Figure 9.3 describes the characteristics of an effective code of conduct.

To make the code of conduct meaningful, you should discuss it with your students, make sure everyone understands its purpose and expectations, and seek agreement from students to follow it. Conduct discussion at a level that your students can understand and provide examples to help them see that this applies to them. You may appreciate the presence of the principal or vice-principal in your classroom for at least part of this discussion. In order for teachers to follow through consistently, there will have to be a shared understanding. This requires discussion by the staff, agreement on what actions will be taken following common incidents, and agreement on emergency responses to violence and aggression (Watson, Poda,

Weblinks

Many schools have Web sites. Visit the Web sites of five schools, searching for their codes of conduct. Are they available? If not, contact the schools to ask how you can obtain copies.

Figure 9.3

CHARACTERISTICS OF AN EFFECTIVE CODE OF CONDUCT

A code of conduct should:

1. Explain rules of student behaviour.
2. Clearly define roles, rights, and responsibilities of persons involved in the school setting, including teachers, administrators, support staff, as well as parents and police.
3. Describe consequences for misbehaviour.
4. Say that striking another person may be considered a criminal act and dealt with as such (especially in secondary school).
5. Say that every student has a right to be safe and secure from threats and harassment.
6. Include a policy against crimes of property, racism, sexual harassment, and sexual assault.

Miller, Rice, & West, 1993). While a code of conduct should involve the entire school community, it is only one strategy to improve the social environment of a school.

STRATEGIES TO INCREASE STUDENT PARTICIPATION IN VIOLENCE REDUCTION

Many schools take actions to involve students directly in setting a positive social tone for the school. This usually means creating a group of school leaders to promote **student responsibility** for a safe school environment. Choosing students who are looked up to and have peer influence is important. Students are more likely to participate in such initiatives if they have been involved in decision making about school rules, development of curriculum highlights, mentoring and tutoring programs, etc. (Gottfredson, Gottfredson, & Hybl, 1993).

You and your colleagues can contribute to student leadership by involving students in decision making at the classroom level. Teach students to take responsibility for their own safety and report suspicious activities or people around the school. Teach students to use conflict-resolution techniques and to act as student mediators for conflicts among their peers. Prepare students to teach peers about violence prevention; many programs involve teachers co-teaching with students. You can involve your students (from kindergarten to grade 12) in community service projects to improve the school and community environment. Primary students can visit seniors in community homes and plant gardens, while junior students can develop peer support programs and Web sites that reach out to others (e.g., http://www.bullying.com). Secondary students can coach teams, volunteer in hospitals, and tutor. These kinds of community involvement help students learn personal responsibility (Kelchner, 1995).

PREVENTING BULLYING

Many schoolwide programs are designed to reduce the incidence of destructive behaviours such as bullying. Schoolwide programs are the most effective response to bullying because it is a problem that occurs in the school's social environment as a whole (Banks, 1997). **Bullying** can take many forms: physical, emotional, and verbal or a combination of these. It involves an imbalance of power, a victim who is upset and a bully who is calm and in control, and a lack of compassion on the part of the bully. Children who lack social skills and do not pick up on social cues are among those likely to be victims. As you know, many exceptional students both lack social skills and miss social cues. They are one of the vulnerable groups who may be bullied. Your efforts to prevent students in your class from bullying or being bullied will be much more effective if your school has a schoolwide anti-bullying program.

All students need to understand that bullying is unacceptable. This means that every class in the school takes part in a consistent program that emphasizes that bullying behaviour and students who bully will be dealt with. All teachers and students need to be alert to recognize bullying. The characteristics of verbal, emotional, and physical bullying should be portrayed around the school, in assemblies, and in classrooms in language that all students can understand. Everyone, adults

Put Into Practice

Develop a code of conduct for your classroom. Make three lesson plans for introducing and two for reviewing the code of conduct with your class.

Further Reading

A.P. Daunic et al. (2000). School-wide conflict resolution and peer mediation programs. *Intervention in School and Clinic, 36*(2), 94–100.

What do you think?

Why do you think involving students in conflict resolution and community service helps reduce violence in schools? Try to observe such a program in operation to answer some of your questions.

Cross-Reference
Chapter 5 includes a framework for analyzing equity incidents in the classroom that could be used to decide how to intervene to prevent future incidents of bullying.

There are many Web sites available to help you and your school tackle bullying on a schoolwide basis. Most of these Canadian sites will also provide links to other international sites.

London (Ontario) Family Court Clinic, http://www.lfcc.on.ca/bully.htm

This site contains extensive information about bullying for parents and teachers. The highly readable information is an excerpt from the second edition of A.S.A.P.: A School-based Anti-Violence Program that is available from the London Family Court Clinic. It consists of a video and 65 lessons.

Bully B'ware Programs (British Columbia), http://www.bullybeware.com

This site contains information about a video (*Bully Beware*), books (*Take Action Against Bullying* and *How Parents Can Take Action Against Bullying*), and posters that can be used around the school to support the anti-bullying program. There are also tips and news articles from Canadian newspapers and magazines about bullying incidents in our schools and communities.

Bullying.org (children at Banded Peak School in Bragg Creek, Alberta, and their teacher, William Belsey), http://www.bullying.org

This very interesting site is part of Canada's SchoolNet GrassRoots Program. It was started after the shooting at W.R. Myers High School in Taber, Alberta, when stories emerged that the accused had been bullied. A group of grades 1 to 8 students who met to provide peer support grew into www.bullying.org, which attempts to help young people help each other. There are contributions from youth and adults around the world who realize they are not alone in their experiences and feelings. The teacher, William Belsey, has won awards for this and other online projects. Not only can you and your students learn by visiting this site, but you might be inspired to commit to an online project that would ensure that your students internalized and lived the lessons you were learning together.

and children, must have strategies for responding. This means teaching all students, including those exceptional students who use alternate forms of communication, to report incidents that occur to them or others. Protecting children who report bullying will be necessary, and care must be taken to convince children and adolescents that there will be no retaliation for reporting. Consistency is necessary, which is why it is preferable for a school to adopt a program and use it widely, making adaptations so presentations and activities are appropriate for various age and ability levels.

A proactive program teaches children to talk about their feelings, rather than lash out at others. As soon as children actively or verbally exclude others, they need to hear, "You don't have to be friends with her/him today. But it is *not* all right to be cruel and exclude her/him." You can teach children to consider how others feel and to speak up on behalf of those who are bullied. Show children how everyone can work together to create a school climate in which bullying is not tolerated (Sjostrom & Stein, 1996). Children must be confident that they have the backing of adults. Canadian research by Debra Peplar of York University and Wendy Craig of Queen's University suggests that teachers respond only about 10 percent of the time (http://www.yorku.ca/lamarsh). In addition to consistent teacher response, children need to role-play and practise proactive and prosocial responses to bullying. Figure 9.4 provides students with strategies for reporting bullying. You can use resources like this one (Stones, 1993) to devise student activities for practice. You may also have to coach your students to include all classmates, especially in playground activities, and to support victims, report incidents, and take part in role-playing to practise leadership and citizenship (Olweus, 1993).

HELPING STUDENTS PRACTISE SELF-PROTECTION STRATEGIES: GOOD WAYS TO TELL TALES

- Remember that not telling helps the bullies go on bullying—and you are almost certainly not the only person who is or will be bullied by them. By telling you will be helping to create an atmosphere where people can feel safe and confident that they will be well treated instead of feeling frightened and insecure because they might be bullied.

- Tell with someone if you can—take a friend or a witness or your mum or dad with you. It's good to have someone there for you.

- Don't suffer bullying for a long time. Perhaps you want to try and stop it on your own—fine. But if you don't manage, don't let it drag on. Get help. The longer bullying goes on, the harder it will be to put an end to it.

- As a last resort and if your school really won't help bullying to stop, it may be possible for you to change schools. Discuss this with your parents.

When there are bullies around, it is sensible to:

1. Stick with your friends whenever you can. Be part of a group.

2. In the playground, keep within sight of a teacher or supervisor.

3. Try not to react to teasing or bullying by showing that you are upset or angry. Try to keep and look calm. Bullies lose interest in bullying people who don't react.

4. Don't show off by wearing expensive jewellery or taking other expensive items into school with you.

5. If bullies take your money or steal something of yours, try not to get into a fight. Tell a trusted adult what happened and who was responsible as soon as you can. Talk through how you're going to ensure that it doesn't happen again.

6. Practice your replies to things that you may be teased or bullied about (embarrassing initials, unusual name, glasses, hearing aid, red hair, black skin, freckles, tall, short, plump, etc., etc.) so that you can give the impression it doesn't bother you.

Source: R. Stones (1993). *Don't Pick on Me: How to Handle Bullying*. Markham, ON: Pembroke Publishers. Used by permission.

Strong programs to improve the school environment also involve individualized interventions with violent, bullying, and at-risk students (Olweus, 1993). You may find that if children in your class are identified as bullies, you will be asked to take part in interventions with a counsellor or resource teacher. This will help you to be consistent with these specialists in your preventive and responsive dealings with such students. Strong intervention programs also involve teachers in ongoing cooperative learning activities that reduce social isolation. They have increased adult supervision at key times such as recess and lunch. Most bullying incidents occur out of the sight of teachers and adult volunteers. Increasing supervision, along with other schoolwide components, contributes to reducing bullying. There are many resources for tackling this important issue in Canadian schools. Reducing bullying through schoolwide efforts is one aspect of creating a school in which social relations can grow between exceptional students and their classmates. Other approaches include peer tutoring and cooperative and collaborative teaching in the classroom.

Using the ADAPT Strategy to Analyze Social Demands in the Classroom: Peer Tutoring and Collaborative Learning

Put Into Practice

Review the ADAPT strategy in Chapter 1. Use it to devise a peer tutoring approach to promote social development, social acceptance, and academic learning of an exceptional student.

You can use the ADAPT strategy to analyze the social demands of classroom organization and tasks and compare them to student strengths and needs. There may be opportunities for students to learn from one another through peer tutoring, as well as through collaborative and cooperative learning.

Peer Tutoring

Peer tutoring can take many forms. Essentially it involves peers as teaching partners. Peers learning together can be especially effective when second-language students translate for one another. In Chapter 5, we read about classwide peer tutoring. Reviews of large numbers of studies show that both tutors and tutees benefit in many different arrangements of peer tutoring (Jenkins & Jenkins, 1982; Osguthorpe & Scruggs, 1986). Fulton and her colleagues (1994) describe a program in which typical grades 4 to 6 students share activities with students with severe disabilities. The tutors received a four-week training program and then tutored an exceptional student for 30-minute sessions, 3 to 5 days per week for a period of 6 weeks. They found that both the typical students and exceptional students rated the experience highly and reported that they learned. Tutors expressed increasingly positive attitudes toward exceptional students with comments like, "If you believe in someone they believe in themselves" (p. 8) and "They can learn anything if they just try hard" (p. 9).

In a program designed to enable students with disabilities to take the role of tutor, Blackbourn and Blackbourn (1993) described how an adolescent with moderate developmental disabilities tutored a grade 1 non-disabled child. The grade 1 boy needed individual teaching and practice adding and subtracting numbers up to nine with manipulatives. The tutor was skilled in addition and subtraction of up to three-digit numbers and demonstrated a desire to help others. A teacher

Learning in pairs is good preparation for cooperative and collaborative learning in groups.

modelled for the tutor how he was to praise the tutee, provided task sheets for the two of them to work on, and demonstrated for the tutor how to use manipulatives to show the young student how to do the tasks. The teacher monitored their progress and provided feedback to the tutor. The grade 1 student improved in mathematics and the tutor became more responsive to learning new and challenging mathematics at his level. Both increased in self-confidence. The additional benefit was that the grade 1 teacher began to view older students with disabilities more positively. "She requested more older students with disabilities as tutors and implemented an expanded peer tutoring program in her classroom" (p. 57). Tutoring programs can take many forms, and they not only teach academic skills but also enhance social interaction, especially between exceptional students and their schoolmates without disabilitites.

Using Cooperative and Collaborative Learning to Meet Academic and Social Goals

Researchers have argued that enhancing social development and acceptance requires sufficient opportunities to practise these skills in a reinforcing environment (Vaughn, 1991). Students prefer to focus on learning and refining social skills within the context of learning "relevant and practical information" (Hutchinson, Freeman, & Quick, 1996). All of these perspectives point to integrating social skills enhancement into ongoing curriculum within the classroom. **Collaborative learning** methods include cooperative learning and problem solving in pairs and groups. These grouping methods usually involve students of varying abilities and skills, that is, heterogeneous groupings rather than homogeneous groupings. Collaborative learning methods have been successful in improving academic performance of students of varying ages, grades, subjects, and abilities (see Scheid, 1993). Research has demonstrated a couple key characteristics of collaborative learning that make it highly effective. Students are more likely to be successful when:

1. They are instructed in well-structured, cognitively oriented programs (Cohen, Kulik, & Kulik, 1982).

2. They are required as part of their group work to give and receive explanations for answers and ideas suggested in discussion (Webb, 1985).

There are a number of simple techniques you can use, starting on the first day of class, to facilitate collaborative learning and more interactive classrooms.

Planning for Formal Teaching of Collaboration

While you won't use collaborative groups exclusively, you will probably want to look for opportunities where they suit the learning goals. Choose a collaborative strategy when you intend to promote positive peer support, social acceptance, and social competence, and especially when the knowledge can be best learned through the contributions of many learners. There are three types of groups. **Base groups** or **home groups** serve as small, long-term, support groups. They may be the groups of peers who sit together at the beginning of each class. You put **infor-**

Further Reading

V.A. Blackbourn & J.M. Blackbourn (1993). An adolescent with moderate mental disabilities tutors a 1st grade, nondisabled child. *Teaching Exceptional Children, 25*(4), 56–57.

L. Fulton et al. (1994). Peer education partners. *Teaching Exceptional Children, 26*(4), 6–11.

mal groups together for a short period of time to complete a particular activity. You assemble **formal groups** with attention to group composition to work together usually throughout a unit (Johnson & Johnson, 1989). Figure 9.5 shows the planning decisions that go into designing collaborative learning.

There are many examples of lesson plans for collaborative learning at the elementary and secondary levels (e.g., Clarke, Wideman, & Eadie, 1990; Johnson, Johnson, & Holubec, 1987; Lincoln County Board of Education, 1993; Villa & Thousand, 1994). These sources contain forms that teachers can use for all aspects of the planning and execution of collaborative teaching. There are also excellent models of planning collaborative teaching for classes that include students with special needs (Nevin, Thousand, & Villa, 1994), for techniques ranging from simple to complex.

TTYPA

A simple method to use during a lecture, film, or reading is called **TTYPA**, or "turn to your partner and…." The teacher stops and tells the students to "Turn to your partner and…introduce yourself…or describe a time when you…Then switch roles" (Fogarty, 1990). It is useful for making connections between prior learning and a new topic. To ensure that all students understand what to do next, you can use

---

Figure 9.5

PLANNING DECISIONS IN DESIGNING COLLABORATIVE LEARNING

1. Academic goals for the group as a whole and adaptations or modifications of goals for exceptional students.
2. Social goals for the group and for exceptional students.
3. Comunicating both sets of goals and teaching rather than assuming social skills.
4. The type of interaction between students to meet these goals.
5. The collaborative learning technique to promote such interaction.
6. Membership of student groups.
7. Room arrangement.
8. Structure of positive interdependence so students get the following messages: We sink or swim together. Do your work; we are counting on you. How can we help each other to do better?
9. Student roles to use.
10. Monitoring student performance.
11. Guidelines for intervening in poorly functioning groups (as little as possible; with questions rather than answers).
12. Individual accountability (during monitoring or in the products).
13. Introducing the lesson, fostering collaboration.
14. How students obtain closure on the content and feedback, and reflect on the social skills.
15. Evaluating the learning and reflecting on the process.

TTYPA for the first partner to describe the instructions and the second partner to describe the first two steps. Such interdependence is easy to achieve and is good preparation for more complex collaborative activities.

PAIRED PARTNERS: THINK ALOUD

In **Partners Thinking Aloud**, you model thinking aloud and ensure that the students understand what is expected of them (Whimbey & Whimbey, 1975). One student is the problem solver and the other the monitor. The problem solver thinks aloud throughout the task, and the monitor cues the "self-talk" of the solver by asking questions, such as: "What is your goal?" "Does this makes sense?" "Why?" Then they switch roles. Hutchinson (1989) demonstrated the effectiveness of this technique for teaching math problem solving to grade 8 students from an inner-city school, in mixed-ability pairs. The students and their teacher successfully adapted the approach to use in their science classes, as well.

COOPERATIVE LEARNING

Cooperative learning has been used extensively to promote interdependence in classrooms of typical and exceptional students (Johnson & Johnson, 1989). Students work together to accomplish shared goals. They are assigned to small groups and instructed to ensure that all members of the group learn the assignment. Students discuss material, help one another understand it, and encourage one another to work hard. You should check individual accountability and learning frequently. You can use this approach for a brief discussion to kick off an activity or in an entire curriculum unit. Johnson and Johnson believe the following five elements are necessary: student interdependence, working face to face, tasks that require everyone's efforts for group success, students knowing how to collaborate, and feedback on social processes in the groups.

You can accept one product from the whole group and give group members a grade based on this product. You can assign roles to ensure that everyone participates (for example, the checker ensures that each member understands, the encourager urges members to speak up, the recorder writes down the ideas of the group, the reporter reports to the rest of the class, etc.). Johnson and Johnson (1985) wrote that the processes that promote higher achievement and liking among students include high-quality reasoning strategies, constructive management of conflict over ideas, and feelings of psychological support and acceptance.

The jigsaw strategy is described in Figure 5.4. It is a structured cooperative learning approach.

Teaching Students to Collaborate

How can students learn to cooperate? You can use ADAPT and observation to decide the behaviours and social skills that students need most. For the most important social skills (such as giving everyone a chance to talk, listening actively, and providing explanations), students need practice. They will probably require effective role models (you can model or use a paired teaching strategy), and you will need to help them persist in the face of deterrents. In her book *Designing*

Weblinks

THE COOPERATIVE LEARNING NETWORK, SHERIDAN COLLEGE
http://www.sheridanc.on.ca/coop_learn/cooplrn.htm

USING COOPERATIVE LEARNING TO TEACH MATH TO STUDENTS WITH LD
http://www.ldonline.org/ld_indepth/math_skills/coopmath.html

CENTRE FOR THE STUDY OF CLASS-ROOM PROCESSES, CONCORDIA UNIVERSITY
http://www.artsci-ccwin.concordia.ca/education/cscp/Try.htm

Further Reading

P.J. Vermette (1998). *Making cooperative learning work: Student teams in K-12 classrooms.* Upper Saddle River, NJ: Merrill.

E. Coelho, L. Winer, & J. Inn-Bell Olsen (1989). *All sides of the issue: Activities for cooperative jigsaw groups.* Englewood Cliffs, NJ: Alemany Press.

J. Clarke, R. Wideman, & S. Eadie (1990). *Together we learn: Cooperative small group learning.* Scarborough, ON: Prentice-Hall Canada.

Put Into Practice

Read the following article and develop an intervention using direct instruction to improve the social skills of an exceptional student: L.K. Elksnin & N. Elksnin (1998). Teaching social skills to students with learning and behaviour problems. *Intervention in School and Clinic, 33*(3), 131–40.

Groupwork: Strategies for the Heterogeneous Classroom, Elizabeth Cohen (1986) provides several examples of activities and games to help students acquire group work skills.

Begin with simple, short activities that provide frequent occasions for participation. Try participation in pairs through TTYPA, Think-Pair-Share (shown in Figure 5.4), and Think Aloud pairs, and progress to short cooperative learning activities such as 10 minutes of group work on a 5-minute mystery. You will learn to form groups and intervene effectively by practising with simple, short collaborative activities. You may find that some of your students need direct instruction in social skills. There are a number of programs available; some of these are described in Figure 9.6. Remember to enlist the help of parents. Children can also learn social skills by taking part in activities with their parents and siblings.

Figure 9.6

USING DIRECT INSTRUCTION TO TEACH SOCIAL SKILLS AND SOCIAL ACCEPTANCE: INSTRUCTIONAL PROGRAMS

The ACCESS Program: Adolescent Curriculum for Communication and Effective Social Skills by Hill M. Walker, Bonnie Todis, Deborah Holmes, and Gary Horton (1988). Pro-Ed, 8700 Shoal Creek Blvd., Austin, TX 78758, 512-451-3246

ACCESS is designed to teach peer-to-peer skills, skills for relating to adults, and self-management skills to students at middle-school and high-school levels. It is designed for use by both regular and special educators and may be taught in small-group or large-group formats. It contains teaching scripts, instructional procedures, and a student study guide.

ASSET: A Social Skills Program for Adolescents by J.S. Hazel, J.B. Schumaker, J.A. Sherman, and J. Sheldon-Wildgen (1981). Research Press, Champaign, IL.

The ASSET program teaches eight social skills, including giving and receiving feedback, negotiation, and conversation. The lessons include teacher explanations, opportunities for student practice of the skills, and homework assignments for students to obtain practice outside school. This program has less emphasis on authentic tasks than programs developed more recently. It is better suited to use with groups of students with learning disabilities rather than inclusive classrooms.

Pathways by Nancy L. Hutchinson and John Freeman (1994). Nelson Canada, 1120 Birchmount Road, Scarborough, ON M1K 5G4 1-800-268-2222.

This highly interactive Canadian program uses collaborative learning methods particularly well suited to mixed-ability groups and inclusive and destreamed classrooms. It consists of an overview booklet and five modules that can be used singly or in combination for a unit or a course of study. It contains teacher scripts; includes modelling, thinking aloud, and group and pair work; and involves students in solving authentic social problems.

Challenges to Collaborative Learning

There are a number of challenges to collaborative learning. Cooperative activities in which all students in a group receive the same grade can result in unfair evaluation outcomes if some students have failed to contribute, or if some knew all the content before the unit began. Occasionally a student may become dependent on the more able members of a cooperative group. Exceptional students and gifted students in inclusive classrooms are more likely to experience these drawbacks than are their peers. You may have to provide alternate evaluation criteria for some students. It may be necessary to modify or adapt the goals and curriculum for some students with special needs.

To meet these challenges, monitor group interaction. Focus on the needs of exceptional students when creating groups. Gifted students can benefit from being placed in a collaborative group with gifted peers, where they can challenge one another (Winebrenner, 1992), especially when they are able pursue tasks at an advanced level. In areas where they are far ahead of the rest of the class, they may be too impatient to be supportive and good models for the lowest achievers. Use heterogeneous groups as much as possible, but consider the best group composition for meeting the academic and social goals of each lesson.

Children with autism can learn to skate, for social participation as well as exercise.

Secondary teachers often feel pressure to "cover the curriculum" (Hutchinson, Freeman, & Quick, 1996). Many teachers find that the gains in motivation, reasoning, and self-directedness more than compensate for the time required to teach students to work collaboratively (e.g., Bellanca & Fogarty, 1991). In upper years, students may be competing for entry to post-secondary education and scholarships. For a variety of reasons, secondary teachers find it challenging to adopt collaborative learning. Some adolescents show a low tolerance for diversity (Rice, 1987) and view conformity as an important requirement for popularity (Sebald, 1981). Collaborative groups can focus the frustration of group members on students who contribute less than their share when the collaborations are unsuccessful (Scheid, 1993). Cohen, Lotan, and Catanzarite (1990) suggest that groups can be dominated by high-status members and may not pay attention to the contributions of low-status members. Cohen et al. (1990) make a number of recommendations for minimizing the impact of status problems:

1. Teach students to listen, take turns, and assume various roles. At this stage, emphasize process as much as content, gradually shifting the emphasis to content.

2. Use stimulating materials and activities that are not entirely dependent on reading. These may include diagrams, videotapes, audiotapes, case studies, and authentic documents that enable students to understand and participate.

> **Cross-Reference**
> Chapter 7 describes adapting teaching to meet adapted and modified goals of exceptional students, and Chapter 8 focuses on adapting assessment.

Children and adolescents with physical disabilities learn to sail.

3. Build on student experience, beyond that typically used in the classroom, with authentic tasks. Bestow status on students who do not often shine in standard academic tasks. For example, students who have had part-time jobs may excel at negotiating resolutions in conflicts. Look for ways to use student expertise in a range of domains.

4. Collaborate with colleagues, seek professional development, and keep an account of your experiences to share with colleagues (Gaskins & Elliot, 1991).

Although there are considerable challenges, there are also benefits in social development and social acceptance when you use collaborative teaching approaches in the classroom. In addition, look to the community for additional opportunities to enhance social relations of exceptional students.

The Community and Social Relations

Increasingly, the community has a role to play in the development of social relationships for exceptional learners. The community newspaper and the newsletters of local associations and organizations may provide you with authentic learning opportunities that are ideal for enhancing social relations. The local swimming pool or bowling alley may provide an inexpensive venue for children or adolescents to learn together. If it is not feasible for the whole class to take part, look for ways to use paraprofessionals and volunteers to accompany approximately three pairs of students (perhaps students who work together in peer tutoring). There are many summer (and some winter) recreation programs, such as learn-to-sail programs, learn-to-swim programs, computer camps, and skating at the community rink, that include spaces for exceptional youth. Watch for opportunities that you and your students can access and opportunities to recommend to families.

You can include a few exceptional students in each monthly trip to the symphony or the local theatre company. Develop activities to be done at the museum in your community (Tam, Nassivera, Rousseau, & Vreeland, 2000). These community integration activities provide you and your students with goals to work toward, special events to share, and evidence of the progress you are making toward inclusion in the community.

Summary

Social development and social acceptance are critical to inclusion because they refer to an exceptional student's ability to take part in the social and academic life of the classroom and their acceptance by classmates. Both exceptional students and their peers without disabilities have expressed an array of views on inclusion and the social processes that accompany it. Friendship is probably much more important to learning than we have understood in the past, enabling students to gradually internalize the ideas they are challenged with by their peers. Both elementary and secondary schools are social environments and schoolwide approaches can ensure that they are inviting and safe for all students. You can analyze social demands and choose a wide range of collaborative and social approaches to learning as well as use the community to enhance social relations.■

Key Terms

social relationships (p. 260)

social development (p. 261)

social acceptance (p. 261)

friendships (p. 261)

interpersonal competence (p. 262)

peer perspectives (p. 263)

(dis)ability awareness program (p. 263)

sociometric rating (p. 263)

social status (p. 263)

schoolwide approaches (p. 271)

discipline code or code of conduct (p. 272)

student responsibility (p. 273)

bullying (p. 273)

peer tutoring (p. 276)

collaborative learning (p. 277)

base groups (p. 277)

home groups (p. 277)

informal groups (p. 278)

formal groups (p. 278)

TTYPA (p. 278)

Partners Thinking Aloud (p. 279)

cooperative learning (p. 279)

LEARNER OBJECTIVES

After you have read this chapter you will be able to:

1. Describe how you can teach strategies to help exceptional students in elementary and secondary schools to become more independent learners (student development).

2. Discuss what can be done to make transitions for exceptional learners as smooth as possible.

3. Describe strategies for enhancing interpersonal development and its contribution to independence.

4. Explain the contribution of career development (including career education and cooperative education) to the development of independence.

5. Discuss community participation and community support approaches to independent living.

Chapter 10

Enhancing Independent Learning and Independent Living

Fran was 16 when she rolled her car. After being in a coma for weeks, she awakened as a different person. The Fran she remembered being was an athlete, a dancer, and a student who could write an entire essay the night before it was due and who didn't know the meaning of can't. While her family, friends, and teachers have struggled to adjust to a Fran who tires easily, can't plan ahead enough to make a sandwich for lunch, and lashes out at those closest to her, Fran has not made the adjustment. Her homeroom teacher describes Fran as a young woman who doesn't know herself. The guidance counsellor who is working with Fran at school keeps reminding her that she won't be studying physical education at university like she had planned. Many adolescents need strategies to improve their self-knowledge and self-advocacy. These strategies are especially important for youth with exceptionalities, and absolutely essential to young people with traumatic brain injury.

Ray is in grade 4 and his next transition will come after grade 5, when he must move from his neighbourhood school, Avon Elementary, to a middle school across town. Ray hates change, unpredictability, and chaos. He has Asperger syndrome. His family started working with the kindergarten teacher about eight months before his transition from preschool to Avon Elementary. To get Ray ready for the move from Avon to Brown Middle School, his family and his teacher have made a plan to start a full year ahead. In September of grade 5, Ray will start going to Brown for an hour per week, then two hours, with a gradual increase. By the end of grade 5, Ray will know his homeroom teacher and resource teacher at Brown, the location of both their rooms, as well as how to eat in the cafeteria, how to borrow a book from the library, and how to use a combination lock. This kind of troubleshooting should help Ray to make the transition without the stress and overreaction that can cause him to fight or flee and hide. Ray's IEP for grade 5 focuses as much on preparing him for the transition as on academic learning. Everyone agrees that if the transition is smooth, Ray can begin learning as soon as he arrives at Brown. Without a smooth transition, his first year will probably be disastrous.

1. Why are transitions so critical to many exceptional students? What is common in the case studies of Ray and Fran?

2. What kinds of strategies can the teachers of Ray and Fran teach them so they can be as independent as possible in their upcoming learning?

3. Describe how schools have become much more focused on the needs of exceptional students for life in the community since the emphasis shifted to inclusion.

4. What strategies do Ray, Fran, and other exceptional students need in order to be aware of their own strengths and needs and to advocate for themselves?

5. How can teachers employ the resources of the community and of others around them to help meet the needs of exceptional students for independent learning strategies and independent living strategies?

Introduction

Cross-Reference
How does this chapter relate to the ADAPT strategy in Chapter 1?

Chapter 10 focuses on enhancing the independent learning and independent living of exceptional students. The two students described in these opening cases, who have traumatic brain injury and Asperger syndrome, respectively, are facing transitions and need strategies to help them function independently to meet the demands of school and life. This chapter prepares you for helping your students to be more independent in meeting both kinds of demands.

Throughout this book, you have read about young people with exceptionalities and their teachers and parents working together to maximize the young people's opportunities for social and academic participation and for playing a valued role in society. You have reflected on our country's high expectations for inclusion in school and in society. In the recent and ongoing educational reforms across the country (see Chapter 1 for a summary focused on exceptional learners), there has been a renewed emphasis on students' developing independence. One of the clearest indications of this emphasis is Ontario's document *Choices into Action* (Ontario Ministry of Education, 1999). The foci and components of these curricula are variously described as guidance, career education, career development, career and personal planning, cooperative education, workplace learning, work experience, and so on. Most of these programs that have been developed or are in development have goals that can be described as:

Cross-Reference
Chapter 4 contains characteristics and strategies specific to students with traumatic brain injury and students with Asperger syndrome.

- student development (personal development or personal independence)
- interpersonal development (social responsibility, citizenship, working cooperatively, or responsible interdependence)
- career development (responsible decision making, employability, successful transitions, independent planning)

All three kinds of development are seen as critical to independent learning and independent living, which are important issues for the education of exceptional learners. However, the career education and workplace learning (or cooperative education) curriculum documents from across Canada were reviewed recently by researchers at Queen's University. Their findings suggest that only the curriculum documents revised within the past few years contain direct references to the needs of exceptional learners (Hutchinson et al., 1998). This chapter enlarges on these three themes (student development, interpersonal development, and career development) for classroom teachers with exceptional learners in their classrooms. The emphasis is on two of these themes—student development of strategies for independent learning and career development for independent living—because Chapter 9 focuses on interpersonal development.

Student Development for Independent Learning

Many people think that development of independence, career development, and the accompanying themes of this chapter are primarily the concerns of secondary teachers. However, the recently revised provincial curricula emphasize the importance of teaching independence throughout the school years from K to 12. **Career** refers to one's progress through life and through the roles appropriate to various ages as well as to the process of making a living by means of a particular occupation (Super & Harris-Bowlsbey, 1979). Thus **career development** refers to students' growing understanding of all aspects of changing roles and responsibilities, including adult responsibilities, roles, and the nature and meaning of work. This understanding encompasses the incredible range of ways in which adults engage independently and interdependently in paid work, volunteer and unpaid work, and other adult roles such as leisure, child rearing, and citizenship. The first theme addressed is enhancing independent learning.

Strategies for Independent Learning

A large body of research in exceptional education focuses on teaching students what are known as learning strategies. The logic underlying this research is that many efficient learners (often students without exceptionalities) have been observed to develop efficient strategies to learn. They find ways to solve problems, comprehend what they read, write what is expected of them, and so on, even if teachers do not make these strategies explicit. These approaches—to understanding what is expected and finding shortcuts to meet expectations effectively—remain invisible in many classrooms. Researchers like Ann Brown, Ann Marie Palincsar, and Bernice Wong have spent much of their careers trying to make these learning strategies explicit and to find ways to teach them explicitly to exceptional students.

What are strategies? Bernice Wong (1996) of Simon Fraser University describes **learning strategies** as techniques or principles that enable a student to learn to solve problems, read, communicate, organize, and so on independently. Learning strategies emphasize the steps necessary to perform a strategy as well as when and why to perform that strategy and how to monitor its use. Often you can teach strategies to your entire class that may benefit many normally achieving students and, with additional opportunities to practise, exceptional students will be better able to participate in your class and in life. Sometimes exceptional students need learning strategies that their classmates have already acquired. This means that you may need to use approaches described in many chapters in this book—for example, teach a "needs group" at what I call "the round table," a place where students are invited to join the teacher for intense teaching. Or enlist the services of a co-teacher (a resource teacher or a paraprofessional) to do this teaching. Perhaps you can model the first session while this co-teacher observes and the co-teacher can conduct the remaining sessions. After years of using "the round table" approach, both as classroom teacher and as resource teacher, I can vouch for its effectiveness as long as your students always leave the round table feeling that they have had your full attention and have learned. Make it a learning privilege—not a punishment—that is used at various times for all students.

Teaching Strategies

Before you can teach learning strategies, you have to plan for this teaching. Six steps in this planning are:

Weblinks

Hint: If you cannot reach a Web site from the URL given, try entering the site name until the first / and after you reach the site, add the additional information one / at a time.

KEVIN'S LEARNING STRATEGIES LINKS AND RESOURCES, CAPE BRETON VICTORIA REGIONAL SCHOOL BOARD
http://www.cbv.ns.ca/sstudies

UNIVERSITY OF KANSAS LEARNING STRATEGIES CURRICULUM
http://www.ku-crl.org/htmlfiles/lscurriculum/ls.html

What do you think?

Learning strategies were originally designed to meet the needs of students with learning disabilities. In recent years they have been found effective for teaching students with many exceptionalities, and are often recommended for teaching entire classes. What is it about learning strategies that makes them effective for so many students?

1. Identify areas in which many students could be working more independently.

2. Specify outcomes you would like to see.

3. List the steps students should follow.

4. Limit the number of steps.

5. Put the strategy steps on cue cards for individual use (students can staple them into their notebooks).

6. Put a poster on the wall for those who need to keep referring to the steps.

For students to use learning strategies independently, they have to learn to do them accurately and fluently. Many studies have shown the steps that are effective in teaching strategies (e.g., Hutchinson, 1993; Schumaker, Deshler, & Denton, 1984; Wong, 1996). First, students must see the need for the strategy, so begin by assessing current strategy use and sharing your observations with the students. Also, consider the pre-skills students' need for what you are teaching. If many students lack the pre-skills, start by teaching these.

Because learning strategies can help students function independently, students may be motivated to work at them. However, you need to clarify expectations for the strategy, point out benefits, and convince students to "give it a try." You might plan four classes in which you will teach the strategy, and then in the fifth class begin a series of activities or a unit in which students will use the strategies. Put up a chart that shows this plan; then students can see that they have four classes in which to master the strategy. This can motivate them to learn as efficiently as they can. Approach it positively; don't threaten.

Model strategy use carefully. Exceptional students will probably use the strategy only as well as you do when you model it. Explain carefully, by thinking aloud, your thinking patterns, how you decide when to use the strategy, and how you do each step. For exceptional students, you are making the invisible (efficient learning strategies) visible to students who may never come up with these strategies on their own. It often helps to demonstrate what *not* to do, but be adamant that these are *not effective strategies*. Stop and discuss with the students why they are not feasible or effective. Then provide additional practice with the steps of the effective strategy.

Guided practice or scaffolded practice, in which students are prompted to do each step, enables exceptional students to learn the strategy. Use an overhead to demonstrate or prompt students and stop for a few seconds after each prompt, or have students work in pairs and remind each other of the steps. Throughout the previous nine chapters there have been many

Hobbies such as competing in plowing matches can turn into careers. Rebecca Woodman, at 15, competed in the 1998 International Plowing Match.

examples of guided practice or scaffolded practice. **Independent practice** is necessary for students to be able to use a strategy independently and fluently. If some students still require scaffolded practice after most have learned the strategy, arrange for them to continue to practise with you or someone else. For a student like Fran in the opening case studies, a paraprofessional could continue to prompt her for weeks or months. The other students would be working independently, with only a quick booster session at the beginning of each week. Give students specific **feedback** about what they are doing correctly and incorrectly, and gradually ask them to assess themselves for efficient strategy use. Self-monitoring is an important aspect of independent strategy use.

You may have to use the ADAPT strategy to adapt or modify the teaching and practice of learning strategies for some students. This could involve the use of Braille, an interpreter, individual explanations, comprehension checks, partnered practice dictation by the student instead of written expression, etc.

There are many effective learning strategies designed for elementary and secondary classrooms. In earlier chapters you have seen strategies for teaching mathematics, spelling, reading, and writing. Table 10.1 lists learning strategies and their locations throughout this book. Look back through the chapters of this book, focusing on the examples of learning strategies. Look for strategies that you can use to teach students to learn more independently in your classroom. Also note strategies that can serve as models for developing your own strategies that meet the circumstances most pressing in your classroom.

Cross-Reference
Look for learning strategies in other chapters that might help students become more independent learners. Start by examining the History Cognitive Credit Card (Chapter 3); a cognitive behaviour modification strategy (SNAP) (Chapter 6); and a strategy for solving algebra word problems (Chapter 7). What others can you find?

Put Into Practice

Choose an area in which exceptional students you have taught would benefit from a learning strategy. Devise a learning strategy and a plan for teaching it to the whole class and providing extra practice for the exceptional students.

Table 10.1

LEARNING STRATEGIES DESCRIBED THROUGHOUT THIS BOOK

Learning Strategy	Chapter
RAP (Read, Ask questions, Paraphrase)	Chapter 1, case of Ben
ADAPT strategy	Chapter 1, introduced; examples throughout
Plan, Write, and Revise Opinion Essays	Chapter 1, Focus on Technology
History Cognitive Credit Card	Chapter 3, Figure 3.2
Class-Wide Peer Tutoring (CWPT)	Chapter 5, Focus on Research
SNAP (See problem, Name plan, Act on plan, Pat on back)	Chapter 6, Figure 6.5
Scaffolded Reading Experience (SRE)	Chapter 7, Table 7.1
Story Planning	Chapter 7
Self-Questions for Representing Algebra Word Problems	Chapter 7
Self-Questions for Solving Algebra Word Problems	Chapter 7
Reciprocal Teaching	Chapter 7

Most universities and colleges across Canada have a student learning service or counselling service that provides learning strategies both on its Web site and in workshops on campus. Many of these learning strategies are practical for learners from about grade 5 and up. Figure 10.1 shows one of the learning strategies from the Web site of Queen's University (http://www.queensu.ca/stser/top_10.html).

Adapting to Change: Transitions and Student Development

While we most often think of **transition** as referring to the move from secondary school into post-secondary endeavours, there are also considerable challenges associated with the move from preschool to elementary school and from elementary or junior high into secondary school (Mallory, 1996).

Families can perceive a loss of support associated with the move from preschool into elementary school. In interviews with three Canadian families, Cheryl Schmid and Nancy Hutchinson (1994) found that all three families reported that this transition was not well coordinated and was jeopardized by poor communication. Two mothers reported on their inability to arrange meetings between the preschool resource teacher and other professionals such as the occupational therapist or speech therapist. Neither of these two mothers had the role she desired in this critical transition. The third mother was about to embark on this vital transition and "planned to compensate for the failure of professionals to consider her a partner in the transition process by continuing to advocate vigorously for Susan [her daughter]" (p. 9).

Weblinks

CANLEARN LISTING OF WEB SITES OF COLLEGES AND UNIVERSITIES
http://canlearn.ca/english/find/college&university/college.cfm

BRANDON UNIVERSITY STUDENT SERVICES (INCLUDING LEARNING SKILLS)
http://www.brandonu.ca/studentssvc/index.html

UNIVERSITY OF VICTORIA SKILLS PROGRAM
http://www.coun.uvic.ca/learn/index.html

UNIVERSITY OF TORONTO COUNSELLING AND LEARNING SKILLS SERVICE (CALSS)
http://www.library.utoronto.ca/calss/

Figure 10.1

TEN TIPS FOR IMPROVING TIME MANAGEMENT

1. Concentrate on one thing at a time.
2. Plan your day each morning or the night before and set priorities for yourself.
3. Keep paper or a calendar with you to jot down the things you have to do or notes to yourself.
4. Try to avoid wasting time—all time can be useful.
5. Try rewarding yourself when you get things done as you had planned, especially the important ones.
6. Be sure and set deadlines for yourself whenever possible.
7. Stop regretting failures and start learning from your mistakes.
8. Remind yourself, "There is always enough time for the important things." If it is important, you should be able to make time to do it.
9. Examine and revise your life goals on a monthly basis and be sure to include progress toward these goals on a daily basis.
10. Put up reminders in your room about your goals.

—
Queen's University Health Counselling and Disability Services. "10 Tips for Improving Time Management." http://www.queensu.ca/stserv/top_10.html via http://www.queensu.ca/stserv/ls.htm>http://www.queensu.ca/stserv/ls/htm

In a companion study with a preschool resource teacher, Amy, who was considered exemplary, Hutchinson and Schmid (1996) found that this teacher saw herself as an advocate, whose focus was on the needs of individual exceptional children. The third theme in the interviews was her focus on partnerships and transitions. She perceived herself to be responsible for the transition between preschool and elementary school, a crucial juncture that she said many parents found disturbing. Her strategies included:

- inviting kindergarten and grade 1 teachers to the preschool to observe an exceptional student, rather than relying on information presented in a case conference;
- videotaping the exceptional child at the preschool and giving the tape to the parents to take to the kindergarten teacher;
- providing in-service to school staff (especially in rural schools where they had not previously taught a child with a particular exceptionality);
- videotaping a parent of a child with an unusual or severe disability (e.g., a feeding machine) as an expert explaining the child's condition in non-technical terms for the teacher.

In a national study of transition practices in the U.S., Paro, Pianta, and Cox (2000) reported that kindergarten teachers implement kindergarten and grade 1 transition practices. However, reported frequencies of the use of transition practices specifically for children with disabilities were not high. The kinds of strategies regularly implemented by Amy, an exemplary preschool teacher (Hutchinson & Schmid, 1996), which foster continuity and give parents a role as partners, were rarely reported. It may be more realistic to expect preschool teachers, who know the needs of the exceptional children, to assume this role—ensure a smooth transition and invite parents to bring together the preschool and elementary educators as well as the therapists. Amy described the transition between preschool and elementary school as "really important because what happens is the child can get lost in the shuffle." Transitions are inherently times of stress (Mallory, 1996). As a kindergarten or grade 1 teacher you can ensure that you are aware and knowledgeable about your exceptional students before they arrive so that the level of stress is as low as possible for you, the student, and the family.

This grade 1 boy ran away from school. When asked why, he said, "School is too hard." Transitions can be tough.

What about the transition from elementary school to middle school, junior high, or secondary school? While this is likely to be stressful for parents, chances are that it is extremely stressful for the exceptional student. For many exceptional students, change causes fear (review Chapters 3 and 4 to see how many descriptions of exceptionalities include this characteristic). The actions taken by the family and teacher of Ray, described in the case studies at the beginning of this chapter, are designed to minimize the trauma of his upcoming transition. This boy with Asperger syndrome will have gradually learned to meet the most challenging social expectations of his new school before he begins classes there. Because his biggest challenges are the social expectations associated with learning in classrooms, these were made the focus of his IEP for the year during which he was being prepared for the transition. His classroom teacher and resource teacher at Avon Elementary have worked as an effective team with Ray, his parents, and the resource teacher at Brown Middle School. An older boy, Marty, who took an interest in Ray while he was visiting Brown and learning to find his locker, offered to serve as a peer tutor and teach Ray to open his combination lock. Schools with peer tutor programs can often supplement the efforts of teachers to welcome new exceptional students. Marty has LD, remembers how difficult his move to Brown was, and appreciates the help he received from his peer tutor.

As a classroom teacher, you do not have to develop and execute transition plans alone. Once you start the ball rolling or respond to the requests of parents, you can usually share the load with a team. If your school does not have a procedure, you should enlist the principal and resource teacher to develop one that would serve many students. Look for resources of all kinds within the school and the community to make transitions smooth. The local Community Living Association or Spina Bifida Association may be willing to help. CNIB has procedures for assisting in transitions and has mobility specialists to help blind students learn their new environment. Consult local organizations, including Big Brothers, service clubs, church groups, and pensioners groups who provide volunteers. Remember that your school board may require a police check of these non-staff volunteers and that those without training may need guidance. The most efficient way to enhance independence for the transitions of exceptional students is to get these goals and strategies into the student's IEP, especially during the final year before they move from one school to another. Then a whole team, including parents and the student, will be making the student independence required for the transition a priority over the year. Some students use assistive devices and computers to enhance their independence. This is the focus of the next section.

Further Reading

Books on Asperger syndrome: B. Myles & R.L. Simpson (1998). *Asperger syndrome: A guide for educators and parents.* Austin, TX: Pro-Ed.

P. Howlin (1998). *Children with autism and Asperger syndrome: A guide for practitioners and carers.* Chichester, NY: John Wiley.

Using Computers and Assistive Devices to Enhance Learning and Independence

It has almost become a truism to say that computer skills are required for independence in today's world. People with disabilities frequently express this view. For examples, consult an issue of *Abilities* magazine online (http://www.abilities.ca/). Adapted technologies and computers play a significant role in enhancing the independence of exceptional children, adolescents, and adults. With information technology advancing daily, many believe that computers will enable youth with disabilities to develop greater independence than has ever been possible.

Computing technologies will influence all your students not only in the classroom but also in every aspect of their lives. These technologies are changing our concepts of education, culture, communication, shopping, and work. This means that we are educating students for a future that includes computers in roles we have not yet imagined and for a life of continuous learning. In spite of the *Charter of Rights and Freedoms* and employment equity initiatives (Coates, 1986), Canadians with disabilities have much higher rates of unemployment than do Canadians without disabilities (e.g., Gower, 1988). The impact of education level on employment rate is profound for all Canadians, but most pronounced for Canadians with disabilities, where only about 30 percent with elementary or no education are employed and over 70 percent of those with post-secondary education are employed (Hollingsworth, 1992). Skills in information technology may be more critical to the employment and economic independence of persons with disabilities than to citizens in general because technologies can serve as "equity tools" to provide access for the disabled (Hollingsworth, 1996; http://www.nlc-bnc.ca/accessinfo/tfpd-e.htm). American data suggest that 70 percent of blind adults of working age were unemployed in 1989, but only 15 percent of those who were technology users were unemployed (Hollingsworth, 1996; Keddy, 1989). Without computer skills and the accessibility they provide, persons with disabilities have yet another handicap.

There are many hardware and software tools designed to serve as "equity tools" to meet the needs of persons with specific disabilities (Hollingsworth, 1996). Their costs and availability were hotly debated on the listserv that was in use during the work of the Task Force on Access to Information for Print-Disabled Canadians in fall of 2000. The report of the Task Force is titled *Fulfilling the Promise* (http://www.nlc-bnc.ca/accessinfo/tfpd-e.htm). A recent study, in the Adaptech Project, conducted by researchers at Dawson College in Montreal, set out to learn why some students with disabilities who could benefit from computer technologies do not use them (http://omega.dawsoncollege.qc.ca/adaptech). The researchers sent questionnaires to 725 post-secondary students with various disabilities from across Canada. Most reported that they use computer technologies (95 percent). Almost half of the respondents needed adaptations to use a computer effectively and less than 60 percent of those who needed adaptations had these. The high cost of acquiring and maintaining computer and adaptive technologies was the problem most often noted by computer users and non-users. Most students were unaware of government programs to absorb or offset the high costs. Table 10.2 contains information about software and hardware from the Adaptech Resource Web page, which also includes a list of free or inexpensive downloads (http://omega.dawsoncollege.qc.ca/adaptech/adlinks.htm).

Assistive technology is defined as "any item, piece of equipment or product system...that is used to increase, maintain, or improve functional capabilities of individuals with disabilities" (Ely, 2000, p. 1). What kinds of assistive technologies, computer technologies, and equity tools might your students be using? The range is large (Lazzaro, 1993; Scott, 1996). For persons with visual disabilities, speech synthesizers allow access to other software tools. For people with low vision, there are magnification systems. The CNIB lists the following high-tech product categories on its Web page: Braille computer access, Braille printers, portable Braille and/or speech note takers, Windows 95 speech computer access, synthesizers, optical scanners and optical character recognition, large print computer access,

Cross-Reference
Chapter 1 contains a chart (Figure 1.1) suggesting how to judge the merit of Web sites.

Table 10.2

CANADIAN VENDORS OF ADAPTIVE TECHNOLOGY AND SERVICES

Company	Web address
Aroga Technologies	www.aroga.com
Assistive Devices Industry Association of Canada (Can ADIA)	www.starlingweb.com
Aurora Systems	www.djtech.com/aurora/
Braille Jymico	www.braillejymico.qc.ca
Betacom Corporation	www.betacom.com/
Biolink Computer Research and Development	www.biolink.bc.ca
Compusult Limited	www.compusult.nf.ca
Diffusion Multimedia	www.diffm.com
Eyecan	www.eyecan.ca
Frontier Computing	www.frontiercomputing.on.ca
Gutmann Ltee.	www.gutmanncorp.com
Neil Squire Foundation	www.neilsquire.ca
Sennheiser Canada	www.sennheiser.com
Textel	www.textel.com
VisuAide	www.visuaide.com
WiVik	www.WiVik.com

Note: Adaptech Resource Page also includes free or inexpensive downloads.

Source: Adaptech Resource Page, http://omega.dawsoncollege.qc.ca/adaptech/adlinks.htm. Used by permission.

closed circuit television readers (CCTVs), and DOS speech computer access (http://www.cnib.ca/tech_aids/index.htm). Technologies for persons with hearing impairments may incorporate fax and electronic mail as well as visual signals to replace auditory signals. Those with motor impairments may have adapted keyboards, programmable keys, and toggle switches, or may wear a headset that tracks head movement and uses a puff and sip switch to replace a mouse (Hollingsworth, 1996).

Assistive technologies can enable students with disabilities to access social, communicative, recreational, and academic opportunities. However, assistive technologies are not without problems. Devices are expensive, sometimes the training needed to use the device well is unavailable, or the device breaks. With the constant changes in technologies, suppliers, and assessment methods, you and your teaching colleagues may be facing questions from parents and students that you cannot answer. Look to your district school board consultants for advice on the interface between the individual with disabilities and the technology; ask them to recommend provincial experts. For example, in Ontario you can consult Bloorview MacMillan Centre (http://www.bloorviewmacmillan.on.ca/) and in Alberta, Alberta Children's Hospital (http://www.crha-health.ab.ca/sites/ach.htm). There are books and Web sites that provide general information about assistive technologies and education (e.g., Ely, 2000; http://at-advocacy.phillynews.com/data/atworkined.html). Figure 10.2 provides a worksheet for parents who think their children might benefit from assistive technologies, available on the Web site of Temple University (http://www.kidstogether.org/at_cmps.htm). Assistive and computer technologies facilitate independence in many ways, including enabling people with physical disabilities to engage in self-advocacy by using the Internet to access information (Wong, 1997), and then use that knowledge to gain some control over their treatment and care (Nagler & Nagler, 1999).

Put Into Practice

Visit a library in a university or college or a public library and familiarize yourself with the assistive devices available there.

Summary of Student Development

To be independent learners, exceptional students need to develop learning strategies and knowledge and skills for adapting to change. Other important aspects of student development include setting goals, monitoring progress, and using school and community resources effectively and appropriately. The IEPs of exceptional students should include these important aspects of student development. Without as much independence as possible in these aspects of their lives, exceptional students are unlikely to be able to use the curriculum learning that schools usually emphasize. Some provinces (including Alberta, British Columbia, and Ontario) emphasize annual goals for all students from about grade 7 upward. If your school has a process for setting annual goals, ensure that these are aligned with their IEP for the exceptional students in your classes.

Computers can serve as "equity tools" as well as sources of knowledge and potential careers for students with disabilities.

Fostering Interpersonal Development for Independence

The key components of interpersonal development include students managing themselves, getting along with others, and assuming social responsibility or citizenship. Chapter 6 focused on how you can create a classroom with a positive

Figure 10.2

COMPUTERS FOR CHILDREN WITH DISABILITIES: A WORKSHEET FOR PARENTS

If you think your child needs a computer for school or home, use the following worksheet as a tool to help you determine and support your child's needs for computer equipment.

Why do you think your child needs a computer?

I think my child needs a computer because…

Have you identified the educational goals that the computer will help your child achieve?   Yes ___ No ___

For example, a computer may help students improve written expression; complete assignments in a reasonable amount of time; assist in electronic research. If the primary purpose of the computer is educational, consider requesting the computer through your local school district.

Have you identified other ways in which a computer will help your child's development?   Yes ___ No ___

For example, a computer may help children to play, socialize, and lengthen attention span.

A computer will help my child …

Has your child had a computer evaluation?   Yes ___ No ___

An evaluation is necessary for determining what type of computer hardware and software are appropriate for your child. An evaluation should also identify any adaptations your child will require in order to access the computer.

An evaluation was provided by _____

The evaluator recommended a computer because …

The evaluator recommended the following equipment, software, or other adaptations for access …

Have you identified when, where, and how often your child will be using the computer?   Yes ___ No ___

The computer may be needed in the classroom, in the library or resource room or at home.

My child will be using the computer during …

Are the computer hardware, software, and services necessary to use them included in your child's Individualized Education Plan (IEP)?   Yes ___ No ___

If you anticipate that the computer your child needs will be provided through your local school district, the computer should be written into your child's IEP.

The following hardware, software, and assistive technology service(s) are included in my child's IEP …

Source: Pennsylvania's Initiative on Assistive Technology, Institute on Disabilities, Temple University. Computers for Children with Disabilities: A Worksheet for Parents. Prepared under a grant from the National Institute on Disability and Rehabilitation Research, U.S. Department of Education.

social climate that makes it easy for students to learn, participate, cooperate, take risks, assume responsibility, and grow interpersonally. In Chapter 9, you learned about enhancing peer relations and about specific strategies for helping students to learn together. However, there are excellent resources for explicitly teaching students so they grow interpersonally and become more independent in this sphere of their lives.

Strategies for Elementary Classrooms

For teachers of elementary students, I recommend *Self-Discipline* by Rob Kerr (1999), a Canadian educator. One of the best-known writers on the topic of interpersonal development is Daniel Goleman (1995). His concept of emotional intelligence caught the imagination of North Americans. He argued that what we need to foster in all children is intelligent self-control of emotions and responses in day-to-day life. You can create learning activities for your class that teach deliberate strategies for responding to interpersonal challenges. For example, the SAT plan (Kerr, 1999) is short for Sensible Acting and Thinking and consists of:

1. Stop. Relax.
2. Think sensibly: …just because…
3. Make a plan: Be calm, be strong.
4. Reward yourself.

By using Kerr's (1999) scenarios as models, you can create scenarios that reflect issues currently important to the life of your classroom, school, and community. Don't make them so similar to real incidents that students are embarrassed or see themselves in scenarios (unless you have the permission of the student and parents and make no reference to them). For example, to teach students to recognize when they overreact, you could change the details of a recent schoolyard incident that you witnessed between the last two students to enter the building. A boy who is known to taunt students who react to him waited for a younger child who was slouching toward the school and happened to be wearing red hand-me-down sneakers from his older sister. The bully taunted him with, "Girls' shoes! You're a loser, wearing girls' shoes." The younger boy punched the aggressor, tore off the sneakers, and threw them into the garbage can beside the door of the school.

Chapter 5 contained an equity strategy to respond to this kind of treatment by bullies (which was an example of "putting down women"). You used this equity strategy, but realized that it is also important to teach students how to minimize the impact of being on the receiving end. After disguising the details of the scenario, you can describe it to your students and explain how the young boy overreacted: we overreact if we become needlessly upset, and/or if we are unfair to others. In their journals, students could reflect on a time they overreacted. You can ask students to draw a cartoon showing someone of their age overreacting to an unfortunate event. Then teach students that what drives our reaction is what we think or believe. If we think this unfortunate event is the "end of the world," then we tell ourselves it is horrible, and engage in negative self-talk that makes us feel worse and worse. If we say to ourselves, "He is a creep. I don't care what he thinks. But

Put Into Practice

Develop three scenarios for your students to use to practise the SAT plan. Make the scenarios appropriate to the age of your students and the context in which you teach.

What do you think?

Should we teach children and adolescents how to respond when they are bullied, or should we put all our energy into preventing bullying?

I don't like these shoes either. I am going to talk to my mom about getting a different pair," we are engaging in sensible self-talk. Advise students not only to get control of their self-talk, but also to report the incident to an adult or peer negotiator as calmly as they can. Then you can continue to teach strategies for relaxing, jumping to the right conclusions, laughing about the things that happen, and being "calm and strong" when responding to people who treat them unfairly or rudely (Kerr, 1999). Kerr's activities on building relationships have students role-playing and reflecting on such skills as active listening, win-win plans, and having courage. Figure 10.3 shows Kerr's activity for helping students to learn to have courage and be a responsible citizen by refusing to go along with the inappropriate actions of others.

Figure 10.3

HAVING COURAGE

Having courage is important to everyone. But acting on our personal values is not always easy. Nor is it always easy to stick up for ourselves or to say "No." We can learn to have courage, to act on our own values, by reminding ourselves to be calm and strong to do the right thing.

Activity

1. Read Randy's story:

   Randy went out with some friends on Tuesday night. Finally Chip said, "Hey guys, let's go over to the school and throw some rocks through the windows. It'll be a riot." Some of the others laughed. Randy felt uneasy. It wasn't his thing. He believed it was wrong and stupid, yet his friends were important to him. He said to himself, *"Be calm, be strong. I have to have some courage here."* He looked at Chip, straight in the eye: "Sorry guys, that's a bit stupid. I'm not up for that." Chip became offended: "Are you saying we're stupid, Randy?" "No," Randy replied. "You guys are great, but that idea is a bit stupid. Breaking windows costs my parents and your parents money. Your taxes, my taxes. I'm not up for it. See you guys tomorrow." Randy smiled, turned, and walked away.

2. Have a brief discussion about Randy. What did he tell himself in order to act with courage? Is it harder to be courageous with friends or non-friends?

3. Ask students to work in small groups to plan and present a skit. They should show a character in the skit acting with courage. These characters think out loud to share courageous self-talk.

Make the point that it is often difficult to act with courage, especially with friends. But, in the long run, people respect courageous individuals. Stress too that courageous action comes from courageous self-talk. Ask: What are some courageous self-statements we might use?

Reflection Journal

Invite students to reflect in their journals on a time when they acted with courage. Have them describe the situation and their courageous self-talk. Ask them how they felt afterwards. Were they proud of themselves?

Source: R. Kerr (1999). *Self-discipline: Using portfolios to help students develop self-awareness, manage emotions and build relationships.* Markham, ON: Pembroke Publishers. Used by permission.

Strategies for Secondary Classrooms

Secondary teachers might want to focus such learning much more on Solving Problems on the Job and Anger Management on the Job. These are the titles of two of the modules in *Pathways* (Hutchinson & Freeman, 1994). The advantage to focusing on the workplace with adolescents is that you can help them look ahead and develop strategies for new challenges that await them, rather than reminding them of failures they have experienced in interpersonal relations in the school context. Both of these modules include school examples and workplace examples, but focus students on preparing for participation in workplace experience within their courses, cooperative learning, part-time jobs, and future careers. Anger Management on the Job includes the CALMER strategy:

C̲heck that there is a problem

A̲ssess the nature of the problem

L̲ist possible alternatives

M̲ake a decision about the best alternative

E̲valuate the consequences

R̲epeat the process, if necessary

Figure 10.4 shows example scenarios and the steps in teaching students to use rehearsed role-play in learning to solve workplace problems (from Solving Problems on the Job). You can use programs like these as models for developing your own activities that are particularly relevant to your students, school, community, and career opportunities.

Summary for Interpersonal Development

Interpersonal development includes children and adolescents learning to take responsibility for the way they interact with others and for their social and civic responsibility. It includes students working cooperatively in the classroom and anticipating what will be required of them in terms of collaboration and cooperation in the workplace. These are all essential for independent learning and independent living. Exceptional students sometimes find responsible interdependence challenging because they need practice in reading social cues, speaking up appropriately, and responding to criticism. IEPs should include goals for interpersonal development. In addition to the strategies discussed here, Chapter 9 includes many suggestions for teaching to enhance interpersonal development, all of which might appear as strategies for implementation on the IEPs of exceptional students.

Career Development and Career Education for Exceptional Individuals

The third area of learning in the recent guidance and career planning curricula is career development. It is clearly related to personal development and to interper-

Further Reading

Canadian Career Counselling Programs: G.A. Charter, D. Persaud, A. Poonwassie, S. Williams, & D. Zinger (1995). *Career counselling for Aboriginal youth: The journey inward; the journey outward.* Toronto: Guidance Centre.

D. Campbell, P. Serff, & D. Williams (1994). *The BreakAway Company.* Toronto: Trifolium. (for at-risk youth)

M. Jamieson, J. Paterson, T. Krupa, E. MacEachern, & A. Topping (1993). *Thresholds: Enhancing the career development strategies of young people with physical disabilities.* Ottawa: Canadian Career Development Foundation.

Figure 10.4

REHEARSED ROLE-PLAY FOR LEARNING TO SOLVE WORKPLACE PROBLEMS

Example Scenarios

- You do maintenance work outdoors at a year-round amusement park. When you come inside to get supplies, a visitor to the park stops to ask you a question. Your supervisor yells at you for not being outside.

- You have a partner in a furniture refinishing business. Your partner leaves the worst jobs for you to do.

- A client is dissatisfied with a layout done by your advertising agency, returns it, and tells you the complaints. Your supervisor created the design.

Activity Plan for the Teacher

1. Model how to use the problem-solving worksheet.

    Choose a scenario and a student partner. Think aloud, with your partner asking for clarification, and record your thoughts on a transparency copy of the worksheet.

2. Discuss with your partner how to role-play the situation.

    The modelled discussion should focus on how each character will react in the problem-solving role-play. In particular, discuss how you will respond to the barriers erected by your partner. Here is a possible script for this step:

    Let's figure out how to role-play this situation. I will play the employee with the problem and my partner will act as the person I'm having difficulty with. To partner: "What do you think?" Partner replies.

    We've listed on the worksheet four possible paths we could follow to reach our goal. We need to decide which paths to follow in which order.

3. Role-play the situation.

    As much as possible, assume the mannerisms of the characters.

4. The class selects a job-related problem from the provided scenarios or from a list they have generated.

5. Students form groups of three.

    Most scenarios involve three characters: the person with the problem, the person with whom the problem must be addressed, and one other character.

6. Each group completes the problem-solving worksheet for the selected problem.

    Stress that the groups should do this quickly and move on to role-playing, because they have already had considerable practice completing the worksheets.

7. Each group discusses and practises a role-play of the situation.

    The discussion will encompass assignment of roles, likely success of each path, order in which paths will be taken, possible barriers to resolution. Then the group practises the role-play to gain self-confidence.

8. The groups present their role-plays to the class.

9. The class discusses the role-plays.

10. Repeat steps 4 through 9 with a new scenario.

Extension: You could videotape the student role-plays.

Figure 10.4

(CONTINUED)

Problem-Solving Worksheet

Group Members:

Job Scenario:

Statement of Problem:

Type of Problem:

Goal:

Who can help you reach this goal?

What paths could you follow to reach your goal?

1. _____
2. _____
3. _____
4. _____

Which path would you try first?

Why would you try this path first?

—

Adapted from N.L. Hutchinson & J.G. Freeman (1994). *Pathways: Solving Problems on the Job.*
Scarborough, ON: Nelson Canada. Used by permission.

sonal development. Like the other two areas, it contributes to independent learning and especially to independent living. Career development is based on the idea that career aspirations are developmental in nature, that is, they develop gradually over time, and require experiences and reflection on those experiences (Gottfredson, 1981). For exceptional individuals, most would agree that career development begins in childhood and extends through adolescence into the adult years (Morningstar, 1997). Super's (1990) life-span theory of career development indicates that career awareness and exploration begin early in life and continue until the mid-thirties. Super suggested adolescence should be spent focusing on career exploration rather than preparation for a specific occupation. He stressed the need for planned exploration, experience, and evaluated trial in order to develop career maturity and planfulness. Most career education programs for adolescents with disabilities include three components: self-awareness/career awareness, career exploration, and career experiences.

Developing Self-Awareness and Career Awareness

Strategies for self-awareness are important to all exceptional learners and should be developed over a number of years so that prior to the arrival of employment or post-secondary education opportunities, individuals can describe their strengths and needs with confidence and clarity (Van Reusen & Bos, 1994; Hutchinson & Freeman, 1994).

Self-awareness refers to one knowing about himself or herself, developing a picture of the kind of person one is. For students with disabilities, self-awareness includes understanding the characteristics associated with their exceptionality— their personal strengths and needs. Students need self-awareness about their interests, preferences, abilities, and anything else that defines them. Career is usually thought to refer to both the process of making a living by means of a particular occupation and the broader notions of one's course or progress through life (Super & Harris-Bowlsbey, 1979). Thus career awareness refers to students' understanding of all aspects of adult responsibilities, roles, and the nature and meaning of work. This includes the incredible range of ways in which adults engage in paid work, volunteer and unpaid work, and other adult roles such as leisure, child rearing, and citizenship.

Counsellors and teachers at secondary and post-secondary levels usually emphasize students knowing themselves. However, this process can and should start much earlier (Clark, Carlson, Fisher, Cook, & D'Alonzo, 1991). Young children can describe their hobbies and interests if asked what they like to do in their spare time, what they save their money for, and what they would most like to do on their next vacation. These activities can be carried out in pairs and small groups with drawings and short pieces of writing showing the results of the deliberations. It is difficult to separate self-awareness from career awareness because many activities designed to help students come to know themselves highlight how characteristics, interests, abilities, etc., are related to choices, roles, and careers.

By inviting adults into the classroom to talk about their work, you can provide lively career education. Prepare questions for children to use as models of what to ask; if you are concerned about inappropriate questions, have a rehearsal session before the first visitor. The school or community librarian can assist by providing or recommending books that match children's professed interests in both hobbies and careers. Remember to invite adults who have pursued non-traditional career paths, adults representing the cultural diversity of the neighbourhood, and adults with disabilities. Avoid reinforcing stereotypes and introduce careers that may be unfamiliar to the children. When your school has visitors, arrange for those adults to visit your class. One of my best career and self-awareness units as an elementary teacher included inviting the musicians from the Montreal Symphony who played in our school in a monthly program that was part of our school's focus on the arts. I invited each musician to speak briefly to my students about him- or herself and

Further Reading

R.S. Hughes & P.C. Kloeppel (1994). *SAIL: Self-awareness in language arts.* Minneapolis, MN: Educational Media Corp.

P. Huggins (1994). *Helping children find their strengths.* Longmont, CO: Sopris West.

J. Kincher & J. Bach (1990). *Psychology for kids: 40 fun tests that help you learn about yourself.* Minneapolis, MN: Free Spirit Pub.

answer the students' questions. The students learned to ask about how the musicians knew that this was the career they wanted, how they turned a hobby into a career, when they learned enough about themselves to say they wanted to be musicians, etc. Then we invited parents, storekeepers, members of our community, the school janitor, and the school principal to visit us. After every session, the students made entries in their "Book About Myself" about what they were learning about themselves through this process. There are many approaches, including using literature to enhance children's self-awareness (e.g., Hughes & Kloeppel, 1994) and series of activities such as Huggins (1994) and Kincher and Bach (1990). Remember to turn the emphasis back to the students learning about themselves—increasing self-awareness—and ensure that you help exceptional students carry out the follow-up tasks in a way that promotes meaningful self-awareness.

Self-awareness and career awareness are more often associated with the developmental tasks of adolescence. Many provinces include courses on study skills, career development, and cooperative education in the secondary curriculum. These courses usually include a component on self-awareness. Kerr (1999) recommends that adolescents develop portfolios in order to learn about themselves. There are also a number of sources for leading discussion groups made up of adolescents with and without disabilities (e.g., Peterson, 1993) and groups composed entirely of exceptional adolescents (e.g., Dennison, 1997). The Canadian program *Pathways* (Hutchinson & Freeman, 1994), includes a module on Knowing About Yourself, Knowing About Careers. This program is designed for heterogeneous groups of adolescents and was pilot tested on groups of exceptional adolescents and in inclusive classrooms. Figure 10.5 contains an activity sheet from *Pathways* called Personal Strengths.

Career Exploration

Career exploration, actions undertaken deliberately or for their own sake that teach about possible careers and adult roles, can take many forms. Engaging in imaginative play, reading, watching films, playing on teams, and developing hobbies and interests all contribute to career exploration. When parents say that their exceptional children or adolescents have too much homework to do and cannot take part in Cubs or extracurricular activities, you may want to speak up. These after-school pursuits are critical in helping young people of all ages and abilities to engage in career exploration. You may have known a gifted young woman who chaired the public relations committee in secondary school and began to consider a career in marketing. Or a boy with developmental disabilities who cooked for the school "family days" and asked if he could visit a cafeteria to learn about possible careers in food preparation. Other adolescents learn that playing the flute will remain a hobby because they are not talented enough to be a professional musician. Students must reflect on the exploration or experience and relate it to themselves. Questions students can ask include: Did I enjoy doing that and why? How good was I at that? How confident do I feel about doing it again? Why was that so interesting? Is this something that makes me feel "in my element?" If I were to do this every day, how would I feel about it? Do I value this experience?

Further Reading

L. Plue, W. Palmer & C. Karakokkinos (2000). *Careers today and tomorrow.* Toronto: Irwin Publishing. (student text and teacher's resource guide)

What do you think?

Read M. Nagler & A. Nagler (1999). *What's Stopping You: Living Successfully with Disability.* Toronto: Stoddart. This comprehensive, Canadian manual for self-advocacy focuses more on adults than on adolescents and children. What would you ask the authors if you had an opportunity to meet them?

PERSONAL STRENGTHS

Name: _____

Partner: _____

Have your partner record your answers to the questions below and list your three greatest strengths.

		Yes	Sometimes	No
1.	Do I value other people's opinions?	___	___	___
2.	Do I make good decisions?	___	___	___
3.	Do I like talking to people?	___	___	___
4.	Do I like fixing things?	___	___	___
5.	Do I organize my time well?	___	___	___
6.	Am I a responsible person?	___	___	___
7.	Do I write about my ideas?	___	___	___
8.	Do I think for myself?	___	___	___
9.	Am I a team player?	___	___	___
10.	Do I work hard?	___	___	___
11.	Do I try to look my best?	___	___	___
12.	Do I finish what I start?	___	___	___

My three greatest strengths:

1. _____
2. _____
3. _____

Source: N.L. Hutchinson & J.G. Freeman (1994). *Pathways: Knowing About Yourself, Knowing About Careers*. Scarborough, ON: Nelson Canada. Used by permission.

You can contribute to career exploration by including discussions of the application of the knowledge you are teaching. When your students are studying history, you can point out how much history is used to create lifelike settings for films and television programs and invite a historian to tell your students what she does. When studying design and technology, discuss with students how engineers, technicians, and construction workers on the teams that design and build bridges apply this kind of knowledge. Invite an array of individuals who work with people, including occupational therapists, child-care workers, and bus drivers. Remember that chefs and pharmacists are applied chemists. Once you begin to act on the connections between your curriculum and possible careers, you are engaging your students in career exploration. Encourage students to ask questions, consult books and Web sites, and learn about the credential requirements, educational qualifications, expectations, demands, wages, and dangers of the careers that interest them. Provide opportunities for children and adolescents to interview adults in careers that intrigue them. Encourage wide exploration of many possibilities rather than premature narrowing to one or two careers.

The Calgary Educational Partnership Foundation (1996) published an excellent resource for secondary students and their teachers to guide and record career exploration called *Employability Skills: Creating My Future*. It is a student portfolio that focuses on career goals, plans, and actions one can take to move toward those goals. It helps students develop a portfolio to record progress and show to employers when applying for part-time or full-time employment, to post-secondary programs that require portfolios, or to cooperative education or workplace experience employers. Table 10.3 shows a career goals chart from *Employability Skills*.

Labour market information provides workers and those aspiring to work with details about current and projected demand for labour services and supply of labour services in the economy (http://www.hrdc-drhc.gc.ca/common/lmi.shtml). Thus, youth who might express interest in work that takes advantage of their numerical abilities could learn about the demand for mathematics teachers, actuarial professionals, chartered accountants, mathematics professors, and mathematical engineers. The same kind of information is available about any cluster of ability-related occupations. While there are complex classification systems of occupations, a simple set of categories that has been effective when teaching adolescents in inclusive classrooms is: (1) generating ideas, (2) mathematics and science, (3)

Table 10.3

CAREER GOALS CHART

People and resources I can go to for more information	Courses required/ recommended	Skills and qualities I need
Career 1	• _____ • _____ • _____ • _____	• _____ • _____ • _____ • _____
Career 2	• _____ • _____ • _____ • _____	• _____ • _____ • _____ • _____
Career 3	• _____ • _____ • _____ • _____	• _____ • _____ • _____ • _____

Source: Calgary Educational Partnership Foundation (1996). *Employability Skills: Creating My Future* (Student Booklet). Scarborough, ON: Nelson Canada. Used by permission.

Weblinks

LABOUR MARKET INFORMATION
MENU (HUMAN RESOURCES
DEVELOPMENT CANADA)
**http://www.hrdc-drhc.gc.ca/
common/lmo.shtml**

CANADA PROSPECTS
**http://www.careerccc.org/
products/cp_99_e/section5/
lmi1.html**

LABOUR FORCE SURVEY (LATEST
RELEASE), STATISTICS CANADA
**http://www.statcan.ca/
english/Subjects/Labour/LFS/
lfs-en.htm**

SKILLNET.CA TODAY (DAILY
PROSPECTS IN CANADA'S LABOUR
MARKET)
**http://www.prospects.skillnet.
ca/**

CANADA WORKINFONET (CANWIN)
**http://www.workinfonet.ca/
cwn/english/main.html**

KIDS TOGETHER, INC.
**http://www.kidstogether.org/
at_cmps.htm**

talking with people, (4) helping people, (5) hands-on training and using equipment (Hutchinson & Freeman, 1994). With the advent of computers and the Internet, it is much easier for educators, counsellors, and youth to access labour market information. While there are Web sites for which one must register and pay, there are also many excellent sites available at no cost.

Parents, teachers, and employers often assume that career exploration and decision making are easy for gifted students, who have high academic achievement, have many abilities, and can access information easily (Achter, Benbow, & Lubinski, 1996). Recent research suggests that as much as 53 percent of academically advanced students experience difficulties and want help with career exploration and decision making (Emmett & Minor, 1993). John Stewart (1999) of the University of New Brunswick reported that the difficulties experienced by gifted students included narrowing career choice, indecision, pressure from others, lack of career role models, and lack of meaningfulness or personal challenge in careers. Michael Pyryt (1992) of the University of Calgary suggests how counsellors and teachers can help gifted students engage in divergent thinking strategies to combine interests and lifestyle issues into a meaningful occupational choice.

Career exploration is a complex and lengthy process of seeking and reflecting on information and experience, setting goals and monitoring progress toward them, and changing direction and pursuing alternatives. There are many competencies and perspectives that young people need to develop and embrace to progress in career development as a result of career exploration. Some of these include self-advocacy and self-determination.

Self-Advocacy

Self-advocacy is essential in every role from student to employee. It enables students to act on career awareness and career exploration. **Self-advocacy** is important for promoting independent learning and independent living and refers to "an individual's ability to effectively communicate, convey, negotiate or assert his or her own interests, desires, needs, and rights" (Van Reusen & Bos, 1994, p. 466). It also involves making informed decisions and taking responsibility for those decisions. For example, if a student is to explain to a teacher the adaptations he needs in order to submit assignments when his cerebral palsy prevents him from writing with a pencil, he will have to know about his own strengths and needs (Nagler & Nagler, 1999). Self-advocacy also contributes to career development. If an employee with a disability is to explain to an employer how her computer will have to be adapted, she must be articulate about her own condition or disability as well as understand the demands and routines of the workplace. In addition, it takes confidence, courage, and determination to be one's own spokesperson.

Research has been conducted on self-advocacy for individuals with every area of exceptionality we have discussed. In a program designed to enhance self-advocacy of adolescents with learning disabilities (Van Reusen & Bos, 1990; 1994), adolescents learn strategies to increase their participation in IEP conferences. They learn specific strategies for inventorying their strengths and weaknesses, recording this information on inventory sheets, listening and responding, asking questions, and naming their goals. Similar approaches have been recommended for teaching other exceptional students to participate in transitions and important decisions: students with physical disabilities (King, Shultz, Steel, Gilpin, & Cathers, 1993), students with visual impairments (Koenig, 1992), students with mental illnesses or emotional disabilities (http://www.nami.org/youth/selfadvc.htm), and students with developmental disabilities (Dybwad & Bersani, 1996; Johnson, 1999), as well as gifted students (Robinson, 1996). Other groups have also emphasized self-advocacy, including persons with traumatic brain injury (http://www.headinjury.com/advocacy.htm), and Epilepsy Ontario (http://epilepsyontario.org/faqs/advocacy.html). Self-advocacy is a skill that adults must use frequently in order to ensure fair treatment in a busy and impersonal world—this is especially so for adults with disabilities. Focus on Advocacy tells of the experiences of Marie Laporte-Stark, a blind woman, who advocated for herself until she succeeded.

Self-Determination

Recently researchers and practitioners have begun to focus on a larger construct in preparing youth with disabilities for independence and for playing a valued role: self-determination. **Self-determination** refers to the abilities, motivation, and volition that enable people to define goals for themselves and take and sustain the initiative to reach those goals (Versnel, 2001). Self-determination entails choosing, and enacting choices, to control one's life to the maximum extent possible based on knowing and valuing oneself, and in pursuit of one's own needs, interests, and values (Campeau & Wolman, 1993).

FOCUS ON ADVOCACY

Marie Laporte-Stark has long been an advocate for access. While Marie and her husband are blind, their children are sighted. She says that "within the home, access to information was rarely a problem" because this was an environment she could shape. For example, she used a kettle that whistles when water has boiled and labelled microwave controls in Braille. However, the neighbourhood school turned out to be a more challenging environment for accessing important information. While students who were blind had access to Braille textbooks and assignments, Marie could not convince the school that she needed Braille copies of her children's textbooks to help them with their homework. She says, "I found ways around most of these barriers to participation in my children's education." The barrier Marie could not overcome was her need for Braille copies of her children's report cards.

The school suggested that the children read the report cards to their parents or that the parents ask a friend to read the report cards to them. However, Marie knew that she had a right to this critical information in an accessible form. Marie persisted and eventually the family filed a complaint with the Human Rights Commission of their province. After many years of Marie's "advocacy for access," the school district adopted an Alternate Format Policy. Marie says, "This policy means that, today, other parents who are blind can obtain report cards, school materials, and school information in a form they can read independently—just as parents with sight have been doing for decades."

Thinking about school–home interactions from the point of view of the parent may not be easy for us as teachers. However, Marie Laporte-Stark's advocacy reminds us what individuals with disabilities need for full participation in our schools and communities—the same access to information, opportunities, and outcomes as people without disabilities. Principals can authorize that schools fund the provision of information to parents in alternate formats. Blind parents have a right to expect principals and teachers to take these actions.

Source: Based on M. Laporte-Stark (1998). Advocating for access. *Abilities, 37* (Winter), pp. 14–17.

"I want the same things as other people—to work and to live on my own."

During the 1990s, a number of research groups in the United States developed curricula under the auspices of Office of Special Education and Rehabilitation Services (OSERS) that were geared primarily to the needs of individuals with developmental disabilities. Weymeyer (1992), one of the leaders in this field, emphasized self-determination as enabling one to act as "the primary causal agent in one's life and making choices and decisions regarding one's quality of life" (p. 305). Each curriculum emphasized the teaching of the skills, behaviours, and dispositions its authors thought necessary for self-determination. These curricula included:

- ChoiceMaker Self-Determination Curriculum (Martin & Marshal, 1995)

- Steps to Self-Determination (Field & Hoffman, 1996)

- Take Charge (Powers, Sowers, Turner, Nesbitt, Knowles, & Ellison, 1996)

A review and synthesis of the best practices, curricula, and research on self-advocacy and self-determination is available from the Self-Determination Synthesis project at the University of North Carolina at Charlotte (http://www.uncc.edu.sdsp/objectives.asp).

Career Experiences

Career experiences refers to the opportunities adolescents have to try out and experience aspects of the working role that is expected of adults. Some describe this as the reality testing of the understanding developed through career exploration. In Canada, the most common forms of career experiences that occur within school programs are cooperative education and work experience. The Canadian Labour Force Development Board (1994) recently recommended cooperative education as a central component of the transition to work.

COOPERATIVE EDUCATION AND WORKPLACE LEARNING

Weblinks

ONTARIO CO-OPERATIVE
EDUCATION ASSOCIATION
http://www.ocea.on.ca

Cooperative education (co-op), in which schools cooperate with employers, involves students in extended periods of time in a workplace (often around 100 hours over a school term) while enrolled in full-time study. Typically students also engage in classroom orientations to the workplace and in reflective seminars. **Workplace experience** is usually of shorter duration, ranging from a one-day job-shadowing experience to a few half-day visits within the context of a credit course. A recent review of the co-op education and career education policies across Canada showed that all ten provinces and three territories provide co-op education and/or workplace experiences; however, a variety of organizations are used (Hutchinson et al., 1998). This review also showed that only recently revised co-op education curricula referred directly to the provision of adapted experiences for exceptional students (or to the needs of women, ESL, and Aboriginal students). There were frequent references to the needs of at-risk students.

Research suggests that adolescents with disabilities can benefit from co-op and career education (Tennant, Hutchinson, & Freeman, 1992). They tend to learn well in structured, hands-on, experiential settings, often much better than in traditional classrooms (e.g., Hutchinson, Freeman, Downey, & Kilbreath, 1992). In a recent study of college and university students from four programs, Chin et al. (in press) found that over 95 percent of those who had *and* had not taken co-op education in secondary school would recommend it to others. Their reasons for taking co-op education were often combinations of career exploration and career experiences, for example, wanting to try out careers that interested them and use the information to help them decide whether to pursue a particular career. A review of representative curriculum documents from school districts in Ontario (Hutchinson et al., in press) showed that school districts saw co-op education as a means of helping students make connections between the classroom and the world of work, as well as a means of career exploration and career experiences.

Research conducted in the United States with students with various disabilities suggests that vocational training or on-the-job-training during the high-school years for a particular entry-level job is premature (e.g., Heal & Rusch, 1995). Morningstar (1997) recommends a balanced program of career development that includes opportunities to develop career maturity, self-determination through meaningful work experiences that are primarily for learning, not on-the-job-training. Morningstar describes an ideal program that is much like co-op education as it is practised in Canada. Encourage your exceptional students and their parents to consider cooperative education as an integral part of their secondary school years. In our research at Queen's University with adolescents in co-op education, we have learned that co-op stretches adolescents—with and without disabilities—in ways that we had not imagined (Munby et al., 2001).

It is important that career development include opportunities for students to dream about their futures and grow enthusiastic about being valued and taking adult roles, because "the specific nature of a youth's dream is less important than the enthusiasm dreaming generates for goal achievement" (Powers et al., 1996, p. 12). Cooperative education enables adolescents to dream, to reality-test their dreams, and to grow into independent adult roles.

Independent Living

Much has been written in the past decade about independent living, particularly about people with developmental disabilities. For some time, the emphasis was on enhancing strategies for community participation. More recently the focus has begun to shift to what is called community support. This evolution toward supported participation in the roles and to meet the goals chosen by individuals with disabilities could lead to immense changes in social policy in the next decade.

Strategies for Community Participation

Community participation demands independent living skills and career development. The needs of exceptional adolescents, in particular, may be different than their peers (Brolin, 1991). While learning these skills in inclusive classrooms is encouraged, it may also be necessary to increase the intensity of teaching and the opportunities for practice in personal, interpersonal, and career development, just as it may be necessary for academic learning. Many writers have suggested recently that aiming for community participation requires community education during the school years and not just classroom education (e.g., Jenkinson, 1997). Community-based instruction is defined by Wehmeyer (1992) as involving "teachers and other educational personnel teaching educational objectives in natural environments, such as work sites, shopping malls, and restaurants" (p. 170). Learning experiences in the community help youth with disabilities to learn authentic tasks in their natural contexts, to develop personally and interpersonally, and to grow to understand career preferences and to develop a work history. These experiences need to enable students to become part of the community culture and workplace culture, alongside other citizens and employees. Throughout this book, there have been many examples of students learning to use the telephone by making authentic phone calls to secure meaningful information, riding the bus in order to learn how, and participating in cooperative education or workplace learning. These are complex arrangements for learning and require the cooperation of a number of educators and members of the community. However, they can become the responsibility of the entire team if they are included in the student's annual goals at the IEP meeting.

Independence: Community Support

Self-determination is consistent with the recent growth of the movement called community inclusion and a new approach to community services based on the concept of support. Knoll and Racino (1994) refer to this as a "new way of thinking" that mobilizes the "unique array of supports each individual needs to live in his or her own home and participate in the life of the community" (p. 301). This reform had its beginnings in grassroots efforts of people with disabilities and their families and service providers who sought to work around the barriers to community membership, true choice, and control or self-determination. Support means working for people with disabilities, meeting their notions of what is supportive to them, and functioning as a community worker (that is, the person who helps make connections, mobilizes resources, and plans backup systems).

The research on best practices from family support, supported employment, and inclusive education shows that central to each of these is a common focus on support (Ferguson & Olsen, 1989). Organizations providing support have made a commitment to self-determination for individuals with disabilities and empowerment of their organizations. An international think-tank suggested the following eight competencies for professionals whose work involves supporting individuals and empowering organizations (based on Cochran, 1990):

- ability and commitment to identify strengths in people and groups
- respect for diverse perspectives and lifestyles

Weblinks

RYERSON DISABILITIES STUDIES PROGRAM
http://www.ryerson.ca/ds

- capacity to listen and reflect
- ability to put one's self aside in the interest of the group
- creativity in helping people become more aware and confident of their abilities
- ability to help individual or group assume decision-making responsibility and action
- knowledge of how to access information
- ability to reflect critically on ongoing process, including one's own role

You may be asking, "What lies ahead?" It is always difficult to predict the future, but we can be fairly confident in predicting change, and if the supported living model gains the endorsement of Canadian citizens, courts, and lawmakers, we could experience great change and increased inclusion on a grand scale.

Weblinks

ACCESSIBILITY GUIDE OF CANLEARN
http://canlearn.ca/English/learn/newaccessguide/index.shtml

CONNECTING CANADIANS—PERSONS WITH DISABILITIES' GUIDE
http://www.connect.cg.ca/en/930-e.htm

NATIONAL SCHOLARSHIPS AND GRANTS FOR POST-SECONDARY STUDENTS WITH DISABILITIES
http://canlearn.ca/english/learn/newaccessguide/scholarships.shtml

Summary

Developing independence for learning and for living is an important goal for every exceptional student. Recent curricula have focused on personal development, interpersonal development, and career development. Personal development includes acquiring strategies to be an independent learner, negotiating transitions, and using computers and, if necessary, assistive devices to maximize independence. Interpersonal development refers to a student's ongoing growth in relating to others. Examples include responding with courage and controlling one's anger. Career development includes growth that enables one to assume the various roles associated with maturing and adulthood, including understanding and participating in the world of work. Usually students take part in career exploration and career experience as ways of coming to understand themselves, to become a self-advocate and to be more self-determined. There are a number of approaches to independent living, and which approach is more appropriate to the adult years of an exceptional individual may depend on the nature and severity of the exceptionality, the context within which the individual lives, and the community, which may encourage participation or provide support. There has been a great deal of change in the way exceptional individuals live and learn in the past decade and we can only expect continuing change in the next decade. ■

Key Terms

career (p. 287)

career development (p. 287)

learning strategies (p. 287)

model strategy use (p. 288)

guided practice (p. 288)

independent practice (p. 289)

feedback (p. 289)

transition (p. 290)

assistive technology (p. 293)

self-awareness (p. 302)

career exploration (p. 303)

labour market information (p. 305)

self-advocacy (p. 306)

self-determination (p. 307)

cooperative education (p. 308)

workplace experience (p. 308)

Conclusion

Thriving as a Teacher

> My first day of teaching finally arrived and I embarked on a completely foreign adventure...I was scared, excited, and (in hindsight) idealistic. The truth is I continue to operate with this mixed bag of emotions, but underneath it all, I love it!
>
> Christa Armstrong (1997, p. 67)

You may be wondering after reading about all the challenges involved in including exceptional students in your classroom whether a teaching career is really for you. This is a good question to ask. Every day somewhere in Canada, a teacher or intending teacher asks this question. However, remember that intending stockbrokers, physicians, and electricians also ask themselves whether they have chosen the right career. I believe that this can be a good thing—for these individuals and for these careers—that people ask hard questions about the choices they have made. As you will see, this question can also signal that teachers have some problem solving ahead in order to thrive in their work.

Succeeding as a Beginning Teacher

You will have already noticed that this conclusion is not about exceptional children and adolescents. This chapter is about you. It is about how you can thrive as a teacher. Teachers enter the profession with high expectations, a vision of the future, and a mission to educate children and adolescents. Years of research, including studies by Alan King (e.g., King, Warren, & Peart, 1988) of Queen's University, suggest that effective and rewarding teaching is most apt to be accomplished by optimistic and self-confident teachers. One study focused on teachers who were successful in their beginning years and seemed to be particularly high in self-confidence and energy levels. All these teachers had a number of characteristics in common, including deep commitment to teaching, genuine caring for students, and the goals to become better teachers and to learn more (Dillon-Peterson, 1982). Other research has found that beginning teachers needed both a positive outlook and the support of their colleagues and administrators to succeed (Mani, 1989).

Teachers who have a greater belief in their ability to teach have been found to be more likely to: (a) try different ways of teaching; (b) be business-like by being organized in their teaching and fair and firm in their dealings with students; and (c) be enthusiastic about teaching. Those high in the belief that students benefit from school experiences were also high in confidence and enthusiasm about teaching (Allinder, 1994). The picture that emerges suggests that some personal characteristics, such as commitment, self-confidence, and a positive outlook, may contribute to thriving in teaching. These are things over which you have some control. As well, some aspects of the teaching environment, such as colleague and administrator support, over which you exert less control, may also be critical, especially in the early years. Figure C-1 was prepared by an early career teacher at the conclusion of her first year teaching secondary French and English.

Figure C-1

SURVIVAL SKILLS FOR THE FIRST-YEAR TEACHER

- Find a mentor—a department head or an experienced teacher—who can offer another perspective on the daily dilemmas you face.

- Find a friend —a new teacher like yourself—so you can support one another and talk out your problems and potential solutions.

- Meet resource teachers and guidance staff—as soon as you arrive at your school, learn about the available resources.

- Don't be afraid to borrow resources—replenish the department files or your colleagues' files with your own creations.

- Make a "sick day" plan—include lesson plans, the required materials, class seating plan, attendance list, and instructions, just in case.

- Keep lines of communication open with parents.

- Maintain a page for each student—document telephone calls made to parents, calls received, conversations with resource personnel, behaviour observation notes, etc.

- Maintain (or ask designated students to maintain) a logbook of each day's lesson and copies of extra handouts so that absent students can be responsible for finding and catching up on missed work.

- Before you start teaching, set your policy on washroom breaks, late assignments, attendance, truancy, lates, your behaviour plan, methods for getting the students' attention, etc. Discuss these with a mentor so that your policies are consistent with the school's code of behaviour, and adapt them as required as the year progresses.

- Remember that you need time to develop all the creative activities that make your classes exciting and rewarding to teach. Develop a manageable number each week (e.g., one or two), borrow when necessary, and accept that some ideas will have to wait until the next time you teach this unit.

- Take off Friday night and at least one full day on the weekend to recharge for the next week.

—
Prepared by Nicole Lévesque, a classroom teacher in Barrie, Ontario. Used by permission.

Teachers cite many rewarding aspects of their work that contribute to their positive outlook. In an Ontario study, teachers reported that the three most satisfying aspects of teaching involved their relationships with their students. These were: (a) experiencing good rapport and relationships with young people; (b) recognizing students suddenly understanding or enjoying their lessons; (c) seeing student success, achievement, and satisfaction. These rewards of teaching reflect the reasons that many teachers give for choosing their profession: "I enjoy children" and "I love history and really want to pass my love of learning on to others." The next most frequently mentioned reward was interacting with and receiving support from colleagues (King et al., 1988).

I encourage you to consider what you need to thrive as an educator. When you listen to experienced teachers who thrive on teaching, what do you hear? The following are all excerpts from interviews with Canadian teachers (King & Peart, 1992)—people who strive to be members of a vibrant community by working closely with colleagues, joining associations, taking on new challenges, and taking care of themselves.

> The most helpful thing is when I go and visit teachers in my field. I think teachers should be encouraged to visit teachers.
>
> *Male teacher, 49 years old, grades 7–12, Alberta (p. 35)*

> It helps to have a supportive family…to go home and talk about things other than teaching.
>
> *Female teacher, 24 years of experience, grade 3, Manitoba (p. 126)*

> I fish, I take pictures. I think that one of the keys to being able to last in teaching for a long period of time is to deal with stress. I think you have to have other types of interest outside the school.
>
> *Male teacher, 17 years of experience, grades 9–12, science/ mathematics/health/computer science, Manitoba (p. 126)*

> [I deal with stress by] being proactive and improving the system on the level that I can work at. Being part of the solution. To actively seek new challenges—I am teaching chemistry this year for the first time in my career. There is also my work with staff committee—helping empower teachers.
>
> *Male teacher, 26 years of experience, grades 10–12, geology/chemistry, British Columbia (p. 126)*

> I think it is important that I not necessarily make money at it, but that I keep my musical skills up. So I perform as much as I can without interfering with the rest of my job; I play in a big band and in the symphony orchestra.
>
> *Male teacher, 4 years of experience, grades 9–12, music, British Columbia (p. 143)*

> [I deal with stress by] having a relaxing period and getting lots of sleep…that is one thing I have to do; if I don't get enough sleep, I am a basket case.
>
> *Female teacher, 4 years of experience, grades 9–12/OAC, music, Ontario (p. 126)*

Being a Change Agent

Like many other professions, teaching in the current era is caught in the throes of massive and continual change. Some teachers find themselves looking back rather than looking ahead and fighting a rearguard action to maintain the profession as they have known it (Sikes, 1992). Michael Fullan (1991) of University of Toronto describes how change has been introduced into Canadian schools without regard for the impact it has on teachers' daily lives. Almost all change, even when we embrace the innovation, results in feelings of loss and grief (Marris, 1986). Change also makes teachers feel incompetent (or less competent than when they were doing what they knew well) and creates confusion and conflict. Unless each of these issues is matched with an appropriate response, change is unlikely to succeed (Bolman & Deal, 1991), even when we want to improve our practice.

"Teachers vastly underestimate their power to change things" (Sarason, 1993, p. 6). In a perceptive analysis of what it takes to be a change agent, Donna Patterson (1996) of the University of Regina suggests that teachers focus on self-care, political astuteness, planning, effective conflict resolution, and humour. With these strengths, Patterson demonstrates how teachers can become agents of change in their own classrooms, lead by example, and earn the respect of their colleagues for their ideas. Patterson closes with sage advice for teachers working to make their classrooms inclusive (see Figure C-2).

Handling Stress

Most teachers thrive on the challenges of the profession. However, for others, the rewards of personal satisfaction and sense of accomplishment do not last. Many of these teachers choose to leave the profession and most often cite stress or burnout as the reason. In the past few decades, the helping professions in many countries have experienced this loss of talented and capable members. A report by Bryan Hiebert of the University of Calgary summarized the research on teacher stress in Canada (Hiebert, 1985). Canadian teachers reported a variety of stressors, but referred most often to work overload (or lack of time) and student discipline problems. Across all the studies, representing all parts of the country, the problems usually seemed to involve some form of personal interaction or time management concerns. A review of the research on reasons for teachers leaving the profession suggested that lack of support, especially from administrators, was a major contributor (Brownell & Smith, 1992). Since Hiebert's report in 1985 the pressures on Canadian classroom teachers have, if anything, increased. For one thing, there have been large increases in the diversity of students in Canadian classrooms (Dei, 1996; Edmunds, 1998; McLeod, 1993). Fullan (1991) described the inclusion of exceptional students in regular classrooms as an example of "the misunderstood complexities and multiple components of change" that challenge teachers (p. 41). This is not surprising. As we have seen, inclusion can involve many of the factors that contribute to teaching being rewarding (e.g., satisfaction in seeing students "get it," collaboration with colleagues) or being stressful (increased workload, discipline problems, lack of administrative support).

TIPS FOR CHANGE AGENTS

- If what you desire in the way of change is not immediately forthcoming, take your time.

- Do the best you can, don't stop trying, and don't be afraid to make mistakes. Mistakes are human.

- Remember to take one step at a time and to build in success.

- Recognize and build on your strengths.

- The initial stages of any significant change involve anxiety and uncertainty and/or involve taking a risk.

- Support is crucial.

- Change involves learning new skills through practice and feedback.

- The most significant breakthrough occurs when you understand how the new way will make things better for you.

Source: Donna Patterson (1996). Becoming a change agent in your elementary classroom, in J. Andrews (ed.), *Teaching Students with Diverse Needs: Elementary Classrooms*, pp. 31–32, Scarborough: ITP Nelson Canada. Reprinted with permission.

Hiebert (1985) also reported that the studies showed that Canadian teachers did not have a large repertoire of strategies aimed specifically at coping with stress. What is stress, and how can you, as a beginning teacher, cope well with this challenge? Much has been written about stress, and there have been many definitions. Historically, stress has been conceptualized in three ways: as an event or stimulus in the environment (e.g., a defiant student), as an individual response (e.g., tension headaches), or as an interaction between the person and the environment. Most modern writers take the interactionist perspective. The best-known author on the subject of stress is probably Hans Selye (1956, 1974). He focused on the intensity of the need for a person to adapt to a demand and wrote about positive stress (eustress that comes from adapting and meeting challenges) and negative stress (distress that occurs when our coping mechanisms are overwhelmed by the challenges).

While we may not find it easy to define stress, we can probably all think of examples from our personal experiences as a teacher. Listen to Maria describe to her support group what she found when she returned to her grade 5 class after recess on the afternoon of October 19:

> I am soooo frustrated. I was late getting to my room yesterday because I had separated four students who were fighting on the playground. I felt my blood pressure soar when I yelled at them, avoided taking any random punches, and led them to the principal's office—only to find the office empty. I couldn't leave them alone, on the verge of tearing each other apart, could I? So I worried about the fights that might be breaking out in my class. And fretted that someone might pick on Josh, who has childhood rheumatoid arthritis and is frail and vulnerable. After what

seemed like an eternity, the principal's secretary came strolling down the hall. When I asked her where the principal was, she laughed and pointed toward my room. How could I have forgotten? He was in my room waiting to observe me teaching. In the excitement, it had slipped my mind completely. All I could think of then was, 'What an idiot he will think I am! I knew I should have asked someone to switch recess duty with me. Why did no one volunteer? They knew I had an observation.' By then I was angry with the whole staff! I was so nervous that my hands were wet, my throat was dry, and my mind was blank. I always feel inadequate when I am evaluated. Especially when it is the first evaluation—I can't seem to stay calm, even though I have taught for five years. I asked myself, 'What was the lesson I planned to teach?' I had to look in my daybook to jog my memory; the lesson involved a complex explanation, hands-on practice, and follow-up written practice in adding fractions. Why did I not choose something simpler? I must have been trying to show off and impress him with my up-to-date methods. What I did was fumbled my way through the explanation, forgot to do the hands-on activity, and had to explain the written activity about a thousand times. To almost every student individually. By the time my principal left, my stomach was almost sick. I dread receiving the evaluation. Even I think I should be fired.

Maria went on to explain to the members of her group that she had moved to this downtown school in September when her partner was transferred to the city from a small town. She found that the teachers were not as friendly as in her previous school and the children fought all the time on the playground, "like gang warfare." Maria's husband was rarely home because he was learning a new job, and her preschool children hated the new daycare, begging every morning to go to Sue's, the home of their previous child minder. To finish her story, Maria added with emphasis, "I'm so stressed!"

Few of us would disagree with Maria's assessment of the situation. This sounds like a case of many threats that together exceed Maria's coping strategies. However, there was reason to be optimistic. To begin to take control of the situation, Maria had called the number on the poster the first day it was tacked on the bulletin board in the staff room. The poster said:

Feel stressed? Need support?

New group starting September 30 at Eastside Teachers' Centre.

Call today!

That is how Maria came to be telling eight strangers about her most frustrating day at work.

Focusing on Your Well-Being

Recently, researchers have studied the stress of large numbers of teachers in Britain and North America. They suggest that stress is triggered and sustained by the cognitive processes we choose to use when we perceive a threat, is affected by the emotions we experience, and affects our health (Gold & Roth, 1993; Vandenberghe & Huberman, 1999). This means that stress affects all our being. We make decisions about how we will cope with a threat; when our coping mechanisms are successful, distress is minimized and we may even feel a positive type of stress, sometimes called eustress. However, when our coping mechanisms are not adequate, we experience negative emotions and feel threatened and our immune system is affected, which may result in illness. While this all sounds menacing, there are many suggestions to assist teachers in handling their stressors and in learning new coping mechanisms (see Figure C-3).

In the *Professional Health* program (Gold & Roth, 1993), problem solving is the focus and personal and professional needs are the content. Teachers are urged to go beyond stress management and focus on their underlying problems and needs. While we all need skills to survive the immediate challenges, we may also need psychological support to grow over the long term and develop professional health. Otherwise, we could be continuously engaged in stress management when what we need is to gain self-control. Maria found that her teacher support group helped her become aware of the factors that were causing difficulties and getting in the way of her teaching. Through the activities of the group, she recognized her feelings, her stressors, and her own abilities to deal with them in effective ways. She realized how much she wanted to be respected by all her students, and how much she had needed to belong to a group of teachers that she could talk to for support. Gold and Roth report that teachers begin to withdraw after they feel isolated from their colleagues. Visit other teachers' classrooms, arrange exchanges, join the local association of science teachers, or find a support group, like Maria did.

Teachers are sometimes surprised to learn that they need to keep mentally active to deal with stress. While teaching offers the promise of intellectual stimulation, it is easy for us to become buried in paperwork and spend the evenings marking, rather than reading about innovative teaching approaches or attending stimulating

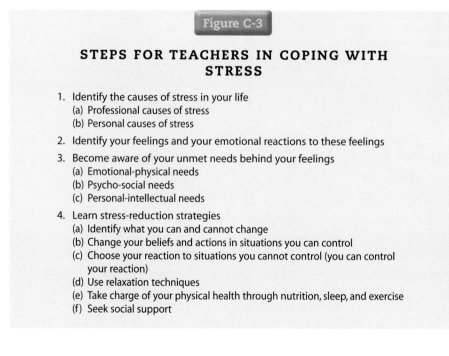

Figure C-3

STEPS FOR TEACHERS IN COPING WITH STRESS

1. Identify the causes of stress in your life
   (a) Professional causes of stress
   (b) Personal causes of stress

2. Identify your feelings and your emotional reactions to these feelings

3. Become aware of your unmet needs behind your feelings
   (a) Emotional-physical needs
   (b) Psycho-social needs
   (c) Personal-intellectual needs

4. Learn stress-reduction strategies
   (a) Identify what you can and cannot change
   (b) Change your beliefs and actions in situations you can control
   (c) Choose your reaction to situations you cannot control (you can control your reaction)
   (d) Use relaxation techniques
   (e) Take charge of your physical health through nutrition, sleep, and exercise
   (f) Seek social support

cultural events. However, discovering new ideas and learning innovative techniques contribute to our personal-intellectual needs. For example, Gold and Roth (1993) encourage teachers to embrace intellectual challenges so they can thrive at work: enrol in professional development or graduate courses, take out a subscription to a concert series, or learn to weave. Rena Upitis, dean of education at Queen's University from 1995 to 2000, always advised teacher candidates and colleagues to learn something new every school year. In recent years, her own projects have included learning to skate, learning to weave, and learning to weld. She argues that not only is this intellectually stimulating but it also allows teachers to become novices and renew empathy for their students who are not experts in everything that is taught in the classroom.

The Last Word

This book has been about teaching and including exceptional children in our classrooms—so they may take their places in Canadian society. This conclusion is about teachers who thrive on challenge, change children's lives, and are never forgotten. This is the kind of teacher many of us aspire to be—a teacher who touches the lives of children or adolescents and who leaves a mark. When I read the obituary reprinted in Figure C-4 in the Globe and Mail on August 3, 1999, I wished I had known Benny Sheardown, and I decided to give him the last word.

Figure C-4

LIFE STORY: HELPED HUNDREDS OF YOUNGSTERS

Benny Sheardown: Father, husband, guidance counsellor, athlete. Born in Whitehorse in 1944. Died of cancer in Calgary aged 55. Cathy Sheardown wasn't surprised by the number of people who paid tribute to her late husband Ben. It was the tenor of it all that caught her off-guard.

More than 1,000 people attended the guidance counsellor's memorial service in Whitehorse, and Ms. Sheardown could easily decorate a huge wall with cards and letters from admirers and friends from all over the Yukon and well beyond its borders. "They feel that he was really there when nobody else could be or cared to be. He felt everybody deserved a second, third and fourth chance depending on the story," said Ms. Sheardown.

Benjamin Clarke Sheardown was born in the Yukon, spent his life there and affected the lives of many, especially young people to whom he devoted so much time. After graduating from the University of Alaska in Fairbanks, the father of two returned to the Yukon and became a gym teacher in 1972. Later on, as a guidance counsellor, he heard more than a few stories of broken homes and suicidal youth.

"He affected a ton of people in different ways, never, ever taking the credit and letting [the kids] almost believe it was their idea," said Ms. Sheardown.

After his death, local newspapers ran letters to the editor from as far away as Mexico City, from people who credited him with shaping their lives, and, in some cases, saving their lives. "I'm getting numerous cards in the mail that start out, 'You don't know me but …' and they're telling me, 'If it wasn't for Mr. Sheardown I would never have become who I am or never been able to do what I've done, I certainly wouldn't have gone through school,'" said Ms. Sheardown.

Last year, Mr. Sheardown was inducted into the Yukon Sports Hall of Fame. It was an award he almost refused to accept, thinking it was out of pity for a man with a terminal illness. But after talking to family and friends, he concluded that the award was as much a tribute to those who helped him accomplish great things in his lifetime as it was to him. A planned sports multiplex in Whitehorse might even be named after him. He always pursued a healthy lifestyle. He played hockey (helping the Yukon to win gold in the Arctic Winter Games in 1972) and basketball. He also took part in running, biking, swimming and Nordic skiing. In winter, he was often seen riding his bike or taking his dog Tacumsa on long walks through downtown trails. On the front of his memorial-service pamphlet, he's photographed with Tacumsa in the shadow of a hilltop called the King's Throne near Kathleen Lake, a pristine area on the cusp of Kluane National Park. He's wearing mis-matched cross-country skis and, according to a childhood friend, couldn't care less.

Jim Perry knew Mr. Sheardown from the age of 10, when he moved to Whitehorse from Ireland. "He took me under his wing. He reached out to this little immigrant boy and we became lifelong friends," said Mr. Perry, who made the trip from Abbotsford, BC, to Whitehorse to speak at the memorial service. "This memorial was a true indication of the kind of support and the number of lives he touched. Ben left a huge footprint on many hearts." Mr. Perry said he always lived life fully and brought the best out of other people.

—

Source: Mario Carlucci (1999). Life story: Helped hundreds of youngsters. *The Globe and Mail*, August 3, p. A17. Reprinted with permission.

Glossary

A

Aboriginal cultures Aboriginal peoples are nations, that is, political and cultural groups with values and lifeways distinct from those of other Canadians.

Aboriginal elders The senior members of an Aboriginal community who are respected and looked to for wisdom.

Aboriginal languages There were 12 language families and about 50 languages when the Europeans arrived in Canada; only about 15 of those are currently in vigorous use.

academic tasks as punishment The practice of assigning students additional homework or lines to write as a punishment.

acceleration An approach for educating gifted students that allows them to move through the curriculum in an area of strength at an accelerated pace or to work at the next grade level.

ADAPT A systematic strategy for adapting teaching to include exceptional learners consisting of five steps: Accounts of students' strengths and needs; Demands of the classroom; Adaptations; Perspectives and consequences; Teach and assess the match.

adapted program An exceptional student's program that retains the learning outcomes of the prescribed curriculum but provides adaptations so the student can participate, including alternate formats, instructional strategies, and assessment procedures.

adaptive skills Areas of participation in the life of the community in which individuals with development disabilities may be delayed: communication, home living, community use, health and safety, leisure, self-care, social skills, self-direction, functional academics, work.

additional practice Providing more opportunities for exceptional learners to practise what has been taught and to develop full understanding of ideas, procedures, etc.

advocate A person who represents or champions the cause of another.

aggression Bold, direct action that is intended to hurt someone else or take property; unprovoked attack.

AIDS (Acquired Immune Deficiency Syndrome) A disease in which there is severe loss of cellular immunity.

allergen-free alternative Refers to the practice of creating an alternative activity or snack that is safe for students with allergies so they can participate in class activities and excursions.

allergic salute Children pushing up on a runny nose; a symptom of allergies.

allergy An abnormal reaction to a normal substance (e.g., peanuts).

American Sign Language (ASL) A manual language system that has its own rule-governed syntactic system.

amniocentesis A test of the fluid surrounding a fetus to check for many kinds of abnormalities.

amplification The process of enhancing sound, usually through the use of hearing aids or FM (frequency modulation) systems.

ANA-KIT® Brand name of an easily administered form of adrenalin often carried by children who have allergies and suffer anaphylactic reactions.

anaphylactic shock See *anaphylaxis*.

anaphylaxis A sudden, severe allergic reaction that causes breathing difficulties; death can occur within minutes unless an injection is administered.

antidepressants Medications for managing attention deficit/hyperactivity disorder.

anti-racist education A program that assumes that existing policies and practices are racist in their impact if not in their intent; provides teachers and students with the knowledge and skills to identify and challenge racism.

applied stream A secondary school program intended to prepare adolescents for entering the workforce rather than for formal post-secondary education.

articulation Word and sound production.

Asperger syndrome Severe and sustained impairment in social interaction with restricted, repetitive patterns of behaviour, interests, and activities, with no significant delays in language acquisition or cognitive development.

assessment Data collection, gathering information of many kinds about a student or a group of students, using a variety of tools and techniques.

assistive technology An item, piece of equipment, or product system that is used to maintain or improve the functional capabilities of individuals with disabilities.

asthma Obstructed airways that hinder the flow of air in and out of the lungs; an attack is characterized by persistent wheezing, tightness in the chest, and excess phlegm, and can be life threatening.

at risk More likely to develop special needs due to poverty and other social conditions, including sexual and physical abuse, exposure to drugs, etc.

attention deficit/hyperactivity disorder (AD/HD) A persistent pattern of inattention and impulsiveness that may be accompanied by hyperactivity and that hinders social, academic, and vocational expectations.

authentic assessment Assessment on tasks that are engaging, contextualized, and represent those expected in the adult world.

authentic tasks Learning activities close to real-world tasks, usually involving problems that are engaging, contextualized, and represent those expected in the adult world.

autism Limited development in communication and social interaction, and a severe delay in intellectual, emotional, and behavioural development.

B

base groups See *home groups.*

basic stream See *applied stream.*

behaviour ratings Scales on which student behaviour is evaluated for frequency and intensity of symptoms.

behavioural or emotional exceptionalities Usually characterized by dysfunctional relationships at home and/or school and at least one of aggression, negative psychological states, and social problems.

blind Characterized by loss of sight and use of auditory and tactile sources of information to replace sight.

Braille A system of raised dots that can be read by touch by persons who are blind.

bullying A pattern of actions that involves an imbalance of power, a victim who is upset, and a bully who is cool and in control and who shows a lack of compassion; can take many forms, including physical, emotional, and verbal.

bypass strategies Teaching and learning approaches that allow students to gain access to, practise, or demonstrate learning of the curriculum in alternative ways.

C

cancer A malignant tumour or growth of body cells.

career Progress through life and through the roles appropriate to various ages as well as the process of making a living by means of a particular occupation.

career development Growing understanding of changing roles and responsibilities, including adult responsibilities, roles, and the nature and meaning of work.

career exploration Actions undertaken deliberately or for their own sake that teach about possible careers and adult roles.

carrel A private space for working, which can be a booth made out of wood or from a cardboard crate that once held a large appliance.

case coordinator Person responsible for ensuring that the various services required by an exceptional student are coordinated; sometimes parents assume this role.

catch 'em being good A strategy developed many years ago in which teachers monitor students and acknowledge and reward behaviour that is consistent with expectations.

CCTV Closed circuit television system consisting of a digital camera and display so that anything placed in front of the camera is magnified on the display to allow visually impaired people to see things that are far away, such as a demonstration at the front of a classroom, or read a book or look at a photograph.

cerebral palsy (CP) A group of disorders impairing body movement and muscle coordination as a result of an interference in messages between the brain and the body.

changing grading criteria Varying grading weights so exceptional students are not disadvantaged by an impossible task; for example, students who are hard of hearing do not have part of their grade determined by their inability to hear during pop quizzes.

Charter of Rights and Freedoms Legislation that protects the rights of all Canadians and, in particular, Canadians who are members of minority groups, including people with disabilities.

checkpoints Checklists for students to complete at quarter- and halfway points of long-term assignments to show progress and receive feedback.

child abuse Physical abuse (use of force on a child's body), emotional abuse (persistent attacks on a child's sense of self), and sexual abuse (any sexual exploitation) by an adult or another child, and neglect of a child by parent or caregiver.

chromosomal abnormalities Chromosomes contain genes with the chemical codes that direct cell function; aberrant chromosomes are those with abnormal numbers or structures.

chronic health condition A qualified medical practitioner has certified that a student requires medical procedures, excluding administration of medication only, to ensure the health and safety of the student while in school or requires ongoing special education interventions due to the student's limited school attendance or because the condition adversely affects the student's educational performance.

chronic health impairment See *chronic health condition.*

chronic medical disorder See *chronic health condition.*

chunking strategies Ways of grouping information; used for remembering important lists.

classroom assessment Day-to-day practices adopted by teachers to describe student learning through portfolios, conferences with students, paper and pencil tests, etc.

classroom procedures Efficient ways of moving all members of a class through the day or the period that are consistent with the teacher's goals and follow from the rules (e.g., transitions and distribution of materials).

climate The general feeling created in a classroom; positive classroom climate usually is thought to develop when people treat each other with respect.

code of conduct Brief guidelines that clearly identify school rules and acceptable student behaviours and contain consequences.

cognitive abilities Processes and knowledge, including vocabulary, verbal fluency, retention, generalizing, making abstractions, organizing, and planning.

cognitive-behaviour management (CBM) Programs that teach students how to use cognition to control their own behaviour by using self-talk and self-instruction.

cognitive complexity The cognitive demands made of the learner by teaching and learning in the classroom.

cognitive strategies Plans and processes designed to accomplish learning or solve problems.

collaboration Teachers and other professionals learning from each other's experiences and working in teams where all members feel that their contributions are valued.

collaborative learning Teaching approaches that include cooperative learning and problem solving in pairs and groups and that usually involve student groups of varying abilities and skills, that is, heterogeneous groupings.

colour-coded A cueing system to enhance the organizational skills of exceptional students by consistently using colours for particular kinds of information.

community A group of people who have shared interests and who mutually pursue the common good.

community agreements Four guidelines for students to use in developing a sense of community in the classroom: attentive listening, appreciation/no put-downs, the right to pass when given an opportunity to speak, and mutual respect (*Tribes*, Gibbs, 1995).

community-based Education that focuses on relating what is learned in school to what occurs in the community; often learning takes place in the community as well as in the school.

community circle The gathering of all students in a class in a large circle where each student is given an opportunity to present himself or herself in a structured way and to reflect on what is happening in his or her world (*Tribes*, Gibbs, 1995).

components of an IEP The seven sections that usually comprise an IEP are present level of functioning, long-term goals, short-term goals, instructional strategies and materials, dates for review, identification of participants (including parents) and their responsibilities, and evaluation procedures.

computation Mathematical skill and understanding in using the four basic operations to combine numbers.

concept maps Graphic organizers that show relationships among concepts as well as essential characteristics of the concepts.

Connections In the ICE model of learning and assessment, the links or relationships that students make among the Ideas, and to the relationships that students establish between new learning and prior learning.

consistency In classroom management, maintaining the same expectations from day to day and applying the same consequences when students fail to meet expectations while honouring adaptations for exceptional students.

contract A behaviour management technique involving a written agreement that states what the teacher and the student agree to do, and specifies the positive rewards and the consequences for failing to live up to the agreement.

contraindications Existing conditions that suggest one cannot take a medication safely.

cooperative education (co-op) Involves students in extended periods of time in a workplace (often around 100 hours over a school term) while enrolled in full-time study as well as in classroom orientations to the workplace and reflective seminars.

cooperative learning A teaching approach that involves students in learning with peers in small groups, taking roles, and working interdependently.

corporal punishment Punishing a student for misbehaving by striking the student or threatening to strike the student.

creativity Demonstrated by students' contributing ideas, transforming and combining ideas, asking questions, and being curious.

credit/no credit See *pass/fail*.

criterion-referenced Data in which a student's work is compared to expected outcomes.

Crohn's disease A chronic inflammatory disease of the intestines.

cueing A method of directing students' attention to specific aspects of the learning environment.

cultural awareness Sensitivity when one makes the effort to become aware and respectful of the beliefs, values, and lives of members of other cultural groups.

cultural relevance Refers to curriculum that represents the cultures and experiences of the students being taught and makes them feel they are at the centre of the society rather than on its margins.

culturally diverse backgrounds Used to refer to students who are not from the majority Anglo-European culture.

culturally relevant curriculum Curriculum in which students see themselves and their cultural group represented in a respectful way that shows their role in Canadian society, history, etc.

cystic fibrosis (CF) Increasingly severe respiratory problems and extreme difficulty in digesting nutrients from food.

D

dates for review On an IEP, these are usually set for the end of the school year in which the IEP is established or renewed.

deaf Characterized by hearing loss that interferes with the acquisition and maintenance of the auditory skills necessary to develop speech and oral language and causes one to use visual sources of information to replace hearing.

deaf community Many deaf adults describe themselves as a cultural minority and use the term *deaf* to designate cultural group membership; the common language is American Sign Language (ASL).

depression A pervasive mood of unhappiness accompanied by long-term difficulties sleeping, feelings of worthlessness, and inability to experience pleasure.

developmental disabilities The development of cognitive abilities and adaptive behaviours at a much slower rate than normal, which results in significant limitations in these areas at mild and severe levels.

developmentally advanced See *gifted*.

diabetes A condition of the pancreas that fails to produce a sufficient amount of the hormone insulin required for proper sugar absorption in the body and may place restrictions on physical activity.

diabetes emergency kits A ration package containing juice, raisins, or dextrose, often carried by an individual with diabetes and sometimes kept in a central location in a school to be used by students with diabetes in an emergency.

disability Defined by the World Health Organization as the nature and extent of limitations to function (e.g., performing the activities required to read) resulting from impairment.

(dis)ability awareness programs Programs developed to foster greater understanding of people with disabilities, to increase students' knowledge about specific disabilities, and to increase students' sensitivity toward individuals with disabilities.

discipline code See *code of conduct*.

discrepancy A controversial method of identifying a learning disability by establishing a difference between ability (usually measured by an intelligence test) and achievement in one or more of the following areas: reading, writing, language acquisition, mathematics, reasoning, or listening.

diversity Variation in culture, ability, and values that characterizes modern Canadian society.

domains Areas of expertise or disciplines within education such as mathematics, science, and literature.

Down syndrome A genetic defect causing limitations in physical and cognitive development; physically, children with Down syndrome have low muscle tone and a generalized looseness of the ligaments.

Duchenne muscular dystrophy (DMD) A musculoskeletal condition with marked physical degeneration that occurs during the school years.

dyscalculia Learning disabilities in arithmetic, especially calculations.

dysgraphia Learning disabilities in writing.

dyslexia Learning disabilities in reading.

E

echolalia Speech that is an immediate imitation of that of some other speaker.

enforcing a rule In teaching classroom rules, enforcement usually follows demonstration and practice and refers to the follow-up and feedback provided by teachers to commend students when they follow the rules and to ensure that consequences are applied when students fail to follow the rules.

engagement The extent to which students embrace learning and throw themselves into the activities of the classroom.

English as a second language (ESL) Students who have learned a language other than English as their first language and must acquire English as a second language, often in the context of school; programs designed to teach English to these students.

enlarged print The practice of increasing the print size for students with vision impairment, usually to 130 percent on a photocopier or 18 font on a computer.

environment Context of learning, composed of both classroom climate and physical layout.

enzyme supplements Medication taken by a person with cystic fibrosis before a meal or snack to replace pancreatic enzymes that the body does not produce and that are essential to digestion.

epilepsy A neurological disorder that occasionally produces brief disturbances in normal electrical functions of the brain that lead to sudden, brief seizures that vary in nature and intensity from person to person.

epinephrine Adrenalin; administered in the event of an anaphylactic allergic reaction; can be life saving.

EPIPEN® Brand name of an easily administered form of adrenalin often carried by children who have allergies and anaphylactic reactions.

equal participation The United Nations (1993) *Standard Rules on the Equalization of Opportunities for Persons with Disabilities* targeted eight areas for equal participation in the local community, including education, health, employment, and social services.

equality rights In Canada, the equality rights that apply to education are contained in section 15(1) of the Charter: "Every individual is equal before and under the law and has a right to the equal protection and equal benefit of the law without discrimination based on race, national or ethnic origin, colour, religion, sex, age, or mental or physical disability."

equipment On an IEP, this usually includes tape recorders, wheelchairs, computers, and other technological devices used by an exceptional student to enhance learning.

equity Equity education means tailoring teaching to challenge inequities and discrimination.

evaluation Making decisions based on the assessment data that have been gathered about a student or group of students; on an IEP, this refers to procedures the in-school team will use to demonstrate accountability by showing that the student is making reasonable progress.

exceptional students Learners who are gifted as well as students with disabilities; used interchangeably with terms like *students with special needs* to describe students in need of special education programs.

experiential learning Learning by doing includes field trips, role-playing, designing and making, and other forms of learning by doing.

expulsion Permanent removal of a student from the classroom as a consequence of the student behaving inappropriately, violating the code of conduct, etc.

Extensions In the ICE model of learning and assessment, the ways that students internalize learning so it becomes part of their perspective; revealed when students use their learning in novel ways.

F

feedback Specific information for students about what they are doing correctly and incorrectly.

fetal alcohol effects (FAE) Describes individuals with a documented history of prenatal alcohol exposure and the presence of some, but not all, of the other diagnostic criteria for fetal alcohol syndrome.

fetal alcohol syndrome (FAS) Physical and physiological abnormalities due to prenatal exposure to alcohol causing delays in development, central nervous dysfunction, and a characteristic pattern of facial features, and learning problems.

form of practice Allowing students to engage in oral or written practice or another form of practice that advances their learning; can be ADAPTed for exceptional students.

formal assessment Assessment using standardized tests; these could include an intelligence test, behaviour observation checklists, vision, hearing or language assessments, and medical tests.

formal groups In collaborative learning, groupings of students assembled, with attention to group composition, to work together for a period of time, for example, throughout a unit.

frequency modulation (FM) systems With a classroom FM system, the carrier wave is transmitted through the air by frequency modulation from a teacher-worn microphone to a student-worn FM receiver; students with hearing impairments can hear the teacher clearly from any location in the classroom.

friendships Close relationships characterized by reciprocity, that is, give and take, and by commitment between individuals who see themselves as equals.

functional curriculum Outcomes for a student are based on life skills such as shopping, banking, and cooking.

G

generalized seizures Epileptic seizures that involve the whole brain.

genetic screening Identification of the risk of a couple having a child with a condition caused by chromosomal abnormalities.

gifted Exceptionally high abilities in one or several areas, including specific academic subjects, overall intellect, leadership, creativity, or the arts.

give-and-take dialogues Problem-solving discussions in which all students feel they can advance ideas, be heard, comment on others' ideas, and feel that the classroom is a safe place.

good behaviour game A strategy for reducing disruptive behaviour and promoting positive behaviour in the classroom in which students work on teams to earn points for appropriate behaviour toward a reward.

grading Symbolic representation of evaluation or judgments based on assessment data, often in the form of letter grades, percentages, or performance levels.

grading contract An agreement between teacher and student on the basis for awarding a grade; may include giving exceptional students credit for attendance, promptness, effort, and cooperative behaviour.

grouping The practice of deliberately placing students in learning or working groups; used extensively in cooperative and collaborative learning approaches.

guided practice Scaffolded practice in which students are prompted to use each step of a strategy; enables exceptional students to learn the strategy.

H

handicap Defined by the World Health Organization as the nature and extent of restrictions on participation (e.g., being employed) that result from impairment and disability.

harassment Communication in any form (e.g., verbal or physical abuse, jokes, slurs, graffiti) that expresses negative attitudes, beliefs, or actions toward an individual or group with the intention of hurting that person or group.

hard of hearing Partial hearing loss that interferes with the acquisition and maintenance of the auditory skills necessary to develop speech and oral language; use visual sources of information to supplement or replace hearing.

head injury See *traumatic brain injury (TBI)*.

hearing aids Systems that amplify all sounds, worn in the ear.

hearing status Description of one's ability to hear; used to describe the parents of children who are deaf.

heart disease In children, most often refers to a congenital defect; these range widely in severity and outcome from few symptoms to totally incapacitating.

hemophilia A hereditary bleeding disorder in which there is a deficiency of a clotting factor.

heritage language The language of one's ancestors; heritage language programs help children learn and maintain their parents' first language.

high blood sugar (hyperglycemia) An abnormally high amount of sugar in the bloodstream; usually associated with diabetes.

high-incidence exceptionalities Frequently occurring exceptionalities, including giftedness, learning disabilities, attention deficit/hyperactivity disorder, communication exceptionalities, behaviour exceptionalities, and mild developmental disabilities.

high-interest low-vocabulary books Written materials designed to interest and engage students while using simple vocabulary and uncomplicated sentence structures.

holding pattern A strategy teachers use when they have a misbehaving student wait (in the office, at the side of the classroom, immediately outside the door) until the teacher is available to meet and talk with the student.

home groups In collaborative learning, these groupings of students serve as small, long-term support groups; may be the groups of peers who sit together at the beginning of each class.

homeless Those who have experienced the loss of their home are often thrust away from community, friends, and support systems and living in hostels or on the street.

homophobia Discrimination against people who are gay or lesbian that often takes the form of taunts, ridicule, and physical assaults.

hundreds chart A chart containing the numbers from 1 to 100 or 0 to 99 in rows and columns; used to help students learn the meaning of place value and relationships among numbers.

hydrocephalus A condition characterized by an excessive accumulation of cerebrospinal fluid in the brain due to an obstruction of its flow.

hyperactivity Characterized by fidgeting, squirming, moving constantly, talking excessively, and finding it challenging to play or work quietly.

hypersensitivity The tendency to be extremely sensitive to sensory stimuli such as touch and to engage in unusual behaviour to obtain a particular sensory stimulation.

I

ICE model Characterizes learning and assessment as consisting of Ideas, Connections among those Ideas, and Extensions of those Ideas and Connections.

Ideas In the ICE model of learning and assessment, the building blocks of learning include such things as the steps in a process, vocabulary, and facts and definitions in the textbook; most fill-in-the-blank and multiple-choice questions assess at the level of Ideas.

Identification, Placement, and Review Committee (IPRC) In Ontario, this committee, consisting of the teacher, special educators, administrators, and parents, meets to consider whether a child is exceptional and recommends a placement prior to the IEP meeting.

immigrant A person who has come to Canada as a permanent resident from a foreign country.

immune system The mechanism that enables a body to resist infections, toxins, etc., owing to the presence of specific antibodies or sensitized white blood cells.

impairment Defined by the World Health Organization as a loss or abnormality of body structure or of a physiological or psychological function (e.g., loss of vision).

impulsivity Characteristics include blurting out answers before the teacher has finished asking a question, not waiting for one's turn, and interrupting other students.

inattentiveness Characterized by ignoring details, making careless errors, having trouble concentrating and staying on task while working or playing.

inclusion The social value and policy that persons with disabilities are entitled to full participation in all aspects of Canadian society, including education.

inclusive education The value system that holds that all students are entitled to equitable access to learning, achievement, and the pursuit of excellence in all aspects of their education; incorporates basic values that promote participation, friendship, and interaction.

increase students' appropriate behaviour Giving positive attention to the student behaviour one wants to maintain or increase; praising students publicly or privately and providing specific feedback.

independent practice Students practising on their own, choosing, using, and monitoring strategies.

Individual Education Plan (IEP) A written plan developed for an exceptional student that describes the adaptations, modifications, and services to be provided.

Individualized Program Plan (IPP) The form that an IEP takes in some provinces (e.g., Alberta).

inflammation A localized physical condition with heat, swelling, and pain.

informal assessment Testing carried out by the classroom teacher or the resource teacher that provides information about an exceptional student's current level of functioning.

informal conference A behaviour management technique in which a teacher and student meet to define the problem clearly, generate solutions together, and agree on what each will do to implement the solution.

informal groups In collaborative learning, groupings of students put together for a short period of time to complete a particular activity.

information processing The human mind's activity of taking in, storing, and using information.

infusion A process of integrating a theme throughout the curriculum such as teaching about Aboriginal culture in various areas of the curriculum rather than exclusively in a course on native studies.

instructional strategies, materials, and services A section of the IEP that usually describes the adaptations to teaching and modifications to curriculum as well as other efforts made to provide an appropriate education for an exceptional student.

insulin injections Shots, often self-administered, of the pancreatic secretion that transports glucose from the bloodstream to the cells.

integration A term used in the 1970s and 1980s that referred to moving exceptional students from segregated settings into classrooms in the mainstream, with the emphasis on physical integration or placement rather than on learning or participating.

intelligence Ability or abilities to acquire and use knowledge for solving problems and adapting to the world.

interest An affective interaction between students and tasks.

interpersonal competence The abilities needed for friendships, including initiating and sustaining conversation, initiating plans to spend time with friends outside of school, disclosing personal thoughts and empathy, and managing conflict effectively.

"invisible" classroom management Techniques used by teachers to increase students' appropriate behaviour so that they rarely have to draw attention to inappropriate behaviour.

J

jigsaw strategy A collaborative learning approach in which students leave home groups to study in expert groups and later teach what they have learned to their home groups.

juvenile arthritis (JA) A chronic arthritic condition with continuous inflammation of one or more joints, stiffness, pain, and possible involvement of the eyes.

L

labour market information Details about current and projected demand for labour services and about supply of labour services in the economy.

large-scale assessment Nationwide, province-wide, or district-wide efforts to provide information about student achievement, usually by means of paper and pencil tests.

learned helplessness The expectation, based on previous experiences with a lack of control, that all one's efforts will lead to failure.

learning disabilities (LD) Dysfunctions in processing information that may occur in reading (dyslexia), writing, or arithmetic calculations; often defined as a discrepancy between ability and achievement despite average or above-average intelligence.

learning strategies Techniques or principles that enable a student to learn to solve problems, read, communicate, and organize independently.

limited range of motion An inability to move affected limbs and grasp a pencil with swollen fingers that is seen in children with juvenile arthritis, for example.

long-term goals A section of the IEP that usually includes learning goals within the curriculum, independence goals within the community, and career goals for a period of at least a year.

low blood sugar (hypoglycemia) The condition in which there is an abnormally low amount of sugar in the bloodstream; a complication of diabetes.

lower reading level materials Text materials that parallel the required or recommended text but are written at a lower reading level and are more accessible to those reading below grade level.

low-incidence exceptionalities Any of the less common exceptionalities, including severe developmental disabilities, hearing impairment, visual impairments, autism, and Asperger syndrome.

low-key interventions Minimal actions taken by teachers to respond to minor misbehaviours so that the teachers' actions do not disrupt the flow of the class and to de-escalate rather than raise the stakes.

M

mainstreaming A term used in the 1970s and 1980s that referred to moving exceptional students from segregated settings into classrooms in the mainstream when they could meet traditional academic expectations or when those expectations were not relevant.

manipulatives Learning materials children can handle to aid learning, such as counters when adding in arithmetic.

McGill Action Planning System (MAPS) A process of gathering key people in the life of a student with a disability to cooperatively support the individual and plan structured friendships.

MedicAlert® An identification bracelet worn by individuals with medical conditions that can help you make fast decisions in an emergency.

metacognition Knowledge about our own thinking.

method of presentation The means used to communicate information to students, including oral, visual, videotaped demonstration, live demonstration, and hands-on techniques.

mild developmental disabilities Delays in physical, cognitive, language, and social development while passing through the same developmental stages as others, but at a much slower rate; reading comprehension, arithmetic reasoning, and problem solving are likely to be most affected, but there may be lower levels of achievement in all curriculum areas.

mnemonics Impose an order on information to be remembered using poems, rhymes, jingles, funny sayings, or images. For example, to remember the names, in order, of the five largest cities in Canada, use Teachers Make Very Odd Exams, for Toronto, Montreal, Vancouver, Ottawa, and Edmonton.

mode of presentation See *method of presentation*.

model strategy use Explain carefully, by thinking aloud, your thinking patterns, how to decide when to use a strategy, and how to do each step.

modified course syllabus A document, perhaps produced by the IEP team, that states specific learning expectations, grading criteria, and other changes made in a course for an exceptional student.

modified program A student's program that has learning outcomes substantially different from the prescribed curriculum and specifically selected to meet the exceptional student's needs in accordance with the IEP.

monitoring The process of the teacher being alert and responsive to student action as part of classroom management.

multicultural education Creating a classroom in which students' cultures are acknowledged and valued and that reflects the diversity of Canadian society.

muscular dystrophy (MD) A group of muscle disorders characterized by progressive weakness and wasting away of the voluntary muscles that control body movement.

musculoskeletal conditions Chronic health conditions that affect the muscles and the skeleton and that can affect all aspects of a student's life (e.g., muscular dystrophy and juvenile arthritis).

N

narrative text Written expression that is intended to tell a story.

natural consequences Punishment in which a student suffers the logical outcome of a misbehaviour (e.g., a student removing pencil marks from a desk after writing on the desk).

nebulizer An aerosol machine that connects to a mask that fits over the mouth and nose to administer medication to persons with asthma.

needs Areas in which an exceptional student has relatively weak abilities and skills that need to be developed or bypassed in his or her education by drawing on or compensating with areas of relative strength; schools often focus on academic, social/emotional, and behavioural needs in preparing a student's IEP.

negative psychological states Often seen in students with behavioural and emotional exceptionalities; include anxiety, depression, and stress-related disorders.

neglect Omission on the part of parent or caregiver to provide a child the basic necessities such as food, clothing, shelter, adequate supervision, or medical care.

neighbourhood schools A policy of educating exceptional students in regular classrooms in neighbourhood or local schools or at least making these the first placement option considered, in consultation with families.

nervous system impairment Results of damage or dysfunction of the brain or spinal cord that may have occurred before, during, or after birth; examples of exceptionalities are cerebral palsy, spina bifida, epilepsy, Tourette syndrome, brain injury, and fetal alcohol syndrome.

neurological dysfunction See *nervous system impairment*.

normalization The concept that all persons, regardless of disability, should live and learn in environments as close to normal as possible.

norm-referenced Data in which a student's work is compared to the work of other students who are comparable in age or grade.

norms for classroom interaction Expectations and rules about how students will initiate interactions with and respond to one another: effective communication and respectful interaction in conversation and discussion.

number sense Essential sense of what numbers mean, how to compare numbers, and how to see and count quantities in the world around us.

O

open-ended assignment Students are given options for completing an assignment and decide how far to take their learning.

organic cause Physical or physiological basis for a disability.

outcomes Learning that is expected of students, often expressed as short-term and long-term goals.

P

pace The rate of presentation of new information or rate of introduction of new skills.

paraprofessional A non-certified staff member employed to assist certified teachers in carrying out the educational program and care of exceptional students; sometimes called teachers' assistant or educational assistant.

parent–teacher conferences Formal meetings of parents and teachers at regular intervals during the school year and more frequent informal discussions that can build a productive partnership.

Parents as Tutors Program A structured set of workshops in which parents learned how to tutor their children, who ranged from 5 to 11 years of age in a number of subjects, including reading, spelling, and arithmetic (Hendrikse, 1999).

partial seizures Epileptic seizures that involve one area of the brain; there may be strange sensations, possibly accompanied by inappropriate movements such as plucking at clothes or books, smacking the lips, or aimless wandering but without complete consciousness being lost.

Partners Thinking Aloud A collaborative learning activity in which students work in pairs, alternating roles of teacher and learner with the learner thinking aloud and the teacher offering prompts and feedback; can be used for guided practice.

pass/fail A designation to show that students have or have not met the minimum requirements for a unit; based on objective specification of requirements, and aided by the use of qualitative rubrics and checklists.

peer-mediated strategies Classroom instructional approaches in which the pattern of interaction is among students with the teacher serving as facilitator.

peer perspectives The views of classmates on their relationships with children and adolescents with disabilities, in the literature on social relationships of exceptional children.

peer tutoring A teaching approach that involves peers as teaching partners.

performance assessment Assessment that provides opportunities for students to demonstrate directly their ability to combine and use their knowledge, skills, and habits of mind.

perseveration Repeating an activity.

Personal Program Plan (PPP) The form that the IEP takes in some provinces (e.g., Saskatchewan).

pervasive developmental disabilities (PDD) General term used to describe children with chronic and severe conditions that affect every aspect of their development.

phonemic awareness Sensitivity to and explicit awareness of individual sounds that make up words, which demands that children analyze or manipulate the sounds (includes early skills such as recognizing rhyming and later skills such as segmenting the sounds in words and synthesizing the sounds in words).

physical disabilities A range of conditions restricting physical movement or motor abilities as a result of nervous system impairment, musculoskeletal conditions, or chronic medical disorders.

physical space The physical layout and areas of a classroom that can make it inviting, accessible, and efficient (including arrangement of furniture, audiovisual equipment, visual aids, etc.).

portfolio A collection of the student's work in an area showing growth, self-reflection, and achievement.

postreading activities Activities following individual, paired, or group reading of an assigned piece of text; usually include application of what has been read and a review of learning by the teacher.

poverty Insufficient access to the basic goods, services, and opportunities accepted as necessary for a decent standard of living in Canada, as defined by the Canadian Council on Social Development and Statistics Canada.

prenatal exposure to alcohol Maternal use of alcohol during pregnancy.

pre-reading activities Activities that occur prior to individual, paired, or group reading of an assigned piece of text and usually include an introduction to the topic and the vocabulary and a preview of the text by the teacher.

pre-referral intervention Actions taken by a teacher, possibly with the aid of a resource teacher, after the teacher has voiced concerns about a student and before the student has been referred for formal assessment.

present level of functioning A section of the IEP that includes recent test results, observations of the student, medical and school history, and degree of participation in current classes.

preteaching The technique of preparing exceptional students, frequently used with students who are deaf or hard of hearing, by teaching them the vocabulary and concepts prior to introducing new material to the entire class.

preventers Anti-inflammatory drugs taken regularly to prevent and treat inflammation in persons with asthma.

primary disability A term that refers to the disability that is the source of an individual's challenges. See *secondary disability*.

principles of fairness Fairness does not necessarily mean sameness; this can be a difficult concept for young children to understand and for adolescents to accept.

"pro-act" The actions of teachers effective at classroom management who appear to respond to misbehaviour at a moment's notice; they actually anticipate and act almost before the behaviour occurs (Bennett & Smilanich, 1994).

problem-solution-effect A text structure used to organize expository content that emphasizes that the problems encountered might be linked to issues, and that the solutions people generate can have broad effects such as new institutions, new problems, or changes in society.

problem-solving approach A behaviour management technique in which the teacher asks students questions about what they think the problem was, what they did to contribute to the problem, how they can make amends, and how they can prevent the problem from recurring, and then the teacher follows up.

prosocial behaviours Behaviours that exemplify the relations of an individual's emotional needs to the social environment.

psychostimulant medications Drugs used to treat AD/HD, most commonly Ritalin, Dexedrine, and Cylert, that may have side effects.

puffer A small device that delivers medication in a pre-measured amount to persons with asthma; sometimes called an inhaler.

punishment A response or consequence aimed at decreasing the likelihood of an inappropriate behaviour.

Q

qualitative rubrics Descriptions of learning that characterize learning at various levels and provide students with information about the next steps they must tackle in order to improve.

quantitative rubrics Descriptions of learning that identify that students with higher achievement have greater quantities of valued responses such as some of the main ideas, most of the main ideas, or all of the main ideas.

R

reading comprehension Reading skill involving understanding the meaning of what has been read.

reading wars Controversies over the whole language versus phonics emphases in teaching early reading (see Stanovich & Stanovich, 1995).

reciprocal teaching A teaching approach that involves enabling students to teach one another by taking turns leading discussion in small groups; usually the teacher models how to lead the discussion and provides scaffolding for the groups as they begin.

referring teacher A classroom teacher who recognizes that a student may need an adapted or modified program, implements pre-referral interventions, and then refers the student to the in-school team for problem solving and possibly an individual assessment and an IEP.

refugee A person who has left his or her home country and seeks refuge in Canada from war, persecution, or a natural disaster.

reinforcers Consequences that cause a behaviour to increase.

related services On the IEP of an exceptional student, this usually refers to services such as speech therapy, physical therapy, and alternate transportation.

relievers Rescue medications to relax the muscles of the airways and provide quick relief of breathing problems for persons with asthma.

remediation Intensive instruction, to address basic skills in an area in which a student has needs, that can be carried out with an individual or a small group in the classroom or in a resource room.

remission Temporary disappearance of the symptoms of a health condition or disease.

reporting The way in which evaluation results are communicated, including individual student report cards, which can be computer generated or written by teachers.

resilient students Students who have risk factors but do not manifest risk outcomes tend to possess four attributes: social competence, problem-solving skills, autonomy, and a sense of purpose and future.

resource teacher A special educator who supports teachers and exceptional students, usually by consulting with teachers and offering some direct services to exceptional students, either in the classroom or in the resource room; can have many titles, including learning assistance teacher, learning program teacher, tutor, and curriculum resource teacher.

reward systems Teachers give students as a group or as individuals tokens or points in a systematic way for appropriate behaviour or work.

right to pass Students having the right to choose the extent to which they will participate in a group activity that requires sharing personal information; teachers acknowledge a pass by saying, "That is fine," and offer a second chance for those who passed (used in community circle; *Tribes*, Gibbs, 1995).

role models Adults who show youths how to assume the roles expected in adulthood.

Royal Commission on Aboriginal Peoples In 1991, four Aboriginal and three non-Aboriginal commissioners were appointed to investigate Aboriginal issues and advise the federal government; one of their major recommendations was to end assimilation of Aboriginal peoples.

rubrics Descriptions of learning at different levels of development; can be quantitative or qualitative descriptions.

rules Expressions of what can and cannot be done in the classroom that are brief and specific, positively worded, and clearly understood by students.

S

Scaffolded Reading Experience (SRE) Designed for classes with students of varying abilities in reading, it involves teachers in ADAPTing the three steps of prereading, reading, and postreading activities by providing varying degrees of support so all students can learn.

scaffolding Support for learning and problem solving; can be clues, reminders, encouragement, breaking the problem into parts, or anything that enables a student to grow in independence as a learner.

school-based team A team of teachers, specialists, and administrators that problem solves about students experiencing academic or behaviour difficulties and decides whether students should be individually assessed for an IEP.

schoolwide approach A program that is adopted, implemented, and enforced throughout a school; for example, a code of conduct or anti-bullying policy that is applied in every part of the school.

secondary disability Exceptionality that results from living with a primary disability in another aspect of one's life; for example, social skills difficulties that arise from being rejected as a result of having a disability. See *primary disability*.

seizures Brief bursts of electrical activity in the brain.

self-advocacy An individual's ability to effectively communicate, convey, negotiate, or assert his or her own interests, desires, needs, and rights.

self-awareness Knowing about oneself; developing a picture of the kind of person one is.

self-care The personal care activities that maintain hygiene and health.

self-concept Our perceptions about ourselves.

self-determination The abilities, motivation, and volition that enable people to define goals for themselves and to take and sustain the initiative to reach those goals.

self-monitoring A strategy in which students are taught to check whether they have performed targeted behaviours.

self-referenced Data that compare a student's progress to where that student started from, regardless of whether that starting point is ahead of, even with, or behind others in the class; often the most appropriate form of data for students on modified programs.

sense of community A feeling of belonging; for example, for Aboriginal students this can be created in a place where Aboriginal is the norm, not the minority, such as a First Nations Centre in a university.

severe developmental disabilities Includes those previously considered to have moderate, severe, or profound disabilities, spanning a range of abilities from those who can acquire academic skills to those who require assistance with self-care.

sexual harassment Includes put-downs and negative comments made about gender or sexual preference, sexist jokes, and calling someone gay or lesbian.

short-term goals A section of the IEP that usually includes learning outcomes that are steps on the way to long-term goals, and may be goals for a term or half-term.

shunt A mechanism installed to drain the fluid that builds up with hydrocephalus, for reabsorption in individuals with spina bifida.

side effects Unwanted results of medication.

signal The means used by teachers to obtain and maintain the attention of students, including flicking the lights, raising a hand, rhythmic clapping or speaking, or even blowing a whistle in the gymnasium; usually taught to classes at the beginning of term.

simple absence seizure (petit mal) This generalized seizure occurs in children; they stare or daydream for 5 to 15 seconds and there may be small muscle movements in the face, the eyes may roll up or to one side, and the child may be confused about the seconds "missed."

"six-hour handicap" A description of students who lag behind their peers at school but meet the everyday demands of living.

social acceptance The response and evaluation by peers of students' social behaviours, including approving of their behaviours, considering them to be members of the group, and including them in social and learning activities.

social competence See *social development*.

social development The ability to implement developmentally appropriate social behaviours that enhance one's interpersonal relationships without causing harm to anyone.

social problems Risk factors often experienced by students with emotional and behavioural exceptionalities, including delinquency, substance abuse, and neglect.

social relationships Friendships, peer relations, and romantic relationships that change with development; for example, by middle childhood, children choose friends on the basis of personality and interests and friendships become increasingly stable.

social skills difficulties A controversial aspect of learning disabilities, not present in all students with LD; for example, teachers report that *most* students with LD experience social skills difficulties and peers report that *many* have low social status; however, only a *few* children with LD report low social self-concept.

social status A rating of a child's or adolescent's popularity with their classmates, that is, how well they are liked.

social stories Describe a situation from the perspective of a student, direct the student to do the appropriate behaviour, and are in the first person; developed by Gray (1993) for children with autism.

sociometric rating A system of collecting data by asking children to indicate which classmates they would choose as best friends, to play with, etc., and which they would not choose; enables researchers to develop ratings of popularity or social status for individual students.

special education Programs or services designed to accommodate students whose educational needs cannot adequately be met through the use of regular curriculum and services only.

spectrum of autistic disorders Refers to the range of characteristics and degrees of severity displayed by individuals with autism.

speech and language exceptionalities Problems encountered in the oral production of language and/or impairment in the use or comprehension of spoken language that interfere with communication.

speech-activated Describes equipment that responds to the human voice, usually computer equipment used by individuals with visual impairments.

speech-reading The skill of understanding speech by watching the lips and face; sometimes called lip-reading.

spina bifida A condition developed prenatally that disturbs proper development of the vertebrae or spinal cord and results in varying degrees of damage to the spinal cord and nervous system.

stigma A negative stereotype.

story planning sheet Scaffolding to help students create narrative text that includes prompts such as the following: setting, main character, character clues, problem, attempts to solve the problem, and resolution.

strengths Areas in which an exceptional student has relatively strong abilities and skills on which to draw in compensating or learning in areas of relative weakness; schools often focus on academic, social/emotional, and behavioural strengths in preparing a student's IEP.

structure Predictability and organization in learning activities that enables exceptional students to feel safe and focus on learning.

student activity log A summary of student activities that may be particularly beneficial in reporting progress for students on modified programs because it can include a summary of key accomplishments shown in the portfolio or performance-based assessments.

student responsibility Making students share the responsibility for a safe school environment by creating a group of school leaders who directly involve students in setting a positive social tone for the school.

students with special needs See *exceptional students*.

study guide A learning aid that tells students what to study for the test and can enable them to be more efficient in their preparation; includes outlines, abstracts, and questions that emphasize important information in texts.

study skills The actions students take to prepare for tests that usually involve reviewing notes and texts.

suspension Temporary removal of a student from the classroom (for a day or more) as a consequence of the student behaving inappropriately, violating the code of conduct, etc.

T

taped books A technique of reading books onto audiotape so they can be used by persons who are print-disabled, usually people who are blind or have learning disabilities in the area of reading (dyslexia).

task commitment The degree to which students set their own goals, embrace challenges, and show perseverance.

Teacher Adviser Groups (TAGs) Formal groups of students who meet with a teacher at regular intervals to plan the students' programs and advise students on study skills, course selections, and career planning.

testing A form of assessment, normally using a paper and pencil test (either designed by the teacher or commercially available) to gather information that describes a student's or a group's level of performance.

theory of mind The notion that others think, feel, and know; Baron-Cohen (1995) hypothesized that people with autism do not have a theory of mind.

thinking aloud Teachers or peers can make the invisible visible by verbalizing their thoughts and showing students how to use a strategy, solve a problem, etc.

think-pair-share A collaborative activity in which the teacher poses a problem, students think and jot down their thoughts, pair with a classmate to discuss the question, and a few students share the thoughts of their pair with the class.

tics Involuntary, rapid, sudden muscular movements; uncontrollable vocal sounds; and inappropriate words (seen in Tourette syndrome).

time out Punishment in which a student is removed from opportunities for reward as a consequence for inappropriate behaviour.

token economy See *token reinforcement.*

token reinforcement Often called a "token economy," a system in which a teacher and a student select a specific appropriate target behaviour for which the student earns points or tokens that are collected and then traded in for some kind of reward once the agreed-upon amount has been earned.

tonic-clonic (grand mal) seizure In this generalized seizure, the individual sometimes gives a sharp cry before falling to the floor, the muscles stiffen, then begin to jerk rhythmically, and there may be loss of bladder control, some breathing difficulty, and saliva may gather at the mouth.

Tourette syndrome A neurological disorder involving motor tics and uncontrollable vocal sounds or inappropriate words that are often accompanied by obsessions and hyperactivity.

transient lifestyle A way of living adopted by homeless people who move from shelter to shelter; often seen in adolescents who have left home.

transition Changing from one stage of life to another; often used to refer to the transition to work that follows formal education.

transition plan A formal, written plan that some provinces require, for students with an IEP, to ensure that preparation for post-secondary endeavours begins early in the high school years.

traumatic brain injury (TBI) Damage to brain tissue as a result of a blow to the head or an accident that can cause physical difficulties (e.g., paralysis) and cognitive problems (e.g., memory loss).

TTYPA A collaborative learning activity in which a teacher stops and tells the students to "Turn to your partner and...introduce yourself...or describe a time when you..." Then the students switch roles.

U

universal design for learning The design of instructional materials and activities that allows the learning goals to be achievable by individuals with wide differences in their abilities to see, hear, speak, move, etc., by means of flexible curricular materials and activities designed to include alternatives for students with diversity in abilities and backgrounds.

V

verbal reprimand Punishment in which a student is reminded of the classroom rules; the most effective reprimands are immediate, unemotional, brief, and backed up with a time out or loss of privileges.

vision teacher A special educator who teaches or tutors students who are blind or have impaired vision.

visual impairment Disability characterized by partial or complete loss of sight and use of auditory and tactile sources of information to supplement or replace sight.

vocabulary The kind and level of language used in oral and written expression to communicate meaning to students; can also refer to the kind and level of language used in oral and written expression by students.

voice synthesizer Converts information typed or scanned into a computer into speech.

W

wheezing Breathing with an audible chesty, whistling sound; a symptom of an asthma episode.

workplace experience Involves students for brief periods of time in a workplace (ranging from one-day job-shadowing experiences to a few half-day visits) within the context of a credit course.

Z

zone of proximal development (ZPD) Learning that the student is just about to appropriate or make their own that they can already understand with support; from the work of Vygotsky.

References

Abilities: Canada's Lifestyle Magazine for People with Disabilities, http://www.abilities.ca (March 12, 2001).

Achter, J.A., Benbow, C.P., & Lubinski, D. (1996). Rethinking multipotentiality among the intellectually gifted: A critical review and recommendations. *Gifted Child Quarterly, 41,* 5–14.

Adams, M.J. (1990). *Beginning to read: Thinking and learning about print.* Cambridge, MA: MIT Press.

Adaptech Project of Canada, http://www.omega. dawsoncollege.qc.ca/adaptech/ (February 19, 2001).

Aiello, B., & Shulman, J. (1988a). *Business is looking up.* Frederick, MD: Twenty-First Century.

Aiello, B., & Shulman, J. (1988b). *Friends for life.* Frederick, MD: Twenty-First Century.

Aiello, B., & Shulman, J. (1988c). *It's your turn at bat.* Frederick, MD: Twenty-First Century.

Aiello, B., & Shulman, J. (1988d). *Secrets aren't (always) for keeps.* Frederick, MD: Twenty-First Century.

Aiello, B., & Shulman, J. (1989a). *A portrait of me.* Frederick, MD: Twenty-First Century.

Aiello, B., & Shulman, J. (1989b). *Trick or treat or trouble.* Frederick, MD: Twenty-First Century.

Ainscow, M., Booth, T., & Dyson, A. (1999). Inclusion and exclusion in schools: Listening to some hidden voices. In K. Ballard (ed.), *Inclusive education: International voices on disability and justice* (pp. 139–51). London, UK: Falmer Press.

Alberta Children's Hospital, Calgary, AB, http://www.crha-health.ab.ca/sites/ach.htm (February 19, 2001).

Alberta Education (1995). *Individualized program plans: Programming for students with special needs.* Edmonton: Alberta Education.

Alberta Education (1996). *Partners during changing times: An information booklet for parents of children with special needs.* Edmonton: Alberta Education.

Alberta Education (1997). Guide to education for students with special needs. Edmonton: Alberta Education. http://www.learning.gov.ab.ca/k_12/specialneeds/ident.asp (March 12, 2001).

Alberta Learning. Provincial Testing, Achievement Testing Program. http://www.learning.gov.ab.ca/k_12/testing/default.asp (March 29, 2001).

Alberta Learning. Approved Accommodations for Students with Special Diploma Examination Writing Needs. http://www.learning.gov.ab.ca/k_12/testing/diploma/dip_gib/sec11_policy_4.htm (March 29, 2001).

Alberta Learning (2000). *Shaping the future for students with special needs: A review of special education in Alberta: Final report.* Edmonton: Alberta Learning. http://www.learning.gov.ab.ca/k_12/special/SpecialEdReview/ (March 12, 2001).

Allen, A.M.A. (1996). "I don't want to read this": Students' responses to illustrations of Black characters. In K.S. Brethwaite & C.E. James (eds.), *Educating African Canadians* (pp. 147–66). Toronto: James Lorimer & Co.

Allinder, R.M. (1994). The relationship between efficacy and the instructional practices of special education teachers and consultants. *Teacher Education and Special Education, 17,* 86–95.

Allingham, N.D. (1992). Antiracist education and the curriculum: A privileged perspective. In Canadian Teachers' Federation (ed.), *Racism and education: Different perspectives and experiences* (pp. 15–29). Ottawa: Canadian Teachers' Federation.

Alper, S.K, Ryndak, D., & Lea, D. (1992). Students with severe handicaps in regular classes. *Elementary School Journal, 92,* 373–88.

Alper, S.K, Schloss, P., & Schloss, C. (1995). Families of children with disabilities in elementary and middle school: Advocacy models and strategies. *Exceptional Children, 62,* 261–70.

Alper, S.K, Schloss, P.J., & Schloss, C.N. (1994). *Families of students with disabilities.* Boston, MA: Allyn and Bacon.

Alster, E.H. (1997). The effects of extended time on algebra test scores for college students with and without learning disabilities. *Journal of Learning Disabilities, 30,* 222–27.

American Association of University Women (1993). *Hostile hallways: The AAUW survey on sexual harassment in America's schools.* Washington, DC: American Association of University Women.

American Association on Mental Retardation (AAMR) (1993). *Mental retardation: Definition, classification, and systems of support* (9th ed.). Washington, DC: AAMR. http://www.aamr.org (March 21, 2001).

American Psychiatric Association (APA) (1994). *The Diagnostic and Statistical Manual of Mental Disorders* (DSM-IV). Washington, DC: APA.

Anderson, J.D. (1994). School climate for gay and lesbian students and staff members. *Phi Delta Kappan, 76*(2), 151–54.

Anderson, J.O., & Bachor, D.G. (1998). A Canadian perspective on portfolio use in student assessment. *Assessment in Education, 5,* 353–79.

Annable, G. (1993). *Perspectives on the journey: The qualifications and experiences of Canadian job seekers with disabilities.* Winnipeg: Canadian Council on Rehabilitation and Work.

Armstrong, C. (1997). My roller-coaster ride with a grade 4–5 class. In D. Featherstone, H. Munby, & T. Russell (eds.), *Finding a voice while learning to teach* (pp. 67–70). London, UK: Falmer Press.

Arnott, K. (1998, Winter). No address, no education: Keeping homeless children in School. *Education Today, 10*(1), 16–17.

Aronson, E., Blaney, N., Stephen, C., Sikes, J., & Snapp, M. (1978). *The jigsaw classroom.* Beverly Hills, CA: Sage.

Assembly of First Nations, http://afn.ca (March 27, 2001).

Assistive and Adaptive Computing Technology in Special Education, http://at-advocacy.phillynews.com/data/atworkined.html (February 19, 2001).

Atlantic Provinces Education Foundation. Education Indicators for Atlantic Canada, http://apef-fepa.org/ (March 29, 2001).

Azmitia, M. (1988). Peer interaction and problem solving: When are two heads better than one? *Child Development, 59,* 87–96.

Azmitia, M., & Montgomery, R. (1993). Friendship, transactive dialogues, and the development of scientific reasoning. *Social Development, 2,* 202–21.

Ballard, K. (ed.) (1999). *Inclusive education: International voices on disability and justice.* London, UK: Falmer Press.

Ballard, K., & McDonald, T. (1999). Disability, inclusion and exclusion: Some insider accounts and interpretations. In K. Ballard (Ed.), *Inclusive education: International voices on disability and justice* (pp. 97–115). London, UK: Falmer Press.

Banks, R. (1997). Bullying in schools. *Eric Digest* ED407154.

Barakett, J.M. (1986). Teachers' theories and methods in structuring routine activities in an inner city school. *Canadian Journal of Education, 11,* 91–108.

Barkley, R. (1990). *Attention-deficit hyperactivity disorder: A handbook for diagnosis and treatment.* New York: Guilford Press.

Baron, J., & Brown, R.V. (1991). *Teaching decision making to adolescents.* Hillsdale, NJ: Erlbaum.

Baron-Cohen, S. (1995). *Mindblindness.* Cambridge, MA: MIT Press.

Barrish, H.H., Saunders, M., & Wolf, M.M. (1969). Good behavior game: Effects of individual contingencies for group consequences on disruptive behavior in a classroom. *Journal of Applied Behavior Analysis, 2,* 119–24.

Battiste, M., & Barman, J. (eds.) (1995). *First Nations education in Canada: The circle unfolds.* Vancouver: UBC Press.

Beddard, J.M. (1996). *Fetal alcohol syndrome: Educators' knowledge and needs.* Unpublished master's project, Queen's University, Kingston, ON.

Bellanca, J., & Fogarty, R. (1991). *Blueprints for thinking in the cooperative classroom.* Palatine, IL: Skylight Publishing.

Bennett, B., & Smilanich, P. (1994). *Classroom management: A thinking and caring approach.* Toronto: Bookation.

Benton-Banai, E. (1988). *The Mishomis book: The voice of the Ojibway.* Saint Paul, MN: Red School House.

Berlak, A., & Berlak, H. (1981). *Dilemmas of schooling: Teaching and social change.* New York: Methuen.

Berscheid, E. (1985). Interpersonal attraction. In G. Lindzey & E. Aronson (eds.), *Handbook of Social Psychology* (3rd ed., Vol. 2, pp. 413–84). New York: Random House.

Beveridge, A. (1997). *Successful inclusion of children with disabilities into regular classrooms: The practices and beliefs of four elementary teachers.* Unpublished master's thesis, Faculty of Education, Queen's University, Kingston, ON.

Beynon, J., & Toohey, K. (1995). Access and aspirations: Careers in teaching as seen by Canadian university students of Chinese and Punjabi-Sikh ancestry. *Alberta Journal of Educational Research, 41,* 435–61.

Blackbourn, V.A., & Blackbourn, J.M. (1993). An adolescent with moderate mental disabilities tutors a 1st grade, nondisabled child. *Teaching Exceptional Children, 25*(4), 56–57.

Blankenship, C., & Lily, M.S. (1981). *Mainstreaming students with learning and behavior problems.* New York: Holt, Rinehart, & Winston.

Bloorview Macmillan Centre, Toronto, ON, http://www.bloorviewmacmillan.on.ca/ (February 19, 2001).

Bluebond-Langer, M. (1996). *In the shadow of illness: Parents and siblings of the chronically ill child.* Princeton, NJ: Princeton University Press.

Blumenfeld, P.C., Puro, P., & Mergendoller, J.R. (1992). Translating motivation into thoughtfulness. In H.H. Marshal (ed.), *Redefining student learning: Roots of educational change.* Norwood, NJ: Ablex.

Bob, G., Marcuse, G., Nyce, D., & Williams, L. (1993). *First Nations: The circle unbroken: The teacher's guide (videos 1–4).* Montreal: National Film Board of Canada.

Bolman, L.G., & Deal, T.E. (1991). *Reframing organizations: Artistry, choice and leadership.* San Francisco: Jossey-Bass.

Bosetti, L., & Watt, D. (1995). Structural marginalization in educational policy: The case of English as a second language. *Exceptionality Education Canada, 5*(1), 24–41.

Bradley, D.F., & Calvin, M.B. (1998). Grading modified assignments: Equity or compromise? *Teaching Exceptional Children, 31*(2), 24–29.

Brethwaite, K.S. (1996). Keeping watch over our children: The role of African Canadian parents on the education team. In K.S. Brethwaite & C.E. James (eds.), *Educating African Canadians* (pp. 107–130). Toronto: James Lorimer & Co.

Bristol, M.M., et al. (1996). State of the science in autism: Report to the National Institutes of Health. *Journal of Autism and Developmental Disorders, 26,* 121–54.

British Columbia Ministry of Education. Provincial Student Assessment Program. http://www.bced.gov.bc.ca/assessment (March 29, 2001).

British Columbia Ministry of Education (1992). *Intermediate program* (draft). Victoria: Ministry of Education.

British Columbia Ministry of Education (1997). *Aboriginal education: Counselling of First Nations students.* http://www.bced.gov.bc.ca/abed/ (March 27, 2001).

British Columbia Ministry of Education (1998). *Shared learnings: Integrating BC Aboriginal content, K–10.* http://www.bced.gov.bc.ca/abed/shared.htm (March 27, 2001).

British Columbia Ministry of Education (1999). *Planning guide and framework for the development of Aboriginal learning resources.* http://www.bced.gov.bc.ca/abed/planguide/toc.htm (March 27, 2001).

British Columbia Special Education Branch (1995a). *Gifted education: A resource guide for teachers.* Victoria: Queen's

Printer for British Columbia. http://www.bced.gov.bc.ca./specialed/gifted/toc.htm (March 12, 2001).

British Columbia Special Education Branch (1995b). *Special education services: A manual of policies and guidelines.* Victoria: Queen's Printer for British Columbia. http://www.bced.gov.bc.ca/specialed/ppandg/toc.htm (March 12, 2001).

British Columbia Special Education Branch (1996). *Individual education planning for students with special needs.* Victoria: Queen's Printer for British Columbia. http://www.bced.gov.bc.ca/specialed/iepssn/toc.htm (March 12, 2001).

British Columbia Special Education Branch (1998a). *Students with intellectual disabilities: A handbook for teachers.* Victoria: British Columbia Special Education Branch.

British Columbia Special Education Branch (1998b). *Students with visual impairment: A handbook for teachers.* Victoria: British Columbia Special Education Branch.

Brolin, D. (1991). *Life-centered career education: A competency-based approach.* Reston, VA: Council for Exceptional Children.

Brookfield, S.D. (1995). *Becoming a critically reflective teacher.* San Francisco: Jossey-Bass.

Brown, J.S., Collins, A., & Duguid, P. (1989). Situated cognition and the culture of learning. *Educational Researcher, 18*(1), 32–42.

Brown, R.T. (ed.) (1999). *Cognitive aspects of chronic illness in children.* New York: Guilford.

Brownell, M.T., & Smith, S.W. (1992). Attrition/retention of special education teachers: Critique of current research and recommendations for retention efforts. *Teacher Education and Special Education, 15,* 229–48.

Bruer, J. (1993). *Schools for thought: A science of learning in the classroom.* Cambridge, MA: MIT Press.

Bryan, T. (1991). Social problems and learning disabilities. In B.Y.L. Wong (ed.), *Learning about learning disabilities* (pp. 195–229). San Diego, CA: Academic.

Bryan, T. (1999). Reflections on a research career. *Exceptional Children, 65,* 438–47.

Bryson, S.E. (1996). Brief report: Epidemiology of autism. *Journal of Autism and Developmental Disabilities, 26,* 165–67.

Bryson, S.E. (1997). Epidemiology of autism: Overview and issues outstanding. In D.J. Cohen & F.R. Volkmar (eds.), *Handbook of autism and pervasive developmental disorders* (2nd ed.) (pp. 41–46). New York: Wiley & Sons.

Bryson, S.E., Clark, B.S., & Smith, I.M. (1988). First report of a Canadian epidemiology study of autism syndromes. *Journal of Child Psychology and Psychiatry, 29,* 433–46.

Buhrmester, D. (1996). Need fulfillment, interpersonal competence, and the developmental contexts of early adolescent friendship. In W.M. Bukowski, A.F. Newcomb, & W.W. Hartup (eds.), *The company they keep: Friendship in childhood and adolescence* (pp. 158–85). New York: Cambridge University Press.

Bullara, D.T. (1993). Classroom management strategies to reduce racially biased treatment of students. *Journal of Educational and Psychological Consultation, 4*(4), 357–68.

Bullock, L.M., & Gable, R.A. (1995). *Perspectives on school aggression and violence: Highlights from the working forum on children and youth who have aggressive and violent behaviors.* Reston, VA: Council for Exceptional Children.

Bullying, http://www.bullying.com/ (April 2, 2001).

Bunch, G. (1992). Teacher attitudes to full inclusion. *Exceptionality Education Canada, 2*(1&2), 117–37.

Bunch, G., Lupart, J., & Brown, M. (1997). *Resistance and acceptance: Educator attitudes to inclusion of students with disabilities.* North York, ON: York University Faculty of Education.

Burney, S. (1995). *Coming to Gum San: The story of Chinese Canadians.* Toronto: D.C. Heath Canada Ltd. & Multicultural History Society of Ontario.

Butler, C., & Swain, M. (1996). *Cultural awareness through the arts.* Unpublished manuscript, Lennox and Addington County Board of Education, Ontario.

Butler, C.M. (2000). *Cultural awareness through the arts: The success of an Aboriginal antibias program for intermediate students.* Unpublished master's thesis, Queen's University, Kingston, ON.

Caduto, M.J., & Bruchae, J. (1988). *Keepers of the earth: Teacher's guide.* Golden, CO: Fulcrum Pub.

Calgary Educational Partnership Foundation (1996). *Employability skills: Creating my future.* Scarborough, ON: ITP Nelson Canada.

Callahan, K., Rademacher, J.A., & Hildreth, B.L. (1998). The effect of parent participation in strategies to improve the homework performance of students who are at risk. *Remedial and Special Education, 19,* 131–41.

Calliou, J. (1995). In M. Battiste & J. Barman (eds.), *First Nations education in Canada: The circle unfolds.* Vancouver: UBC Press.

Campbell, D.S., Serff, P., & Williams, D. (1994). *BreakAway company.* Toronto: Trifolium Publishing.

Campbell, P., & Stewart, E.L. (1993). Calculators and computers. In R. Jensen, *Early Childhood Mathematics, NCTM Research Interpretation Project* (pp. 251–68). New York: Macmillan.

Campeau, P., & Wolman, J. (1993). *Research on self-determination in individuals with disabilities.* Palo Alto, CA: American Institutes for Research.

Canadian Association of Independent Living Centres, http://www.cailc.ca (March 21, 2001).

Canadian Council on Social Development (1998). *Progress of Canada's children.* http://www.ccsd.ca/pcc98/ (March 28, 2001).

Canadian Council on Social Development (2000). *The Canadian fact book on poverty 2000.* Ottawa: Canadian Council on Social Development. http:www.ccsd.ca/briefs.html (March 28, 2001).

Canadian Global Almanac (2000). Toronto: Macmillan Canada.

Canadian Labour Force Development Board (1994). *Putting the pieces together, toward a coherent transition system for Canada's labour force: Report.* Canadian Labour Force Development Board.

Canadian National Institute for the Blind (CNIB). *Technical aids: High technology product categories.* http://www.cnib.ca/tech_aids/index.htm (February 19, 2001).

Canadian School Boards Association (1996). *Anaphylaxis: A handbook for school boards.* Ottawa: Health Canada.

Canadian Task Force on Mental Health Issues Affecting Immigrants and Refugees (1988). *After the door has been opened: Mental health issues affecting immigrants and refugees in Canada.* Ottawa: Department of the Secretary of State of Canada, Multiculturalism Sector.

Canning, P.M. (1996). *Special matters: The report of the review of special education.* St. John's: Newfoundland Department of Education and Training.

Cantwell, D.P. (1996). Attention deficit disorder: A review of the past 10 years. *Journal of the American Academy of Child and Adolescent Psychiatry, 34,* 1262–71.

Careless, J. (1994). A checklist for caring. *University Affairs,* May, pp. 6–7.

Carnine, D., Silbert, J., & Kameenui, E. (1990). *Direct instruction reading.* Columbus, OH: Merrill.

Carter, B., & Mok, W.Y. (1992). *Newcomer children: Rights, needs, and adjustment.* Ottawa: Employment and Immigration Canada.

Case, R. (1998, April). *A psychological model of number sense and its development.* Paper presented at the annual meeting of the American Educational Research Association, San Diego, CA.

Celano, M.P., & Geller, R.J. (1993). Learning, school performance, and children with asthma: How much at risk? *Journal of Learning Disabilities, 26,* 23–32.

Centra, J.A. (1986). Handicapped student performance on the Scholastic Aptitude Test. *Journal of Learning Disabilities, 19,* 324–27.

Chan, J.S. (2000). *The social skills of two elementary students with learning disabilities: A participant observational study across seven school contexts.* Unpublished master's thesis, Queen's University, Kingston, ON.

Chin, P., & Members of the STAO Safety Committee. (1995). Teaching science safety in the ESL classroom. *Crucible, 27*(1), 24–25.

Chin, P., Munby, H., Hutchinson, N.L., & Steiner-Bell, K. (in press). Meeting academic goals: Post-secondary students' intentions for participating in high school co-operative education programs. *Journal of Vocational Educational Research.*

Chomicki, S., & Kysela, G. (1993). Teacher attitudes toward mainstreaming: What do they think and what do they need? A literature review. *Exceptionality Education Canada, 3*(4), 61–79.

Christiansen, J., & Vogel, J.R. (1998). A decision model for grading students with disabilities. *Teaching Exceptional Children, 31*(2), 30–35.

Clark, G., Carlson, B.C., Fisher, S., Cook, I.D., & D'Alonzo, B.J. (1991). Career development for students with disabilities in elementary schools: A position statement of the Division of Career Development. *Career Development for Exceptional Individuals, 14,* 109–120.

Clarke, J., Wideman, R., & Eadie, S. (1990). *Together we learn.* Scarborough, ON: Prentice-Hall Canada.

Coates, M.L.J. (1986). *Employment equity: Issues, approaches and public policy framework.* Kingston, ON: Queen's University Industrial Relations Centre.

Cochran, M. (1990). The transforming role. *Networking Bulletin: Empowerment & Family Support, 1*(3), 25.

Coelho, E. (1994). *Learning together in the multicultural classroom.* Markham, ON: Pippin Pub. Ltd.

Coelho, E. (1998). *Teaching and learning in multicultural schools.* Clevedon, UK: Multilingual Matters.

Cohen, E. (1986). *Designing groupwork: Strategies for the heterogeneous classroom.* New York: Teachers College Press.

Cohen, E., Lotan, R., & Catanzarite, L. (1990). Treating status problems in the cooperative classroom. In S. Sharan (ed.), *Cooperative learning: Theory and research* (pp. 203–229). New York: Praeger.

Cohen, P., Kulik, J., & Kulik, C. (1982). Educational outcomes of tutoring: A meta-analysis of findings. *American Educational Research Journal, 19,* 237–48.

Colangelo, N. (1991). Psychological development of gifted students. *Exceptionality Education Canada, 1*(1), 103–117.

Coleman, M.R., Gallagher, J.J., & Nelson, S.M. (1997). *Cooperative learning and gifted students: Report on five case studies.* Washington, DC: National Association for Gifted Children.

Collicott, J. (1994, Winter). Multi-level instruction: A guide for teachers. *Keeping in Touch* (Quarterly Newsletter of CEC Canada).

Collins, W.A., & Repinskie, D.J. (1994). Relationships during adolescence: Continuity and change in interpersonal perspective. In R. Montemayor, G. Adams, & T. Gullotta (eds.), *Personal relationships during adolescence* (pp. 7–36). Thousand Oaks, CA: Sage.

Collins-Williams, M.A., & Willows, D. (1998, December). *A longitudinal study of the effects of inservice teacher education on primary students' literacy success.* Paper presented at the National Reading Conference, Austin, TX.

Conderman, G. (1995). Social status of sixth- and seventh-grade students with learning disabilities. *Learning Disability Quarterly, 18,* 13–24.

Connell, J.P., Spencer, M.B., & Aber, J.L. (1994). Educational risk and resilience in African-American youth: Context, self, action, and outcomes in school. *Child Development, 65,* 493–506.

Conte, R., & Andrews, J. (1993). Social skills in the context of learning disability definitions: A reply to Gresham and Elliott and directions for the future. *Journal of Learning Disabilities, 26,* 146–53.

Cooper, M., Griffith, K.G., & Filer, J. (1999). School intervention for inclusion of students with and without disabilities. *Focus on Autism and Other Developmental Disabilities, 14,* 110–115.

Council of Ministers of Education of Canada. School Assessment Indicators Program. http://www.cmec.ca/saip/indexe.stm (March 29, 2001).

Council of Ministers of Education of Canada (1999). *1998 Report on reading and writing assessment: School achievement indicators program.* Toronto: Council of Ministers of Education of Canada.

Cripps, S. (1991, Spring). An examination of the role of paraprofessionals in three New Brunswick school districts. *New Brunswick Teachers' Association News,* 11–12.

Cummins, J. (1981). *Bilingualism and minority language children*. Toronto, ON: Ontario Institute for Studies in Education.

Cunningham, A.E., & Stanovich, K.E. (1997). Early reading acquisition and its relation to reading experience and ability 10 years later. *Developmental Psychology, 33*, 934–45.

Daiute, C., & Dalton, B. (1992). *Collaboration between children learning to write: Can novices be masters?* Eric Document ED 354522.

Davidson, I., & Wiener, J. (1991). Creating educational change: The in-school team. *Exceptionality Education Canada, 1*(2), 25–44.

DeBettencourt, L. (1999). General educators' attitudes toward students with mild disabilities and their use of instructional strategies. *Remedial and Special Education, 20*, 27–35.

DeClements, B. (1985). *Sixth grade can really kill you*. New York: Viking Penguin.

Dei, G.J.S. (1996a). *Anti-racism education: Theory and practice*. Halifax: Fernwood.

Dei, G.J.S. (1996b). Listening to voices: Developing a pedagogy of change from the narratives of African-Canadian students and parents. In K.S. Brethwaite & C.E. James (eds.), *Educating African Canadians* (pp. 32–57). Toronto: James Lorimer & Co.

Delisle, J.R. (1992). *Guiding the social and emotional development of gifted youth: A practical guide for educators and counselors*. New York: Longman.

Delong, J., & Wideman, R. (eds.) (1998). *Action research: School improvement through research-based professionalism*. Mississauga, ON: Ontario Public School Teachers' Federation.

Dennison, S.T. (1997). *Creating positive support groups for at-risk children*. Torrance, CA: Jalmar Press.

Deno, S.L., & Mirkin, P.K. (1977). *Data-based program modification: A manual*. Reston, VA: Council for Exceptional Children.

Deshler, D.D., Ellis, E.S., & Lenz, B.K. (1996). *Teaching adolescents with learning disabilities: Strategies and methods*. Denver: Love Publishing.

Developmental Disabilities Program, University of Western Ontario Psychiatry. http://www.psychiatry.med.uwo.ca/ (March 21, 2001).

Dever, R.B. (1990). Defining mental retardation from an instructional perspective. *Mental Retardation, 28*, 147–53.

Dewey, J. (1916). *Democracy and education: An introduction to the philosophy of education*. New York: Macmillan.

Dickason, O.P. (1992). *Canada's First Nations: A history of founding peoples from earliest times*. Toronto: McClelland & Stewart.

Dillon-Peterson, E. (1982). *Sameness drives me up the wall*. Paper presented at the annual meeting of the American Educational Research Association, New York.

Dodge, K.A. (1985). Factors of social interaction and the assessment of social competence in children. In B.H. Schneider, K.H. Rubin, & J.E. Ledingham (eds.), *Children's peer relations: Issues in assessment and intervention* (pp. 3–22). New York: Springer-Verlag.

Doyle, W. (1990). Classroom management techniques. In O.C. Moles (ed.), *Student discipline strategies*. Albany: State University of New York Press.

Duhaney, L.M.G., & Salend, S. (2000). Parental perceptions of inclusive educational placements. *Remedial and Special Education, 21*, 121–28.

Dunn, L. (1968). Special education for the mildly retarded: Is much of it justifiable? *Exceptional Children, 35*, 5–22.

Duquette, C. (1992). Integrating mildly and moderately handicapped children: What goes on in a successful school? *Exceptionality Education Canada, 2*(1&2), 139–53.

Duquette, C. (1996). Behaviour and procedures of secondary teachers in the integrated classroom. In J. Andrews (ed.), *Teaching students with diverse needs: Secondary classrooms* (pp. 146–59). Scarborough, ON: ITP Nelson Canada.

Duquette, C., & O'Reilly, R. (1988). Perceived attributes of mainstreaming, principal change strategy, and teacher attitudes toward mainstreaming. *Alberta Journal of Educational Research, 34*, 390–402.

Durham, P.H., & Dick, T.P. (1994). Research on graphing calculators. *Mathematics Teacher, 87*, 440–45.

Dworet, D., & Rathgeber, A. (1998). Confusion reigns: Definitions of behaviour exceptionalities in Canada. *Exceptionality Education Canada, 8*(1), 3–19.

Dybwad, G., & Bersani, H.A. (eds.) (1996). *New voices: Self-advocacy by people with disabilities*. Cambridge, MA: Brookline.

Dyson, L. (1992a). Adjustment of siblings of handicapped children: A comparison. In M.C. Roberts & J.L. Wallander (eds.), *Family issues in pediatric psychology* (pp. 165–79). Hillsdale, NJ: Erlbaum.

Dyson, L. (1992b). Siblings of children with learning disabilities. In Z. Stoneman & P.W. Berman (eds.), *The effects of mental retardation, disability, and illness on sibling relationships: Research issues and challenges* (pp. 235–52). Baltimore: Paul H. Brookes.

Dyson, L. (1993). Response to the presence of a child with disabilities: Parental stress and family functioning over time. *American Journal on Mental Retardation, 98*, 207–218.

Earl, L., & Cousins, J.B. (1995). *Classroom assessment: Changing the face, facing the change*. Toronto: Ontario Public School Teachers Federation.

Earl, L., & Lemahieu, P.G. (1997). Rethinking assessment and accountability. In A. Hargreaves (ed.), *Rethinking educational change with heart and mind* (pp. 149–68). Alexandria, VA: Association for Supervision and Curriculum Development.

Eaton v. Brant (county) Board of Education (1995). 22 O.R. (3d) 1 O.C.A.

Edgar, E. (1988). Employment as an outcome for mildly handicapped students: Current status and future directions. *Focus on Exceptional Children, 21*, 1–8.

Edmunds, A. (1998). Classroom teachers are not prepared for the inclusive classroom. *Exceptionality Education Canada, 8*(2), 27–40.

Edmunds, A. (1999). Acquiring learning strategies. *Teaching Exceptional Children, 31*(4), 69–73.

Education Quality and Accountability Office (Ontario), http://www.eqao.com (March 29, 2001).

Edwards, K.L. (2000). *"They can be successful too!" Inclusive practices of secondary school science teachers.* Unpublished master's thesis, Faculty of Education, Queen's University, Kingston, ON.

Elbaum, B., Moody, S.W., & Schumm, J.S. (1999). Mixed-ability grouping for reading: What students think. *Learning Disabilities Research and Practice, 14,* 61–66.

Elliott, J., Ysseldyke, J., Thurlow, M., & Erickson, R. (1998). What about assessment and accountability? Practical implications for educators. *Teaching Exceptional Children, 31,* 20–27.

Ely, S. (2000). *What is assistive technology? A basic guide for individuals with disabilities and their families.* Bloomington, IN: Indiana Institute on Disability and Communication, Indiana University.

Emmer, E.T., Evertson, C., & Worsham, M.E. (2000). *Classroom management for secondary teachers* (5th ed.). Boston: Allyn & Bacon.

Emmett, J.D., & Minor, C.W. (1993). Career decision-making factors in gifted young adults. *The Career Development Quarterly, 41,* 350–66.

Epilepsy Association of Metro Toronto. *What teachers should know about epilepsy.* (Brochure.) Toronto: Epilepsy Association of Metro Toronto.

Epilepsy Ontario, http://epilepsyontario.org/faqs/advocacy.html (February 19, 2001).

Espin, C.A., Deno, S.L., & Albayrak-Kaymak, D. (1998). Individualized education programs in resource and inclusive settings: How "individualized" are they? *Journal of Special Education, 32,* 164–74.

Evans, D.D., & Strong, C.J. What's the story? Attending, listening, telling in middle school. *Teaching Exceptional Children, 28*(3), 58–61.

Evans, M., McDonald, J., & Nyce, N. (1999). Acting across boundaries in Aboriginal curriculum development: Examples from northern British Columbia. *Canadian Journal of Native Education, 23,* 190–205.

Evers, R.B., & Bursuck, W. (1993). Teacher ratings of instructional and setting demands in vocational education classes. *Learning Disability Quarterly, 16,* 82–92.

Evertson, C.M., Emmer, E.T., & Worsham, M.E. (2000). *Classroom management for elementary teachers* (5th ed.). Boston: Allyn and Bacon.

Faltis, C.J. (1993). *Joinfostering: Adapting teaching strategies for the multilingual classroom.* Don Mills, ON: Maxwell Macmillan Canada, Inc.

Fasano, J.H., & Brown, M.E. (1992). Facilitating inclusive secondary classrooms through curriculum adaptation. *Exceptionality Education Canada, 2*(1&2), 155–80.

Featherstone, D., Munby, H., & Russell, T. (eds.) (1997). *Finding a voice while learning to teach.* London, UK: Falmer Press.

Ferguson, P.M., & Olsen, D. (1989). *Supported community life: Connecting policy to practice in disability research.* Eugene, OR: Specialized Training Program.

Field, S., & Hoffman, A. (1996). *Steps to self-determination.* Austin, TX: Pro-Ed.

Fine, E.S., Lacey, A., & Baer, J. (1995). *Children as peacemakers.* Portsmouth, NH: Heineman.

Fitzsimmons, M.K. (1998). Including students with disabilities in large-scale testing: Emerging practices. *ERIC/OSEP Digest* E564.

Flanigan, B.O. (1991). Peer tutoring and second language acquisition in the elementary school. *Applied Linguistics, 12,* 141–58.

Flatow, I. (1985). The king of storms. In M.W. Aulls & M.F. Graves (eds.), *In another world* (pp. 57–63). New York: Scholastic.

Fogarty, R. (1990). *Designs for cooperative interactions.* Palatine, IL: Skylight Publishing.

Ford, A., Davern, L., & Schnorr, R. (1990). Inclusive education: "Making sense" of the curriculum. In S. Stainback & W. Stainback (eds.), *Curriculum considerations in inclusive classrooms: Facilitating learning for all students.* Baltimore: Brookes.

Forest, M., & Lusthaus, E. (1987). The kaleidoscope: Challenge to the cascade. In M. Forest (ed.), *More education/integration* (pp. 1–16). Downsview, ON: G. Allen Roeher Institute.

Forness, S.R., & Kavale, K.A. (1988). Psychopharmacologic treatment: A note on classroom effects. *Journal of Learning Disabilities, 21,* 144–47.

Forness, S.R., Swanson, J.M., Cantwell, D.P., Guthrie, D., & Sena, R. (1992). Response to stimulant medication across six measures of school-related performance in children with ADHD and disruptive behavior. *Behavioral Disorders, 18,* 42–53.

Fostaty Young, S.F., & Wilson, R.J. (2000). *Assessment and learning: The ICE approach.* Winnipeg: Portage & Main Press (Peguis Publishers).

Foster, G. (1995). Discipline and exceptional students. *Principals in-council: The Newsletter of the Principals' and Vice-principals' Council of the New Brunswick Teachers' Association, 22*(2), 7–9.

Freeman, J.G. (1998). *Interest and special education: The role of interest in teaching children with learning disabilities.* Unpublished doctoral dissertation, University of Michigan.

French, C. (1999). *Report summary: Teachers' perceptions of the IPP process.* http://www.nstu.ns.ca/aviso/Winter99/research.html (March 13, 2001).

Friedel, T.L. (1999). The role of Aboriginal parents in public education: Barriers to change in an urban setting. *Canadian Journal of Native Education, 23,* 139–58.

Friend, M., Bursuck, W., & Hutchinson, N.L. (1998). *Including exceptional students: A practical guide for classroom teachers,* Canadian edition. Scarborough, ON: Allyn & Bacon.

Fullan, M. (1991). *The new meaning of educational change.* New York: Teachers College Press.

Fullwood, D. *Chances and choices: Making integration work.* Sydney, AU: Paul H. Brookes.

Fulton, L., et al. (1994). Peer education partners. *Teaching Exceptional Children, 26*(4), 6–11.

Furman, W., & Bierman, K.L. (1984). Children's conceptions of friendship: A multimethod study of developmental changes. *Developmental Psychology, 20*, 925–31.

Furman, W., & Robbins, P. (1985). What's the point? Issues in the selection of treatment objectives. In B.H. Schneider, K.H. Rubin, & J.E. Ledingham (eds.), *Children's peer relations: Issues in assessment and intervention* (pp. 41–54). New York: Springer-Verlag.

Gallegos, A.Y., & Medina, C. (1995). Twenty-one ways to involve families: A practical approach. *Rural Special Education Quarterly, 14*(3), 3–6.

Garnett, K. (1992). Developing fluency with basic number facts: Intervention for students with learning disabilities. *Learning Disabilities: Research and Practice, 7*, 210–16.

Gaskins, I., & Elliot, T. (1991). *Implementing cognitive strategy instruction across the school.* Cambridge, MA: Brookline.

Gauldnau, C. (1996). *An examination of collaboration practices in schools, in relation to teachers' efficacy and their beliefs about the inclusion of children.* Unpublished master's thesis, University of Toronto, Toronto, ON.

Gauthier-McMahon, S.L., & Hutchinson, N.L. (1998). *Adolescent beliefs about teachers who help them learn: Gender differences.* Paper presented at the annual meeting of the American Educational Research Association, Montreal, QC.

Geary, D.C. (1993). Mathematical disabilities: Cognitive, neuropsychological, and genetic components. *Psychological Bulletin, 114*, 345–62.

Gehret, J. (1991). *Eagle eyes: A child's guide to paying attention.* Fairport, NY: Verbal Images Press.

Gerber, P.J., Ginsberg, R., & Reiff, H.B. (1992). Identifying alterable patterns of employment success for highly successful adults with learning disabilities. *Journal of Learning Disabilities, 25*, 475–87.

Gersten, R., & Chard, D. (1999). Number sense: Rethinking arithmetic instruction for students with mathematical disabilities. *The Journal of Special Education, 33*, 18–28.

Gibbs, J. (1995). *Tribes: A new way of learning and being together.* Sausalito, CA: Center Source Systems.

Gidney, R.D. (1999). *From Hope to Harris: The reshaping of Ontario's schools.* Toronto: University of Toronto Press.

Gilchrist, W. (1986). Teaching statistics to the rest of humanity. *Proceedings of the Second International Conference on Teaching Statistics* (pp. 494–97). Victoria, BC: University of Victoria.

Gilliland, H. (1995). *Teaching the Native American* (3rd ed.). Dubuque, IA: Kendall/Hunt Pub.

Gilmore, R. (1994). *Lights for Gita.* Toronto: Second Story Press.

Gold, Y., & Roth, R.A. (1993). *Teachers managing stress and preventing burnout: The professional health solution.* London: Falmer Press.

Goleman, D. (1995). *Emotional intelligence.* New York: Bantam Books.

Good, T., & Brophy, J. (1987). *Looking in classrooms* (4th ed.). New York: Harper & Row.

Gottardo, A., Chiappe, P., Siegel, L.S., & Stanovich, K.E. (1999). Patterns of word and nonword processing in skilled and less skilled readers. *Reading and Writing: An Interdisciplinary Journal, 11*, 465–87.

Gottfredson, D.C., Gottfredson, G.C., & Hybl, L.G. (1993). Managing adolescent behavior: A multiyear multischool study. *American Educational Research Journal, 30*, 179–215.

Gottfredson, L.S. (1981). Circumscription and compromise: A developmental theory of occupational aspirations. *Journal of Counseling Psychology Monographs, 28*, 545–79.

Gouvernement du Québec Ministère de l'Éducation. Uniform Ministry Examinations. http://www.meq.gouv.qc.ca/GR-PUB/m_englis.htm (March 29, 2001).

Gouvernement du Québec Ministère de l'Éducation (1993). *A reference guide for developing individualized education plans for students with handicaps or learning or adjustment difficulties.* Québec: Dépôt légal—Bibliotèque nationale du Québec.

Gouvernement du Québec Ministère de l'Éducation (1999). *Adapting our schools to the needs of all students: Draft policy on special education.* Québec: Dépôt légal—Bibliotèque nationale du Québec.

Government of Canada (1982). *The Charter of Rights and Freedoms: A guide for Canadians.* Ottawa: Minister of Supply and Services. http://canada.justice.gc.ca/Loireg/charte/const_en.html (March 13, 2001).

Government of Canada (1991). *Learning well … living well.* Ottawa: Minister of Supply and Services.

Government of Newfoundland and Labrador (2000). *Ministerial panel on educational delivery in the classroom.* St. John's: Government of Newfoundland and Labrador. http://www.gov.nf.ca/edu/EDUPUB.HTM (March 13, 2001).

Government of Nunavut (2001). http://www.gov.nu.ca (March 12, 2001).

Gower, D. (1988, Summer). Employment of disabled Canadians. *Canadian Social Trends—Statistics Canada.*

Gracenin, D. (1993). Culture clash in San Francisco: Reconnecting youth who are homeless with education. *Intervention in School and Clinic, 29*(1), 41–46.

Graham, L., & Wong, B. (1993). Two modes of teaching a question-answering strategy for enhancing reading comprehension. *Journal of Learning Disabilities, 26*, 270–79.

Grant, I. (1997). Life, liberty and peanut butter. *Globe and Mail.* November 26, p. A24.

Grant, L.R. (2000). A framework for professional learning and the Ontario College of Teachers. In R. Upitis (ed.), *Who will teach? A case study of teacher education reform* (pp. 245–58). San Francisco: Caddo Gap Press.

Graves, M.F., & Braaten, S. (1996). Scaffolded reading experiences: Bridges to success. *Preventing School Failure, 40*, 169–73.

Gray, C. (1993). *How to write social stories.* Jenison, MI: Jenison Public Schools.

Greenwood, C.R., Delquadri, J.C., & Carta, J.J. (1988). *Classwide peer tutoring (CWPT).* Seattle, WA: Educational Achievement Systems.

Greenwood, C.R., Delquadri, J.C., & Hall, R.V. (1989). Longitudinal effects of classwide peer tutoring. *Journal of Educational Psychology, 81*, 371–383.

Griffin, S., & Case, R. (1997). Re-thinking the primary school math curriculum: An approach based on cognitive science. *Issues in Education, 3*, 1–49.

Guay, D.M. (1993). Cross-site analysis of teaching practices: Visual art education with students experiencing disabilities. *Studies in Art Education, 34*, 233–43.

Haager, D., & Vaughn, S. (1995). Parent, teacher, peer, and self-reports of the social competence of students with learning disabilities. *Journal of Learning Disabilities, 28*, 205–215, 231.

Hall, L.J., & McGregor, J.A. (2000). A follow-up study of the peer relationships of children with disabilities in an inclusive school. *Journal of Special Education, 34*, 114–26.

Hammeken, P.A. (1996). *An essential guide for the paraprofessional.* Minnetonka, MN: Peytral Publications.

Hampton, E. (1995). Towards a redefinition of Indian education. In M. Battiste & J. Barman (1995) (eds.), *First Nations education in Canada: The circle unfolds* (pp. 5–46). Vancouver: UBC Press.

Hardy, M.I., McLeod, J., Minto, H., Perkins, S.A., & Quance, W.R. (1971). *Standards for education of exceptional children in Canada: The SEECC Report.* Toronto: Leonard Crainford.

Harniss, M.K., Hollenbeck, K., Crawford, A., & Carnine, D. (1994). Content organization and instructional design issues in the development of history texts. *Learning Disability Quarterly, 17*, 235–48.

Harper, M., O'Connor, K., & Simpson, M. (1999). *Quality assessment: Fitting the pieces together.* Toronto: Ontario Secondary School Teachers Federation.

Hartas, D., & Patrikakou, E.N. (1997). Friendship and conversational skills of adolescents with behavioral or emotional disorders. *B.C. Journal of Special Education, 21*(2), 5–30.

Hartmann, T. (1995). *ADD success stories: A guide to fulfillment for families with attention deficit disorder.* Grass Valley, CA: Underwood Books.

Hartup, W.W. (1993). Adolescents and their friends. In B. Laursen (ed.), *Close friendships in adolescence* (Vol. 60, pp. 3–22). San Francisco: Jossey-Bass.

Hartup, W.W. (1996). The company they keep: Friendships and their developmental significance. *Child Development, 67*, 1–13.

Hartup, W.W., Daiute, C., Zajac, R., & Sholl, W. (1995). *Collaboration in creative writing by friends and nonfriends.* Unpublished manuscript, Harvard University.

Hartup, W.W., French, D.C., Laursen, B., Johnston, M.K., & Ogawa, J.R. (1993). Conflict and friendship relations in middle childhood: behavior in a closed-field situation. *Child Development, 64*, 445–54.

Harvey, J.G., Waits, B.K., & Demana, F. (1995). The influence of technology on the teaching and learning of algebra. *Journal of Mathematical Behavior, 14*, 75–109.

Hayes, F.B., Hynd, G.W., & Wisenbaker, J. (1986). Learning disabled and normal college students' performance on reaction time and speeded classification tasks. *Journal of Educational Psychology, 78*, 39–43.

Head Injury Hotline, http://www.headinjury.com/advocacy.htm (February 19, 2001).

Heal, L.W., & Rusch, F.R. (1995). Predicting employment for students who leave special education high school programs. *Exceptional Children, 61*, 472–87.

Heath, N.L. (1995). Distortion and deficit: Self-perceived versus actual academic competence in depressed and nondepressed children with and without learning disabilities. *Learning Disabilities Research and Practice, 10*, 2–10.

Heath, N.L. (1996). The emotional domain: Self-concept and depression in children with learning disabilities. *Advances in Learning and Behavioral Disabilities, 10A*, 47–75.

Heath, N.L., & Ross, S. (2000). The prevalence and expression of depressive symptomatology in children with and without learning disabilities. *Learning Disability Quarterly, 23*, 24–36.

Heath, N.L., & Weiner, J. (1996). Depression and nonacademic self-perceptions in children with and without learning disabilities. *Learning Disability Quarterly, 19*, 34–44.

Heller, K.W., Alberto, P.A., Forney, P.E., & Schwartzman, M.N. (1996). *Understanding physical, sensory, and health impairments.* Boston: Brooks/Cole.

Hendrikse, J. (1999). *Parents as tutors of their own children: Effects of a training program on children's achievement and confidence of parents.* Unpublished doctoral thesis, University of Toronto.

Hendrickson et al. (1995). Creating community: A promising concept for preventing and eliminating aggressive and violent behaviors. In L.M. Bullock & R.A. Gable (eds.), *Perspectives on school aggression and violence: Highlights from the working forum on children and youth who have aggressive and violent behaviors* (pp. 45–48). Reston, VA: Council for Exceptional Children.

Hess, M. (1991). *Children, schools, and poverty.* Ottawa: Canadian Teachers' Federation.

Hiebert, B. (1985). *Stress and teachers: The Canadian scene.* Toronto: Canadian Education Association.

Higenbottam, J. (1998). What is a brain injury? In S. Acorn & P. Offer (eds.), *Living with brain injury* (pp. 7–19). Toronto: University of Toronto Press.

Hoffman, J. (1999). The learning channels: How to navigate the special-ed system. *Today's Parent, 16*(3), 56–62.

Hoge, R.D. (1988). Issues in the definition and measurement of the giftedness construct. *Educational Researcher, 27*(7), 12–16.

Hollingsworth, M.G. (1992). Computing technologies: A cornerstone for educational and employment equity. *The Canadian Journal of Higher Education, 12*(1), 14–26.

Hollingsworth, M.G. (1996). Computers in secondary education: Practices today, preparing for tomorrow. In J. Andrews (ed.), *Teaching students with diverse needs: Secondary classrooms* (pp. 243–74). Scarborough, ON: Nelson Canada.

Holmes, M. (1998). *The reformation of Canada's schools: Breaking the barriers to parental choice.* Kingston, ON: McGill-Queen's Press.

Hoo Kong, N.A. (1996). Confronting a history of exclusion: a personal reflection. In K.S. Brethwaite & C.E. James (eds.), *Educating African Canadians* (pp. 58–68). Toronto: James Lorimer & Co.

Huggins, P. (1994). *Helping kids find their strengths*. Longmont, CO: Sopris West.

Hughes, C., et al. (1999). "They are my best friends": Peer buddies promote inclusion in high school. *Teaching Exceptional Children, 31*(5), 32–37.

Hughes, L. (1999). Action research and practical inquiry: How can I meet the needs of the high ability student within my regular education classroom? *Journal for the Education of the Gifted, 22*, 282–97.

Hughes, R.S., & Kloeppel, P.C. (1994). *Self-awareness in language arts (SAIL)*. Minneapolis, MN: Educational Media.

Human Resources and Labour Canada (1993). *Leaving school*. Ottawa: Queen's Printer.

Human Resources Development Canada, http://www.hrdc-drhc.gc.ca/common/lmi.shtml (February 19, 2001).

Hunt, P., Alwell, M., Farron-Davis, F., & Goetz, L. (1996). Creating socially supportive environments for fully included students who experience multiple disabilities. *Journal of the Association for Persons with Severe Handicaps, 21*(2), 53–71.

Hutchinson, N.L. (1989). Strategy instruction research in one domain: Algebra. *Canadian Journal of Special Education, 5*, 169–77.

Hutchinson, N.L. (1993). Effects of cognitive strategy instruction on algebra problem solving of adolescents with learning disabilities. *Learning Disability Quarterly, 16*, 34–63.

Hutchinson, N.L. (1997). Creating an inclusive classroom with young adolescents in an urban school. *Exceptionality Education Canada, 6*(3&4), 51–67.

Hutchinson, N.L., Chin, P., Munby, H., Mills de Espana, W., Young, J., Edwards, K.L. (1998). How inclusive is co-operative education in Canada? Getting the story and the numbers. *Exceptionality Education Canada, 8*(3), 15–43.

Hutchinson, N.L., & Freeman, J.G. (1994). *Pathways*. Scarborough, ON: ITP Nelson Canada.

Hutchinson, N.L., Freeman, J.G., Downey, K.H., & Kilbreath, L. (1992). Development and evaluation of an instructional module to promote career maturity for youth with learning disabilities. *Canadian Journal of Counselling, 26*, 290–99.

Hutchinson, N.L., Freeman, J.G., & Quick, V.E. (1996). Group counseling intervention for solving problems on the job. *Journal of Employment Counseling, 33*(1), 2–19.

Hutchinson, N.L., Freeman, J.G., & Steiner-Bell, K. (2001). Children and adolescents with learning disabilities: Case studies of social relations in inclusive classrooms. In B.Y.L. Wong & M. Donahue (eds.), *The social dimensions of learning disabilities*. Mahwah, NJ: Lawrence Erlbaum.

Hutchinson, N.L., & Martin, A.K. (1999). Fostering inclusive beliefs and practices during preservice teacher education through communities of practice. *Teacher Education and Special Education, 22*, 234–50.

Hutchinson, N.L., Munby, H., Chin, P., Edwards, K.L., Steiner-Bell, K., Chapman, C., Ho, K., & Mills de España, W. (in press). The intended curriculum in co-operative education in Ontario secondary schools: An analysis of school district documents. *Journal of Vocational Educational Research*.

Hutchinson, N.L., & Schmid, C. (1996). Perceptions of a resource teacher about programs for preschoolers with special needs and their families. *Canadian Journal of Research in Early Childhood Education, 5*(1), 73–82.

Hutchinson, N.L., & Taves, R.A. (1994). *Why not me? Career development and learning disabilities*. Ottawa: Canadian Guidance and Counselling Foundation.

Hynd, G., Hern, K.L., Voeller, K.K., & Marshall, R.M. (1991). Neurobiological basis of attention-deficit hyperactivity disorder (ADHD). *School Psychology Review, 20*, 174–86.

Ignatieff, M. (2000). *The rights revolution*. Toronto: House of Anansi Press.

Jackett, E., & Willows, D. (1998, December). *Development of story schemata in the written compositions of primary students: A longitudinal study of the balanced and flexible literacy diet*. Paper presented at the National Reading Conference, Austin, TX.

James, J. (1996). *Phonological processing in early reading and invented spelling*. Unpublished master's thesis, Queen's University, Kingston, ON.

James, K. (1996). Dear high school teacher. In K.S. Brethwaite & C.E. James (eds.), *Educating African Canadians* (pp. 302–04). Toronto: James Lorimer & Co.

Jenkins, J., & Jenkins, A. (1985). Peer tutoring in elementary and secondary programs. *Focus on Exceptional Children, 17*(6), 1–12.

Jenkinson, J.C. (1997). *Mainstream or special? Educating students with disabilities*. London: Routledge.

Johnsen, S.K., & Ryser, G.R. (1996). An overview of effective practices with gifted students in general-education settings. *Journal for the Education of the Gifted, 19*, 379–404.

Johnson, D.W., & Johnson, R.T. (1985). The internal dynamics of cooperative learning groups. In R. Slavin et al. (eds.), *Learning to cooperate, cooperating to learn* (pp. 103–124). New York: Plenum Press.

Johnson, D.W., & Johnson, R.T. (1989). Cooperative learning and mainstreaming. In R. Gaylord-Ross (ed.), Integration strategies for students with handicaps (pp. 233–48). Baltimore, MD: Paul H. Brookes.

Johnson, G. (1997). Resilient at-risk students in the inner city. *McGill Journal of Education, 32*(1), 35–49.

Johnson, J.R. (1999). Leadership and self-determinants. *Focus on Autism and Other Developmental Disabilities, 14*(1), 4–16.

Johnson, R.T., Johnson, D.W., & Holubec, E.J. (eds.) (1987). *Structuring cooperative learning: Lesson plans for teachers*. Edina, MN: Interaction Book Co.

Jordan, A. (1994). *Skills in collaborative classroom consultation*. New York: Routledge.

Jordan, A., Lindsay, L., & Stanovich, P.J. (1997). Classroom teachers' instructional interactions with students who are exceptional, at risk, and typically achieving. *Remedial and Special Education, 18*, 82–93.

Jordan, A., & Stanovich, P.J. (1998). *Exemplary teaching in inclusive classrooms*. Paper presented at the annual meeting of the American Educational Research Association, San Diego, CA.

Jory, D. (1991). Principles of change: A parent's perspective on the education system. In G.L. Porter & D. Richler (eds.), *Changing Canadian schools: Perspectives on disability and inclusion*. North York, ON: Roeher Institute.

J.P. Das Developmental Disabilities Centre, University of Alberta, http://www.quasar.ualberta.ca/ddc/INDEX.html (March 21, 2001).

Kagan, S. (1992). *Cooperative learning.* San Jaun Capistrano, CA: Kagan Cooperative Learning.

Kamann, M.P., & Perry, N.E. (1994). Amalgamating support services to support integration. *Exceptionality Education Canada,* 4(3&4), 91–106.

Kaprielian-Churchill, I., & Churchill, S. (1994). *The pulse of the world: Refugees in our schools.* Toronto: OISE Press.

Kauffman, J.M., & Hallahan, D.P. (eds.) (1995). *The illusion of full inclusion: A comprehensive critique of a current special education bandwagon.* Austin, TX: Pro-ed.

Kauffman, M. (1995). *Easy for you to say: Questions and answers for teens living with chronic illness or disability.* Toronto: Key Porter Books.

Kavale, K.A., & Forness, S.R. (1996). Social skill deficits and learning disabilities: A meta-analysis. *Journal of Learning Disabilities,* 29, 226–37.

Kearney, M., & Ray, R. (1999). *The great Canadian book of lists.* Toronto: The Dundurn Group.

Keating, D.P. (1990). Adolescent thinking. In S.S. Feldman & G.R. Elliott (eds.), *At the threshold: The developing adolescent* (pp. 54–89). Boston: Harvard University Press.

Keating, D.P. (1991). Curriculum options for the developmentally advanced: A developmental alternative to gifted education. *Exceptionality Education Canada,* 1(1), 53–83.

Keddy, B.A.S. (1989). Methods of adapting computers for use by disabled students. *Journal of Postsecondary Education and Disability,* 7(1), 17–26.

Kelchner, T.R. (1995). Strategies to reduce school aggression and violence. In L.M. Bullock & R.A. Gable (eds.), *Perspectives on school aggression and violence: Highlights from the working forum on children and youth who have aggressive and violent behaviors* (pp. 36–38). Reston, VA: Council for Exceptional Children.

Kerr, R. (1999). *Self-discipline: Using portfolios to help students develop self awareness and manage emotions and build relationships.* Markham, ON: Pembroke.

Kim, Y.Y. (1988). *Communication and cross-cultural adaptation.* Clevedon, UK: Multilingual Matters.

Kimber, J.L., & Kysela, G.M. (1998). Parental perceptions of care, satisfaction and goal achievement. *Exceptionality Education Canada,* 8(2), 3–26.

Kincher, J., & Bach, J. (1990). *Psychology for kids: 40 fun tests that help you learn about yourself.* Minneapolis, MN: Free Spirit.

King, A.J.C., & Peart, M. (1992). *Teachers in Canada: Their work and quality of life.* Kingston, ON: Canadian Teachers' Federation and Queen's University Program Social Evaluation Group.

King, A.J.C., Warren, W., & Peart, M. (1988). *The teaching experience.* Toronto: Ontario Secondary School Teachers' Federation.

King, G.A., Shultz, I.Z., Steel, K., Gilpin, M., & Cathers, T. (1993). Self-evaluation and self-concept of adolescents with physical disabilities. *American Journal of Occupational Therapy,* 47, 132–40.

Kirby, J.R., & Parrila, R.K. (1999). Theory-based prediction of early reading. *The Alberta Journal of Educational Research,* 45, 428–47.

Kleinert, H.L., Haig, J., Kearns, J.F., & Kennedy, S. (2000). Alternate assessments: Lessons learned and roads to be taken. *Exceptional Children,* 67, 51–66.

Kleinfeld, J., & Westcott, S. (1994). *Fantastic Antoine succeeds! Experiences in educating children with fetal alcohol syndrome.* Anchorage, AK: University of Alaska Press.

Klesmer, H. (1994). *ESL achievement project: Development of English as a second language achievement criteria as a function of age and length of residence in Canada.* North York, ON: North York Board of Education.

Klinger, J.K., & Vaughn, S. (1999). Students' perceptions of instruction in inclusion classrooms: Implications for students with learning disabilities. *Exceptional Children,* 66, 23–37.

Knoll, J.A., & Racino, J.A. (1994). Field in search of a home: The need for support personnel to develop a distinct identity. In V.J. Bradley, J.W. Ashbaugh, & B.C. Blaney (eds.), *Creating individual supports for people with developmental disabilities: A mandate for change at many levels* (pp. 299–323). Baltimore, MD: Brookes.

Koenig, A.J. (1992). Framework for understanding the literacy of individuals with visual impairments. *The Journal of Visual Impairment and Blindness,* 86, 277–84.

Kohn, A. (1996). *Beyond discipline: From compliance to community.* Alexandria, VA: Association for Supervision and Curriculum Development.

Korneluk, Y.G., MacDonald, N.E., Cappelli, M., McGrath, P., & Heich, C.E. (1996). *CF and you: A guide for adolescents.* Ottawa: Carleton University Press.

Krogness, M.M. (1995). *Just teach me, Mrs. K.: Talking, reading, and writing with resistant adolescent learners.* Portsmouth, NH: Heineman.

Kruger, A.C. (1992). The effect of peer and adult-child transactive discussions on moral reasoning. *Merrill-Palmer Quarterly,* 38, 191–211.

Kuhne, M., & Wiener, J. (2000). Stability of social status of children with and without learning disabilities. *Learning Disability Quarterly,* 23, 64–75.

Lam, C.S.M. (1996). The green teacher. In D. Thiessen, N. Bascia, & I. Goodson (eds.), *Making a difference about difference: The lives and careers of racial minority immigrant teachers* (pp. 15–50). Toronto: Garamond Press.

LaMarsh Centre for Research on Violence and Conflict Resolution, http://www.yorku.ca/lamarsh/ (April 2, 2001).

Lamont, I.L., & Hill, J.L. (1991). Roles and responsibilities of paraprofessionals in the regular elementary classroom. *B.C. Journal of Special Education,* 15(1), 1–24.

Landucci, S., & Bachor, D. (1992). Reconsidering the feasibility of service delivery for learning disabled students. *Exceptionality Education Canada,* 2(3&4), 5–25.

Larkin, J. (1994). *Sexual harassment: High school girls speak out.* Toronto: Second Story.

Lazzaro, J.J. (1993). *Adaptive technologies for learning and work environments.* Chicago: American Library Association.

Learning Disabilities Association of Ontario (2001). *About LD, promoting early intervention: Draft definition.* http://www.ldao.on.ca/defdraft.html (March 21, 2001).

Lederer, J.M. (2000). Reciprocal teaching of social studies in inclusive elementary classrooms. *Journal of Learning Disabilities, 33,* 91–106.

Lee, E. (1985). *Letters to Marcia: A teacher's guide to anti-racist education.* Toronto: Cross-Cultural Communication Centre.

Leithwood, K., Begley, P., & Cousins, J.B. (1992). *Developing expert leadership for future schools.* London: Falmer Press.

Lennon, G. (1995, March/April). Inclusion: Adapting the curriculum. *FWTAO Newsletter,* 22–26.

Lennox, C., & Siegel, L.S. (1996). The development of phonological rules and visual strategies in average and poor spellers. *Journal of Experimental Child Psychology, 62,* 60–83.

Lepofsky, M.D. (1997). A report card on the *Charter's* guarantee of equality to persons with disabilities after 10 years—what progress? What prospects? *National Journal of Constitutional Law, 7,* 263–431.

Lévesque, N.L. (1997). *Perceptions of friendships and peer groups: The school experiences of two adolescents with learning disabilities.* Unpublished master's thesis. Queen's University, Kingston, ON.

Levin, B. (1994). Strategies for working with children from low income families. *Canadian School Executive, 14*(2), 23–25.

Levin, E. (1994). *Teaching young children in violent times: Building a peaceable classroom.* Cambridge, MA: Educators for Social Responsibility.

Lewis, S. (1992). *Report on race relations.* Toronto: Government of Ontario.

Lightfoot, C. (1997). *The culture of adolescent risk-taking.* New York: Guilford.

Lincoln County Board of Education (1993). *Growing collaboratively.* Scarborough, ON: Prentice-Hall Canada.

Lord, C. (1995). Facilitating social inclusion: Examples from peer intervention programs. In E. Schopler & G.B. Mesibov (eds.), *Learning and cognition in autism* (pp. 221–40). New York: Plenum Press.

Lovitt, T.C., Plavins, M., & Cushing, S. (1999). What do pupils with disabilities have to say about their experience in high school? *Remedial and Special Education, 20,* 67–76.

Lowenthal, B. (1993). The use of medication for children with attention deficit disorders. *B.C. Journal of Special Education, 17*(2), 135–40.

Lung Association of Canada, http://www.lung.ca/ (March 25, 2001).

Lupart, J.L., Barva, C., & Cannon, M.E. (2000). *What happens when girls, gifted in science, grow up?* Paper presented at the CCWEST Conference for the Advancement of Women in Engineering, Science, and Technology, St. John's, NF.

Lupart, J.L., & Cannon, M.E. (2000). *Gender differences in junior high school students towards future plans and career choices.* Paper presented at the CCWEST Conference for the Advancement of Women in Engineering, Science, and Technology, St. John's, NF.

Lupart, J.L., & Pyryt, M. (1996). Identifying the hidden gifted. *Journal for the Education of the Gifted, 20*(1), 7–16.

MacCuspie, P.A. (1993). Short-term placements: A crucial role for residential schools. *Journal of Visual Impairment and Blindness, 87,* 193–98.

MacCuspie, P.A. (1996). *Promoting acceptance of children with disabilities: From tolerance to inclusion.* Halifax: Atlantic Provinces Special Education Authority.

Mackey & Associates (n.d.). *Report of the review of special education: Prince Edward Island.* Charlottetown: Mackey & Associates. http://www2.gov.pe.ca/educ/publications/reports/se/toc.asp (March 13, 2001).

MacLeod, S. (1997). How to talk—and listen—to your child's teacher. *Today's Parent, 14*(7), pp. 52–59.

MacRae, L., & Lupart, J.L. (1991). Issues in identifying gifted students: How Renzulli's model stacks up. *Roeper Review, 14*(2), 53–58.

Mallory, B.L. (1996). The role of social policy in life-cycle transitions. *Exceptional Children, 62,* 213–23.

Mani, M.N.G. (1989). Analysis of the factors contributing to the retention of special education teachers in Colorado. (Doctoral dissertation, University of Northern Colorado.) *Dissertation Abstracts International, 50,* 07A.

Manitoba Education and Training. Assessment and Evaluation, http://www.edu.gov.mb.ca/metks4/curricul/assess/index.html (March 29, 2001).

Manitoba Education and Training (1989). *Special education in Manitoba.* Winnipeg: Manitoba Education and Training.

Manitoba Education and Training (1995). *Towards inclusion: A handbook for modified course designation, Senior 1–4.* Winnipeg: Manitoba Education and Training.

Manitoba Education and Training (1998). *Individual education planning.* Winnipeg: Manitoba Education and Training.

Manitoba Special Education Review Initiative (SERI), http://www.edu.gov.mb.ca/metks4/instruct/specedu/review/default/htm (March 12, 2001).

Marris, P. (1986). *Loss and change.* London: Routledge and Kegan Paul.

Martin, G., & Pear, J. (1992). *Behavior modification: What it is and how to do it* (4th ed.). Englewood Cliffs, NJ: Prentice Hall.

Martin, J., Dworet, D., & Davis, C. (1996). The secondary student with behaviour disorders: A puzzle worth solving. *Exceptionality Education Canada, 6*(3&4), 183–201.

Martin, J., & Sugarman, J. (1993). *Models of classroom management: Principles, applications and critical perspectives* (2nd ed.). Calgary: Detselig Enterprises.

Martin, J.E., & Marshal, L.H. (1995). *ChoiceMaker.* Longmont, CO: Sopris West.

Martinussen, R., Kirby, J.R., & Das, J.P. (1998). Instruction in successive and phonological processing to improve reading acquisition skills of at-risk kindergarten children. *Developmental Disabilities Bulletin, 26*(2), 19–39.

Maté, G. (2000). *Scattered minds: A new look at the origins and healing of attention deficit disorder.* Toronto: Alfred A. Knopf Canada.

Matthews, D.J. (1996). Giftedness at adolescence: Diverse educational options required. *Exceptionality Education Canada, 6*(3&4), 25–49.

Matthews, D.J., & Steinhauer, N. (1998). Giftedness, girls, others, and equity: Theory-based practical strategies for the regular classroom. *Exceptionality Education Canada, 8*(2), 41–56.

Mawhinney, H.B. (1998, January/March). Patterns of social control in assessment practices in Canadian frameworks for accountability in education. *Educational Policy, 12*, 98–109.

McBurnett, K., Lahey, B.B., & Pfiffner, D. (1993). Diagnosis of attention deficit disorders in DSM-IV: Scientific basis and implications for education. *Exceptional Children, 60*, 108–117.

McCaleb, S.P. (1994). *Building communities of learners: A collaboration among teachers, students, family, and community.* New York: St. Martin's Press, Inc.

McIntosh, R., & Vaughn, S. (1993). So you want to teach social skills to your students: Some pointers from the research. *Exceptionality Education Canada, 3*(1&2), 39–59.

McLaughlin, M. (1992). *Employability skills profile: What are employers looking for?* Ottawa: Conference Board of Canada.

McLaughlin, T.F., & Vacha, E.F. (1993). In-class and district programs for at-risk students. *Canadian School Executive, 13*(4), 27–29.

McLeod, K.A. (ed.) (1993). *Multicultural education: The state of the art* (National Study, Report #1). Toronto: Canadian Association of Second Language Teachers.

McNiff, J., Lomax, P., & Whitehead, J. (1996). *You and your action research project.* London, UK: Routledge.

McQueen, T. (1992). *Essentials of classroom management and discipline.* New York: HarperCollins.

Merritt, S.E. (1992). *Her story: Women from Canada's past.* St. Catharine's, ON: Vanwell Pub.

Merritt, S.E. (1995). *Her story II: Women from Canada's past.* St. Catharine's, ON: Vanwell Pub.

Merritt, S.E. (1999). *Her story III: Women from Canada's past.* St. Catharine's, ON: Vanwell Pub.

Mervis, B.A. (1998). The use of peer-pairing in schools to improve socialization. *Child and Adolescent Social Work Journal, 15*, 467–77.

Meyers, M. (1993). *Teaching to diversity: Teaching and learning in the multi-ethnic classroom.* Toronto: Irwin Pub.

Miller-Chenier, N. (1996). *Bioethics, medical technologies and the health of Canadians: Some policy considerations.* Ottawa: Library of Parliament, Research Branch.

Mittag, K.C., & Van Reusen, A.K. (1999). One fish, two fish, pretzel fish: Learning estimation and other advanced mathematics concepts in an inclusive class. *Teaching Exceptional Children, 31*(6), 66–72.

Montague, M. (1997). Cognitive strategy instruction in mathematics for students with learning disabilities. *Journal of Learning Disabilities, 30*, 64–177.

Morningstar, M.E. (1997). Critical issues in career development and employment preparation for adolescents with disabilities. *Remedial and Special Education, 18*, 307–320.

Munby, H., Hutchinson, N.L., Chin, P., Steiner-Bell, K., Versnel, J., & Chapman, C. (2001, May). *The value of workplace learning: Multiple perspectives on secondary co-op education programs.* Paper presented at the annual conference of the Canadian Society for the Study of Education, Quebec.

Muscular Dystrophy Association of Canada, http://www.mdac.ca (March 26, 2001).

Nagler, M., & Nagler, A. (1999). *What's stopping you? Living successfully with disability.* Toronto: Stoddart.

Napier, E. (1995). *Integrating students with special needs: Effective strategies to provide the most enabling education for all students.* Vancouver: EduServ.

National Alliance for the Mentally Ill, http://www.nami.org/youth/selfadvc.htm (February 19, 2001).

Neuharth-Pritchett, S., & Getch, Y.Q. (1999). Children with asthma: Strategies for educators. *Teaching Exceptional Children, 31*(3), 30–36.

Nevin, A., Johnson, D.W., & Johnson, R.T. (1982). Effects of group and individual contingencies on academic performance and social relations of special needs students. *Journal of Social Psychology, 116*, 41–59.

Nevin, A., Thousand, J.S., & Villa, R.A. (1994). Introduction to creative cooperative group lesson plans. In J.S. Thousand, R.A. Villa, & A. Nevin (eds.), *Creativity and collaborative learning* (pp. 131–225). Baltimore, MD: Paul H. Brookes.

New Brunswick Department of Education (n.d.). *Guidelines for a special education plan.* Fredericton: New Brunswick Department of Education

New Brunswick Department of Education (1988). *Working guidelines on integration.* Fredericton: New Brunswick Department of Education.

New Brunswick Department of Education (1991). *Position statement on inclusive, quality education.* Fredericton: New Brunswick Department of Education.

New Brunswick Department of Education (1997). *Gifted and talented students: A resource guide.* Fredericton: New Brunswick Department of Education. http://www.gov.nb.ca/education/orgs/e/stuserv.htm (March 12, 2001).

Newfoundland Classroom Issues Committee (1995). *Report to the Social Policy Committee of the provincial cabinet.* St. John's: Government of Newfoundland.

Newfoundland Department of Education (1996). *Programming for individual needs: Pre-referral intervention.* St. John's: Government of Newfoundland.

Newfoundland Department of Education (1997). *Coordination of services to children and youth in Newfoundland & Labrador.* St. John's: Government of Newfoundland. http://www.edu.gov.nf.ca/issp/table.htm (March 13, 2001).

Newfoundland Department of Education (1998). *Pathways to programming and graduation: A handbook for teachers and administrators.* St. John's: Government of Newfoundland.

Northwest Territories Department of Education, Culture, and Employment (1995). *Bill 25: Education act summary.* Yellowknife: Northwest Territories Department of Education, Culture, and Employment.

Northwest Territories Department of Education, Culture, and Employment (1996). *Educating all our children: Departmental directive on inclusive schooling.* Yellowknife: Northwest Territories Department of Education, Culture, and Employment. http://siksik.learnnet.nt.ca/ECE/ECSS/office/D/8/directve.htm (March 12, 2001).

Notman, D. (2000). *Another way of coming downstairs: The effects of portfolio assessment and student led conferences on ownership, control and learning.* A paper presented at the annual meeting of the Ontario Education Research Conference, Toronto, ON.

Nova Scotia Association for Spina Bifida and Hydrocephalus, http://chebucto.ns.ca/Health/SBANS/index.html (March 26, 2001).

Nova Scotia Department of Education (1996). *Special education policy manual*. Halifax: Nova Scotia Department of Education. http://doc-depot.ednet.ns.ca (March 13, 2001).

O'Brien, J., Forest, M., Snow, J., & Hasbury, D. (1989). *Action for inclusion*. Toronto: Frontier College Press.

Office of Disability Issues, Human Resources Development Canada, http://www.hrdc-drhc.gc.ca/bcph-odi/content/about.shtml (April 2, 2001)

Olweus, D. (1993). *Bullying at school: What we know and what we can do*. Oxford, UK: Blackwell.

Ontario Association on Developmental Disabilities, http://oadd.icomm.ca/ (March 21, 2001).

Ontario Ministry of Education (1987). *Vision: Resource guide.* Toronto, ON: Queen's Printer for Ontario.

Ontario Ministry of Education (1998). *Individual education plan (IEP) resource guide.* Toronto: Ontario Ministry of Education. http://www.edu.gov.on.ca/eng/general/elemsec/speced/individu.html (March 12, 2001).

Ontario Ministry of Education (1999). *Choices into action.* http://mettowas21.edu.gov.on.ca:80/eng/document/curricul/secondary/choices/index.html (February 19, 2001).

Ontario Ministry of Education (1999, January 15). *Updates to categories of exceptionalities and definitions: Memorandum.* Toronto: Ontario Ministry of Education.

Ontario Ministry of Education (2000). *Individual education plans: Standards for development, program planning, and implementation.* Toronto: Ontario Ministry of Education. http://www.edu.gov.on.ca/eng/general/elemsec/speced/iep/iep.html (March 29, 2001).

Ontario Ministry of Education, Regulation 181/98. http://www.edu.gov.on.ca/eng/general/elemsec/speced/hilites.html (March 12, 2001).

Ontario Ministry of Health (1978). *You and your hearing.* Toronto: Ontario Ministry of Health.

Ontario Public School Teachers Federation (1996). *Act, reflect, revise, revitalize: Action research, moving beyond problem solving to renewal.* Mississauga, ON: Ontario Public School Teachers Federation.

Ontario Public School Teachers Federation (1998). *Action research: Improving schools through action research* (video). Mississauga, ON: Ontario Public School Teachers Federation.

Ontario Secondary School Teachers' Federation (1995). *The joke's over: Student to student sexual harassment in secondary schools.* Toronto: Ontario Secondary School Teachers' Federation.

Osguthorpe, R., & Scruggs, T. (1986). Special education students as tutors: A review and analysis. *Remedial and Special Education, 7*(4), 15–25.

Ottewell, C.G. (1998). A survivor's view. In S. Acorn & P. Offer (eds.), *Living with brain injury* (pp. 20–33). Toronto: University of Toronto Press.

Palincsar, A.S., & Brown, A. (1984). Reciprocal teaching of comprehension-fostering and comprehension-monitoring activities. *Cognition and Instruction, 1*, 117–75.

Palmer, H. (1997). *…But where are you really from? Stories of identity and assimilation in Canada.* Toronto: Sister Vision.

Parke, B.N. (1992). Challenging gifted students in the regular classroom. *ERIC Digest #E513.*

Parker, J.G., & Asher, S.R. (1987). Peer relations and later personal adjustment: Are low-accepted children at risk? *Psychological Bulletin, 102,* 357–89.

Paro, K.M., Pianta, R.C., & Cox, M.J. (2000). Teachers' reported transition practices for children transitioning into kindergarten and first grade. *Exceptional Children, 67,* 7–20.

Patchett, R., & Gauthier, Y. (1991). Parent and teacher perceptions of giftedness and a program for the gifted. *B.C. Journal of Special Education, 15*(1), 25–38.

Patterson, D. (1996). Becoming a change agent in your elementary classroom. In J. Andrews (ed.), *Teaching students with diverse needs: Elementary classrooms* (pp. 14–37). Scarborough: Nelson Canada.

Pearson, P.D. (1996). Reclaiming the center. In M.F. Graves, P. van den Broek, & B.M. Taylor (eds.), *The first r: Every child's right to read.* New York: Teachers College Press.

Peel Board of Education (1990). *Looking at assessment, more than marks: Adapting tests and assignments for exceptional students* (Book 4). Mississauga: Peel Board of Education.

Peterson, J.S. (1993). *Talk with teens about self and stress: 50 guided discussions for school and counseling groups.* Minneapolis, MN: Free Spirit.

Phelan, P., Davidson, A., & Cao, H. (1992). Speaking up: Students' perspectives on school. *Phi Delta Kappan, 73,* 695–704.

Pincivero, E.E. (2000). *An analysis of the implementation of the new IEP in an Ontario secondary school setting.* Unpublished master's thesis, Faculty of Education, Queen's University, Kingston, ON.

Pletsch, V.C. (1997). *Not wanted in the classroom.* London, ON: Althouse Press.

Pohl, A. (1997, April). Teaching Native studies. *OPSTF News.*

Powers, L.E., Sowers, J., Turner, A., Nesbitt, M., Knowles, A., & Ellison, R. (1996). *Take charge.* Portland, OR: Oregon Health Sciences University.

Prince, A. (1996). Black history month: A multi-cultural myth or "Have-Black-History-Month-Kit will travel." In K.S. Brethwaite & C.E. James (eds.), *Educating African Canadians* (pp. 179–98). Toronto: James Lorimer & Co.

Prince Edward Island Department of Education (1995). *A model of special education service delivery* (Draft). Charlottetown: Prince Edward Island Department of Education.

Prince Edward Island Department of Education (1997a). *A handbook on special education service delivery* (Draft). Charlottetown: Prince Edward Island Department of Education.

Prince Edward Island Department of Education (1997b). *Minister's directive No. MD97-07: Special education.* Charlottetown: Prince Edward Island Department of Education.

Prince Edward Island Minister of Education (1990). *Special education policy statement.* Charlottetown: Prince Edward Island Department of Education.

Proactive Information Services (1998). *The Manitoba special education review.* Winnipeg: Proactive Information Services.

Pyryt, M.C. (1992). *Career development for the gifted and talented.* Proceedings of the SAGE, 6th Canadian Symposium.

Qualifications of paraprofessionals (1999, Spring/Summer). *Keeping in Touch: A Newsletter from the Canadian CEC Office,* p. 6.

Queen's University Learning Strategies Development. *10 Tips for Improving Time Management.* http://www.queensu.ca/stserv/top_10.html (February 19, 2001).

Rabby, R., & Croft, D.L. (1989). *Take charge: A strategic guide for blind job seekers.* Boston: National Braille Press Inc.

Rafferty, Y. (1998, January). Meeting the educational needs of homeless children. *Educational Leadership,* 48–52.

Reed, D.F., McMillan, J.H., & McBee, R.H. (1995). Defying the odds: Middle schoolers in high risk circumstances who succeed. *Middle School Journal, 27,* 3–10.

Reed, K. (1999). *Aboriginal peoples: Building for the future.* Don Mills, ON: Oxford University Press Canada.

Reis, S.M., & Renzulli, J.S. (1985). *The secondary triad model: A practical plan for implementing gifted programs at the junior and senior high school levels.* Mansfield Center, CN: Creative Learning Press.

Reithaug, D. (1998a). *Orchestrating academic success by adapting and modifying programs.* Vancouver: Stirling Head Enterprises.

Reithaug, D. (1998b). *Orchestrating positive and practical behaviour plans.* Vancouver: Stirling Head Enterprises.

Renzulli, J.S. & Reis, S.M. (1985). *The schoolwide enrichment model: A comprehensive plan for educational excellence.* Mansfield Center, CN: Creative Learning Press.

Report of the Royal Commission on Aboriginal Peoples (1996). Ottawa: Government of Canada. http://www.inac.gc.ca/ch/rcap/ (March 26, 2001).

Resource Foundation for Children with Challenges, http://www.specialchild.com (March 26, 2001).

Rice, F.P. (1987). *The adolescent: Development, relationships, and culture.* Needham Neights, MA: Allyn & Bacon.

Riendl, P.A., & Haworth, D.T. (1995). Chemistry and special education. *Journal of Chemical Education, 72,* 983–86.

Roberts, C.A., & Lazure, M.D. (1970). *One million children: A national study of Canadian children with emotional and learning disorders.* Toronto: Leonard Crainford.

Roberts, M., White, R., & McLaughlin, T.F. (1997). Useful classroom accommodations for teaching children with ADD and ADHD. *B.C. Journal of Special Education, 21*(2), 71–90.

Robinson, N.M. (1996). Counseling agendas for gifted young people: A commentary. *Journal for the Education of the Gifted, 20*(2), 128–37.

Roffey, S., Majors, K., & Tarrant, T. (1997). Friends, who needs them? What do we know and what can we do? *Educational and Child Psychology, 14*(3), 51–56.

Rosenthal-Malek, A., & Greenspan, J. (1999). A student with diabetes is in my class. *Teaching Exceptional Children, 31*(3), 38–43.

Rosenthal-Malek, A.L. (1997). Stop and think: Using metacognitive strategies to teach students social skills. *Teaching Exceptional Children, 29*(3), 29–31.

Ross, D., & Roberts, P. (1999). Income and child well-being: A new perspective on the poverty debate. Ottawa: Canadian Council on Social Development. http://www.ccsd.ca/pubs/inckids/ (March 28, 2001).

Ross, D., Scott, K., & Kelly, M. (1996). *Child poverty: What are the consequences?* Ottawa: Canadian Council on Social Development.

Ross, J.A., & Smyth, E. (1995). Differentiating co-operative learning to meet the needs of gifted learners: A case for transformational leadership. *Journal for the Education of the Gifted, 19,* 63–82.

Rubin, D.H., Erickson, C.J., San Agustin, M., Cleary, S.D., Allen, J.K., & Cohen, P. (1996). Cognitive and academic functioning of homeless children compared with housed children. *Pediatrics, 97,* 289–94.

Runyan, M.K. (1991). The effects of extra time on reading comprehension scores for university students with and without learning disabilities. *Journal of Learning Disabilities, 24,* 104–108.

Ruppert, E.S., & Buhrer, K. (1992). Ohio's infant hearing screening and assessment program. *Clinical Pediatrics, 31,* 19–22.

Ryndak, D.L., Downing, J.E., Morrison, A.P., & Williams, L.J. (1996). Parents' perceptions of educational settings and services for children with moderate or severe disabilities. *Remedial and Special Education, 17,* 106–118.

Rynders, J.E., & Horrobin, J.M. (1990). Always trainable? Never educable? Updating educational expectations concerning children with Down syndrome. *American Journal on Mental Retardation, 95,* 77–83.

Ryser, G.R., & Johnsen, S.K. (1996). Toward more research on effective practices with gifted students in general-education settings. *Journal for the Education of the Gifted, 19,* 481–96.

Salend, S.J. (1998). *Effective mainstreaming: Creating inclusive classrooms* (3rd ed.). Upper Saddle River, NJ: Merrill.

Salend, S.J., & Gajria, M. (1995). Increasing the homework completion rates of students with mild disabilities. *Remedial and Special Education, 16,* 271–78.

Sandieson, R. (1994). Developmentally-based instruction for mentally challenged learners. *Exceptionality Education Canada, 4*(1), 73–88.

Sarason, S.B. (1993). *You are thinking of teaching? Opportunities, problems, realities.* San Francisco: Jossey-Bass.

Saskatchewan Education (1996). *Special education policy manual* (Draft). Regina: Saskatchewan Education.

Saskatchewan Education (2000a). *Directions for diversity: Final report of the Saskatchewan Special Education Review Committee.* Regina: Saskatchewan Education. http://www.sasked.gov.sk.ca/k/pecs/se/whatsnew.html (March 12, 2001).

Saskatchewan Education (2000b). *Strengthening supports: Minister's response to the report of the Special education Review committee.* Regina: Saskatchewan Education. http://www.sasked.gov.sk.ca/k/pecs/se/whatsnew.html (March 12, 2001).

Saskatchewan Education Indicators Program, http://www.sasked.gov.sk.ca/k/pecs/ae/pub1.html (March 29, 2001).

Saskatchewan Education, Special Education Unit (1998). *Teaching students with autism: A guide for educators*. Regina: Saskatchewan Education Special Education Unit. http://www.sasked.gov.sk.ca/k/pecs/se/docs/autism/def.html (March 26, 2001).

Saskatchewan Education, Special Education Unit (2001). *Challenges, choices, and changes*. http://www.sasked. gov.sk.ca/k/pecs/se/newsletter.html (March 12, 2001).

Scales, P.C. (1992). From risks to resources: Disadvantaged learners and middle grades teaching. *Middle School Journal, 23*(5), 3–9.

Scheid, K. (1993). *Helping students become strategic learners: Guidelines for teaching*. Cambridge, MA: Brookline.

Schmid, C., & Hutchinson, N.L. (1994). *The role of the family in programs for preschoolers with special needs: A case of three Canadian families*. Paper presented at the annual conference of American Educational Research Association, New Orleans, LA.

Schneider, B.H. (1993). *Children's social competence in context: The contributions of family, school, and culture*. Oxford, UK: Pergamon.

Schneider, W., Ennemoser, M., Roth, E., & Kuspert, P. (1999). Kindergarten prevention of dyslexia: Does training in phonological awareness work for everybody? *Journal of Learning Disabilities, 32*, 429–36.

Schumaker, J.B., Deshler, D.D., & Denton, P. (1984). *The learning strategies curriculum: The paraphrase strategy*. Lawrence, KS: University of Kansas.

Schumm, J.S., Vaughn, S., Haager, D., McDowell, J., Rothlein, L., & Saumell, L. (1995). Teacher planning for individual student needs: What can mainstreamed special education students expect? *Exceptional Children, 61*, 335–52.

Scott, B.J., Vitale, M.R., & Masten, W.G. (1998). Implementing instructional adaptations for students with disabilities in inclusive classrooms: A literature review. *Remedial and Special Education, 19*, 106–119.

Scott, W. (1996). *The accessible Canadian library II: A resource tools for libraries serving persons with disabilities*. Ottawa: National Library of Canada.

Searcy, S. (1996). Friendship interventions for the integration of children and youth with learning and behavior problems. *Preventing School Failure, 40*(3), 131–34.

Sebald, H. (1981). Adolescents' concept of popularity and unpopularity. *Adolescence, 16*, 187–93.

Seidel, J.F., & Vaughn, S. (1991). Social alienation and the learning disabled school dropout. *Learning Disabilities Research and Practice, 6*, 152–57.

Selye, H. (1956). *The stress of life*. New York: McGraw-Hill.

Selye, H. (1974). *Stress without distress*. New York: Harper and Row.

Sharan, S., & Sharan, Y. (1976). *Small group teaching*. Englewood Cliffs, NJ: Educational Testing Publications.

Shriner, J.G., Spande, G.E., & Thurlow, M.L. (1994). *State special education outcomes 1993*. Minneapolis, MN: University of Minnesota, National Center on Educational Outcomes.

Siegel, L.S. (1999). Issues in the definition and diagnosis of learning disabilities. *Journal of Learning Disabilities, 32*, 304–319.

Sikes, P.J. (1992). Imposed change and the experienced teacher. In M. Fullan and A. Hargreaves (eds.), *Teacher development and educational change*. London: Falmer Press.

Simmons, D.C., Dickson, S.V., & Chard, D. (1993). *Integrating narrative reading comprehension and writing instruction for all learners*. Paper presented at the annual meeting of the National Reading Conference, Charleston, SC.

Sjostrum, L., & Stein, N. (1996). *Bully proof: A teacher's guide on teasing and bullying for use with fourth and fifth grade students*. Boston, MA: Wellesley College Center for Research on Women and the NEA Professional Library.

Smith, D.H. (1998). *Early warning: Cases and ethical guidance for presymptomatic testing in genetic diseases*. Bloomington, IN: Indiana University Press.

Smith, M.A., & Mirsa, A. (1992). A comprehensive management system for students in regular classrooms. *Elementary School Journal, 92*(3), 354–71.

Smith, T.E.C., Polloway, E.A., Patton, J.R., & Dowdy, C.A. (1995). *Teaching students with special needs in inclusive settings*. Needham Heights, MA: Allyn & Bacon.

Smith, T.E.C., Polloway, E.A., Patton, J.R., & Dowdy, C.A. (1998). *Teaching students with special needs in inclusive settings* (2nd ed.). Boston: Allyn and Bacon.

Smith, W.J. (1991). *Inclusive education: Recent experiences in Québec*. Montreal: Learning Centre of Québec.

Smith, W.J., & Foster, W.F. (1993). Educational opportunity for students with disabilities in Canada: A platform of rights to build on. *Education and Law Journal, 5*, 193–223.

Smith, W.J., & Foster, W.F. (1994). Educational opportunity for students with disabilities in Canada: Beyond the schoolhouse door. *Education and Law Journal, 5*, 305–335.

Solomon, R.P. (1992). *Black resistance in high school: A separatist culture*. Albany, NY: State University of New York Press.

Solomon, R.P. (1996). Creating an opportunity structure for Blacks and other teachers of colour. In K.S. Brethwaite & C.E. James (eds.), *Educating African Canadians* (pp. 216–33). Toronto: James Lorimer & Co.

Stairs, A. (1991). Learning processes and teaching roles in Native education: Cultural base and cultural brokerage. *Canadian Modern Language Review, 47*, 280–94.

Stanovich, K.E. (1994). Constructivism in reading education. *Journal of Special Education, 28*, 259–74.

Stanovich, K.E. (1996). Toward a more inclusive definition of dyslexia. *Dyslexia, 2*, 154–66.

Stanovich, K.E., & Stanovich, P.J. (1995). How research might inform the debate about early reading acquisition. *Journal of Research in Reading, 18*, 87–105.

Stanovich, P.J. (1996). Collaboration: The key to successful instruction in today's inclusive schools. *Intervention in School and Clinic, 32*(1), 39–42.

Stanovich, P.J. (1999). Conversations about inclusion. *Teaching Exceptional Children, 31*(6), 54–58.

Stanovich, P.J., & Jordan, A. (1995). *Integrated education: A resource guide for including students with special needs in the regular classroom.* Toronto: Federation of Women Teachers' Associations of Ontario.

Stanovich, P.J., & Jordan, A. (1998). Canadian teachers' and principals' beliefs about inclusive education as predictors of effective teaching in heterogeneous classrooms. *Elementary School Journal, 98,* 221–38.

Steiner-Bell, K. (1998). *Teaching emotion and belief as adapted curriculum for children with autism: A first step in addressing mind-blindness.* Unpublished master's thesis. Queen's University, Kingston, ON.

Stewart, J. (1999). Career counselling for the academically gifted student. *Canadian Journal of Career Counselling, 33,* 3–12.

Stoch, S.A. (2000). *Zak: An adolescent with learning disabilities at home, at camp, and at school.* Unpublished master's thesis, Queen's University, Kingston, ON.

Stones, R. (1993). *Don't pick on me: How to handle bullying.* Markham, ON: Pembroke Publishers.

Streissguth, A. (1997). *Fetal alcohol syndrome: A guide for families and communities.* Toronto: Brookes.

Super, D.E. (1990). A life-span, life-space approach to career development. In D. Brown, L. Brooks, & Associates (eds.), *Career choice and development: Applying contemporary theories to practice* (2nd ed.), pp. 197–261. San Francisco: Jossey-Bass.

Super, D.E., & Harris-Bowlsbey, J.A. (1979). *Guided career exploration.* New York: Psychological Corporation.

Sweeney, D.P., Forness, S.R., Kavale, K.A., & Levitt, J.G. (1997). An update on psychopharmacologic medication: What teachers, clinicians, and parents need to know. *Intervention in School and Clinic, 33*(1), 4–21, 25.

Tam, K.Y., Nassivera, J.W., Rousseau, M.K. & Vreeland, P. (2000). More than just a field trip: Using the museum as a resource for inclusive secondary science classrooms. *Teaching Exceptional Children, 33*(1), 70–78.

Task Force on Access to Information for Print-Disabled Canadians. *Fulfilling the Promise.* http://www.nlc-bcn.ca/accessinfo/tfpd-e.htm (February 19, 2001).

Taylor, R., & Reeves, J. (1993). More is better: Raising expectations for students at risk. *Middle School Journal, 24,* 13–18.

Teens: The Company They Keep fact sheet, http://www.nimh.nih.gov/publicat/teens.cfm (March 21, 2001).

Temple University Institute on Disabilities, http://www.kidstogether.org/at_cmps.htm (February 19, 2001).

Tennant, B., Hutchinson, N.L, & Freeman, J.G. (1992). Employers' expectations of adolescents with learning disabilities in co-operative education. *Exceptionality Education Canada, 2*(3&4), 129–42.

Thiessen, D., Bascia, N., & Goodson, I. (eds.) (1996). *Making a difference about difference: The lives and careers of racial minority immigrant teachers.* Toronto: Garamond Press.

Tourette Syndrome Foundation of Canada, http://www.tourette.ca/ (March 26, 2001).

Trent, S.C., Artiles, A.J., & Englert, C.S. (1998). From deficit thinking to social constructivism: A review of theory, research, and practice in special education. *Review of Research in Education, 23,* 277–307.

Turnbull, A.P., Pereira, L., & Blue-Banning, M. (2000). Teachers as friendship facilitators. *Teaching Exceptional Children, 32*(5), 66–70.

Turnbull, A.P., & Turnbull, H.R. (1990). *Families, professionals, and exceptionality: A special partnership* (2nd ed.). Columbus, OH: Merrill.

United Nations (1993). *Standard rules on the equalization of opportunities for persons with disabilities.* http://unescap.org/decade/st-rules.htm (March 29, 2001).

University of North Carolina at Charlotte, Self-Determination Synthesis Project, http://www.uncc.edu.sdsp/sd_curricula.asp (February 19, 2001).

Upitis, R. (ed.) (2000). *Who will teach? A case study of teacher education reform.* San Francisco: Caddo Gap Press.

Vacc, N.N. (1995). Gaining number sense through a restructured hundreds chart. *Teaching Exceptional Children, 28*(1), 50–55.

Valeo, A., & Bunch, G. (1998). Teachers, attitudes, inclusion, and the curriculum. *B.C. Journal of Special Education, 21*(3), 6–19.

Valpy, M. (1998). Sticks and stones: The ugly truth about beauty. *The Globe and Mail.* May 23, pp. D1, D2.

Vandenberghe, R., & Huberman, A.M. (eds.) (1999). *Understanding and preventing teacher burnout: A sourcebook of international research and practice.* New York: Cambridge University Press.

Van Reusen, A.K., & Bos, C.S. (1990). I PLAN: Helping students communicate in planning conferences. *Teaching Exceptional Children, 22*(4), 30–32.

Van Reusen, A.K., & Bos, C.S. (1994). Facilitating student participation in individualized education programs through motivation strategy instruction. *Exceptional Children, 60,* 466–70.

Vaughn, S. (1991). Social skills enhancement in students with learning disabilities. In B.Y.L. Wong (ed.), *Learning about learning disabilities* (pp. 407–40). San Diego, CA: Academic.

Vaughn, S., Schumm, J.S., Klinger, J., & Saumell, L. (1995). Students' views of instuctional practices: Implications for inclusion. *Learning Disability Quarterly, 18,* 236–48.

Vermette, P.J. (1998). *Making cooperative learning work: Student teams in K–12 classrooms.* Upper Saddle River, NJ: Merrill.

Versnel, J. (2001). *Self-determination in career education: A journey toward a proposed curriculum framework.* Unpublished paper, Queen's University, Kingston, ON.

Villa, R.A., & Thousand, J.S. (1994). One divided by two or more: Redefining the cooperative education team. In J.S Thousand, R.A. Villa, & A. Nevin (eds.), *Creativity and collaborative learning* (pp. 79–102). Baltimore, MD: Paul H. Brookes.

Vygotsky, L. (1978). *Mind in society.* Cambridge, MA: Harvard University Press.

Vygotsky, L.S. (1986). *Thought and language.* Cambridge, MA: MIT Press.

Waggoner, K., & Wilgosh, L. (1990). Concerns of families of children with learning disabilities. *Journal of Learning Disabilities, 23*(2), 97–98, 113.

Walczyk, E.B. (1993). Music instruction and the hearing impaired. *Music Educators Journal, 80,* 42–44.

Waldron, N.L., McLeskey, J., & Pacchiano, D. (1999). Giving teachers a voice: Teachers' perspectives regarding elementary inclusive school programs (ISP). *Teacher Education and Special Education, 22,* 141–53.

Ward, A. (1996). Beyond "sharing time": Negotiating Aboriginal culture in an urban classroom. *English Quarterly, 28*(2/3), 23–28.

Watson, R.S., Poda, J.H., Miller, C.T., Rice, E.S., & West, G. (1993). *Containing crisis: A guide to managing school emergencies.* Bloomington, IL: National Educational Service.

Webb, N. (1985). Student interactions and learning in small groups: A research summary. In R. Slavin, S. Sharan, S. Kagan, R. Hertz-Lazarowitz, C. Webb, & R. Schmuck (eds.), *Learning to cooperate, cooperating to learn* (pp. 147–72). New York: Plenum.

Weber, K. (1993). *Special education in Ontario schools* (3rd ed.). Thornhill, ON: Highland Press.

Wehmeyer, M.L. (1992). Self-determination and the education of students with mental retardation. *Education and Training in Mental Retardation, 27,* 302–14.

Weidmer, T. (1998, March). Digital portfolios: Capturing and demonstrating skills and levels of performance. *Phi Delta Kappan,* 586–89.

Weisgerber, R.A. (1993). *Science success for students with disabilities.* New York: Addison-Wesley.

Welch, A.B. (2000). Responding to student concerns about fairness. *Teaching Exceptional Children, 33*(2), 36–40.

Western Canada Protocol for Collaboration in Basic Education (2000). *Common Curriculum Framework for Aboriginal Language and Culture Programs, Kindergarten to Grade 12.* http://www.wcp.ca/languages/abor.pdf (March 27, 2001).

Western Canadian Protocol for Collaboration in Basic Education (1996). *Aboriginal Languages Project Proposal.* http://www.wcp.ca/languages/abor.pdf (March 27, 2001).

What Is Mental Retardation? fact sheet, http://www.aamr.org.

Whimbey, A., & Whimbey, L. (1975). *Intelligence can be taught.* New York: Innovative Science.

Whitmore, J.R. (1988). Gifted children at risk for learning difficulties. *Teaching Exceptional Children, 20*(4), 10–14.

Wiener, J. (1994). Social and affective impacts of full inclusion. *Exceptionality Education Canada, 4*(3&4), 107–117.

Wiener, J., Harris, P.J., & Duval, L. (1993). Placement, identification and subtype correlates of peer status and social behaviour of children with learning disabilities. *Exceptionality Education Canada, 3*(1&2), 129–55.

Wiener, J., Harris, P.J., & Shirer, C. (1990). Achievement and social-behavioral correlates of peer status in LD children. *Learning Disability Quarterly, 13,* 114–27.

Wiener, J., & Manuel, C. (1994). Attitudes of students with learning handicaps toward in-class resource and pull-out withdrawal educational models. *Exceptionality Education Canada, 4*(2), 53–75.

Wiggins, G. (1993). Assessment: authenticity, context, and validity. *Phi Delta Kappan, 75*(3), 200–14.

Wilgosh, L. (1990). Issues in education and daily living for families of children with disabilities. *The Alberta Journal of Educational Research, 36,* 299–309.

Wilgosh, L. (1992). Integration of children with special needs. *The Canadian Administrator, 31*(4), 1–9.

Wilgosh, L. (1993). Implications of Alberta Education policies and practices for gifted students. In *Nurturing Potential, Proceedings of the Society for the Advancement of Gifted Education Annual Conference* (4th, Edmonton, Canada, September 24–25, 1993).

Wilgosh, L., & Chomicki, S. (1994). Parents' views on inclusive education for young people with disabilities. *Developmental Disabilities Bulletin, 22*(2), 29–35.

Williams, L., Henderson, M., & Marcuse, G. (1998). *First Nations: The circle unbroken: The teacher's guide (videos 5, 6, 7).* Montreal: National Film Board of Canada.

Wilson, R.J. (1996). *Assessing students in classrooms and schools.* Scarborough, ON: Allyn and Bacon Canada.

Winebrenner, S. (1992). *Teaching gifted kids in the regular classroom: Strategies and techniques every teacher can use to meet the academic needs of the gifted and the talented.* Minneapolis: Free Spirit Publishing.

Winzer, M. (1999). *Children with exceptionalities in Canadian classrooms* (5th ed.). Scarborough, ON: Prentice-Hall Canada.

Witt, N. (1998). Promoting self-esteem, defining culture. *Canadian Journal of Native Education, 22*(2), 260–73.

Wolfensberger, W., Nirge, B., Olshansky, S., Perske, R., & Roos, P. (1972). *The principle of normalization in human services.* Toronto: National Institute on Mental Retardation.

Wong, B.Y.L. (1996). *The ABCs of learning disabilities.* Toronto: Academic Press.

Wong, B.Y.L., & Hutchinson, N.L. (in press). *Learning disabilities in Canada.* In D.P. Hallahan & B.K. Keogh (eds.), *Research and global perspectives in learning disabilities: Essays in honor of William M. Cruikshank.* Mahwah, NJ: Erlbaum.

Wong, J. (2000). Alisha is not a genius, but she is smart. *The Globe and Mail.* May 6, p. R7.

Wong, M.A. (1997). Disability and the Internet: Access and use as means toward greater self-advocacy. *Physical Disabilities: Education and Related Services, 15*(2), 23–36.

Woodward, J. (1994). The role of models in secondary science instruction. *Remedial and Special Education, 15,* 94–104.

Working Forum on Inclusive Schools (1994). *Creating schools for all our children: What 12 schools have to say.* Reston, VA: Council for Exceptional Children.

World Health Organization (1997). *ICIDH-2 international classification of impairment, activities and participation: A manual of dimensions of disablement and functioning B Beta-1 draft for field trials.* Geneva, Switzerland: World Health Organization.

Wright, R. (1991). *Stolen continents: The "New World" through Indian eyes since 1492*. Toronto: Penguin Canada.

Yang Lam, M.L. (1996). Of "scattered beads": Reflections on my teaching career from the periphery of Canadian society. In D. Thiessen, N. Bascia, & I. Goodson (eds.), *Making a difference about difference: The lives and careers of racial minority immigrant teachers* (pp. 15–50). Toronto: Garamond Press.

Yates, S. (1994). *Nobody knows!* Winnipeg, MB: Gemma B. Pub.

Yau, M. (1995). *Refugee students in Toronto schools: An exploratory study*. Toronto: Toronto Board of Education.

Yewchuk, C. (1993). The case for ability grouping of gifted students. Implications of inclusive education for gifted and talented children. In *Nurturing Potential, Proceedings of the Society for the Advancement of Gifted Education Annual Conference* (4th, Edmonton, Canada, September 24–25, 1993).

Yssel, N., & Hadadian, A. (1998). Paraprofessionals in inclusive settings. *Exceptionality Education Canada, 8*(1), 39–44.

Ysseldyke, J., & Olsen, K. (1999). Putting alternate assessments into practice: What to measure and possible sources of data. *Exceptional Children, 65*, 175–85.

Yukon Education (1995). *Special programs services: A handbook of procedures and guidelines*. Whitehorse: Yukon Education.

Yukon Education (1996). *Partners in education: The Yukon Education Act*. Whitehorse: Yukon Education.

Zajac, R.J., & Hartup, W.W. (1997). Friends as coworkers: Research review and classroom implications. *Elementary School Journal, 98*, 3–13.

Zentall, S.S. (1990). Fact-retrieval automatization and math problem solving by learning disabled, attention-disordered, and normal adolescents. *Journal of Educational Psychology, 82*, 856–65.

Zimmerman, B., Gold, M., Lavi, S., & Feanny, S. (1991). *The Canadian allergy and asthma handbook*. Mississauga, ON: Random House.

Name Index

Subject Index

Photo Credits

Chapter 1: p. 2, Bernard Clark Photography; p. 6, Eric Hayes; p.7, Tibor Kolley/*The Globe and Mail*; p. 16, Canadian Press; p.27, Angela Solar; **Chapter 2**: p. 32, Angela Solar; p. 36, Bernard Clark Photography; p. 44, Paul Schliesmann/*The Kingston Whig Standard*; p. 51, Bayne Stanley; p. 57, Christopher Grabowski. **Chapter 3**: p. 62, Phil Hossack/*Winnipeg Free Press* February 2, 1996, reprinted with permission; p. 68, Tibor Kolley/*The Globe and Mail*; p. 73, © Todd Korol; p. 87, Angela Solar; p. 97, Ian MacAlpine/*The Kingston Whig Standard*. **Chapter 4**: p. 100, Bernard Clark Photography; p. 105, Edward Regan/*The Globe and Mail*; p. 113, Ian MacAlpine; p. 120, Tibor Kolley/*The Globe and Mail*; p. 135, Angela Solar. **Chapter 5**: p. 140, Angela Solar; p. 144, Anne Marie Beaton/CP Picture Archive; p. 156, Christopher Grabowski; p. 162, Karen Kilbride/Seventh Heaven Photo Tours; p. 165, Tibor Kolley/ *The Globe and Mail*. **Chapter 6**: p. 170, Bernard Clark Photography; p. 175, Angela Solar; p. 181, *The Manitoba Teacher*, © Marilyn Nolt; p. 189, Angela Solar; p. 192, Angela Solar. **Chapter 7**: p. 196, Angela Solar; p. 199, Michael Lea/*The Kingston Whig Standard*; p. 212, Michael Lea/ *The Kingston Whig Standard*; p. 218, Jack Chiang/ *The Kingston Whig Standard*; p.222, Angela Solar. **Chapter 8**: p. 228, Marc Gallant/Canadian Press; p. 234, Angela Solar/Photograph from Canada: *Understanding Your Past*, copyright © 1990 by Irwin Publishing. Reprinted by permission of the publisher; p. 244, Ian MacAlpine; p. 250, Michael Lea/*The Kingston Whig Standard*; p. 251, Stephanie Taylor. **Chapter 9**: p. 258, Pete Gaffney; p. 262, Michael Lea/ *The Kingston Whig Standard*; p. 276, Bernard Clark Photography; p. 281, Ian MacAlpine/*The Kingston Whig Standard*, © Jack Chiang; p.282, Michael Lea/ *The Kingston Whig Standard*. **Chapter 10**: p. 284, Ward Perrin/*The Vancouver Sun*; p.288, Michael Lea/*The Kingston Whig Standard*; p.291, Paul Schliesmann/*The Kingston Whig Standard*; p.295, © Aaron Harris/*The Globe and Mail*; p. 308, Fred Lum/*The Globe and Mail*.